Tonal Structures in Early Music

CRITICISM AND ANALYSIS OF EARLY MUSIC
VOLUME 1
GARLAND REFERENCE LIBRARY OF THE HUMANITIES
VOLUME 1998

Criticism and Analysis of Early Music

Jessie Ann Owens, *Series Editor*

Tonal Structures
in Early Music
edited by Cristle Collins Judd

Counterpoint and
Compositional Process
in the Time of Dufay
*Perspectives from German
Musicology*
edited and translated by
Kevin N. Moll

Tonal Structures in Early Music

Edited by
Cristle Collins Judd

Garland Publishing, Inc.
A member of the Taylor & Francis Group
New York and London
1998

First paperback edition published in 2000 by
Garland Publishing Inc.
A Member of the Taylor & Francis Group
19 Union Square West
New York, NY 10003

10 9 8 7 6 5 4 3 2 1

Library of Congress Cataloging-in-Publication Data

Tonal structures in early music / edited by Cristle Collins Judd.
p. cm. — (Criticism and analysis of early music ; v. 1)
(Garland reference library of the humanities ; v. 1998)
Includes bibliographical references and index.
ISBN 0-8153-3638-1 (alk. paper)
1. Tonality. 2. Musical analysis. 3. Music—Theory. 4. Style, Musical. I. Judd, Cristle Collins. II. Series. III. Series: Garland reference library of the humanities ; vol. 1998.
ML3811.T66 1998
781.2'58'09—dc21 97–49499
CIP
MN

Cover illustration: Angelo da Picitono. *Fior angelico di musica.* Venice, 1547, f. Cii^r. By permission of the Music Division of the Library of Congress.

Printed on acid-free, 250-year-life paper
Manufactured in the United States of America

For
Harold Powers

Contents

Series Editor's Foreword

Jessie Ann Owens

Recent years have seen a critical reassessment of our approach to early music. Musicians, scholars, and critics have been searching for ways of talking about and reacting to the music that engage it not from the perspectives of later music but rather on its own terms. These new approaches would not be possible without the scholarship of the previous decades. The discovery and cataloguing of musical sources, the preparation of critical editions, and the investigation of archival documents have furnished important information about composers, performers, patrons, and institutions that supported the creation and performance of early music. Building on this work, the editors of these volumes now seek to develop and explore analytical methodologies for the discussion of early music as music.

Analytic methods are not easily found for early music. The theorists of the time had their own agendas, and they do not provide models that suit our purposes. As a consequence, many twentieth-century scholars have chosen approaches that reflect their own beliefs about early music and its relation to later music. While some continue to rely on common practice tonality as a prism through which to view early music, others have begun to explore methods that respect the integrity and self-sufficiency of the languages of early music.

We offer a forum for exploration of particular topics, from both a methodological and critical viewpoint. Our premise is that we can best develop new methodologies by encouraging debate. We will explore compositional procedures, tonal structures, musical borrowing, and other topics, focusing both on individual compositions and on theoretical systems. We seek to encourage critical writing about music that will be useful to performers, listeners, and scholars.

Brandeis University

Acknowledgments

I gratefully acknowledge the support of the University of Pennsylvania in the preparation of this volume. The Music Department underwrote the conference that preceded this book in March 1996 and the University of Pennsylvania Research Foundation provided a publication subvention for the preparation of camera-ready copy. My colleagues Lawrence Bernstein, Christopher Hasty, Norman Smith, and Gary Tomlinson chaired sessions, advised on conference matters, and read preliminary drafts of essays. As both colleague and husband, Robert Judd did all this and more. The graduate students in my "Analysis of Early Music" seminar provided help in hosting the conference. In addition, I would like to acknowledge Jessie Ann Owens and Harold Powers, participants with me in the roundtable that concluded the conference, and Leeman Perkins, a session respondent, for their generous and practical advice. Thanks are also due to Jessie, not only for inviting me to edit this volume, but also for her unswerving encouragement during the process of preparing it. Sue Cole offered support in matters many and sundry. Regina Christian assisted with page layout and formatting, David Osbon prepared camera-ready copy of music examples in SCORE, and Scot Grogan assisted in proofing and indexing. Ann Dixon and Jay Treat of Educational Technology Services at Penn provided advice on numerous technical matters. I owe a special word of thanks to Richard Hoffman for his invaluable (and good-humored) close reading of the entire manuscript in the final stages of production.

Introduction: Analyzing Early Music

Cristle Collins Judd

Analyzing early music is a venture with a rich history of provoking spirited exchanges within the musicological community. Articulating the problems associated with analyzing early music while proposing new analytical methods and techniques, as the present volume aims to do, brings a number of previously unstated assumptions about the activity of music analysis to the fore and highlights its place in intellectual inquiry. Exploring less conventional methods of analysis while reexamining the relevance of more traditional analytical approaches subjects many currently accepted views of the role of analysis to scrutiny and opens the possibility that analysis can critique and affect established ways of practicing musicology.

The formulation "early music analysis" captures the difficulties of the enterprise in its inherent ambiguities. Does "early" modify the activity of music[al] analysis, suggesting a search for historical precedents? Or does the phrase perhaps suggest an addition (and implicit corrective) to "tonal" and "post-tonal" analysis—the concerns of much present-day music theory and analysis? Neither emphasis is as straightforward as might at first seem and each is contingent on the other for an understanding of its meaning.

The former understanding—*early* music analysis—draws into question the ways in which musical analysis is defined and the ways in which we read theoretical and musical texts. Ian Bent has suggested that while analysis as "an approach and method can be traced back to the 1750s . . . [i]t existed as a scholarly tool, albeit an auxiliary one, from the Middle Ages onwards."[1] In particular, Bent points to the study of modal systems and theories of musical rhetoric as the site of such activity, emphasizing theorists' supplementation of verbal description with musical citations. Yet teasing out the implications of such verbal discourse proves to be complex. The analyst must unravel not only musical, theological, pedagogical, and philosophical strands of rhetoric, but also individual contexts that may impinge on the imputed analytic activity of the theorist in question. Theorists' citations of musical examples, if anything, prove even more resistant than the texts in which they are situated to yielding an obvious analytical context or model. When considered as appropriated texts, such examples' inclusion in a treatise may just as easily represent an unstated political or social agenda as an overt, if merely secondary, analytical activity. Then there is the problematic issue of how a modern reader is to negotiate the chasm between "our world" and "theirs" in using theoretical sources as a model for analytical activity while avoiding the pitfalls of the "authentic anachronism."

The second understanding implicit in this formulation—*early music* analysis—is equally multifaceted, both in its position in mainstream theoretical parlance and in the way it defines repertory. When seen to complete a trilogy including the tonal and post-tonal analysis that are mainstays of undergraduate and graduate theory curricula, it may appear to equate "early music" with "pre-tonal," easily fixing expectations in a teleological frame that suggests not only that the subject matter of "pre-tonal" analysis is chronologically prior to, but part of, a progression towards a tonal arrival. Ironically, scholars from both sides of an institutionally entrenched historical / theoretical divide might argue against such a subject heading, albeit from profoundly different perspectives. On the one hand, historians who work with so-called "early" repertories have been deeply and rightly skeptical of analytical appropriations by the theoretical community: the crimes charged have ranged from anachronism, to lack of familiarity with repertory and sources, to the universal nature of the analytical act.[2] But many theorists have been equally cool to such study, seeing the repertories as "under-theorized" in coeval sources and, more essentially, lacking associated theoretical apparatus of similar (presumed) explanatory power as those which provide the cohesion in study of later repertories, whether the chosen model is functional harmony, Schenkerian theory, or cognitive hypotheses, to name just a few. The charges by both parties (insofar as the camps I've described can be said really to exist in so pure a state) are not without merit, but with closer examination reveal tensions playing out more broadly in academic music study. Further, the moniker "early music" tacitly suggests that there is some common identifying trait in all music before a given date (ranging anywhere from 1500 to 1700 depending on who applies the term) sufficient to justify such a label.

In such a climate, the title of this volume—*Tonal Structures in Early Music*—may immediately set off alarm bells for music historians, performers of early music, and theorists alike. Indeed, I searched long and hard for a title for this collection (and the conference that preceded it), troubled because "tonal," "structure," and "early music" have all come to be such tremendously loaded terms in musical discourse. But I intend the use of the plural—structure*s*—to be telling. The essays in this volume consider the issue of tonal structure from historical, analytical, theoretical, and cultural perspectives. These essays share a common concern of dealing with "the notes," but the very act of defining those notes immediately raises a number of crucial concerns. It is worth emphasizing that the notation in which earlier music survives is only a trace of musical practice. It is clear that to attend to the notes in these repertories requires approaches that include the meta-theoretical (speculative considerations such as the conceptualization of pitch and the role of notation in relation to our understanding of tonal structure); historical and cultural (the context of the composition and its contingency on interpretation); history of theory (study of critical language and theoretical formulations in conjunction with practical manifestations); abstractly theoretical representations (the conceptual system within which tonal structure operates); and analytical models (detailed study of individual compositions or groups of compositions). Of course, these concerns are not mutually exclusive and all are represented—often in a deliberately uneasy balance—to some degree in the essays collected here.

In part, the discomfiting position occupied by these essays may be traced to a musicological tradition inherited from nineteenth-century perspectives on early music. In 1840, François Joseph Fétis recognized phenomena which he described as *tonalité ancienne*, the tonality of plainchant and Palestrina, and *tonalité moderne*, the tonality of Monteverdi and his successors.[3] Although Fétis's typology might, out of context, seem a simple adaptation of the seventeenth-century *stile antico / stile nuovo* dichotomy, his specific connection of the ancient and modern "tonality" not only with Palestrina and Monteverdi respectively, but as identified by the presence (or absence) of the dominant seventh chord set the direction for numerous studies of the last century and a half. Indeed, his description of "plainchant tonality" as a kind of diatonicism in which relations between tones were without tendency and lacking a pitch hierarchy driven by the possibility of modulation—a placidness he equated with the spiritualism of Palestrina's music—is still a pervading image in popular descriptions of early music from Gregorian chant to sixteenth-century polyphony.

One response to this ancient-modern tonal dualism was the recognition by scholars of "modern tonality" in ever-earlier repertories as these repertories were "colonized" and "familiarized" in modern editions and positioned along the inexorable march toward tonality.[4] To cite a well-known example, Lowinsky claimed for Josquin the dominant seventh and pushed the "moderns" back another couple of generations from Fétis's emphasis on Monteverdi.[5] But while the dominant seventh chord (and more specifically the affinity for resolution held within it by $\hat{4}$ and $\hat{7}$) was central to Fétis's formulation, the search for modern "tonal" composers and theorists was by no means so restricted among later writers. Thus, Riemann saw

Zarlino as a "harmonic dualist" (and therefore a modern). Indeed, Riemann fixed the "transition" from modal to tonal by insisting on a disposition of *musica ficta* that placed the tonic (shown boxed here) in a central position flanked by the subdominant and dominant (encircled) thus:

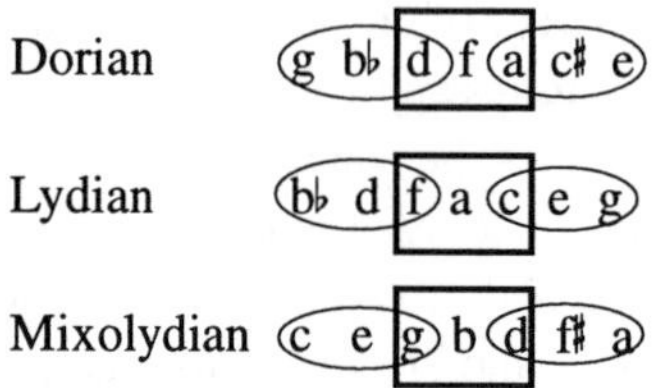

The identification of the cadence as the locus of tonal impulse, particularly the V–I cadence, motivated the "emerging" tonality debate. Lowinsky described the cadence as the "cradle of tonality," and Besseler argued for the implications of harmonic function in Dufay's contratenors.[6]

Ironically, the extensions of such arguments ultimately led to a *de facto* rejection of the "ancient" / "modern" opposition from neo-Schenkerians whose analyses sought to demonstrate ever earlier instances of repertories bearing the universal hallmarks of tonality as understood via eighteenth- and nineteenth-century music in a continuum from earliest times. Put simply, Fétis's underlying hypothesis that all tonality was on the march toward the modern arrival (and ultimately dissolution in what he described as *omnitonique* music) received analytical justification in analyses such as those of Salzer, Novack, and Stern,[7] even though such a view was at odds with the firmly inscribed emphasis in Schenker's own work on the "Bach to Brahms" repertory. Indeed, Schenker was at pains to point out the ways in which earlier repertories failed to meet his criteria of tonality.

But there has, no doubt, been a certain non-critical comfort associated with analyzing works from the "common-practice" period, an assumption of continuity of tradition that provides a veneer of "intuitive knowing" to the enterprise. The attempt to annex earlier works to such tonality not only appeared to provide a much-desired critical vocabulary for describing such works, but also served as a useful means by which to elevate them to membership in the canon of artistic masterpieces.

Thus the significance and meaning of the phrase "early tonality" has ranged from the pejorative to the laudatory depending on context. A now well-established reception history frequently placed the year 1500 as a watershed in the history of music, a time in which composers like Josquin displayed a new awareness of harmonic possibilities and of the organizing force of tonality.[8] Such a position minimizes the distance in both time and tradition that separates us from such music by trying to place it in a context that forms a link with present understandings and concerns rather than acknowledging its differences. Hence the quest to discover tonality, the focus on cadential pitch, and concerns with voice-leading. Yet recognizing the distance that separates us from the music discussed in this volume may prove a beneficial situation, forcing us to confront the distance and difference of repertories that appear to be more "familiar."

One response to "anachronistic" Schenkerian readings firmly reinscribed the ancient / modern polarity via the appropriation of the "authentic" mantle of contemporaneous theorists and modality as the system that described the pitch organization of "ancient" tonality.[9] The trend toward more "historically-informed" analysis and the privileging of modal over tonal theory arose in part from the same reception history of music by composers like Josquin and Palestrina that fueled the search for "early tonality." Meier's *The Modes of Classical Vocal Polyphony* is the classic exposition of this view of the works of mid-sixteenth-century composers' music as expressive paradigms of modality.[10] His last work, *Alte Tonarten*, explicitly recognized the "old" tonality in its title. The view that Meier represents accords well with Fétis's original formulation of the ancient tonality as that of Palestrina and plainchant and has been readily and widely embraced in studies of Renaissance music. The tonal / modal dichotomy has also been reinforced to a certain extent by disciplinary boundaries: exponents of the tonal view tended to be music theorists, while the modal view was most keenly espoused by historical musicologists. Works attributed to Josquin proved central to both positions, with his authorship serving not only as a kind of stamp of validation of the quality of the individual works under discussion but also for fixing the crucial date at about 1500.[11]

Enlightening though Meier's work was, it was not without its critics.[12] Over the last two decades, a series of increasingly skeptical articles by Harold Powers attempted to demonstrate the artificiality of the modal / tonal dichotomy enshrined in this debate.[13] And while Powers's pathbreaking work has indeed eroded the modal / tonal paradigm, his work has only hinted at the paradigm with which a modal / tonal, ancient / modern binarism is to be replaced.[14]

A final group of studies that might be loosely described as empirical or structuralist in orientation needs to be added to the modal / tonal mix I have just described in exploring the current climate of early music analysis. One approach to such studies has been the "cataloguing" of tonal materials in a work or group of works.[15] While these collections may be measured against either coeval or modern theories, the impulse is essentially empirical.[16] And early music has been seen as particularly hospitable to an exploration of analytical techniques derived from language models and structuralist linguistics.[17] Most notable have been attempts stemming from Ruwet's analysis of a *Geisslerlied*, and the work of Lidov and Vaccaro.[18]

It is primarily these analytical traditions of exploring the organization of pitch—tonal, modal, and structural—that the essays in this volume partake of, respond to, and attempt to move beyond.[19] Five of the essays in this volume were first presented at a conference of the same name at the University of Pennsylvania (March 29–30, 1996).[20] The other four essays in this volume had been presented in various forms on earlier occasions. Two large studies on critical language, those by Powers and Owens, provided the starting point for companion essays by Dodds and Bailey, respectively, that explore the application of such language to specific repertories.

These essays traverse (and re-traverse) some of the same routes as their predecessors. Highlighting the names Josquin, Zarlino, Palestrina, and Monteverdi, as two sessions at the conference did, harks back to the Lowinsky, Riemann, Fétis scenario I described above. There is also a very real sense in which many of these essays respond to the analyses that form the final chapter of Dahlhaus's *Studies on the Origins of Harmonic Tonality*. Yet the collection of essays presented here is anything but repertorially or chronologically comprehensive. One will be disappointed if looking for the "great men" of early music: Palestrina, Lasso, and Monteverdi, for example, although works of Josquin are represented in two essays. Machaut is here, but he is keeping company with the likes of anonymous composers of seventeenth-century English keyboard music and lesser-known figures like Murschhauser. The essays on the more well-known composers focus on individual pieces (Fuller, Judd, Steele) while the more methodological studies deal with less usual repertories (and theorists) in this field.

Instead what unites these essays is a shared concern with a historically driven interpretation and its role in analysis. It was abundantly clear at the conference and reinforced here that, as a community, we have not thrown out "mode"—and are unlikely to any time soon—despite Powers's remonstrances, not least because it remains (or appears to remain) a useful descriptive tool for repertories for which we feel in possession of so few adequate analytic tools.[21] What does emerge from these essays are models of interpreting modal theory in nuanced and pluralistic readings that contrast with what Owens aptly describes as "neo-modal" theory—a relatively recent abstraction of diatonic scale types corresponding to modes but lacking the explanatory richness of contextualized modal theory. Frans Wiering places the modal debate in a new context by describing what he terms "internal" and "external" views of the modes, contrasting the minimal knowledge one might rightly expect any musician to have of the modes, with the much deeper understanding one *might* have, and suggesting the range of possibilities this could lead to in composition and performance. My own essay, on Josquin's *In principio erat verbum*, argues that the tonal structure of a group of motets has been fundamentally misconstrued by the inappropriate application of modal labels. Owens and

Bailey suggest the different conceptual framework in which English musicians operated, unadulterated, as it were, by continental modal theory. The concluding essays (Powers and Dodds) demonstrate that understanding the complicated interplay of modes (of both the eight- and twelve-fold variety), psalm tones, and church keys in the seventeenth (and into the eighteenth) century may be the way that we begin to defamiliarize the major-minor tonality that we once thought we understood.

These essays also point in a number of new directions. At a basic level, all confront, directly or indirectly, the ways in which so-called "historical theory" informs analytic and interpretive endeavors. That no easy consensus on the topic comes out of reading these essays together, is, I am convinced, not only a good thing but a salutary reminder of the complexity of the endeavor. Thus Margaret Bent argues passionately and persuasively on the efficacy of mastering the "grammar" of polyphony—dyadic counterpoint—while Sarah Fuller cautions on the difficulty of such a task, implicated as we are as modern readers and listeners.

Not surprisingly, too, consensus is equally lacking on analytical strategies, tied as most of these essays are first and foremost to interpreting particular theoretical traditions and specific repertories. Despite the "historical perspective" that characterizes this volume, there is no out-of-hand rejection of modern analytical techniques but the uneasy—almost schizophrenic at times—relationship is negotiated with no little difficulty. Yet, these essays do not pretend to be the "authentic analyses" which Peter Schubert has recently criticized.[22] Schubert's reductive view of the privileging of historical evidence in analysis as a kind of cosmetic sham does a disservice to historians and theorists alike. The essays in this volume succeed by engaging the perspectives of past and present as only possible when one possesses a thorough knowledge of theoretical sources and manuscript traditions, a deep awareness of repertory and the culture which surrounded it, and a willingness to attempt to understand the music not only as it might have been understood by its contemporaries but also as modern historian and listener—to position one's self not only as critic but as advocate. The essays presented here do not aim at "re-creation"— indeed the creative impulse, either compositional or performative, is not the focus of those essays that deal primarily with critical language—instead they challenge us to a dialogue with the past rather than a definitive "solution" to its "problems." Further, these essays confront the questions of what the works discussed here have in common beyond a chronological frame and what these repertories can mean to twentieth-century listeners. Conventional notions of expectation, tension and release, segmentation, narrative, and perceptual salience are all highlighted, indeed become areas of contention as they are re-focused by the perspectives offered here.

The essays in this volume are unashamedly preoccupied with tonal structure, a bias toward pitch and pitch materials as quantifiable analytical material.[23] But the re-examinations presented here place that focus on pitch in a new light. Principles of tonal structure are here described within narrow geographical or chronological confines. No "universal" theory of the "tonality" of early music emerges from these essays. Far from it! Fuller, for example, makes clear that "signature" and "systems"— "etic" markers for mid-sixteenth-century continental polyphony— are objective only within that cultural context. The association between tonal structure and generic conventions recurs in several essays. Most significant perhaps is the conceptual transformation heralded by the positions of the essays which open and close this volume. While Margaret Bent deftly illustrates the interrelationship of counterpoint and performer's accidentals in fourteenth- and fifteenth-century polyphony via a Guidonian conception of pitch, the final essays by Powers and Dodds rely on a conceptualization linked to the keyboard.

The notion of *tonalité moderne* (by whatever name we wish to give it) has no doubt led to painting with broad brush strokes that have made to seem trivial distinctions that are anything but. The historical, theoretical, and cultural groundwork laid by many of these essays is crucial to even an approximate understanding of the repertory with which we are concerned. Although the repertory discussed in this volume spans some 450 years, it is (relatively) narrowly construed and the chronological boundaries may seem to extend to a surprisingly late date (into the eighteenth century). All of the theoretical and musical sources considered here focus on polyphony, undoubtedly music that constituted only a small fraction of the music from this period, but a fraction preserved on account of notational exigencies. The earliest examples discussed here are chosen from fourteenth-century song (Machaut), the latest from a keyboard repertory printed at the beginning of the eighteenth century (Murschhauser). It is not coincidental that the focus of the essays at the beginning of the book are on vocal music while those that conclude the volume consider instrumental (and specifically keyboard) music. These essays bridge a crucial conceptual shift from the Guidonian hand to the keyboard as an explanatory model of pitch relationships. It is a shift that is by no means straightforward, but one which proves central to understanding the traces of earlier musical practices transmitted to us by notation, for it fundamentally alters the meaning of that notation.

* * *

Finally, a word about the dedication. It seemed only fitting to offer this volume to Harold Powers (b. August 5, 1928) as an unofficial "Festschrift," and I am delighted to have the opportunity to do so. I feel certain that Harry will appreciate the quirkiness of being presented with a volume containing one of his own seminal essays (an essay that has been circulating far too long in a pre-publication typescript). Two essays in the volume were individually dedicated to him and references to Powers's work are liberally sprinkled throughout the book. Indeed, he is the one author cited in *every* essay. Although "mode guru" is only one of the hats Harry wears so interchangeably,[24] his undeniable impact on the field of analyzing early music is ever-present and warmly attested in this volume.

NOTES

1. Bent, "Analysis," 342.

2. See, for example, Aldrich, "Approach," and Treitler, "To Worship that Celestial Sound."

3. Fétis, *Esquisse de l'histoire de l'harmonie*. Fétis was of course not the first to discuss tonality or to propose this distinction, but the particular historical context in which he clothed it was extremely influential.

4. Indeed, it is this teleological perspective which is perhaps the central (if in the present context, dubious) contribution of Fétis's history of tonality. For a recent, Hegelian, interpretation, see Christensen, "Fétis and emerging tonal consciousness."

5. Lowinsky, *Tonality and Atonality*. The work in question was the motet *Benedicite omnia opera*. Dahlhaus refuted Lowinsky's claims in *Studies*, showing not only that the dominant seventh highlighted by Lowinsky failed to function as tonal theory would suggest, but also noting the late provenance of the motet and questioning the reliability of its attribution to Josquin.

6. The "emerging tonality" debate, with its attendant emphasis on the ways in which cadences and harmonic function are identified and described, polarized a generation of scholars. This is not the place to summarize the debate, but only to highlight the sources central to it in recent years: Lowinsky, *Tonality and Atonality*; Besseler, *Bourdon und Fauxbourdon*; Randel, "Emerging Triadic Tonality"; Crocker, "Discant and Counterpoint"; Dahlhaus, *Studies*; Meier, *The Modes*; and Rivera, "Harmonic Theory."

7. Salzer, "Tonality in Medieval Polyphony" and *Structural Hearing*; Novack, "The Analysis of Pre-Baroque Music" and "The History of the Phrygian Mode"; and Stern, "Tonal Organization in Modal Polyphony."

8. E. g., Brown, *Music in the Renaissance*.

9. For one of the strongest statements in opposition to "anachronistic" analysis, see Aldrich, "Approach."

10. On the ways in which the analyses in Meier's *The Modes* evolved from his earlier work, see Wiering, "Language of the Modes." Meier's work has been extended beyond the central mid-century repertory on which he focused to both earlier and later repertories as in Krantz, "Rhetorical and Structural Functions," and McClary, "Transition from Modal to

Tonal." Of course, Meier himself discussed both Josquin and Monteverdi in "Musica Reservata," and "Zur Tonart."

11. Ironically, it is the same works about which questions of authorship, date, and geographic provenance have arisen that are central to debate.

12. Meier and Dahlhaus engaged in a lengthy verbal sparring match that culminated in Dahlhaus's position statement in his *Studies*, particularly his insistence on the concept of *Gesamtmodi* and Meier's refutation and (equally strong) insistence on the plagal / authentic distinction in *The Modes*. That both stances were problematic was demonstrated in Powers, "Modal Representation." On Meier, see Owens' review. On the Meier-Dahlhaus debate, see Judd, review of Dahlhaus, *Studies*. More recently, see the lengthy discussion of the evolution of Meier's thinking on modes in Wiering, "Language of the Modes," 31–54.

13. Most notably in "*Vestiva I colli*," "Mode," "Tonal Types," "Modal Representation," "Cultural Construct," "Monteverdi's Model," and "Is Mode Real?". Powers's work is cited extensively in this volume; I will not summarize his position here.

14. His article "From Psalmody to Tonality," in this volume, goes some way toward suggesting a new model.

15. The extreme forms of this approach were the computer-generated studies associated with the Princeton Josquin project in the late 60s and 70s. See, for example, Mendel, "Towards Objective Criteria."

16. For example, I would describe Treitler's "Tone System" in this way whereas Perkins's "Mode and Structure," although superficially similar, is motivated by a desire to confirm the relevance of theoretical descriptions by demonstrating their appearance in a coeval repertory.

17. On the problems of language models for analysis, see Powers, "Language Models."

18. Ruwet, "Méthodes" (Ruwet later recanted this analysis but it had a profound influence on musical semiotics as seen in the writings of Nattiez. See Everist's discussion in his translation of Ruwet's "Methods."); Lidov, "Lamento"; Vaccaro, "Proposition."

19. Everist, ed., *Music before 1600* offers a cross-section of these analytical approaches, taking individual pieces intended to serve as models as their starting points.

20. The essays by Bailey, Dodds, Fuller, Steele, and Wiering. This volume is by no means a "proceedings" of the conference which included four sessions entitled "Fourteenth- and Fifteenth-Century Song," "Mode and Beyond," "Monteverdi," and "Instrumental Music" comprising thirteen papers and concluding with a roundtable discussion.

21. Most recently, see Perkins, "Modal Species."

22. Schubert, "Authentic Analysis." Schubert's essay is directed primarily at Meier, *The Modes*. The problems of Meier's use (misprision) of sources have long been noted in reviews and responses to his work, most notably in Dahlhaus, *Studies*, but see also Owens's review of *The Modes*, Powers, "Modal Representation," and Wiering, "Language of the

Modes." Meier simply functions as a fitting straw man for the thesis against which Schubert wishes to argue.

23. The exclusive focus on pitch is also a practicality of the organization of the present series in which volumes have been grouped by analytical concerns that will include musical borrowing, compositional procedures, and so forth.

24. Powers, "Three Pragmatists."

The Grammar of Early Music: Preconditions for Analysis*

Margaret Bent

For Harold Powers
on his seventieth birthday

> Given my present belief in the much greater range of variability as to both order and kind of complexity in the world's musics versus the world's languages, I can hardly imagine how a model developed really satisfactorily for the detailed structural explanation of one musical language is so easily modified to another, and all the more so if the original model be evolved from linguistics rather than from the musical disciplines.
>
> (Powers, "Language Models and Musical Analysis," 48.)

> "Objective" analysis is a tool, primarily useful for suggesting or confirming putative relationships between different musical styles. . . . "Critical" analysis results not in a statistical measurement of style or proof of relationship but rather, ideally, in a formal model for a relatively independent and artistically controllable style within a culture, and should then be viable for accounting for individual manifestations of that style. . . .
>
> [The author] neglects to take sufficiently into account the possibilities of critical musical analysis as though from within the culture, be it by a native or a native-trained foreigner.
>
> (Powers, review of A. Merriam, *The Anthropology of Music*, 171, 167.)

HISTORY AND ANALYSIS

Fifteen years ago, Philip Brett pleaded for more attention to "the music itself": "I do think," he wrote then," we need insights into the intentions and the anatomy of early music derived from close reading of the music itself and related not to some abstract method but to the realities of the matter in hand."[1] He acknowledged the different place and importance of external factors, but argued that we should face the music's internal logic on its own terms, not importing extraneous standards or extrinsic "method," whether analytical or critical. He questioned new critical fashions which "seem to one observer at least to have a tendency to direct attention on to the critic and on to the mechanics of the critical response, thus once again deflecting it from the work and from the composer's intentions and conception." He didn't pursue or exemplify how he thought this should happen, and his own work has taken a different direction since then. His statement was, in part, a response to Kerman's plea for criticism to take the place of analysis.[2] Kerman also observed a tendency for early-music studies to be consciously deflected from consideration of the music itself. "The music itself" sounds like a good thing, uncontroversially so. But by this is often meant the modern dress in which we now hear early music, through modern transcriptions or with the conditioning of intervening centuries and especially of nineteenth-century harmonic pedagogy, overlaid with how we now like it to sound; all this is assuredly not the same thing as considering it "in its own terms." It has become axiomatic for some that we should attend rather to our—necessarily present-day—experience-centered response than to object-centered investigation. (Process-centered might be a better term.) For others, the wish to assimilate medieval "masterpieces" to the western canon on equal terms with the symphonies of Beethoven has implied that they can be listened to and analyzed in the same way. There is room for many diverse endeavors and objectives that bear different fruit, address different questions, and have different limitations; no activity need invalidate any of the others. This essay sets out to show how we might indeed set about recovering, to the greatest extent possible, the work's own grammatical sense, in terms proper to it. Pursuit of that particular goal *does* exclude some other incompatible enterprises, and it qualifies certain pre-analytical assumptions as valid or invalid. It reaffirms a role for historically appropriate theory in the analysis of early music, specifically with regard to its elementary contrapuntal foundations. It suggests how we might develop theoretically informed habits of construing early music at the most basic level, habits built on those foundations that go on to project them beyond counterpoint manuals without violating their teaching, and are in turn informed by composed music and carried through into intelligible performance. Generalizations in what follows apply (unless otherwise stated, and *mutatis mutandis*) mostly to fifteenth-century music, with some glances to the fourteenth and sixteenth centuries. If we are to develop an ear for music of the period, if we would hear what remains of their voices rather than overwriting them with our own, let it be an ear properly attuned to *their* musical syntax rather than cobbled *ad hoc* from *ours*.

In different ways, Kerman and Treitler have championed kinds of writing about music that get away from the analyst's close focus on the notes, Kerman by urging humane criticism,[3] and Treitler by emphasising cultural and historical context.[4] Following these leads, attention to the notes themselves has indeed taken a back seat in much recent critical writing by musicologists, thus widening the gap between criticism and analysis and dislocating their shared spectrum of competence. These positions have contributed to the polarization of two extremes: on the one hand, contextual music history conducted at some remove from the scores, even dispensing with them, and on the other, formalist analysis of those scores with no attention to historical factors. The camps more often appear to be embattled than complementary, and not only when it comes to the analysis of early music; this is unnecessary and regrettable. Fashionable stampedes are invariably followed by famine in vacated fields. Historians and critics are rightly suspicious of extrinsic analytical methods claimed to be formalist, positivist, or universal: "By removing the bare score from its context in order to examine it as an autonomous organism, the analyst removes that organism from the ecology that sustains it."[5] Recently, this ecology has been placed above all in the domain of historical and cultural or social context,[6] an essential part of musical and historical investigation, but usually separable from the notes themselves. Good scholarship has always combined wide-ranging consideration of context with deep attention to the notes, and needs no new labels to justify it. I include in this the best work of such as Kerman and Lowinsky, despite their ideological differences.[7] But—again—I charge Kerman with causing no little mischief towards such scholarship by dismissing as positivism (simplistically defined) much well-founded and innovative work which in fact has the opposite orientation.[8]

The historical ingredient in approaching early music is generally understood as twofold: first, the provision of historical contextual information—about the composer, the circumstances of performance and patronage, and second, the main subject of this essay, the application of "historical" theory contemporaneous with the music. The former is what we might call the biographical level, and treats the historical ingredient in music analysis as mainly or solely verbal and descriptive. Some aspects of "biographical" enquiry may indeed be central to the musical substance; these might include choice of cantus firmus, available performing forces as a determinant of texture, and aspects of text, genre, and musical style that are determined by context or patronage. But the more external cultural or sociological aspects may be of very limited relevance for understanding the actual musical substance of medieval polyphony. Contextual and biographical work does not constitute a role for history that bears very directly on editing, performance, listening and on the professional extension of listening in analysis. Critical writing often leans heavily on words and programs and verbalized reception, operating at some remove from the language of the note-content and avoiding technical engagement with the workings of the actual fabric of the music. It does no disrespect to such writing to say that it has little to offer to the discipline of analysis.[9] A further distinction: contextual history is a very different matter from the use of early theory. Both have been included as "historicist" and set up as straw men vulnerable to ridicule by theorists who urge an ahistorical view,[10] and by students of medieval music who adopt the perspective of modern listeners.[11] In outlining the relationship between music analysis and music history, Ian Bent presents "historical and analytical inquiry [as] locked together in mutual dependency, with all things common as to subject matter and with completely complementary methods of working."[12] But in practice, despite this counsel of perfection, the historical ingredient in analysis is often merely contextual, promoting knowledge *about* the music rather than knowledge *of* the music.

One aspect of these dislocations has been constructively addressed by Reinhard Strohm, who observes that the music historian's traditional interest in style has been supplanted by [formalist] interest in structure, on the authority claimed for technical advances in analysis.[13] He argues against the reductionist views that historians and analysts often have of each other's activities: views of the historian as a sort of cataloguer whose results are of little interest to the analyst, and views of the analyst as committed to developing systematic, "scientific," ahistorical universals that are not helpful to the historian seeking to resolve particular connections for music contextually rooted in place and time. Indeed, he even claims that many analytical practitioners do what historians have been unfairly blamed for: "they reduce their methodologies to one specific technique, so that they no longer need to worry about individual pieces of music." The overwhelming question arising from universal analytical systems, "How does music work?", is usually too large and general to field within a historian's immediate concerns; it inhabits the area where analysis meets philosophy and aesthetics. The historian, says Strohm, needs to ask not only "How does this music work?" but "How *did* this music work?", seeking "to place the work in a history of musical thought; it connects the investigator himself with that string of thought." He goes on to distinguish this both from "criticism" and from "historical context," the goals advocated by Kerman and Treitler, both of whom oppose "structural analysis," and encourages music historians—with examples—to devise methods of analysis tailored to their own concerns, to trace the "string of compositional thought in history." Strohm cites Dahlhaus's advocacy of "an analysis which takes as its point of departure matters of compositional technique, instead of painting a panorama of cultural history into which music can be inserted."[14] I also propose to address this middle ground as defined by Dahlhaus, in ways that complement the contribution of Strohm. I shall advocate historically appropriate technical approaches to the analysis of early music, grounded in the theory and in the corresponding musical repertories, simple techniques that need to be mastered and internalized at the grammatical level before valid further analytical activity or interpretation can take place. In addition, we might ask not only how a particular theory works in contexts to which we choose to apply it, but how their theory worked for them.

> No critic, not even a topical analyst, can escape seeing the musical past from a present perspective. But . . . the common-language approach of the topical-analysis critics permits a separation between present sensibility and the general sensibilities of the late eighteenth century, allowing for an ever-evolving dialogue between the vanished past and the evanescent present.
>
> (Powers, "Reading Mozart's Music," 43.)

It has also been argued that analysis as a part of historical investigation should be conducted as a dialogue with the past.[15] Although the hermeneutic model may sometimes be helpful, it can offer an uneasy compromise; the voice of the past has often not been an equal partner in the dialogue. Pieces of music will only unfold their secrets within the dialogue process if the questions are sufficiently refined: "Sonate, que me veux-tu?" is not enough. No "neutral" modern criteria or ahistorical methodologies are going to give relevant answers with respect to a piece of fifteenth-century music unless the "grammar" specific to that music informed the question. A methodology cannot be sensitive to the particular language of pre-tonal music unless that language was taken into account in formulating the analytical method—in which case it would indeed be to some extent a historically sensitive method. The task is to reconstruct, as precisely as possible in the absence of native witnesses, the languages, grammars and dialects proper to specific repertories, as we would in dealing with their verbal counterparts, if we aspire not to a ventriloquized monologue but to a true dialogue. In the case of music from whose performing traditions we have not been severed, "we have stored up from childhood an unconscious fund of comparative material which has coalesced into a working norm for criticism and comparative analysis" (Kerman); this fund cannot help us with music much older and very differently premised from that to which we do have such a connection. It is no accident that printed scores and recorded performances of Mozart are now almost free of wrong notes, whereas in editions and performances of Machaut barbarisms still abound. The problem is widespread in less familiar styles, and its least kind interpretation is that editors and performers do not understand the grammar of those styles well enough to distinguish, as they can in Mozart, between notes that are clearly right and notes that are clearly wrong.

Analytical methods are sometimes discussed as though the choice were simply a matter of the preference or school of the analyst, in which any analytical methodology may be applied to any music. Different analyses may indeed be equally valid, but not if they proceed from faulty premises.[16] Certain kinds of analysis or analytical statements may qualify as right or wrong, appropriate or inappropriate, depending whether or not they take account of the music's particular underlying grammar. Examples of right or appropriate analysis are those that proceed from such objective preliminaries as correct identification of a cantus firmus or of the note-row of a serial composition, the key of a tonal piece, the counter-subject of a fugue, the discant-tenor core of a fifteenth-century song, the model of a parody mass, the resolution of a mensuration canon; and that recognize those things as primary or pre-analytical constraints, either of pre-existent material or of technique. True statements can also be made about the structural divisions of an isorhythmic motet as defined by its color and talea repetitions, their temporal relationship to each other, and the boundaries between texts, i.e. the number of words or lines in the triplum and duplum respectively. Similar weight could also be carried where the honoree of a motet was named at a significant proportional node of the words or lines of the text, marked with fermata chords or placed at a structural division of the music. Such observations and choices must usually have been part of the composer's conscious plan for a piece, and must be taken into account as pre-analytical facts. Where the analyst's premises or statements are of a type that can be judged either true or false, a first level of compositional intent can be assumed that has nothing to do with the "intentional fallacy" of interpretation. Barring occasional disputable cases, such areas can be incontrovertible, unlike subsequent acts of interpretation that reflect the analyst's own biases or concerns and may depart from those of the composer. To understand such fundamentals properly is as essential to correct interpretation of the music as is knowledge of sexagesimal calculation to understanding early astronomy, or knowledge of the relationship of pounds, shillings, and pence to understanding pre-decimal British currency. After that, interpretative editing, performance, and analysis can begin.

> [I]n applications of the music-as-language metaphor we should attend to diverse musical traditions in musical terms, including not only traditions of the music we study but also traditions of how we study music.
>
> (Powers, "Language Models and Musical Analysis," 54–55.)

> A tonal type is minimally identifiable by its three markers and thus objectively observable completely apart from its musical or cultural context; it is "scientific," it is "etic." "Mode" conversely is all bound up in sixteenth-century musical culture, not as a living doctrine of the music of the church and a heritage from the Middle Ages but also as a musical construct being experimented with by members of the culture, from both humanistic and traditional points of view; it is thoroughly "emic" and requires study on its own terms. . . .
>
> (Powers, "Tonal Types," 439.)

Harold Powers has brought some important distinctions to the fore in distinguishing etic tonal types from emic modes, and in contrasting determinable keys with highly indeterminate modal judgments.[17] His work uncovers the individual agendas that disqualify many early theorists from being normative, showing them to be mere informants. An analysis may be judged wrong or inappropriate not so much because it conflicts with one or another contemporary theoretical statement, but rather if it requires us to override the mainstream of counterpoint teaching by many theorists over a long period, teaching which is complemented and corroborated in the music. Powers has stressed that basic counterpoint teaching remains rather constant over a long period, and should not be confused with "creative and ingenious theorizing: how things *ought* to be regarded, not how they *were* regarded":

> Counterpoint texts tend to resemble one another both in the underlying principles of voice-leading they espouse and in the kinds and orderings of rules they provide, but no one could accuse the harmony texts of, let us say, Heinrich Schenker and Hugo Riemann, or of Allen Irvine McHose and Walter Piston—or for that matter, of Arnold Schoenberg, Paul Hindemith, and Roger Sessions—of being mutually compatible, either in premise or in practice.[18]

A wrongly identified note-row, fugue subject, start of recapitulation, rondeau repetition, the failure to acknowledge a discant-tenor duet—all these can invalidate an analysis built upon them. Indeed, a proper analytic foundation should not only underpin an analysis but in turn have informed the edition or version that is being analyzed. In the case of early music this may often mean taking account of multiple versions of the "same" piece, with and without added or optional parts. Analyses may also be wrong according to ethnic tradition, as in the discovery of harmonic-tonal patterns in Indian music, the equivalent, in displacement, of the anachronism that claims serial patterns in Liszt or Mozart,[19] tonal harmony in Du Fay[20] (or perhaps, even in certain cases, modes in polyphony). A time-neutral analysis may observe the presence of constellations that resemble note-rows, or triads, but that does not ensure that they conform to the way that serial or tonal composers use them, nor that they were designed as such. Separations of grammatical and semantic sense are explored by Steven Pinker through analyses of statements as word-trees.[21] Chomsky used "Colorless green ideas sleep furiously" to embody semantic nonsense in a grammatically correct structure. Even more germane to the present concerns in music are (1) examples that deal with transitive and intransitive verbs, where inbuilt rules permit "Melvin dined" but not "Melvin dined the pizza," and "Melvin devoured the pizza" but not "Melvin devoured" (p. 112); and (2) grammar-dependent ambiguities of a kind that often generates humor, such as "discuss sex with Dick Cavett" (pp. 102–03) and many more culled from headlines ("Reagan wins on budget, but more lies ahead," p. 119). In such examples there is always a primary sense as well as a secondary meaning that is intentionally or unintentionally incongruous. We are, of course, far from defining semantic sense in music, but grammatical ambiguity is often present, where a progression construed in terms of early-music grammar may lend itself to a different—but usually imperfect—construction in terms of eighteenth-century harmony, inverting tension and resolution, antecedent and consequent, in much the same way that these examples exhibit differently demarcated sense units, or the use of the same word as either a noun or a verb. The musical examples later in this essay exemplify some of these points. An interesting musical example of cross-cultural miscomprehension is given in an experiment by P. Hopkins, reporting the response of three culturally diverse listeners to Norwegian Hardanger fiddle music, and the differences and levels of incomprehension that arose from their inability to construe it according to the primary expectations of each for coherence.[22] The western musician failed to realize his preconception of the subordination of rhythmic to pitch structures; the Indian musician failed to find the expected extended rhythmic patterns; the Greek rationalized what he heard in terms of Balkan additive rhythmic structures. The "basic interpretational framework that each musician brought to the task proved incapable of structural modification; all he could do was try out different ways of configuring what he heard within that framework."

A recent article invoked Thor Heyerdahl's Kon-Tiki expedition, which tested whether a particular voyage using a balsa-wood raft could be technically replicated. The author rightly distinguished such an experiment from the quite different exercise of pure antiquarianism—trying to *be* the ancient explorers, to think and eat like them, but neglected to allow for historically-informed technical validity, and scathingly relegated history to its "biographical" role: "Historical evidence in the analysis of early music is privileged only in that it provides a backdrop that happens to be chronologically consistent with the music . . . it gives local color and a "feel" for the period. . . . Heyerdahl in a grass skirt."[23] Such a view of "analysis in period costume"[24] fails to get beyond the cosmetic aspect; sentimental antiquarianism and creative anachronism are precisely not appropriate concerns of analysis, which should not be a Merchant Ivory costume drama production with the television aerials airbrushed out. Rather, failure to be fully cognizant of historically demonstrable constraints and differences would be like putting an outboard motor on the Kon-Tiki raft and navigating by computer. Not only the destination but the journey is important, not only the "what" but the "how," which places the destination in a different light. Certain things can be established in purely technical terms without requiring us to eat the diet of early explorers, wear their dress, or enter into their heads—which of course we couldn't do even if we chose to try. But technical understanding is a realistic if modest goal, a necessary basis for any valid analysis; and it is precisely this dimension that is conspicuously scarce in contrapuntally-oriented analyses of early music.[25]

If most analysts have failed to come to grips with early music in any significant way, despite several attempts to forge new tools, it is precisely because dealing with "the music itself" without proper historically grounded technical preparation, whether in an allegedly neutral way with necessarily universal assumptions, or whether as "we" hear or see it, is doomed to failure. An ahistorical approach can only be sterile for repertories which did not inform its techniques. This has nothing to do with historical information *about* the pieces, but with how we engage with the specifics of their musical language, starting by internalizing the fundamentals of their internally coherent but distinctive musical grammar. Whatever its current status in other respects, and whatever degree of universalism permeates some of its claims, Lerdahl and Jackendoff's generative theory of tonal music did not claim to be universal, even for European music. It described the goal of a theory of music as a "formal description of the musical intuitions of a listener who is experienced in a musical idiom," going on to define various gradations of listener experience, from less sophisticated to "perfect."[26] It is precisely such experience in idiom that I advocate here.

Now we need to grasp the nettles of formalism and of anachronistic (or "presentist") analysis. Few will admit without qualification to being a "presentist" or a "historicist"; I borrow these slightly pejorative terms merely as a short-hand.[27] So-called "presentist" analysts see attempts to reconstruct the music's own terms as futile. It's how we now hear it that counts, they say; we should explain "what we currently see and hear in the music . . . in terms which make sense to us."[28] Some feel that because "the music itself" is not completely recoverable—an undeniable fact—it is not even worth attempting a partial reconstruction. The domestication of early music, the minimizing of its differentness, the maximization of what its modern surface sound has in common with later styles—all this may have a role in elementary music appreciation, but it is not good enough for serious scholarship. To adopt a presentist position because of the difficulty of embracing a historical one is defeatist. And to discredit or disqualify all aspects of the quest for historical appropriateness because it is not completely realizable is to throw the baby out with the bathwater. These two extremes fail to distinguish the etic and emic ends of the spectrum and confound irrecoverable surface aspects of the musical sound with its underlying and recoverable grammatical sense. To seek "relevant" echoes of our own training and listening habits in music composed on quite other premises is to engage in a form of identity politics that subscribes to a naive evolutionary view whose climax is mature tonality; our cultural and technical values may simply not be there to find, and in looking for early corroboration of that process we may miss what is intrinsic. I believe that wrong reasons have been given for rejecting a historical ingredient in analysis, and I shall try to suggest what that role can be.

The "formalist" claims to put analysis on a scientific basis, to be objective about the very things that he says disqualify "historicism" (and presumably, by the same token, "presentism"), notably our inability to travel in time. But formalist methods can no more escape the conditioning of their own time than any who reach out to the past can hope entirely to escape modern conditioning. Allen Forte has declared that "a knowledge of history is totally inadequate for understanding musical documents" and that "it is only now, with the development of contemporary modes of theoretical thought, that scholars are beginning to understand more fully many of the classic documents of music theory."[29] Indeed a mere "knowledge of history" is inadequate for dealing with the notes, but such knowledge has not been sufficiently distinguished from historically appropriate techniques. Others are impatient with the reluctance of anti-formalist musicologists to come to grips with "the purely technical advance of music-analytical method."[30] And it has been alleged that historicists seek to confine analytical tools to contemporaneous ones; that is decidedly not the same as requiring (as I do) that analytical tools be harmonious with early techniques and vocabulary, to the extent that these can be recovered and extended, just as what is incompatible with how they parsed their music should be avoided. To the extent that they *do* exist, they should underpin any methods we develop. We can at least trouble to take available right tools, to guard against a demonstrably wrong analysis, and adapt those tools to the case in hand without danger of short-circuiting. "The past is a foreign country: they do things differently there."[31]

Presentist anachronism and ahistorical formalism converge. Formalism cannot achieve the neutrality to which it aspires because, as far as early music is concerned, it is created out of an alien set of expectations. Both formalist approaches and those that seek the origins of tonal harmony in "modal" early music set out to demonstrate qualities assumed *a priori* to be there, such as tonal coherence, goal-directed motion, prolongation, and elaboration, but without showing either from within that music or from relevant theory that these are appropriate categories to be looking for, without telling us why we should expect to find the particular kind of coherence that the analyst seeks to demonstrate in that particular repertory, and even worse, without setting out clearly the criteria of tonal schemes, consonance and dissonance, closure, tension and resolution by which such qualities, and deviations from them, are being defined. It assumes the outcome of an evolutionary process of which medieval harmony was an early or primitive step, not a different world. Some features from that world indeed survived and became transformed into features in ours; but the particular ones that happen to have survived in that way could not then have been foreseen, and they are not the only ones that merit our interest and understanding. All modes of analysis that draw their criteria and their procedures from musical languages (notably tonal harmony) other than that of the music under consideration, or from allegedly neutral universal principles, are doomed to anachronism, and in fact do a rather poor job of identifying let alone explaining the central and recurrent musical phenomena. It was against such importation of alien methods, whether presentist or formalist, that Brett registered his plea for appropriate analysis, matched to the music in hand.

THE DYADIC GRAMMAR OF COUNTERPOINT

> Rules for simultaneous ensemble constraint can't be assumed a priori to be the kinds of rules or rest on the same foundations as rules for constraint on succession. They may well be similar, but they may well not be similar also. It seems to me that ensemble constraints must first be understood in their own terms, within musical cultures individually and comparatively, looking to what appear to be basic principles in each in light of the others. I would call such a study "comparative counterpoint."
>
> (Powers, "Language Models and Musical Analysis," 39.)

It is through notation, their notation, that a first encounter with the music comes, whether at first hand, or via editors and performers; access to the sound of the music is lost. Within the limits of notated music, many perspectives become clear when we thus "face the music" on its own terms and in its own notational language.[32] Renaissance notation is under-prescriptive by our standards; when translated into modern form it acquires a prescriptive weight that overspecifies and distorts its original openness. Accidentals, then accidental rather than essential, like fingering today, may or may not have been notated, but what modern notation requires would then have been perfectly apparent without notation to a singer versed in counterpoint. Singers read their own parts, construing cadential formulas and melodic fourths according to a first default of melodic principles with an expected (but not yet known) simultaneous dimension (ex. 1a, 2a-c). When singers hear the other part(s), the expected default may be overruled by the high-priority correction of a simultaneous imperfect fifth or octave (ex. 2d),[33] or it may have to yield to a prior decision (in ex. 1b the *mi-fa* cadence is encouraged by the tenor's descent, while in ex. 1c it yields to a suspended *fa-mi*). Thus it is from the combination of notated music and learned counterpoint that the music can take shape; the two are complementary. We can understand it fully neither from the rules of counterpoint alone, nor from notation read at "face value."[34]

The most important key to successful realization of weakly prescriptive notation is to complement it as they must have done, armed with an approximation of the elementary training shared by composers and singers, and which composers

Example 1 Cadential formulas

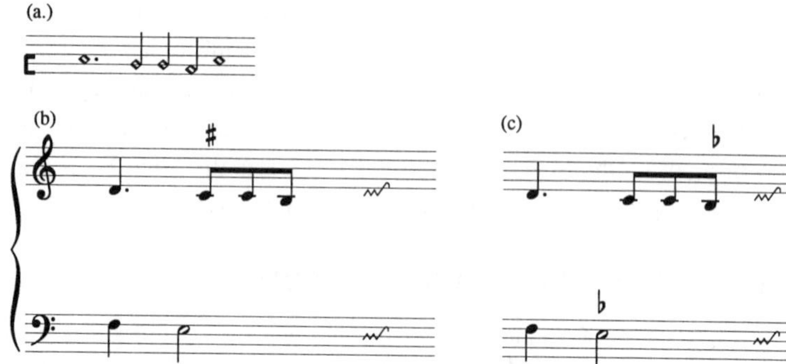

Example 2 Melodic fourths

presumed in their singers when they committed their compositions to notation; namely, for these purposes, fluency in practical counterpoint. Taken in partnership, notation and counterpoint create a more strongly prescriptive basis for realization. Ideally, we should develop the (for us very different) musical skills that are dictated by singing from the original, acquiring first-hand experience of the constraints and freedoms inherent in the notation, as well as a sense of the violence done by putting "weak-default" (early) notation (without the complement of a strengthening counterpoint training) into a (modern) form that demands to be read by the standards of modern notation as a "strong" default. The singer reads his own part in a state of readiness to reinterpret, of readiness to change his expectation of how to read the under-prescriptive notation (not to *change the notation*!) in prompt reaction to what he *hears*. The "default" of the visually scanned line with its implied melodic articulations (perfecting linear fourths, making cadential semitones) is controlled and sometimes overruled by the counterpoint heard. The "default" that is "changed" is not the *notation as transcribed*, but the expectation of how the original notation is to be realized.[35]

Even with experience, this takes longer than the more passive reading of an edited score. For pieces in manuscripts that are damaged, miscopied, or hard to read, an edition may provide the only realistic access. But in using modern scores—as we will and must—we can nonetheless learn to invest them with the experience gained from using original notation.

The rules of counterpoint that most often require alert response from singers (otherwise known as the rules of *musica ficta*) are few and simple: perfect consonances should *be* perfect and should be approached correctly. Counterpoint was learned by the young, practiced, drilled, and internalized, alongside their learning of Latin grammar. As the grammar that governs intervallic progressions, it was primarily a practical and pedagogic exercise. The precepts of counterpoint govern dyadic intervals arranged in note-against-note successions, point counter point (a tradition that persisted to Fux and the codification of species counterpoint). The linear aspect is as incidental (i.e., subsidiary but not negligible) as it is in later harmonic theory. The two-voice or dyadic basis of fourteenth- and fifteenth-century counterpoint can be readily diagnosed from examining the music. It explains many things that receive weak, forced, or no explanations from triadic premises, such as why incomplete triads without thirds are so prominent, absence of theoretical discussion of qualities of triads and the identity they retain through inversion, and the unarguable grammatical completeness of discant-tenor duets. Until the sixteenth century, theorists devote very little explanation to additional voices or elaborations of the dyadic foundation. There is no conflict between counterpoint and composition; composition builds on the foundations of counterpoint. One can learn to hear the discant-tenor strand in a fifteenth-century song as readily as one can learn to hear fugal entries, or to recognize a ground bass in later music. That dyadic training is the shared basis of the musical communication between composers and singers; it is what the notator assumed in the readers. Our access to the grammar of late-medieval polyphony comes in generalized and elementary terms through the theory, and in specific and advanced terms through the music. The task of codifying the development of this musical grammar and of charting its many chronological shifts over two centuries, through many generic and dialect changes, still lies ahead. The rules of early music grammar are easily extrapolated from the music itself, guided by elementary counterpoint theory and by the changing face of that theory in composed music. Theoretical precepts are not artificially imposed on the music, nor do they alone dictate the terms of the investigation. Elementary theory permits simple diagnostic parsing of the first level of the music's own hierarchies. Just as the basic grammar of an ancient language can be reconstructed from elementary and insufficient manuals and vocabulary and then amplified on the basis of literary usage, so with music; principles drawn in common from music and theory can be tested on composed music, refined and extended, gradually codifying irregular general usages and idiosyncratic or personal idioms. While the starting premises of analysis should include the relevant musical grammar, if it is found in practice that the composer departs from that grammar, in such a way that we are sure is not simply a manuscript error with a ready solution, we may add it to a vocabulary of extended or exceptional usage. I intend here comparable licenses to those by which Palestrina and Bach occasionally stretch or break the rules, allowing leading notes to fall, or writing parallel fifths, while in general subscribing to a grammar that avoids these progressions. Proper evaluation of exceptional locutions depends on mastery of standard usage, indeed makes no sense without such a background. The wings of music and literature are not clipped by the grammars that are nevertheless their essential foundation.

Early musical grammar exists, is recoverable, and differs from that of later music. Failure to appreciate its distinctness is like taking a piece of old English and assuming that any words that look like their modern equivalents, and have counterparts in a modern dictionary, do in fact mean what they do now, leaving only those words and usages that are obviously different to require special treatment. This might sometimes work, but would be misleading in the case of words whose sense has altered, such as "lewd" or "gay." It would be dangerous to assume that merely by putting Chaucer into modern spelling we have rendered his meaning in modern English. Likewise with music; it cannot be assumed (as many do) that respelling the musical notation in modern score means that it can then be treated "as is," as if it were modern notation.[36] And a further step would be to pick out configurations that look like triads and treat them as if they behaved like triads in a context of tonal harmony.[37] In language as in musical editing, the magnitude of the conceptual difference is easy to underestimate when the surface similarities sound and look comfortably familiar. To resist particularities of musical grammar and syntax is rather like treating a piece of verbal text as though it could be construed indifferently either as Latin or Italian. I am asking not that we approach analysis in vaguely pious historical terms, and certainly not in period costume, but that we tailor precise tools according to the particular music under examination, as opposed to applying a methodology from a different time and culture, however well formed, however sophisticated or powerful, however objective or neutral that methodology is claimed to be, however well it works on other repertories. Any theory brought to the music needs to be sensitive to peculiarities of grammar and syntax in the musical genre, language, and dialect under consideration. Expectations can be aroused, to be met or side-stepped; implications can be realised or diverted, all within definable conventions. This is the opposite of assimilating the "harmony" of early music to something familiar to us, and "letting the music speak for itself" in a universal musical language requiring no retooling for its full comprehension. Only by taking account of norms and departures can we avoid over-assimilating individual locutions to standard ones and, in turn, feed individual usages into an anthology of experience or extended grammar that can then be used to refine analytical approaches to other works. We do need to understand why the individual work is this way and cannot be otherwise, why the individual note is thus and not other, and to distinguish these things from the general and the commonplace. Music, of course, goes beyond counterpoint just as literature goes beyond grammar; grammar and counterpoint are in each case necessary but not sufficient conditions for understanding the basic level of sense, and hence informing correct articulation or punctuation, factors that can radically affect performance.[38] Individual utterance can only be evaluated against a knowledge of conventional utterance, so far as we can recover that. Saussure's *parole* is the individual utterance that is drawing on *langue*, a system of rules and oppositions in terms of which the individual utterance is understood. We can't get close to the individual work without some knowledge, native or acquired, of its general principles; and we can't adopt general principles that lack a foundation in the works. There is no hope of discovering the individuality of a piece of music, the voice of an individual poet, until it is understood in terms of the specifically musical conventions and common parlance of its time. There are historical differences not only in what we loosely call style, but in the musical equivalents of vocabulary, grammar, and semantic usage. Our forebears distinguished in language between *recte loquendi* (*correct* locution, grammar) and *bene loquendi* (*good* locution, rhetoric, or style). Their musical equivalents, *recte* and *bene modulandi*, are occasionally paired,[39] and *musica est ars bene modulandi* became a widespread commonplace. These terms may correspond to the ends of the etic / emic spectrum respectively, and offer points of orientation for general versus individual style features.

Verbal grammar and syntax indeed afford some analogies, especially with regard to synonyms and homonyms. Chomsky gave the example "Flying planes is dangerous" versus "Flying planes are dangerous." "Flying planes" has an identical surface structure but two very different deep structures, as though the two instances were (so to speak) grammatical homonyms.[40] If we say: "the dogs bark," the context of the sentence, and our understanding of grammar, tell us whether it is the bark of a single dog (noun with apostrophe s) or plural dogs that are barking (verb). At different periods in the writing of English these different senses may or may not have been distinguished in writing by an apostrophe. Another example: in English, "man bites dog" and "dog bites man" mean entirely different things. But in an inflected language like Latin the word order is interchangeable because case endings and other indicators can make it clear which is the subject, which the object: *virum canis mordit* means the same as *canis virum mordit*.[41] Italian "casa" can be pronounced with hard or soft s without a change of meaning, but English "phase" and "face" are different words. "Casa" and "cassa" are different Italian words but English and American pronunciations of "dance" are the same word. And so on. To recognise synonyms and distinguish homonyms, to construe the sense correctly, one needs to know which language it is, and to be sensitive to context, as well as to regional and chronological shifts in pronunciation. So with apparent triads, so with the phonemes of music. We might bear this in mind when a $\hat{5}$–$\hat{1}$ bass progression is assumed to be a V–I: see the different harmonizations of 6–8 (ex. 3a) in example 3 b-c, and the different Tenor/ Contratenor underpinnings of the superficially similar examples 4 a-b.

EXAMPLE 3 Imperfect to perfect consonances

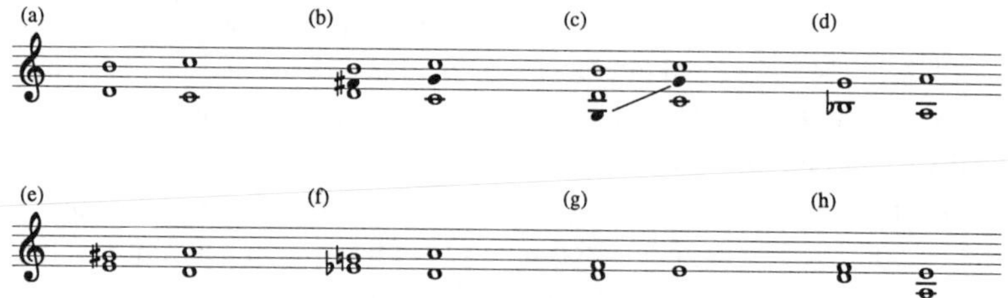

EXAMPLE 4 Roles of tenor and contratenor

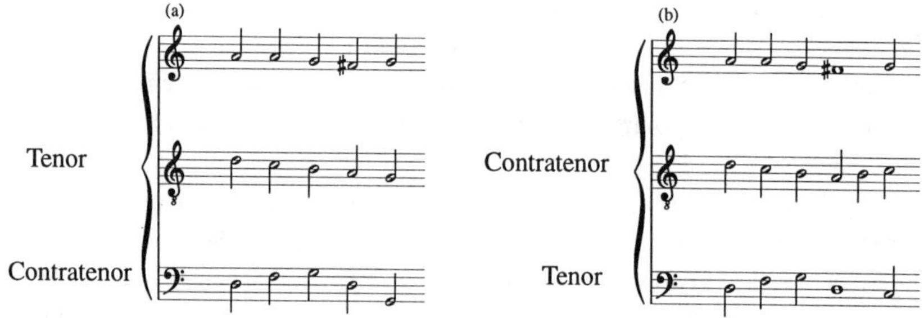

Powers is not the only scholar to allege that

> The primary tonal elements of Renaissance music are pitch-classes and triads, to all intents and purposes acoustically the same as those of eighteenth- and nineteenth-century music.[42]

Strong claims have been made for the explanatory power of the triadic tonality assumed to follow from those triads.[43] Superficial similarities between medieval and later phenomena (things that sound like triads and V–I cadences) have placed us in danger of ignoring major differences in the grammar and syntax which govern their use. This is one area where some of Pinker's Chomskian verbal examples may serve as approximate analogies. Again, it is not so much a question of what we see but of how we look, not of what we hear but of how we listen. Of course there are in early music configurations that are, shorn of context, indistinguishable from triads, configurations of three different notes. But their context can only be seen as triadic by extending our view or perverting theirs. Early theory provides no corroboration for the affinity of triads in root position and in inversion, or for us to talk about the chains of first inversions in fauxbourdon; indeed, it doesn't give identity or function to triads at all, which are presented only as dyads with added parts. The mere presence of a triad as a phoneme does not guarantee that the laws governing its succession will be those we have come to expect. By seeing things in terms of the nearest comparisons and going on to assume that they "mean" the same thing irrespective of context, we fail to guard against an elementary confusion of homonyms—"flying planes." Just as we are concerned with uncovering by analysis the distinctness of different works, so it is our prior business to identify the different premises of early music, rather than assimilating it to our current expectations. Are we now prepared to overwrite the languages of medieval music with those of later cultures, expressed in the technical terms of the traditional western canon that engulfed them by selecting and redirecting some of the same surface features? We should not be too faint-hearted to put out an endangered species warning when the effort to hear that voice is discounted. Analyses that bring to a piece of music or a repertory an external theory devised outside that repertory that is historically and technically inappropriate to it tend to have weaker explanatory power than ones harmonious with the diagnosed characteristics of the music. Insofar as the inbuilt technical assumptions of a theory were not devised for and do not fit the repertory to which that theory is applied, the results will be at best weak, at worst dishonest, as for example when triadic prolongation is alleged in music conceived without triads as functional units.

The idea of "successive composition" is but a poor and misunderstood shorthand for dyadic grammar. Structural priorities varied by genre, and in the case of songs one can often say that the discant and tenor probably did exist, or were at least written down, before the contratenor. This is sometimes borne out by clear evidence from manuscripts that a two-part song was later adorned or "harmonized" with an added triplum or contratenor part; see example 5. But in other genres, particularly those that involve multiple constraints, such as isorhythm coupled with a cantus firmus tenor that is not necessarily the same as a counterpoint-bearing "grammatical" tenor, it is not always so easy to detect such a clear priority. The discant-tenor function may indeed migrate between various voice-pairs, as it clearly

EXAMPLE 5 *J'ayme bien celui qui s'en va*, ed. Besseler (changes in [ ])

does in certain genres from the fourteenth century onwards, and in multi-voice imitative or duet-based compositions of the late fifteenth century. Cadencing pairs may be superimposed.[44] So-called "successive" composition has been caricatured by those who resist the notion it stands for as somehow insulting early composers by limiting their aural skills to two-part processes.[45] Not so, although the terminology could be improved; "dyadic" probably conveys better to a modern reader the essential features of medieval counterpoint. It is not a corollary of dyadic procedure that it limits what can be heard or conceived in the mind. The order of conception is not confined by the grammar. When a native speaker utters a complex and grammatically correct sentence, he surely did not start by thinking of it as a simple subject-verb-object sentence, only then expanding it, even though the sentence can be parsed in an order other than that of its devising. Internalized grammar permits correct articulation of a complex thought, whether in words or music, without violating or necessarily consciously invoking that grammar. As with speech, we need not assume that musical ideas occurred to a composer in grammatical order. While "successive" composition should not necessarily be taken to mean that the piece was composed in that order (although sometimes it almost certainly was), it does mean that the piece was conceived in such a way that the grammatical skeleton was not violated. Exceptions and anomalies can then be isolated, will take on greater interest, and lead to extended formulations of the rules; grammars have irregular verbs or idioms and tolerate exceptions, and advanced accounts of them take account of such experience in usage. "Successive" in music should refer to the procedure uncovered by analysis and inherent in its grammar, and not necessarily to the order of working or compositional process of a native-speaking composer. To talk in terms of triadic harmony no more means that we cannot cope with the five components of a dominant ninth (or the seven or eight of a dominant thirteenth), than dyadic counterpoint means that medieval composers could not conceive sonorities of three, four, five parts as extensions of the underlying dyadic grammar. A dyadic basis doesn't confine composers to hearing only two parts at a time any more than triadic harmony means that its practitioners cannot hear polychords.[46]

If their terminology and concepts are judged by some modern writers to be inadequate for them to deal with their music, how would we answer the future scholar who will come to the music of the eighteenth and nineteenth centuries with only the slightest knowledge of the tonal harmony by which we construe it, and find it quaint that we continued to explain configurations of four, five, six notes in terms of extended triads, dominant ninths and thirteenths? Will he shake his head, shades of M. Jourdain, and say, ah, if only they had realized that they were writing quadratic harmony, but they didn't have a name for it and so they didn't know that's what it was? Would we not point out, in a conventional harmonic analysis, that all can be explained by triadic extension, and that to impose a different and conflicting system on it was not helpful to understanding? Would our medieval colleague not similarly have defended their dyadic technique in response to a champion of triadic terminology? Might he not have pointed out that absence of a term may be not a lack but a pointer, not an impoverishment but a clue to their categories of thought, as are the absence of a medieval word for isorhythm, and of single umbrella words for pitch, for rhythm, for long-term tonal coherence and so on? To say that the musical language is based not on triads but on dyads does not deny that three-part configurations exist, nor does it mean that they could not hear or conceive them; it just means that we don't have to go to triadic harmony to explain them, any more than we have to devise a system of quadratic harmony to explain four-part chords within the language of tonal triadic harmony. Nearly all the music of the fourteenth and fifteenth centuries reveals its two-part framework to simple observation and to the ear that has learned to hear it.

For music in more than two parts, we need to develop hierarchical analytical listening—as we do for many other kinds of music: *Hauptstimmen* and *Nebenstimmen*, outer versus inner voices of figured bass pieces or early string quartets, subject versus episodic material in fugues, principal versus "filler" orchestral parts. Such subsidiary parts are not unimportant to the sound and conception, but they are less important to the musical argument. It is clear from some of Mozart's autograph orchestral scores that he first wrote the principal parts, leaving wind chords to be filled in later, and in some fifteenth-century songs the contratenor was demonstrably a later, variable, or dispensable addition.[47] Indeed, it has been asserted that Schenker requires a new way of hearing: Felix Salzer said that Schenkerian analysis can be done from the sound, given sufficient training. So can proper construing of fifteenth-century music, at first by listening for sixths expanding to octaves, and attending to legal handling of perfect intervals. This may be done by singing or listening successively to a paired discant and tenor, a paired tenor and contratenor, then superimposing the pairs; this may or may not be related to the composer's order of conception, but it certainly could have been. Rather than attempting to adapt Schenkerian techniques for the quite different languages of early music, we would be better employed in developing models for listening and analysis that are specifically tailored to early music, and through which we will learn to discriminate between individual styles. After all, the details of Schenker's method derive indisputably from his intimate knowledge of the particular repertories to which he applied it.

The compositional process is, and perhaps should remain, mysterious. It has been usefully distinguished for Mozart from his "standard operating procedure";[48] applied to our case, this would refer not to how the composer conceived his music, but the basic grammar and conventions in terms of which and against which he did so. Music, obviously, is not to be reduced to its grammar. But the grammar is there, and must be internalized, significantly different as it is from ours, before we proceed to more advanced analysis. That analysis should respect, and proceed in harmony with, the underlying grammar, and should avoid claims that violate the grammar. A composer will constantly go beyond the rules of the basic grammar; we too can go beyond them, extending our store of stylistic rules to enhance our understanding and analysis.

THEORY AND PRACTICE

> The fact that such analyses in traditional Western musicological and theoretical studies have been used primarily in the discussion of individual examples . . . should not be allowed to obscure the fact that in most cases the analyses have really as much or more to do with the presuppositions of the music being studied as with the items themselves.
>
> (Powers, review of A. Merriam, *The Anthropology of Music*, 168.)

> [F]rom the 13th to the 15th centuries chant theory and handbooks of the mechanics of counterpoint and mensuration coexisted without cohabiting. In those treatises that deal with both chant and polyphony, counterpoint and modality are always treated in separate sections, completely independently one of the other.
>
> (Powers, "Modality as a European Cultural Construct," 210.)

Some allege that historical theory is inadequate or too primitive for sophisticated modern analysis, and can therefore be safely ignored. Presentists claim on the one hand that early theory fails to fit the music well, and on the other that it is insufficient for it. Theorists are charged with being inconsistent among themselves and incompatible with the music. Such conflict between theory and practice has been used to justify bypassing theory. We hardly expect a consistent view from modern theorists, but then we are not placing on them the burden of being witnesses on whom we depend for the recovery of a unitary tradition. Harold Powers has eloquently demonstrated this distinction with respect to mode.[49] A few examples can illustrate that the theory may fit the music better than has been realized, often because the theorists have been misread, and indeed that early theory, not surprisingly, fits early music better than do modern impositions upon it. Of course the theory is insufficient, as is any grammar or primer with relation to actual music or literature, but it is a necessary premise.[50] The theory needs to be extended in practice for our purposes, as I have suggested, but on its own foundations, and not by borrowing from modern theory. Medieval theory is not *a priori* incompetent, and we should not lose sight either of ways in which it is richer than ours, or of ways in which the absence of an early term may be eloquent. Mode, counterpoint, solmization, and tuning operated on separate tracks whose points of interdependence are not those that lead us to prioritize not only pitch, but a frequency-biased notion of pitch.[51]

One example of a perceived conflict between music and theory concerns testimony on "accidentals." In a long-running debate on partial signatures, too long to signal more than briefly here, Apel had given priority to melodic considerations drawn from the testimony of German keyboard intabulations, rejecting the theorists as irrelevant because they only dealt with two-part progressions and primarily with "harmonic" reasons for inflection.[52] The many "inflections" specified in those manuscripts were also seen as being irreconcilable with the theorists' call for restraint. Lowinsky treated partial signatures as having something of the same force as later key signatures, discouraging the raising of a note that was flat in the signature and reflecting during the fifteenth century a "gradual change of harmonic structure, as evidenced by the change of cadential formulas."[53] Richard Hoppin urged attention to the theorists and to "harmonic" criteria drawn from them, while leaving open the possibility of "bitonal" readings. All voices in this debate rested on the premise that absence of a notated inflection or presence of a signature were prescriptive, as in modern notation, and only subject to weighty and conscious change by early performers and modern editors. The premises inevitably colored their readings of the theorists and led them to see manuscript and theoretical evidence as being in conflict.[54] Instead, taking a signature as weakly prescriptive, it is easily overruled by contrapuntal necessity, while a proper understanding of the nature of notation and signatures, the truly accidental nature of accidentals, and the irrelevance of mode to fixing actual pitches, can all soften many of the apparently immovable conflicts raised in that debate.

Another example of an allegedly poor fit between theory and practice concerns the prohibition of parallel perfect intervals. Treatises begin to prohibit parallel perfect intervals "in counterpoint" in the fourteenth century, while parallel fifths and octaves are still frequently observed in the music, over a long period, in such basic configurations as the standard parallel four-part cadence of the fourteenth century (ex. 6). Observations like this have fuelled the belief that theorists are

EXAMPLE 6 Four-part cadence

undependable—though they might equally have fuelled a view that the music was incompetent. Neither is the case; the integrity of both can be rescued. When theorists forbid parallel intervals "in counterpoint" they do not mean "anywhere in the texture." Counterpoint is not a general synonym for the musical fabric, but a specific underlying technique: *contrapunctus est fundamentum discantus.*[55]

> Quinta conclusio est quod in suo contrapuncto non debet dare duas decimas, nec duas octavas, nec duas quintas, nec duos unisonos, simul et semel.[56]
>
> The fifth conclusion is that in counterpoint there ought not to be two tenths, octaves, fifths, or unisons (or: two perfect intervals) together in succession.

Prosdocimus, third rule:

> quod insimul cum cantu supra vel infra quem contrapunctamus nunquam ascendere vel descendere debemus cum eadem combinatione perfecte concordante, ut cum unisono vel quinta maiori vel octava maiori vel cum hiis equivalentibus, licet bene cum diversis vocum combinationibus perfecte concordantibus hoc agere possumus . . .
>
> we ought never to ascend or descend in identical perfectly concordant intervals with the melody above or below which we make counterpoint—in a unison or a major fifth or a major octave or in their equivalents—though we may well do so in different perfectly concordant intervals . . . [57]

The qualification "in counterpoint" means that the underlying dyadic duet should avoid parallel perfect consonances. In some genres (most song forms), this duet is the fundamental two-part progression between discant and tenor throughout; but in other genres it may also cover a contrapuntal relationship achieved between the tenor (or its proxy) and any other part. Thus in example 6 all the three upper parts are moving in contrary motion with the tenor at the bottom, and each part individually is creating correct counterpoint with the tenor. The rule says nothing about relationships between other parts. That means not that those other relationships were not subject to scrutiny in other ways, but that they were not bound specifically by the grammatical rules for two-part counterpoint. The rule is occasionally broken between the fundamental parts, but it is not broken in the standard cadences, where all the parts move in contrary motion with the tenor. None makes parallels with it, they only make parallels with each other. To remove this standard cadential situation from the fray permits a closer reconciliation between theory and practice than has usually been acknowledged, and also enables us to isolate actual infractions of the rule to a much smaller number of cases, small enough to attract interest as departures from a newly-defined norm. They can then be negatively classified as deliberate defiance or incompetence, or they can become a positive addition to our vocabulary of licenses, as we show how the rules are extended in practice, in larger musical textures, and what other considerations affect relationships with parts other than the tenor. It permits a finer calibration of the use of parallels and, far from dismissing the theorists who guided this realization, it explains a prominent feature of the music that had caused embarrassed puzzlement and whose explanation had indeed been resistant to recognition from the music alone.

Another example concerns the prohibition of *mi contra fa* in perfect intervals, and again in the contrapuntal relationship strictly defined, which is widely quoted in modern literature without such qualifications, or as a general discouragement of false or cross relations. Some writers have even understood it as pertaining to an oblique or even a linear non-harmonic interval, which is not a sustainable reading of "contra."[58] Theorists are careful to confine the prohibition to perfect intervals, and "in counterpoint," counterpoint having already been defined as a two-part procedure. It would be nonsense for the prohibition to apply universally.[59] One even still finds occasional modern conflations between the tritone (augmented fourth) and the diminished fifth such as can only spring from presuming their enharmonic equivalence in equal temperament. Rules governing the avoidance of one or the other and further restrictions on simultaneous or horizontal usage only make sense when the distinctions are precisely observed. Their theorists cannot be blamed for our careless reading. A more attuned reading of the theorists can help in setting priorities between *ficta* rules and in defining more precisely the circumstances in which diminished intervals were tolerated.

> . . . quia nullibi talibus perfectis concordationibus potest poni mi contra fa, cum insimul discordarent; sed si contra illud mi ponitur fa, confortetur hoc fa sive perficiatur ♮ duro, et sic insimul bene concordabunt.
>
> That in no perfect concords should mi be placed against fa, since together they will be discordant; but if fa is placed against that mi, let that fa be strengthened or perfected by means of hard b, and then they will concord well together.
>
> . . . .
>
> Breviter dicendo in contrapunctu, supra perfectas species nullibi contra mi potest poni fa, nec e contra, in contrapunctu, supra perfectas species nullibi contra fa potest poni mi.

> Speaking briefly, in counterpoint in perfect intervals nowhere should mi be placed against fa, nor vice versa, in counterpoint in perfect intervals nowhere should fa be placed against mi.[60]

> Pro ordinatione autem harum combinationum in contrapuncto proprie sumpto has nota regulas . . . quod in combinationibus perfecte consonantibus nunquam ponere debemus mi contra fa, nec e contra, quoniam statim ipsas vocum combinationes perfecte consonantes minores vel maximas constitueremus, que discordantes sunt, ut supra dictum est.

> For the ordering of these rules in counterpoint defined in the proper sense . . . rule five: in perfectly consonant intervals we ought never to place mi against fa or vice versa, because we would straightway make the perfectly consonant intervals minor or augmented, which forms are discordant, as was said above.[61]

The fault in these cases is not that of the theorists, but ours, in failing to understand sufficiently the context of the statement and failing to qualify it as carefully as they did. Alternatively, sometimes too much weight can be placed by modern readers on isolated or eccentric statements by theorists that may not have universal prescriptive value.[62]

LISTENING AND PERFORMANCE

> [T]he ultimate cause of failure in many musicological analyses . . . is the fact that one does not analyze music but only a representation of music. Notation as a source of data for analysis is always a transcription . . . One of the crucial problems in historical musicology is to know what notation means in terms of performance, both because of insufficiencies and ambiguities in the notation and, even more, because important stylistic features are often taken for granted within the musical culture, and hence need not be, and often are not, notated.
>
> (Powers, review of A. Merriam, *The Anthropology of Music,* 167.)

> We now consider real music to be something performable as opposed to something theoretical. It would not be hyperbole to claim that the very idea that performable music might be susceptible to rational analysis was originally a consequence of making the analogy between language and music.

> The dodecachordal theory of modality survived on the periphery of musical thought into the 18th-century German organ tradition, and into the early 19th century as the simple theory of "modal scales" or "church

> modes." Thereafter the "church modes," and other exotic scales as well, were occasionally picked up as a new musical resource by composers from Beethoven to Debussy and beyond. And more than that, a form of dodecachordal modal theory, reduced to six modes by ignoring the distinction between authentic and plagal, came in for a true revival. It was applied to Anglo-American folksong by Cecil Sharp and others, and as in its medieval and Renaissance phases, here too the theory was picked up by the musicians. Nowadays professional folksingers and composers of folksongs talk glibly about their Dorian and Mixolydian tunes, just as composers and theorists of art music used to compose using "dominants" with "flatted leading-tones" and call it "modal harmony. . . ."
>
> (Powers, "Modality as a European Cultural Construct," 212.)

The performance conventions implicit in traditions of notated music are the contract between composer and performer by which the realization of that notated music is governed and enacted.[63] Some of them (notably in that area of counterpoint commonly understood as *musica ficta*) form an essential part of the functional musical grammar of the composition which, as we have seen, is two-part counterpoint. The performer had to understand this grammar in order to decode the notation within the limits and with the freedoms that the composer envisaged. These recognitions have profound implications for how performers listen, how they construe the music, and hence how it is presented to listeners. We shall deal here with "V-I cadences," triads, and grammatically subsidiary voices. For me as for Dahlhaus "the subject under discussion is not whether one encounters chord progressions in the fourteenth and fifteenth centuries that sound like functional cadences to a twentieth-century listener, but whether their interpretation as functional cadences can be historically justified."[64]

The presentist might say: if we hear a bass line motion $\hat{5}$–$\hat{1}$ from G to C that would in tonal music be associated with the progression V–I, the chords that form a perfect or authentic cadence, there is no reason not to treat it in the earlier music as if it were indeed a tonal V–I progression.[65] Example 7 shows how Heinrich Besseler presented Du Fay's *Helas ma dame*. He observed triads, modulation, and V–I bass motion, and labelled these as tonal functions. But the song has a perfectly self-contained discant-tenor duet, a fact that Besseler chose to suppress in favor of treating its functionally subordinate contratenor as a tonally functional bass, simply because it lies below the tenor and has leaps of fourths and fifths. The fact that it does lie mainly below the tenor, which was why Besseler chose it, makes the self-sufficiency of the discant-tenor duet all the more striking.[66] Besseler's short-circuit to Roman numeral harmonic analysis has lingered, increasingly apologetically, behind even quite recent informal descriptions of early music. Although, forty years on, few scholars would assent to such a full-blown tonal reading, few

EXAMPLE 7 Besseler's harmonic analysis of Dufay, *Helas ma dame* (Besseler, *Bourdon und Fauxbourdon*, p. 41, ex. 9)

have challenged the underlying premises of a position that simply turns compositional technique on its head. Lowinsky, in refuting Leeman Perkins, mocked the stance that amounts to "I see harmony, I hear harmony, but I cannot admit that it is harmony, for I know that the composer did not intend harmony."[67] Lowinsky's rhetoric, as always, was impeccable, but the context of this particular passage arose from his own anachronistic application of the words harmony and counterpoint to chordal and linear techniques respectively. And its flaw is that his recognition of tonal harmony stopped at what we could all agree in isolation to call "triads," and did not go on to admit that, although individually homonymic, their use was quite different from triadic tonal harmony. The configuration may sometimes contain three different pitches, but its actual musical functions lead those three notes in different directions with different places in the hierarchy. This is a musical counterpart to "flying planes."

Although the bottom line of that score may look like a harmonic bass line (with the significant exception of the octave-leap cadence at mm. 14–15), and although special rules govern relationships with the lowest voice, it is, *pace* Besseler, not necessarily a grammatically fundamental voice; the so-called triads over that bass line are often not complete, nor are they resolved like triads in tonal harmony. In some cases this obviously means learning to listen to the musical sense from the inside out rather than, as we are more accustomed to, from the top down or the bottom up. The upper two voices of Du Fay's song, the discant and tenor, make perfect self-contained sense without the lower contratenor, which therefore could not have been grammatically fundamental. Cadence in this music is defined not by bass leap but by tenor step. Its two-part progressions are most fundamentally expressed in cadences; it is cadences that the ear most readily grasps, and that embody the two principal rules, namely, that the closure on a perfect interval should be a perfect unison, fifth or octave; and that it should be approached by an imperfect interval (a third or a sixth) of which one part makes the approach by a semitone or half-step. The primary cadences are made by discant and tenor, usually and most decisively proceeding from a sixth to an octave. Example 3a (p. 30) could be harmonized in two main ways in the fifteenth century.[68] The contratenor can superimpose a third to a fifth, as in example 3b, or leap an octave to create the illusion (for a listener not experienced at hearing tenor functions) of a V–I bass progression (ex. 3c). The privilege of being a harbinger of the perfect cadence is sometimes extended to this octave-leaping contratenor, never mind about the parallel fifths that result from ignoring the crossed parts and their particular functions. Whatever happened later, the cadence in this progression is made by the stepwise tenor descent in a sixth to octave progression with the discantus and not by the contratenor. The choice between the two forms of examples 3b-c were less sharply differentiated for them (as we can tell from different versions of the same piece) than they are for us by tonal hindsight. Fifteenth-century compositions often treat the third to fifth succession (ex. 3b) as more final than the octave leap (ex. 3c), which never wholly supersedes the $^{6}_{3}$ - $^{8}_{5}$ cadence in a clean chronological way. Examples 3 d-h give other progressions of imperfect to perfect intervals, with the mandatory semitone in one or other voice. Example 8 counted for Aron as a cadence on E by tenor step, not on A by bass leap, as it would be from our perspective.[69] Of course, the two lower parts make a correct approach from a third to a fifth with a semitone in one voice, but in a cadence that is subsidiary to the main progression of sixth to octave.

EXAMPLE 8 Aron, cadence on E

When current performances fail to approach octaves via major sixths (usually needing the semitone step at the top, a raised "leading note"), they neglect to articulate significant points of closure within pieces or at ends of sections. This practice cannot be defended either as being modally or notationally faithful. The first resort should be to assume that all sixth-to-octave progressions will be major, and only then to decide which ones, if any, and for whatever reaons, should *not* be handled in that conventional way. Performers can help listeners to a correct hearing of the music's physiognomy with articulations that are the equivalent of punctuation. By singing the C of example 1b (p. 26) as C♯, they will lead the listener to expect an octave resolution following the major sixth; or, with the semitone descent in the tenor, leading the top part to suspend the seventh to a major sixth as in example 1c. But a delay or diversion of octave resolution ought to be signalled by *not* raising the sixth (the first F in ex. 9), by not raising the

EXAMPLE 9 Delay of octave resolution from * to ↓

listener's cadential expectation. The discant singer may have had to find out by trial and error that his suspended seventh was not cadential. However, if many cadential sixths are performed as minor, the listener will not learn to trust the performer's signals. As a good actor can communicate by inflection and intonation the implicit punctuation and sense of a potentially ambiguous sentence, so performers can help listeners to anticipate a cadence correctly by sounding the right intervals, approaches and markers. Where singers select just some cadences for proper approach (by "raised leading note"), they impose an arbitrary hierarchy of importance. The choice may sometimes be dictated by a misplaced desire to leave the notation "as is," adding as little as possible, in turn related to a misplaced notion of modal fidelity.

Dahlhaus's chapter on fifteenth-century harmony reviews how the twentieth-century German tonal-harmonic view evolved through Riemann and Korte, culminating in Besseler and his followers. In America, these followers have included Sanders, Lowinsky, and Randel. Dahlhaus demonstrates very clearly that to analyze example 10 as a primitive dominant seventh (V_7–I) is bad analysis.[70] It is not only objectionable because it disregards theorists, but because it is less satisfactory than an explanation that takes the theoretical context into account. The "seventh" is not resolved downwards but rises, contrary to tonal function, so that it fails to meet the basic criteria for describing a dominant seventh. Moreover, the V lacks its root and the I its third. Dahlhaus shows that the dominant seventh was foreign to composers of the fifteenth and even the sixteenth centuries. He might have added that the concept of triadic inversion on which this reading depends is also not present, and not even triads *tout court*. To give such reasons for avoiding G♯ reduces the choice of notes to subjective judgment or wishful thinking, while avoiding primary contrapuntal precepts; the third to the fifth would on contrapuntal grounds override the "as is" notated version.

EXAMPLE 10 Not V_7 – I

So long as dyadic grammar is foremost, the cadences should in the first instance be realized as given; the sixth expanding to the octave is not controversial, but a third expanding to a fifth should normally be major, not left minor in order the better to qualify it as a proto-dominant seventh or to make it more "modal." With weakly prescriptive notation and signatures, and the exhortation to vary sizes of successive imperfect intervals, determinate thirds and stable triads cannot be counted upon. This aspect of fifteenth-century music has often been noted (as *Terzfreiheit*), though its incompatibility with functional harmony has less often been remarked. So long as such cadences are written in the fifteenth century, they should be so handled, irrespective of chronology, irrespective of partial signatures. The first default position should be that whenever a third expands to a fifth or a sixth to an octave, those imperfect intervals should be major, proceeding by semitone step in one of the parts. That default may be overruled by other considerations, and often will be, but the choices should be driven by the internal needs of the music, not imposed on it from outside by such irrelevant defaults as "not adding too many accidentals." Regardless of whether or not it incurs "accidentals," the G of example 10 has a primary claim to be G♯ if it rises, and must be G♮ if it descends. The time to change to a less angular contrapuntal realization is when composers change the form of the cadence itself, to avoid that progression. By applying these principles, performers will communicate to listeners the cadential physiognomy of the music that they have come to understand by learning the piece in rehearsal.

The way we hear language is conditioned by what is most familiar. As English speakers *we* hear a big difference between the different words sheep and ship, but Italians, lacking a short "i," find this hard to hear and to pronounce.[71] There are many lessons to be learned here, about how to hear affinity between things that to us sound different, and sometimes to hear differences between things that look or even sound similar (compare the example of cross-cultural miscomprehension given above, from Hardanger fiddle music). Examples 4a and 4b (p. 30) may sound quite similar to our ears and expectations: but the functions of the parts are more different than an unprepared modern listener may realise. Conversely, the differently harmonized cadences (exx. 3b, 3c) sound quite different to us. In both cases, hierarchical listening that would have drawn the ear to hear discant-tenor dyadic cadence function as primary may have led to examples 4a and 4b sounding more different to them than to us, examples 3b and 3c more similar.

The opposite fault of neglecting cadences is to treat as a point of closure what is in fact a point of tension aspiring to closure. To render such passages as arrivals turns the sense of the music upside down. Clearly the music does contain three-part simultaneities that look to us like triads and sound to us complete and final. But some of what the harmonic analyst sees as triads and points of resolution or arrival are, in terms of fifteenth-century musical grammar, points of maximum tension and anticipation, awaiting resolution. I have often observed listeners unfamiliar with medieval music react to a progression like example 11a, and think that they have reached the point of arrival, only to be surprised when it continues as example 11b. For the listener who construes this in tonal terms the actual cadence sounds as if it has been tacked on the end of something that has already arrived, on a plagal or imperfect cadence, an example of what makes medieval music weird or exotic. But clearly this is an essential and symptomatic point. If our classically trained ears can mistake tension for resolution, anticipation for arrival, we are getting it badly wrong. However our exposure to later music may encourage us to construe the sounds in more familiar terms, it is clear that, to use another grammatical analogy, even if the vocabulary seems familiar, we must be hearing, so to speak, nouns as verbs and therefore not construing the grammar correctly, missing its basic sense, never mind about going further to build interpretations on that understanding.

EXAMPLE 11 Misconstrued closure

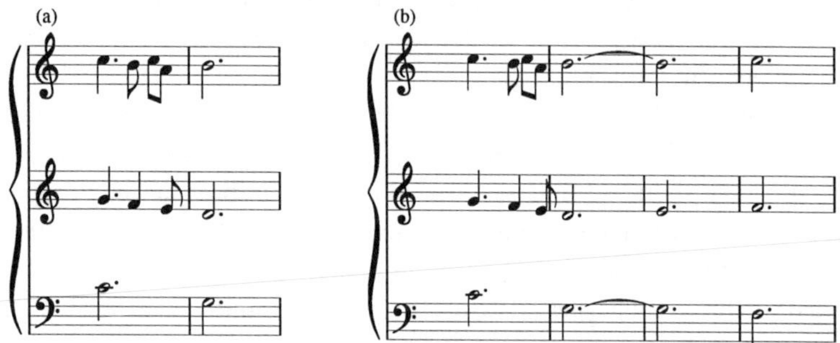

Example 12 shows the transition from the texted portion to the Amen in Ciconia's motet *Venecie mundi splendor.* Singers usually treat measure 89 as a point of rest, take a breath, and then sing the Amen. In fact, the musical grammar indicates that it is a point not of rest but of tension, and should drive forward, possibly without a break, or with an expectant rather than a terminal pause, to the Amen, the first bar of which resolves the tension rather than providing a new beginning, as indeed at the final cadence.

EXAMPLE 12 Ciconia, *Venecie*

EXAMPLE 12 (*cont.*)

In the Gloria and Credo of Machaut's Mass, performers often treat the long held notes as points of arrival, full and half closes, after which they breathe before proceeding to the next phrase. The "half closes" are not that at all in fourteenth-century terms, but penultimates, driving towards the resolutions that inevitably follow—on the first beat of the following measure. Thus in example 13, *Laudamus te* resolves into *Benedicimus te* and cannot in itself be a point of rest, and if the word sense demands a breath or articulation, this will be of a different quality if it links an anticipation to its resolution than if it joins the end of a closed phrase to the beginning of a new one. Sarah Fuller has argued this case compellingly for the Credo of the Mass.[72]

EXAMPLE 13 Machaut, Gloria

Thirds in final chords are rare, but they do exist from an early time. Learning to hear most thirds not as arrival points but as anticipatory should shift the way they are viewed as "harmonic" phenomena, and make us more alert to the revolution when they do begin to appear commonly at points of rest. This happens in English music long before anywhere else, and may therefore turn out to mark an even deeper distinctiveness of English style than has yet been grasped, rather than an external coloristic mannerism.

Example 13 can illustrate another point about how sense is construed. The non-isorhythmic Gloria and Credo of Machaut's Mass make almost perfect sense as three-part compositions (two superimposed discant-tenor duets), ignoring in the first instance the bottom part, the contratenor.[73] It is this contratenor that is responsible for all the spicy dissonances that give the work its exotic quality. If we do not appreciate the regular structure and technique onto which this part is grafted, we will give Machaut less than his due. The most recent study of the Mass has argued that the harmony is built up chordally from the bass and sees no evidence of dyadic part-writing.[74] I believe that such a view fundamentally misconceives the basic sense of the composition by inverting the grammar.

Ciconia's *O virum omnimoda*, like several other of his motets, has a problematic contratenor that may have been added later to his original three-voice composition. Example 14 shows several places where the contratenor creates insoluble problems by sounding a fourth below the tenor and in dissonance with the upper

EXAMPLE 14 Ciconia, *O virum omnimoda*

parts. Some performers have fixed this by emendations that do worse violence to the tenor relationships. The contratenor makes perfect sense with the tenor, and the tenor makes perfect sense with the top parts. At measure 80, this results in a "bifocal" dissonance with the contratenor a fifth below the tenor and the triplum a fifth above. It brooks no emendation and must be accepted either as incompetent or as an example of the different licenses that can apply to contratenor superimpositions. In both the Machaut and Ciconia cases, we can at least observe that contratenor dissonance seems to be guided by rules different from those of tenor counterpoint, rules that we have yet to formulate. That editors, analysts and performers can turn the problem upside down only shows how far we still have to go.

The length of that journey is attested by large numbers of wrong notes in published editions of early music—not merely misprints, but ungrammatical editorial decisions or failure to diagnose the need for correction; these are dutifully passed on by those performers who are in turn insufficiently adept to challenge them. Editors and performers are frequently faced with dissonance, of which their failure to make sense may betray faulty construing of the hierarchy of parts, as does faulty emendation. A test of trained hearing is the ability to make sense out of something that initially sounds wrong or has been wrongly construed in performance. A further test is the ability to diagnose notes as wrong in an unfamiliar piece within a familiar style, for to hear notes as wrong implies thwarted expectation and the possibility of correction in relation to a known language. Example 15 shows an apparently unemendable dissonance in the three-part version of Machaut's ballade *De toutes flours:* the discant and tenor cadence with a sixth to octave followed by a fifth (C–G), with which the contratenor sounds an A. But that A forms a sixth with the tenor C, which resolves on the next breve on an octave B♭. This may need more radical emendation, but if this version is to stand, it requires onward movement in the middle of this phrase, not (as often performed) a general breath-pause after the dissonant "chord," which is senseless as a point of arrival.[75]

EXAMPLE 15 Machaut, *De toutes flours*

A modern edition usually fixes a single version where the early performer had several, or knew one of several. Example 5, *J'ayme bien celui qui s'en va*, survives in three different manuscripts, one as a self-sufficient and contrapuntally correct two-part piece by Pierre Fontaine (discant and tenor) in GB-Ob 213. Perhaps the earliest copy, in I-Bc 15, has those same two parts with the contratenor marked BL. Finally, the latest version (in EscA) has the same two parts with the *contratenor trompette* attributed [by Besseler] to Du Fay (for no better reason than that Du Fay was supposed to have been the originator of the six-line contratenor and bass-generated harmony). Besseler turned this piece, too, on its head. He projected the demonstrably later contratenor trompette as the foundation of the harmony, and that is why he printed it this way. He did not explain how the piece managed until this underpinning was provided, and indeed his writings on Du Fay are completely silent on this basic fact of discant-tenor grammar. This is not a neutral edition; no performer who doesn't know about dyadic harmony would be led to think of using the two-part version, which has a perfectly good pedigree and could be diagnosed as such even apart from the testimony of a source containing it. Most analyses address only one set of permutations of several possible transliterations of the piece as originally notated, usually the most complete possibility, which is not necessarily the version that presents the musical argument most succinctly. A beginning has hardly been made on methods of analysis that are sensitive to plural solutions and plural versions of the same piece.[76]

These are fundamental matters, equivalent to grammatical parsing, and to making correctly the distinctions in language illustrated above by "flying planes" and "dogs bark." Performers can no more conceal a failure of comprehension at this level than can an actor conceal if he doesn't understand a sentence. Insofar as musical grammar, like verbal grammar, controls sense, it must be respected as the foundation of any valid analysis and indeed any valid performance. Whatever new sense modern performers, editors, and analysts may have made out of these passages by approximating them to more recent idioms and expectations, they do less than justice to the terms, and the sense in which that music was devised.

The deep familiarity with idiom advocated above cannot be gained quickly, nor can it be acquired only from listening, because to depend on modern performances is to be informed by a process that in certain respects lags behind scholarship rather than leading it; and to hear original performances is impossible. Lacking native speakers, we have to deal with the available witnesses, namely the notated music taken together with the written theory that supports it. Christopher Page has recently exhorted us to develop an "ear" for medieval music by listening to performances. But whose performances? The ear is fickle and susceptible. Performers may be following bad advice, or following their own ears schooled on modern performances that in turn depend on other modern performances that are directly or indirectly informed by wrong assumptions, leading to a circular mistraining of the ear, as in performances that are virtually free of cadence markers—"leading notes." This sound (it used to be called modal) is in its own way beautiful, and it can get under the listener's skin so that anything else sounds too angular; we and the performers will come to like it, and impose some different kind of sense upon it. We are exposed to the beautiful intonation and high quality of early music performances, many of which have been filtered through modern misunderstandings of the grammar and notation of that music. These performances are seductive, but may lower the performers' and listeners' sensitivity to ungrammatical locutions because they have an insufficient understanding of the grammar, and because we are conditioned to hearing the results of a misplaced belief that "white notes" generally have priority.

Performance is the arena where defaults come into action; indeed, performance of this music is analysis in action. Only at the most preliminary level does the uninflected transcription of the notation have any default status, unlike its more mandatory modern form. The first real level of default may be the singer's silent or sounding construing of his own part, which will include applying melodic defaults such as tritone avoidance and raised leading notes. The second level of default—which may in practice be elided with the first—comes when the singer sings with the other parts. Some of his earlier provisional decisions may now feel wrong; he may prefer, or even be forced, to yield to stronger priorities in another part, or to the greater good of a perfect simultaneity. His cadential discant cadences, if suspended, may yield their semitones in favour of a semitone tenor descent. The third level of default could be, knowing all these things, a conscious departure from them. Only at this stage might one determine that a piece was written in such a way as to *discourage* raised leading notes.

The qualitative difference between tenor and contratenor can be listened for, together with the discant-tenor relationship wherever it occurs in the texture. To recognize norms and deviations is an essential tool not only for analysis but for editing the very versions we analyze. If positivism involves a separation between fact-gathering and interpretation, note-based analysis is the very opposite process because it should entail mutually supporting complementary considerations. This view of how we should set about analyzing early music has much to do with how to learn to listen to it, how to recognize its primary anatomy before we are seduced by its unstable and all-too-mortal flesh. The bones are its bones, the fallible flesh is, inevitably, ours, however well informed; but we will clothe it more fittingly if we take account of the bone structure. A knowledge of the anatomy empowers us to eliminate as impossible certain analytical readings, and to make different judgments about others.

Such recognitions can crucially affect performance, the notes that are sung, and how they are connected and prioritized. What kind of analytical directions may be based on these fundamentals? While there may still be room for some methodological pluralism, the particular notes of constraint which this essay has sounded very considerably narrow the range within which such pluralism can legitimately operate. The first hierarchical level of discant-tenor counterpoint needs to be freed from simplistic claims about successive composition, and recognized for what it is, a grammar which is the starting point for detecting musical sense.[77] Once that duet, or duet network, is isolated, it can be further reduced to an underlying succession of contrapuntal intervals whose adjacent progressions are governed by the rules of counterpoint.

> Relationships between theory and practice are not *a priori*, they are *ad hoc*, so any eventual confrontation of theory and practice ought to be pragmatic, and on a case-by-case basis. We cannot naively adduce the writers on music in a given musical culture as straightforward testimony to musical practice.
>
> (Powers, "Three Pragmatists," 14–15.)

Counterpoint rules are local and tell us nothing directly about long-term goals. Their application, however, furnishes the materials for investigating goals; they fix the intended notes more precisely and on better authority than can be done retrospectively by making the choice of notes conform to their presumed goals. Long-term "coherence" is often invoked to support anachronistic readings of notation. But any consideration of long-term goals in sound (as apart from on paper) must be informed by the workings of counterpoint, and not vice versa, hobbling the counterpoint by imposing a modal strait-jacket of doubtful applicability.

Indeed, the question what kind of tonal planning, if any, may be present has not yet been examined on sound foundations. Anachronistic views of mode will no longer do. If any concept of long-range sounding tonal coherence has the authority to override local grammatical logic, that has yet to be demonstrated. To explore elliptical or long-range relationships with a completely open mind is the most urgent task ahead. That involves full assimilation of the seminal work of Harold Powers, a clear and authoritative position that differs so radically from received views that its consequences have not yet displaced the misconceptions that it replaces. I leave the last word to Harry, in the last words of one of his most seminal articles:

> And above all, theorists from other musical cultures, including ones ancestral to our own, should be allowed to speak as much as possible in their own voices, and we should do them the courtesy of regarding them as advocates rather than wit-

nesses. We may need to explicate or interpret their briefs but we should not rewrite them. We can learn nothing from our distinguished predecessors if we take their elegant and novel constructions as mere descriptions of the commonplace. There are crucial differences between them and us in musical premises and methodological presuppositions alike, but the ingenuity with which they worked out their hypothetical models and theoretical fabrications is right up there with the fancies and elaborations of the tonal and atonal theorizing with which we are more familiar. Plus ça change . . .[78]

NOTES

*Long-term gratitude for years of formative conversation that lie behind this essay goes to my friend and colleague Harold Powers, to whom it is dedicated. He is nevertheless not responsible for the views expressed, nor for formulations he would have put better himself, nor indeed for my use of bleeding chunks from his writings taken and used out of context in a spirit of admiring tribute.

Further thanks for fruitful discussions over the years go to many students, friends, and colleagues including, most recently, for comments on earlier drafts of this paper: Bonnie Blackburn, Patrick Boyde, Suzannah Clark, Cristle Collins Judd, Andrew Kirkman, Elizabeth Leach, Adelyn Peck Leverett, John Milsom, Jonathan Walker, and Rob Wegman. They are not responsible for and may not in some cases agree with the positions I have adopted here. Earlier statements of this thesis and related examples have been given as papers to the New York Chapter of the American Musicological Society in 1989, as the Geiringer lecture at Santa Barbara, April 1995 (with illustrations by Alejandro Planchart and Musica Antiqua), at the University of North Carolina, Chapel Hill, and in London to the Royal Musical Association in 1996, and in Princeton on the occasion of Harry's 65th birthday in 1993.

1. Brett, "Facing the Music," 348.
2. Kerman, "How we got into Analysis" and *Contemplating Music.*
3. Kerman, "How we got into Analysis" and *Contemplating Music.*
4. Treitler, "Music Analysis," "On Historical Criticism," and "Present as History."
5. Kerman, *Contemplating Music.*
6. Treitler, "Music Analysis," "On Historical Criticism," and "Present as History," and Tomlinson, "The Web of Culture."
7. Kerman, "Profile for American Musicology"; Lowinsky, "Character and Purposes"; Kerman response.
8. In *Contemplating Music.* See my response published as "Fact and Value."
9. Agawu, "Does Music Theory Need Musicology?" and "Analyzing Music."
10. "Schenkerian analyses of fifteenth-century chansons fill a gap in documentation. That gap exists because we have questions we want answered about things we have found

in the music, things we were able to find because of our experience (training, etc.) of tonal organization. Given the limits of Renaissance treatises, one way to "explain" large- and small-scale pitch organization is through analogy to tonal music. At worst such analyses are inconsistent, inefficient or unpersuasive, but never *a priori* wrong. Even if they contradict what historical evidence we have, they may be intellectually viable." Schubert, "Authentic Analysis," 17.

11. "In attempting to talk about medieval music we face, among several ideologically imposed restrictions, two which are particularly effective in inhibiting attempts to come to grips with anything more than the surface of the music. The first is the view that the only acceptable reading (or 'interpretation') of a work of music is that current at the time it was produced. The second is the belief that polyphony was constructed successively, one part at a time, and that, as a result, vertical relationships within the music are of very much less significance than is the integrity of horizontal lines." Leech-Wilkinson, "Machaut's *Rose, Lis*," 9.

12. I. Bent, "Analysis," 342.

13. Strohm, "Musical Analysis."

14. Cited and translated by Strohm, "Musical Analysis," 69, fn 24, from Dahlhaus, "Aristoteles-Rezeption," 146–48.

15. Treitler, and most recently Christensen, "Music Theory."

16. Cook, *Guide to Musical Analysis*, 228.

17. Powers, "Tonal Types"; "Modal Representation"; and "Is Mode Real?".

18. Powers, "Is Mode Real?" 18, 10.

19. For a discussion of the finale of the G minor symphony, K550, see Jalowetz, "Spontaneity," 387.

20. See, for example, Lowinsky, "Canon Technique," 190–91.

21. Pinker, *Language Instinct*. See especially Chapter 4, "How Language Works," which presents many examples of distinctions that have approximate musical equivalents. Some sentences used by Chomsky may not originate with him: my proximate source here is Pinker.

22. Cited in Cook, *Music, Imagination and Culture*, 140–42, in a chapter which deals with very similar points in relation to the transcription of non-western musics and jazz. He goes on to say "In so far as we listen to Indian music or Machaut's music as music, we are bound to misinterpret it, because our concept of 'music' is a contemporary Western one" and "listening to music for the purpose of establishing facts or formulating theories and listening to it for purposes of direct aesthetic gratification are two essentially different things" (151–52). I agree, with the important distinction that whereas we can listen to Indian music performed by Indian musicians who "speak" the native language, we have no native performers of Machaut, and the performances of Machaut that we hear are not correspondingly informed. My point here is that we can make some progress with improving the level of grammatical literacy we will tolerate in performances, even though we can never retrieve native sound.

23. Schubert, "Authentic Analysis," 18.

24. Strohm, "Musical Analysis."

25. A lone exception is Sarah Fuller, whose series of thoughtful analyses on Machaut does take cognizance of appropriate theory, though she does not address it at quite the basic level that is my purpose here and sets a higher value on modern "intuitive perception" alongside "fourteenth-century modes of thought." See especially "On Sonority."

26. Lerdahl and Jackendoff, *Generative Theory*, 1.

27. Christensen, "Music Theory."

28. Leech-Wilkinson, "Machaut's *Rose, Lis*," 9.

29. Forte, letter, 335.

30. Agawu, "Does Music Theory Need Musicology?" 90.

31. Hartley, *The Go-Between*, Prologue.

32. For some of the differences see my "Editing early music."

33. For an example of this see Aron's from Josquin's *l'homme arme* mass *super voces musicales*, discussed in my "Accidentals, counterpoint and notation," 312 and ex. 13.

34. Bent, "Diatonic *Ficta* Revisited," para [5], where it is argued that "face value" is an unsustainable characterization of modern notation.

35. Ibid.

36. See my "Editing early music."

37. As Besseler does in ex. 7 and throughout *Bourdon und Fauxbourdon*; Lowinsky, *passim*, especially in *Tonality and Atonality*, and "Canon Technique"; and Randel in "Emerging Triadic Tonality."

38. A telling parallel may be found in Berlin's essay "On Political Judgment":

> To be a good doctor it is necessary, but not sufficient, to know anatomical theory. For one must also know how to apply it to specific cases—to particular patients, suffering from particular forms of a particular disease. This cannot be wholly learned from books or professors, it requires considerable personal experience and natural aptitude. Nevertheless, neither experience nor natural aptitude can ever be a complete substitute for knowledge of a developed science—pathology, say, or anatomy. To know only the theory might not be enough to enable one to heal the sick, but to be ignorant of it is fatal. By analogy with medicine, such faults as bad political judgment, Utopianism, attempts to arrest progress, and so on were duly conceived as deriving from ignorance or defiance of the laws of social development—laws of social biology (which conceives of society as an organism rather than a mechanism), or of the corresponding science of politics.

39. The terms are paired by the fourteenth-century theorist Petrus *dictus* palma ociosa.

40. I am indebted for this example to Harold Powers. He developed this idea on a musical level by demonstrating the homonymous C majors, like-sounding but different-meaning, of Iago and Desdemona, in "Il do del baritono."

41. For the implications of this example see Pinker, *Language Instinct*, 84, 115.

42. Powers, "Tonal Types," 428.

43. Novack, "Pre-Baroque Music," 133:

> The discovery of the prolongation of the triad in polyphony was a momentous historical event. For that reason it may very well be that the era from the School of Compostela to Perotinus is perhaps the most exciting period in the history of Western music. It shaped the future course of musical composition through the nineteenth century . . . we could not begin to understand the historical process without a Schenkerian approach to triadic tonality. This is the only way we can cut across the boundaries of eras of style that have distorted much of our understanding of the history of the art of music. . . . We have no other recourse for understanding the music of the past but to rely upon what Schenker has taught us. Its validity is unquestionable; its limitations none.

44. A good and standard example is given by Dahlhaus, *Entstehung*, 82; *Studies*, 91.

45. See Leech-Wilkinson, "Machaut's *Rose, Lis.*"

46. A timely and eloquent defense of dyadic counterpoint was made by Crocker, "Discant."

47. See ex. 5, *J'ayme bien.*

48. Levin and Leeson, "On the Authenticity of K.Anh.C14.01(279b)."

49. "Is Mode Real?" See also the last paragraph of the present article.

50. See note 38.

51. "Diatonic *Ficta* Revisited," para [28] and n.29.

52. Apel, "Partial Signatures."

53. Lowinsky, "Conflicting Signatures," 245.

54. See "Musica Recta," 75, for a defense of how the theorists' contribution can be reconciled with manuscript evidence, in part by recognizing the overlapping territory between parts with and without signature, and the subjection of both to overriding contrapuntal correction. I there upheld the idea of "successive composition," whereas I would now see a pervasive dyadic contrapuntal basis even in music that was not in the strict sense successively composed. I advocated "applying melodic rules and supplementing them with harmonic adjustment"; the implications of the nature of notation for this practice were further developed in "Diatonic *Ficta*" and now I think improved by the newer "default" hypothesis, which allows first-stage melodic reading to yield to high-priority simultaneous considerations.

55. J. de Muris, *Cum notum sit*, 60b.

56. J. de Muris, *Cum notum sit*, 61. Variant reading: . . . quod in suo contrapuncto non dentur due species perfecte, ut puta 12, 15, 8, 5, et unisoni semel et simul . . . .

57. *Prosdocimo de' Beldomani, Contrapunctus*, 60–63. Herlinger calls the prohibition of parallel perfect intervals in counterpoint "the cardinal rule of counterpoint in the fourteenth and fifteenth centuries," and gives further references on p. 63, note 3.

58. Berger, *Musica ficta* deals in chapter 5 with vertical and cross relations, including tritones, all under the *mi*-against-*fa* rubric.

59. See Bent, "Musica Recta," 93. This strict interpretation of the contrapuntal relationship provides a license for many of the examples given by Boorman, "False Relations," for which he says there is "no theoretical support."

60. J. de Muris, *Ars discantus*, 71.

61. *Prosdocimo de' Beldomani, Contrapunctus*, 58–59, 62–63. Similar statements by other theorists are listed in note 6—Leno, Ugolino, Tinctoris, Hothby, G. Monachus.

62. Powers, "Is Mode Real?" explicates some of the eccentric positions taken by Pietro Aron, which could be taken to illustrate this point. Powers urges that we do our earlier colleagues "the courtesy of regarding them as advocates rather than witnesses," 43.

63. Such "contracts" are not new, and numerous examples exist in more recent music: all opera, certainly from Mozart to Verdi, where arias were written for specific singers, even leaving aside the cases of composers (Beethoven, Mozart, Bartók, Messiaen) who performed their own works, we might mention well-known collaborations (Stravinsky/ Craft, Britten/ Pears), and notable cases, such as compositions written for David Tudor by Morton Feldman and others where the notation counts on largely unwritten expectations of the performer's knowledge of the limits within which realization would be acceptable.

64. Dahlhaus, *Entstehung*, 75, fn 11.

65. This is the view of Randel, "Emerging Triadic Tonality."

66. Besseler selected Du Fay's *Helas ma dame* (ex. 7) precisely because the Contratenor stays below the Tenor and becomes in Besseler's view the *Harmonieträger*, the herald of later bass-driven harmony. After considering the two-part grammatical core of the song, just the discant and tenor parts, observe that there are no structural fourths; the cadences are according to one of the set patterns. There are only three cadences of the strongest type, at measures 5, 15, and the end. This song is a bit unusual by being so economical with its cadences, avoiding formal cadences at the intermediate line-ends and overlapping them. The verse line-end at measure 10 is *not* a cadence, but leads on in musical and verbal sense to the second line. Measure 20 is not a cadence; measure 23 is a subsidiary cadence with a third descending to a fifth.

67. Lowinsky, "Canon technique," 184.

68. Dahlhaus, *Entstehung*, 75–6, *Studies* 85, 340–41 (fn 11): "the effect of this progression was supplemented but not altered by the contratenor, regardless of whether in filling out the discant-tenor framework it resulted in a double-leading-tone, octave-leap, or fourth-leap cadence."

69. Dahlhaus, *Entstehung*, 82; *Studies*, 90–91.

70. In Dahlhaus's statement "displacement of the double-leading-tone cadence C♯–D by the tritone cadence [with G♮] ," double-leading-tone cadence is acceptable insofar as it is understood to involve superimposed dyads and not tonal functions; "tritone cadence," how-

ever, overstresses the relationship between the upper parts at the expense of their relationship to the lower.

71. Leofranc Holford-Strevens points out that this example can be taken further. Italians may not be able to tell the two sounds apart; Danes have both, but whereas they would hear the "ee" of "sheep" as an *i*-sound, they hear the "i" of "ship" as a narrow *e*.

72. In her excellent article "Tendencies and Resolutions," 48–51. Of modern analysts, Fuller comes closest to realizing the counsels of perfection set out here. My points of difference with her arise more from questions of emphasis than of principle, and concern the weight placed on the third and fourth voices, and on longer-term harmonic goals.

73. I will defend this observation at greater length elsewhere. The contrapuntal perfection is qualified by a few self-defining extensions, that will serve as a more detailed application in practice of how a different starting point (such as that suggested here) can produce a radically different reading from that usually given by analysts and performers.

74. Leech-Wilkinson, *Machaut's Mass*.

75. After observing this explanation of an awkward moment, I found that Sarah Fuller implied the same interpretation in "*De toutes flours*."

76. Elizabeth Leach's dissertation on Machaut's ballades (Oxford University, forthcoming) will make an important contribution to this question.

77. In the case of nearly all fifteenth-century songs, recognition of this layer simply involves stripping away the contratenor and considering the discant-tenor duet alone. In other genres it is a bit more complicated, as the functions may migrate between parts in mass and motet composition from the fourteenth and fifteenth centuries, and in all genres by the late fifteenth century. Special definition of these procedures is needed, for example, in the case of canonic and cantus-firmus works.

78. Powers, "Is Mode Real?" 10.

Exploring Tonal Structure in French Polyphonic Song of the Fourteenth Century*

Sarah Fuller

What are we seeking when we set out to identify tonal structure in a composition or within a defined repertory of music? What are we *expecting* to find? Our responses to these questions will largely determine our results, for they will set the course for how we apprehend and configure the phenomena at hand.

A quest for tonal structure often amounts to a search for coherence and unity of pitch relations within a composition or for standard templates of order observed in a repertory. Few scholars wish to entertain the notion that a tonal structure might be disparate or incoherent in nature. The very word "structure" engages associations with regulated order and, in some quarters, predictable pattern. In English, the adjective "tonal" carries weighty associations of hierarchy in which one pitch or sonority dominates over others and controls scale configurations or matrices of relationship. Hence, twentieth-century scholars have tended to describe tonal structure in early European polyphony in terms of coherence about a central pitch (a final or a tonic) or adherence to a template of mode or tonal type identified by a referential final pitch.

Because French polyphonic song of the fourteenth century incorporates no chant melody to betoken and secure its tonal foundation, this repertory pointedly invites investigation of its tonal characteristics. The approach to tonal structure sketched in this exploratory study suspends some of the premises commonly adopted in investigations of "tonal structure" in *ars nova* song, and suggests an alternative mode of examining pitch relations in that repertory. Provisionally, this approach puts aside the criterion of "unity" and accepts the possibility of construing pitch relations within a polyphonic ballade, rondeau, or virelai as other than "coherent and unified." Rather than granting the "privilege of the final" *a priori,* the approach concerns itself with the temporal projection of pitch relationships, with how the events in a song invite a listener to perceive a tonal orientation as they unfold in time.[1] This approach may be characterized as contextual and process-based. Its aim is not to reconstruct compositional procedures but to understand how listeners and singers might become aware of tonal relationships in hearing or performing a song. Perforce, these listeners and singers are (like myself) unavoidably of the present, but the kind of awareness I evoke entails perceptions that were arguably within the capacities of their fourteenth-century counterparts, even though they would not have articulated them explicitly in words.[2]

I begin my exploration with a brief comparison designed to bring into focus guiding tenets that differentiate a system-based from a process-based approach to tonal structure. There follows an analysis of a Machaut ballade intended to illustrate a process-based approach and to communicate its capacity to register nuances of shifting tonal orientation. This exercise itself raises the vexed problem of establishing a "text" for analysis, a problem illustrated through one representative issue, that of *musica ficta*. Finally, I examine commonalities between tonal structures in the Machaut ballade already examined and in a second song said to belong to the same tonal type.

A typical strategy for those concerned with tonal structure in fourteenth-century French song is to focus on what David Lidov has called "culturally inherited abstractions."[3] Such investigations typically deal with tonalities, modal systems, or hexachord patterns as templates governing both single pieces and entire repertories. The investigator regards individual pieces as expressions of a mode, a tonal type coded in final and key signature, or a hexachord construct, and produces taxonomies that to a large extent represent tonal structure within the repertory as fundamentally definite and unambiguous. The mode or tonal type fixes the tonal stance of pieces in a particular class. In such approaches, the "culturally inherited abstractions" guide observation, and aspects of music that fit with those abstractions are singled out for attention.

In contrast, a process-based approach to fourteenth-century secular song investigates how pitch relations become constituted during performance of a song. It does not rely (in the first stages) on received taxonomies, but focuses on the construction of pitch emphases and relational connections among pitches and sonorities as a piece proceeds. It regards tonal structure not as an external property to be assessed rapidly from written notation or a score, but as a perceptual category that becomes constituted in the course of performance, in the course of concentrated listening. Such an approach might be characterized as "performative" as well as process-based, since it takes perception during performance to be a central action in the apprehension of pitch relations.[4] Although analysis from this perspective focuses on individual songs, the results from observation of many pieces can lead toward general hypotheses about the nature of tonal structures in the repertory. Ultimately, the results of a process-oriented, "performative" approach might be expected to mesh with those of a well-conceived "systematic" approach—but where fourteenth-century French song is concerned, that stage of consensus has yet to be attained.

Two recent studies—Christian Berger's *Hexachord, Mensur und Textstruktur: Studien zum französischen Lied des 14. Jahrhunderts* and Peter Lefferts's "Signature-systems and tonal types in the fourteenth-century French chanson"—exemplify approaches to tonal structure in *ars nova* polyphony framed in terms of "culturally inherited abstractions." Their researches lead them to decisively different conclusions about the compositional premises adopted by those who created French secular polyphony in the fourteenth century. Berger argues for the ecclesiastical modes as the shaping force in fourteenth-century French song, while Lefferts argues for conception in terms of tonal types. Lefferts's study can serve to typify a systematic approach whose goal is a comprehensive taxonomy.[5]

Following a path charted in Harold Powers's influential study of tonal types in sixteenth-century polyphony,[6] Lefferts construes fourteenth-century French polyphonic song in terms of established precompositional tonal types. Within a repertory of close to four hundred items (384), he identifies twenty-two tonal types, each of which takes its definition from a final and a "key signature."[7] The final he chooses is the pitch on which the texted cantus ends (not the final tenor pitch or the lowest tone of the concluding sonority). The signature is that presented in standard modern editions of the repertory, usually the one inscribed in the tenor. Figures 1 and 2 summarize his results in graph form.[8] The statistics provoke reflection. Eleven of the twenty-two categories (50% of the types) are represented by a scant four songs or less (fig. 1). Indeed, seven of them owe their existence to a single song. In the aggregate, half of the tonal types postulated on systematic grounds account for only five percent of the repertory (fig. 2, group C). Seventy-three percent of the repertory is distributed among five types (fig. 2, group A), while the remaining twenty-two percent disperses itself among six other types (fig. 2, group B). With such erratic distribution across categories, one cannot but question the degree to which all twenty-two categories are empirically significant, and wonder whether all twenty-two types can reasonably be claimed as operative guides to composition.

Such queries apart, the nature of this approach is that it must be systematic (cantus final and "signature" are inviolable markers) and that it must account for every song in terms of the chosen markers.[9] Such an approach distances itself from direct observation of how songs unfold and privileges external signs that bear the appearance of objective markers. Lefferts claims that through tonal types one may gain "a systematic and largely consistent view of how chanson polyphony operates" (p. 118), and come to know "the paradigms or fundamental givens, the constraints understood at the outset, the range of choices available to the

FIGURE 1 Lefferts's tonal types: Number of items in categories

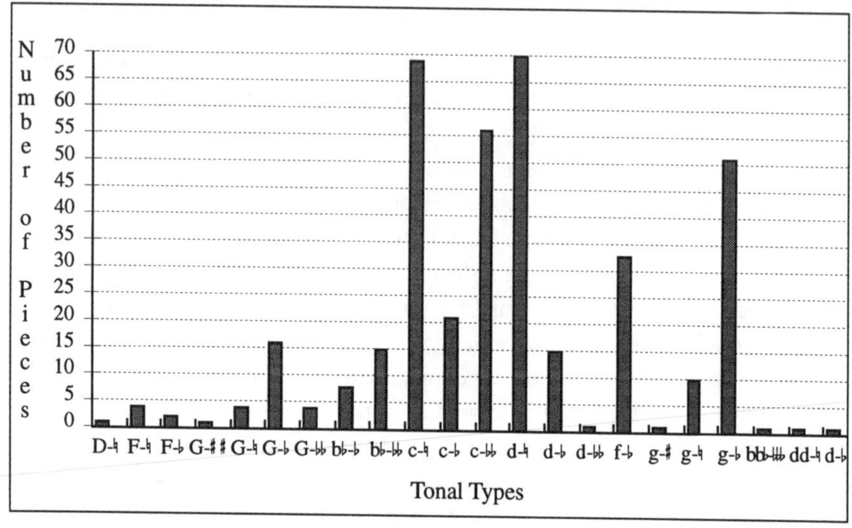

FIGURE 2 Lefferts's tonal types: Distribution within the song repertory

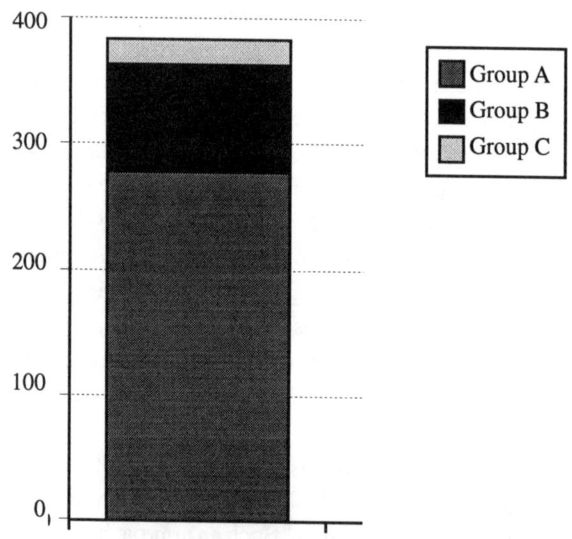

Group A — 5 types with 33–70 representatives (8%–18% of the repertory)
c-♮; c-♭♭; d-♮; f-♭; g-♭

Group B — 6 types with 8–21 representatives (2%–5% of the repertory)
G-♭; b♭-♭; b♭-♭♭; c-♭; d-♭; g-♮

Group C — 11 types with 1-4 representatives (.2%–1% of the repertory)
D-♮; F-♮; F-♭; G-♯♯; G-♮; G-♭♭; d-♭♭; g-♯; bb♭-♭♭♭; dd-♮; dd-♭

composer" (p.117). Such remarks imply that fourteenth-century chanson composers were guided by consistent precompositional tonal templates and that by identifying a song's cantus final and compositional signature a present-day scholar or performer will have discerned the operative pitch and scale hegemony within it. The results of a more nuanced analytic strategy call this position into question.

To approach tonal structure from a perceptual and performative perspective is to adopt a fundamentally different mode of awareness from that entailed in categorization by tonal types. This awareness begins with attention to sonic and temporal qualities projected from the inception of a musical setting, a process I have elsewhere called the "definition of tonal space."[10] As a polyphonic song unfolds in performance, it brings into existence a registral spectrum of sounds and timbres. Within this spectrum, certain pitches, sonorities, and pitch relationships stand out in relief as more salient than others. The delineation of prominent pitches, sonorities, and their relationships is accomplished through many factors, including linear movement of individual voices, distinctions among more and less stable sonorities, voice-leading, text syntax, design, and declamation, all of which are conditioned by temporal factors (phrasing, durations, position).[11] The process through which tonal space is defined may be brief or extended, its outcome clear or ambiguous. An initial definition may set a tonal orientation that holds for the remainder of the piece or may present a reference point from which a future shift in orientation departs. The final impression may be of a uniform tonal center, maintained throughout the piece, or of a pliant tonal situation in which relationships shift and orientations change. In a performative approach, attention turns to the process of definition and to how subsequent events relate to an initial orientation. The larger metaphysical question of how we—as scholars and theorists—make the move from an impression of a particular ordered pitch space to statements about tonal structure is also pertinent, but can here be only tangentially addressed through concrete observations.

Machaut's ballade *Pas de tor*, Ballade 30 in the Ludwig and Schrade editions, may serve to illustrate a process-based approach to tonal structure in a fourteenth-century song.[12] An edition that differs in some respects from those previously printed appears as example 1.[13] *Pas de Tor* is cast in the standard ballade form of $a^{o}a^{c}$ b, where the superscripts indicate *ouvert* (unstable) and *clos* (stable) cadences respectively.[14] Recognition of the a-section repetition is particularly significant in this instance because of the turn to an unanticipated sonority at the *clos*.

The opening sound and the first cantus cadence (br. 9) at first define G–d–g as the axis of tonal space in *Pas de tor*.[15] This G orientation seems at odds with Lefferts's classification of the ballade as a d–♭ tonal type.[16] How it is constituted and subsequently modified is worth exploring first in individual lines, then in the texture of counterpoint and sonorities.

EXAMPLE 1 Guillaume de Machaut, *Pas de tor*

See the Appendix for notes to Example 1 (pp. 80–81).

The cantus plays a major role in defining an initial G orientation (ex. 2).[17] The opening phrase outlines a descent from g to d down to G, passing through b-natural. A delay on a (br. 6–7) coupled with deferred completion of the poetic line arouses anticipation for the G arrival and projects the a as an upper neighbor to the cadential G.[18] The cantus line next gravitates again from g to G, retracing the span in a slightly different way (best grasped from ex. 2b). Its second phrase descends from high g to d to an open-sounding a that resolves in phrase 3a with a well-defined descent to G (br. 21). Yet another descent from g brings the cantus to the unstable *ouvert* pitch, a (br. 24). As the reduction in example 2c shows, the cantus traverses the full g-G octave twice in the course of the first section, and does so twice more on the repeat. Within the cantus, inflected f♯s and c♯s heighten g and d respectively, contributing to the overall impression of a central G–d–g matrix in the principal melodic line as it completes its first delivery of the a section.

EXAMPLE 2 *Pas de tor* Cantus section 1 with two levels of reduction

The first phrase of the tenor supports the cantus focus in its outline of the G–d fifth (ex. 3). Save for an excursion to low D at the end of phrase 2 (ex. 1, br. 17), it remains largely within the G–d fifth up to the final moment of the *clos* cadence (br. 29). The contratenor (whose trajectory is easily tracked by inspection) covers fourth and fifth spans cognate to those in the cantus, but a fourth lower: d–G–D. G is emphasized by its lower half step at breves 3–5 and by duration, br. 15. Contratenor descents to low D at br. 6 and br. 11 take their point of departure from a G context. In the first section, then, tenor and contratenor lines concur in defining a tonal space with G as central reference pitch flanked by its upper fifth d and lower fourth D, a profile consonant with the G–d–g cantus outline.

EXAMPLE 3 *Pas de tor* Tenor, br. 1-9 with reduction

Simultaneities between voices also support this reading of initial tonal orientation toward G. Sonorities in fourteenth-century polyphony fall along a spectrum from extremely stable, consisting only of perfect consonances, to quite unstable, either consisting entirely of imperfect consonances or combining a mix of consonances with chromatic pitch inflections (see ex. 4).[19]

EXAMPLE 4 14th-century sonority types

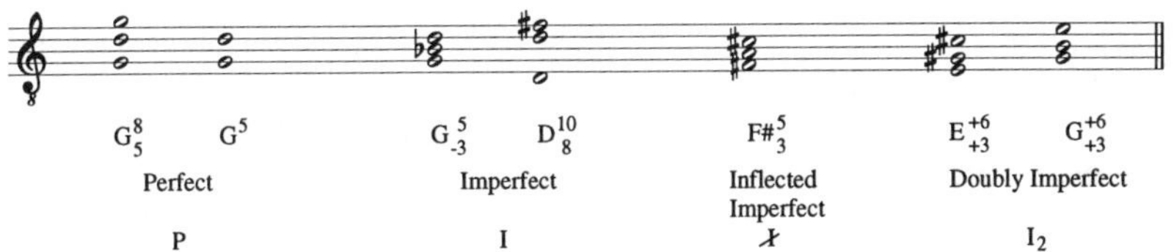

The more unsettled sonorities (doubly imperfect and inflected imperfect) frequently constitute the first component of a directed progression from an unstable to a stable sound.[20] Example 5 illustrates some common directed progressions. The arrows following the intervals of third and sixth indicate a tendency toward perfect consonance, an inclination described (and ascribed) by fourteenth-century theorists. Because they focus attention toward a sonority of resolution, directed progressions function to create salient focal pitches or sonorities within tonal space. That distinct resolutions lie within a fourteenth-century horizon of expectations may be gleaned from theoretical writings of the time.[21] In the first section of *Pas de tor* (example 1), a directed progression at br. 4–5 reinforces the sense of a G center as does the progression of br. 7–8 with its third resolving to unison G.[22] Again at breve 20–21, F[♯] and a converge on G. The F[♯]–a third of the *ouvert* sets up a smooth return to the perfect G sonority of the opening.[23]

EXAMPLE 5 Directed progressions

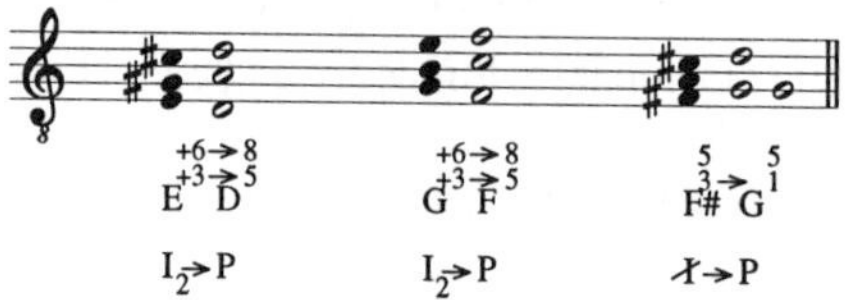

It is at the *clos* cadence that sonority undercuts the prevailing tonal orientation, for the penultimate F[♯]–a–c♯ sonority moves not to a G-d fifth as at breve 4, but to a D–a–d octave and fifth (ex. 6). With this turn of events, the tonal orientation of *Pas de tor* becomes equivocal. Throughout the first section and its repetition, G seems central by virtue of melodic outlines, motion from imperfect to perfect consonance, and reiteration, but at the last moment, with the *clos* progression, D–a–d overrides G–d–g by virtue of its terminal position. By definition, by its status as *clos*, this final sonority must be heard as stable and conclusive. To be sure, D sonorities have appeared before, notably at the beginning and the end of phrase 2, but in contexts that give them an "open" quality, subordinate to the recurring G–d fifth. From a melodic perspective, the *clos* cantus gesture, phrase 3b, could be heard as just another partial descent toward G (exx. 2b and 2c) were it not for the decisive supporting tenor D. The first two sections of *Pas de tor*, a° aᶜ in the formal design, thus present an ambiguous tonal situation in which one pitch—a prominent cantus goal supported by perfect sonorities—seems central but another turns out to be the stable end point.[24]

EXAMPLE 6 *Pas de tor* directed progression at *clos*

Figure 3 attempts to portray this ambiguous tonal situation as a constellation of relationships among pitches. The bold-face large type and the rectangular frame indicate the central position of the G–d–g sonority. The circled pitch units and smaller type show supporting imperfect sonorities. Arrows indicate resolution of these constellations to the G sonority. Standing apart at the end is the terminal D–a–d sonority. The dotted-line rectangle suggests its ambiguous status as a final, but not an anticipated, event. The lack of supporting tendency sonorities underscores its fragility as a determinant of tonal structure.

FIGURE 3 *Pas de tor* tonal configuration: section 1

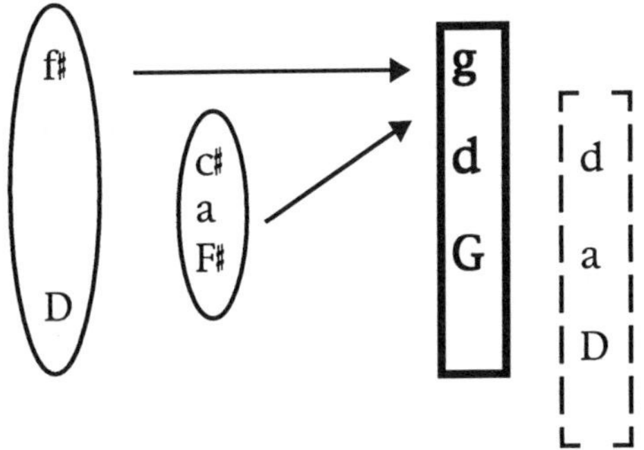

Oscillation between G and D orientations continues in the concluding part of the ballade. The relationship is too subtly drawn to be viewed as an overt conflict between competing centers. It is rather a matter of alluring shifts in balance between two nodes. Until the *clos*, the listener has probably not even regarded D/d as a possible primary locus of tonal orientation. After the *clos,* tonal structure takes on a new dimension in *Pas de tor.*

A sense of this "new dimension" may be grasped from the cantus melody in section 2, which retains many traits imprinted in the first section, including a penchant for descent. The melody even begins with a descent from high g to d familiar from phrase 2 (compare phrase 4, ex. 7 a,b with phrase 2, ex. 2 a,b), but it subsequently avoids completing the octave with arrival on G. The segments of the next phrase (5) close successively on c♯, F♯ and high e. Phrase 6a reinstates the d upon which phrase 4 ended, but in descent turns back from G to a. (This echoes the end of phrase 2; compare exx. 2b and 7b.) When the penultimate segment of the cantus finally closes on G, that pitch is short and weakly positioned in the middle of a breve (phrase 6b, br. 54).

In the last section of the song, then, the cantus clearly traverses paths traced before, but these paths now bypass the low G. The avoidance of that pitch, previous goal of descent, confers a new status upon the high d. Because it remains fixed in place, the d begins to acquire an aura of stability. Compared with the predictable, octave-based cantus outlines in section 1 (ex. 2c), the cantus structure in section 2 seems fractured (ex. 7c). In consequence, the perceived focal point in the cantus line shifts up a fifth from the low G (which is no longer the main goal of melodic motion) to the high d (which remains stable).

EXAMPLE 7 *Pas de tor* Cantus section 2 with two levels of reduction

Within the realm of sonority also, the second section rearranges pitch relations. Phrase 4 reinforces the *clos* cadence on D, with a concentration of D sonorities positioned at beginning, middle, and end (br. 31, 34, 36).[25] Subsequent phrases present G sonorities supported by F♯s and c♯s, but these occur in medial positions (e.g. br. 39, 46). In the refrain, phrases 6a and 6b both move to D octaves and fifths, aurally preparing the final cadence. Whereas in section one the *clos* arrival point was scarcely predictable, in section two it is prepared by a series of prior articulations on D–a–d (br. 47, 50).

It is in phrase 5 that the flux between G and D orientations surfaces most plainly in the three-voice texture. As already noted, phrase 4 begins to emphasize D sonorities through reiteration and position within the phrase unit. Phrase 5, however, turns again toward G, sounding G sonorities on first and third breves (br. 37, 39) and supporting them with F♯–a–c♯ neighbors (br. 38, 41).[26] In Machaut ballades, stable arrivals conventionally occur just before the text refrain, and here the inflected sonority on breve 41 promises a solid phrase ending on a G–d fifth.[27] But the voice-leading goes askew, as shown in example 8. Instead of observing the conventional pattern I-Ɨ-P, and achieving closure on a stable G–d fifth, cantus and tenor sound an imperfect sixth, G–e, that is joined by contratenor B[♮] to create a highly unstable doubly-imperfect sonority on G.[28] Extension of the preparatory inflected sonority over two breves (40–41) delays the arrival of the imperfect G sonority, enhancing its effect as an unexpected event. This adroit mensural gambit also enlarges the span over which contrapuntal tension is sustained without resolution.

EXAMPLE 8 *Pas de tor* directed progressions, phrase 5, br. 37–44

In its inclination toward resolution at the start of the refrain, the $^6_3$ sonority at br. 43 unequivocally dethrones G as a locus of stability. *Contrapunctus* theory as expounded by Johannes Boen (1357) teaches that an imperfect major sixth heralds the perfection of the octave.[29] Intervallic hierarchy here decrees the subordination of the G–b–e sonority to its resolution, F–c–f. This is a key moment in the ballade with regard to tonal structure. Embedded within a doubly imperfect sonority, G becomes a mobile, unstable tone and its status as a locus of resolution dissolves.[30] Oscillation between G and D sonorities continues in the refrain, but both prior experience of the *clos* and the two extended arrivals on D already noted (br. 47 and 50) project tonal orientation toward D. The major sixth-to-octave progression, breves 49–50, is the only standard contrapuntal approach to the D octave in *Pas de tor*.[31] This moment might be regarded as the conclusive polyphonic affirmation of D that overrides the persistent "open" quality of the cantus a. Yet, placed as it is on the penultimate syllable of the text line, and associated motivically with the precadential melodic figures of section one, this internal cadence does not come across as strongly assertive in tonal effect. Still, the new context it provides does alter perception of the final short sequential phrases, which now sound more settled toward D than did their cousins in the approach to the *clos*.[32]

Overall, the second section reorients *Pas de tor* toward D, while yet alluding in its central phrase to the G focus set in the first section. The tonal structure of the second section can be depicted schematically as in figure 4. In contrast to figure 3, the terminal D sonority is now in bold type and enclosed in a solid-line rectangle. It has its own satellite, the E–c♯ sonority. The lowered status of the G sonority is indicated by the dotted-line rectangle. Arrows from the F♯–a–c♯ sonority show other aspects of synoptic voice-leading about the D sonority.

FIGURE 4 *Pas de tor* tonal configuration: section 2

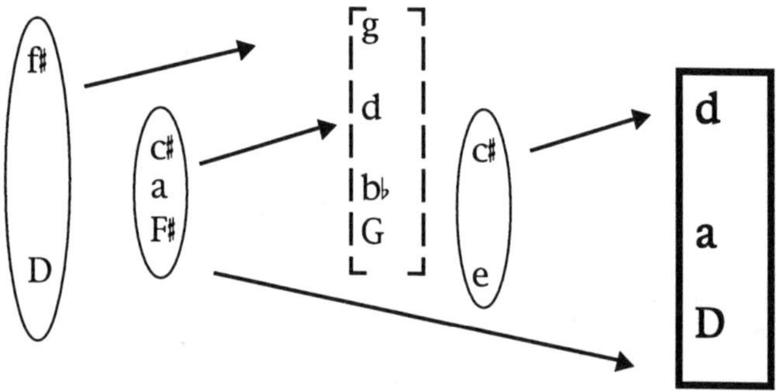

Figures 3 and 4 summarize the chief pitch relationships in *Pas de tor*, and portray the shift in relationships that takes place over the course of the song. Together, the two diagrams could be said to represent the tonal structure of *Pas de tor*.

The interplay between G and D in this ballade, the shifts in their salience, raise questions about classifying *Pas de tor* directly in a d tonal type as though d were the controlling pitch locus throughout and as though the song (considered either as polyphonic complex or as primary cantus) were composed according to a "tonality" framed in terms of that pitch.[33] Even in the second section, the cantus line continues to gravitate down toward G, only settling on d in its final phrase. The very end of the tenor (breves 50–56) might be taken as emblematic of relations between G and D in this song (ex. 9). It outlines two interlocked fifths: one on G followed by one on the D below. Upper and lower neighbor tones surround the top pitch of each fifth. Through this gesture, the G foundation of the first fifth is pulled into the orbit of the D–a fifth as lower neighbor to the a. But this local linear activity in the tenor is more an emblem of relations than a definitive tonal assertion. The effect of the final D–a–d sonority remains more that of an acceptable end point than an inevitable tonal center.[34]

EXAMPLE 9 *Pas de tor* interlocking fifths, end of tenor

Clearly, a process-based approach to tonal structure in *Pas de tor* attends to details and complexities of pitch relations that are beneath the purview of a tonal types classification. The perspectives of "system" and of "process" yield quite different observations about songs. But to ascertain whether a specific tonal type might consistently exhibit the matrix of pitch relations observed in a process-oriented approach, other songs in the same category must be examined. Before turning to another d-♭ song, however, one additional issue critical to analysis of tonal structure in fourteenth-century music must be confronted. This is the issue of the "text" adopted for analysis. For purposes of illustration, only one facet will be addressed here, that of *musica ficta* choices.

As is evident from comparison of the various editions, pitch inflection in *Pas de tor* is fairly pliant. To what degree might the tonal structure descried above and sketched in figures 3 and 4 be said to depend upon choices of *musica ficta*? How much might it be altered or compromised by a decision to continue (or not to continue) a particular written inflection beyond the note to which it is attached, or by strict observance of theorists' admonitions to inflect imperfect consonance in the shortest path to a subsequent perfect consonance? Lacking sure fourteenth-century counsel on this issue, scholars have a wide range for dispute about the influence of *ficta* on tonal structure. In my opinion, the duality of G and D orientations in *Pas de tor* is unchanged by optional *ficta* decisions. Lines, sonorities, phrase articulations, and notated accidentals from the sources all concur on a G orientation up to the *clos* on the hitherto subordinate D sonority. The delicate balancing between D and G orientations in the second section exists independent of elective *ficta* choices. Although I claim that the tonal fluctuation is inscribed in *Pas de Tor* as notated, I maintain that singers (and editors) have power to affect perception of that flux through choices of *ficta*. A rendition that selects F♯–a–c♯ as penultimate sonority of both the *clos* and the final cadence will dramatize the turn from a G to a D orientation far more than one that chooses F–a–c as penultimate.[35] Neither choice will alter the fact that the D octave and fifth is not preceded by its usual tendency sonority (E–G♯–c♯), but the first one will make a point of providing a penultimate tendency element and will highlight the redirection from its usual path (heard at br. 4–5) to a new resolution. Without changing the G/D duality or transgressing the precepts of fourteenth-century theory, *ficta* choices can either bring the tonal reorientation of *Pas de Tor* into the foreground of experience or can convey a more noncommittal, even oblivious, stance toward it. This fits within my general stance that any modern representation of a fourteenth-century polyphonic song (whether performance, edition, or analysis) is inescapably a product of present notions (implicit or explicit) about how the music should go, how theoretical dicta contemporary with the piece are to be implemented.[36]

The systematic tonal-types approach to tonal structure need not concern itself about *musica ficta* matters, since the cantus final and chosen signature operate at a level elevated above such details. That approach does, however, hold out the promise that pieces of the same tonal type will exhibit "similar tonal behaviour."[37] Examination of another song in Lefferts's d-♭ category will give some indication whether a process-oriented approach confirms similarities avowed in a tonal-types classification. *Et je ferai*, example 10, is an anonymous virelai from the manuscript Cambrai 1328.[38] A glance at the end of the refrain (br. 19) and the *clos* of the verse (br. 36) reveals a significant relationship between d and G in this song, an observation that might be taken to ally it with *Pas de tor* in tonal terms. Viewed from the perspective of tonal process, however, the pitch relationships projected in the two songs appear to have quite different profiles.

As before, I begin with individual voices. In the opening refrain section, the cantus of *Et je ferai* outlines an aa–d fifth, and consistently gravitates to d. Example 11 sketches its trajectory over the first two phrases. The following phrases reiterate this direction of motion and confirm the terminal points of the controlling aa–d fifth. Simultaneously, the tenor outlines a descent from d that first terminates on F and finally ends on G (ex. 12).In the verse couplet it traverses the d–G fifth

EXAMPLE 11 *Et je ferai* Cantus outline, br. 1–10

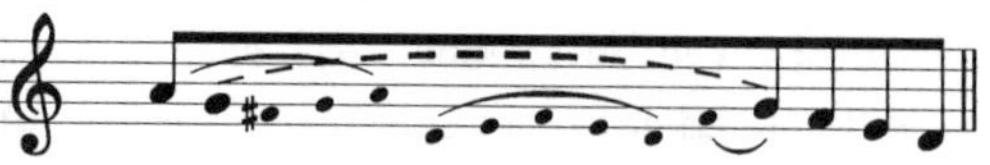

EXAMPLE 12 *Et je ferai* Tenor outline, br. 1–19

EXAMPLE 10 *Et je ferai* anonymous virelai

several times, without sounding the F. In the refrain, differing rates of descent in the two voices produce a staggered counterpoint that keeps the lower goal tones of the two lines separate. For example, the tenor reaches the bottom of its first descent at breve 8, the cantus not until br. 10. By that time, the tenor has begun another descent, and its b♭ greets the cantus d arrival with imperfect consonance. It is not until the very end of the refrain (br. 19) that lower goal tones of cantus and tenor match up in a stable cadence interval. That arrival is then reiterated midway through the verse couplets (br. 26), and at the verse *clos*.

What might we make of tonal structure in this piece? It is not difficult to identify a simple parallel structure of descent through a fifth in each voice. Beginning on pitches a fifth apart, cantus and tenor also end a fifth apart.[39] Figure 5 offers a sketch of the song's tonal structure based on this phenomenon. The fifth is the guiding interval within each voice and between voices. The cantus ends where the tenor begins. In this rendition, tonal space is rather geometric, governed by a prevailing perfect consonance and by directionality. The virelai does not, however, feature interplay between pitch loci analogous to that in *Pas de tor*, nor do inflected intervals guide the ear, except those few that conventions of *musica ficta* would very likely supply. Comparison between figure 5 and figures 3 and 4 (with their complex depictions of pitch relationships) invites us to interrogate the claim that *Pas de tor* and *Et je ferai* share the same tonal type.[40]

FIGURE 5 *Et je ferai* tonal configuration

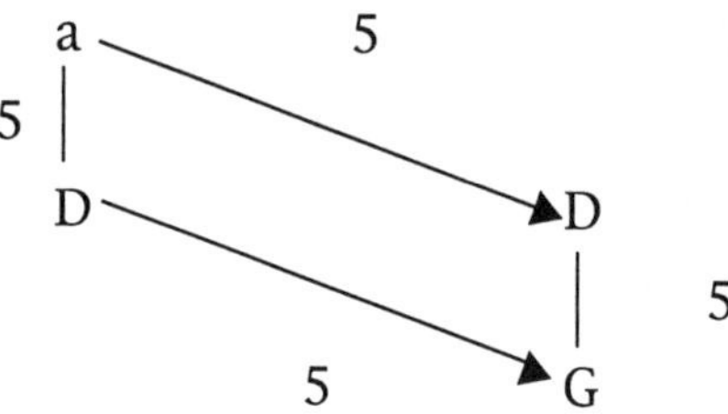

The "signature system" classification of *Et je ferai* also deserves scrutiny, considering that the cantus consistently sings b♮ until (perhaps) the *ouvert* cadence (br. 33) when either the cantus or the tenor must yield to constitute a perfect B octave. If the cantus final is the selected index of tonal type with regard to pitch, it would seem appropriate to take the cantus hexachord profile as the "system" index, in which case *Et je ferai* would be placed in the d-♮ category. Yet in his system of tonal types, Lefferts frequently privileges the "signature" of the tenor or tenor-contratenor complex. The issue of a true "signature" arises also in *Pas de tor,*

where only tenor and contratenor are notated consistently with b♭. The cantus begins each section with b-naturals and shifts to b-flats in approaching the cadence of each. The notations of these songs suggest that just as classification according to a single prime final may not aptly convey the constitution of pitch relations in each, so classification according to a uniform "signature" may not suffice to characterize scale and intervallic configurations within some songs' polyphonic textures.[41]

To return to the opening question: What are we seeking when we set out to identify tonal structure in a piece or within a defined repertory of music? Do we expect to find single, hegemonic tonal centers, or are we open to shifting or ambiguous tonal orientations? Do we hold to a model of a consistent "key signature," or do we recognize differences in scale configuration between voices or shifts in hexachord profile over the course of individual voices? Before we, as a scholarly community, can certify templates and paradigms for tonal structure in fourteenth-century polyphonic French song, we need to become better acquainted with how tonal orientations emerge in individual pieces and to examine quite explicitly the premises we bring to our construction of "tonal structure." If *a priori* we seek uniformity in tonal structures, we will make different observations and will arrive at different conclusions than if we are open to heterogeneous structures or shifting orientations. Even the notion of tonal structure as a level of abstraction beyond "pitch relations" is worth examining, as are possible ways of representing such structures.

No approach escapes the constraints of guiding axioms (however deeply examined these may be). As scholars functioning largely within academic institutions, we tend to want to discover set principles and *modi operandi* observed by past artists and artisans. A process-based approach to analysis of tonal structure in *ars nova* polyphony does not take the existence of a systematic array of tonal or modal templates for granted. In turning attention to the concrete processes by which tonal emphases and hence tonal structure may be constituted, the approach aspires to engage individuals in the qualities of pieces, to raise consciousness about the manifold factors bearing upon what we identify as "tonal structure," and to stimulate critical thought about the degree to which considerations of coherence/diversity, consistency/mutability may enter into (re)construction of images of tonal structure appropriate to music of fourteenth-century France. Some general patterns will emerge from such observations (and some of these may largely conform with some of Lefferts's tonal types), but a process-based approach will also allow diversity of conceptions and images to stand forth within the repertory.

APPENDIX

Notes to Example 1

Sources of *Pas de tor*

F-Pn fr. 1584	f. 469'	(siglum: **A**)
F-Pn fr. 1585	f. 311'	(siglum: **B**)
F-Pn fr. 9221	f. 156	(siglum: **E**)
US-NY*w*	f. 312'	(siglum: **Vg**)

In the edition, breve units are indicated by short strokes on top of each staff. The count is given in the cantus line. An asterisk above a note indicates the probable or possible continuation of a preceding written inflection (sharp or flat). Phrases are identified by numbers in square boxes above the staff.

Variants

(Abbreviations used: Br = breve; L = long; m = minim; om = omitted; SB = semibreve.)

Cantus

12–13	**E**: m m m m m SB m m SB SB g aa g aa f[♯] aa g f♯ g d
14	**B**: SB, first d.
16	**B, Vg**: ♭ on b, beginning of line; **E**: ♭ on e· none on b.
18	**B**: rest om.
22–24	**A**: copied a third too low. ♭ notated on the "B."
25	**B**: ♭ reentered on b.
27	**A**: SB f.
28	**A, E**: no ♯; **B**: ♯ placed low in b space, appears to apply to c.
35	**A**: no ♯.
48	**E**: ♭ on b.
50	**B,E**: SB a.
53–54	**B, E, Vg**: om.
55	**A**: SB f.

Tenor

11–13	All sources: 2 SB ligature SB. I follow Keitel in supposing that the oblique ligature originally had no stem (ascending or descending) and was to be read as L-B.
14	**B, E, Vg**: ♯ on F. Because of the rhythmic error in the tenor, the alignment among voices is uncertain. If the tenor F♯ indicated in three sources were to be observed, then the cantus f and contratenor c would

be raised. This is a plausible reading, but since it emphasizes the tendency sonority more strongly than in any previous edition and might be seen to "weight" the tonal argument unduly, I have refrained from indicating it in the edition.

Contratenor

6	**E**: om.
9	**A**: m SB SB.
26	**B**: SB rest om.
34	**B**: G.
37	**E**: SB rest om.
49–50	**B**: c♯ and d not included in ligature.

NOTES

* I am grateful to Jessie Ann Owens who read an earlier draft of this paper and provided perceptive comments on it.

1. With its focus on the listener, this approach views tonal structure as in part a quality constructed by a perceiver (or by performers) rather than entirely as an immanent property of a composition or group of works. Earlier expressions of this approach may be found in Fuller, "Line, *Contrapunctus*, and Structure," and "*De toutes flours*."

2. Since, ultimately, the relationships claimed arise from features coded in the original notation—such as selection of cadence points, distinction between *ouvert* and *clos* endings, *initia* of phrase units, qualities of consonance and dissonance, durational and registral emphases—they may be imagined as accessible to an "ideal" fourteenth-century musician, whether functioning (in modern terms) as composer, performer, or listener. Recent studies of tonal structure in *ars nova* music generally base their claims regarding systematic pre-compositional constraints observed by fourteenth-century composers on thorough empirical examination of an extant repertory. Yet those examinations are themselves carried out with present-day concerns (including a sense of the centrality of pitch relations in music) a motivating force. Particularly since fourteenth-century writings on *musica mensurabilis* do not address the topic of tonal structure to any significant degree of consistency or detail, the attribution to fourteenth-century composers of systems discovered in the twentieth century is not unproblematic. The situation resembles the ethnomusicologist's problem of representing non-Western musics through Western academic discourse. For one recent statement concerning representation of African musics, see Kofi Agawu, "The Invention of 'African Rhythm.'"

3. "The *Lamento di Tristano*," 67.

4. The "performance" or "listening" can be either actual or mental. I use "performance" here as a code for "the temporal unfolding of a complete musical event," the journey a piece takes, the course it traverses, from beginning to end.

5. Berger's book poses problems that are well beyond the scope of this inquiry which I addressed in a paper, "Modal Discourse and Fourteenth-Century French Song," delivered at the Annual Meeting of the American Musicological Society in New York City, November 4, 1995 (publication forthcoming).

6. Powers, "Tonal Types."

7. The quotes around "key signature" are mine, not his. This reflects my skepticism over the status of "signatures" in the fourteenth-century sources, see below. One attraction of the key signature concept is that signatures have been claimed as objective markers in Hermelink's and Powers's classic studies of tonal structure in sixteenth-century polyphony. Whatever one may think of the sixteenth-century situation (and it is subject to debate), there is real question about extending the sway of a marker so historically situated as "signature" is to a period much earlier than that with which it was originally associated, and to a time of manuscript, not print, transmission.

8. Figures 1 and 2 are based on the data supplied in the Appendix to "Signature-systems," 145–47. I invoke Lefferts's article here only as a representative type of systematic investigation. Full consideration of the claims explicit and implicit in his study goes beyond the present purpose.

9. Lefferts does briefly "explore the tensions inherent in our choice of markers" (131), but the nomenclature of his categories projects a high degree of exactitude.

10. Fuller, "Machaut and the Definition of Musical Space," 1–15. My original characterization of tonal or musical space involves rhythmic and formal characteristics as well as pitch elements. In the present context, this poses an unavoidable duality of sense between that broad and generalized sense of "tonal" and the restricted, pitch-related sense implicated in "tonal structure" as used in the conference and in this paper.

11. By position, I mean location within formal units; for example, an initial position at the begining of a phrase or a principal section, or a terminal position as cadence of a phrase or of a song. From the foregoing, it should be clear that temporal conditions are inevitably implicated in the constitution of tonal space.

12. Ludwig, *Guillaume de Machaut: Musikalische Werke*, 1: 33–34; Schrade, *The Works of Guillaume de Machaut*, 3: 94–95. This ballade has also been edited by Elizabeth A. Keitel as "Seur toute creature humeinne." Both performance choices and editorial decisions can impact upon constructions of tonal organization. This problem is briefly discussed below.

13. *Pas de tor* may be heard on the compact disc *Lancaster and Valois : French and English Music, c. 1350–1420*, Gothic Voices, Christopher Page, director, Hyperion CDA66588 (1992), track 10. The singers follow Keitel's edition, the *ficta* in which differs from that in the Ludwig and Schrade editions and from my own example 1. An instrumental rendition according to Schrade's edition appears on the LP *Ah Sweet Lady: The Romance of Medieval France*, New York Pro Musica Antiqua, John White, director, Decca DL 9431 (1967), side 2, band 5. I chose *Pas de tor* for consideration at the conference preceding this volume partly because of the existence of a polished recording and partly because the song raises representative issues about tonal structure.

14. For more on the ballade form within an analytic context, see my "*De toutes flours*," 42–43. In *Pas de tor*, the final section might well be represented as b[c], since it echoes the a *clos*; compare breves 21–30 with 51–58.

15. This paper uses the Guidonian nomenclature prevalent in Machaut's day that identifies pitches in spans of alphabetic letters a through g: A–G for the low or grave register, a–g for the high or acute register, and aa–ee for the highest, superacute, register. Locations in the score are designated according to the breve count indicated above the cantus staff in example 1.

16. In figure 1, this category appears as the ninth bar from the right. It has fifteen members.

17. Example 2 shows (a) the cantus for the first section of the ballade; (b) a phrase-by-phrase reduction of the cantus, showing the general melodic trajectory with principal pitches in large note-heads; (c) a schematic representation of cantus structure in terms of the octave descents it traverses on the two hearings. The *ouvert* and *clos* endings are designated "o" and "c" respectively.

18. This relationship is already adumbrated in the upper register at the very opening of the line (br. 1). The contrapuntal context makes clear that g, not aa, is the consonant, structural, pitch.

19. See Fuller, "On Sonority." Three-voice sonorities consisting only of imperfect intervals (viewed from the lowest note upward) I designate as "doubly imperfect" (notated I_2), those with only one imperfect interval but one or more inflected pitches, I designate as "inflected imperfect" (notated *I*).

20. See Fuller, "Tendencies and Resolutions."

21. Johannes Boen (1357), for example, speaks of imperfect consonance as attracting and alluring the ears toward a subsequent octave-fifth sonority (quoted in Fuller, "Tendencies and Resolutions," 229). The author of "Cum notum sit" remarks that "the mind would remain suspended" were a *contrapunctus* to end on an imperfect rather than a perfect consonance (quoted in Fuller, "On Sonority," 44).

22. It is a matter of choice whether previous inflections on F and c continue through breve 7, but singers observing standard *contrapunctus* theory would sound a minor third between tenor and contratenor on breve 7 because the two voices converge on a unison.

23. Whether or not one chooses to perform these intervals as minor thirds by raising the F, the effect is still of a progression of third to unison. The dissonant cantus opening transfers the a *ouvert* pitch up an octave and in the resolution of aa to g echoes the a–G hierarchy of the lower octave.

24. Lefferts's emphasis on the conceptual priority of the cantus line is compatible with my attention to processes within the chief melodic line ("Signature systems," 119–22). His reckoning of tonal type strictly according to the cantus final downplays the effects of polyphonic texture and precludes any element of surprise or "play" in pitch relations.

25. The overt parallel between phrase 4's initial D–d–f♯ and the opening of phrase 2 serves to bring out the reorientation toward and reiteration of D.

26. Note that the sense of musical phrasing overlaps verse and syntactic units, severing the prepositional phrase "de vostre | bonte" and placing the terminal rhyme of verse 5 at the beginning of a new musical unit.

27. Such a progression would be parallel to the one heard in br. 4–5.

28. In the annotations below the staff in example 8, I indicates an imperfect sonority, *I* a doubly-imperfect sonority, and P a perfect sonority. The exclamation point marks the moment where the progression takes a surprising new direction.

29. See Fuller, "Tendencies and Resolutions," 229–30.

30. As already noted, this happens also in the cantus line, which avoids strong descents to G from phrases 5–6b. Here the domains of cantus line and three-part sonority concur in attenuating the secure sense of tonal orientation projected in the first section of the ballade.

31. Note that this occurs between the tenor and contratenor rather than in the basic discant pair of cantus and tenor. E–c moves to D–d also in the first section, breves 10–11, but the tenor c is unlikely to be raised there because of the contratenor F.

32. A similar "new context" is provided for the refrain in Machaut's ballade *De toutes flours;* see Fuller, "*De toutes flours*," 56. The disjunctions between primary rhythmic and tonal events fit with my metaphor of "intersecting planes" rather than a "one-track core" advanced in Fuller, "Line, *Contrapunctus*, and Structure," 55. Regarding parallelism between closing segments of first and second sections, note that my terminal phrase partitions in example 1 arise from analytic decisions. If one were to partition according to cantus parallelism, phrase 3b would start at br. 22 and look consistent with 6b. This, however, results in an unusually short phrase 3a and divides into constituent motives what appears to be a single textual trajectory br. 19–24. To begin phrase 6b at br. 53 (parallel to br. 25) divides the refrain melisma in unsatisfactory fashion. I have chosen to privilege textual boundaries over melodic parallelisms in this instance. The chosen partitioning is not inconsistent with my contention that in any case the *clos* of section 2 emerges from a different context from that of section 1 and hence is heard differently. It incidentally lends visibility to the one "proper" cadence toward D in the ballade by situating it at the end of a subphrase.

33. Lefferts, "Signature-Systems," speaks of "the selection of signature-system and final in particular, as a series of deliberate choices by the composer" (144). For his use of the term "tonality," see pp. 129–30. Yolanda Plumley's ambitious study *The Grammar of 14th Century Melody* appeared too late to be addressed in this paper. She does say of *Pas de tor* that "there is some ambiguity as to the identity of the principal pitch area." Rather than perceiving here a challenge to the nomenclature of tonal types, she judges the phenomenon as "entirely typical of the beta tonal types" (157).

34. Heterogeneous tonal characteristics of the sort observed in *Pas de tor* occur also in other polyphonic songs of the fourteenth century, such as Machaut's *Python, le mervilleus serpent* (B 38), *Dame de qui toute ma joie vient*, and *Vos doulz resgars* (R8). Tonal structure in such songs is not well represented by language or categories that imply a monolithic tonal situation. See Fuller, "Line, *Contrapunctus*, and Structure," 50–54.

35. Keitel, "Seur toute creature," remarks of her *ficta* that "editorial accidentals are applied conservatively so that the subtle shifts in modes may be best emphasized" (6). Her choice of uninflected F–a–c at both *clos* and final cadences, performed on the *Gothic Voices* recording, gives a rather bland effect that downplays the sense of "cadence" at both moments.

36. This position will doubtless appear radical to some of my historian colleagues. Yet a review of practices in fourteenth-century manuscripts, a sober sense of indeterminate

aspects of the original notation, and comparison of *ficta* decisions made by modern editors and performers will reveal a considerable range for choice. Helpful as they are, the comments and rules about *ficta* advanced by thirteenth- and fourteenth-century theorists are insufficiently detailed and precise to stifle debate about exactly how and to what degree of consistency *musica ficta* should be implemented.

37. See Lefferts, " Signature-systems," 130 and 144.

38. The edition is from Apel, *French Secular Music* 3, 17. Another edition that differs somewhat from Apel's is in Hasselman, *The French Chanson* 2, 84-85. The virelai survives only in a corrupt state in which the opening of the tenor is lost as well as, possibly, a third voice. For the conference preceding this volume, this song provided a relatively compact example through which a point could be succinctly made.

39. For present purposes, this synopsis represses the tenor F that is rather strong in the refrain and that coincides with significant textual articulations. A process-based approach would give more weight to the F, at least in a first level of analysis.

40. At the conference preceding this volume, Alice Clark noted that the genre discrepancy between a courtly ballade and a virelai with rustic text could account for the differences in complexity of tonal structure observed here. I concur that genre could well play a role. The tonal-types approach, however, operates at a level above genre differences, and classifies ballades, rondeaux, and virelais according to a uniform set of criteria.

41. Given scribal inconsistency in notating inflections, one may doubt whether the whole tribe of fourteenth-century composers and scribes thought in terms of "signature." Lefferts acknowledges scribal inconsistencies, but characterizes them as "relatively few in number." His determinations of signature are based on the standard modern editions ("Signature-systems," 131, note 24).

Internal and External Views of the Modes

Frans Wiering

INTRODUCTION

It has often been asserted that the modal system was self-evidently the basis of "classical vocal polyphony." The standard objection to this view is the existence of all manner of contradictions in the theoretical sources. And the standard refutation is that these contradictions arise at the level of intellectual discourse, not of practical musicianship. But, to follow Harold S. Powers's important distinction, the modal system is not objective, "etic," but "emic," that is, borrowed from another cultural context.[1]

Mode represents a concept that could never have been developed from a study of the music only. Theoretical, or better, textual sources are indeed emphatically "sources" in that they do not only offer raw materials or supporting evidence for our own constructions, but the basic concept as well. Inspired particularly by the work of Bernhard Meier,[2] many scholars have used modality as a tool for the analysis of Renaissance music. But such second-hand knowledge never comes with a certificate of warranty. We acquire it at our own risk: if modality were a second-hand car, we would think twice before buying. Therefore, before we decide to use modes in analysis, we must find out if there are real or apparent contradictions, or other problems, in the sources. And since they undoubtedly exist, they must be investigated, not ignored or explained away, as has been done too often. To apply the image once more: we must not just make a test drive and accept the odd noises from the engine, but take it to pieces, inspect each part, and then reassemble it. In this study I will demonstrate for some parts, notably the modal final, how this can be done.

But my purpose is not simply to admonish a "pro-modal" readership; I also wish to address the "anti-modal" party. Powers answered the rhetorical question "is mode real?" with a well-argued "no."[3] Yet the answer to this question, while it is valid for many of us with regard to analytical pursuits, cannot apply universally. No doubt Aron, an important source for Powers's arguments, would be surprised by this conclusion. For him and his contemporaries the "reality" of the modes as such was beyond question. The problem is rather which form this reality assumed under different circumstances.

For the purposes of this article, I would like to rephrase Powers's question as, "how real *was* mode?," taking the emic "musical mind" rather than the etic musical work as a point of reference. I believe that much of the answer—a full answer is beyond the scope of this article—can be found in the variety, contradictions, or confusion (whichever term one prefers) displayed by the textual and musical sources. I also believe that it may lead in the end to a more balanced application of the modes in analysis.

THE TWO VIEWS

There is not a single aspect of the modal system about which all sources agree. Some of the disagreements concern attributes of the modes such as cadence disposition and melodic patterns; others are about fundamentals of the system, such as the number of modes and the way in which they are constructed. This is also true for modal finals: not only do some finals "belong" to different modes in different theories—the treatment of the finals A and C is notorious, but these are not the only cases—but there are also different viewpoints on the role of the final in the realization of the mode.

The existence of such different views is acknowledged by, among others, the Venetian theorist Gioseffo Zarlino. In chapter iv:30 of his *Le istitutioni harmoniche* (1558), he points out that many compositions that appear to belong to mode 3 display deviant interval species. The expected ones are e–b and b–e^1, harmonically dividing the octave species e–e^1, while in such works this octave is divided arithmetically in e–a and a–e^1, as is proper to mode 10 (see ex. 1a). This is indeed the mode the listener perceives, says Zarlino, even when the piece ends on e:

> La onde vdendosi tali specie tante, & tante volte replicate, non solamente la maggior parte della compositione viene a non hauere parte alcuna del Terzo: ma tutta la cantilena viene ad esser composta sotto'l Decimo modo . . . Di maniera che quella compositione, che noi giudichiamo esser del Terzo modo, non viene ad hauer cosa alcuna, per la quale possiamo far giuditio, che sia di tal Modo, se non il fine: percioche finisce nella chorda E.

> Since these species [e–a and a–e^1] are heard so often and are repeated so many times, not only does the greater part of the composition no longer share anything

> with mode 3, but the entire composition turns out to be composed in mode 10 . . . In this way the composition that we judge to be in mode 3 no longer has anything by which we can judge it to be in this mode, except for the final, for the composition ends on the note e.[4]

Zarlino cites no composition to illustrate this instance of "species shift,"[5] however, Rore's *Ancor che col partire* would be a possible candidate. Lodovico Zacconi observed that this madrigal displays the interval species e–a and a–e^1, most notably in the phrases "de la vita ch'acquisto nel ritorno" (see ex. 1b) and "tanto son dolci", while its final is e. Zarlino could have assigned the piece to mode 10 for this reason. Zacconi, however, considers it to be in mode 4, shaped after the psalmtone.[6]

EXAMPLE 1A Modes 3 and 10, and the ambiguous octave species (Finals are shown as whole notes.)

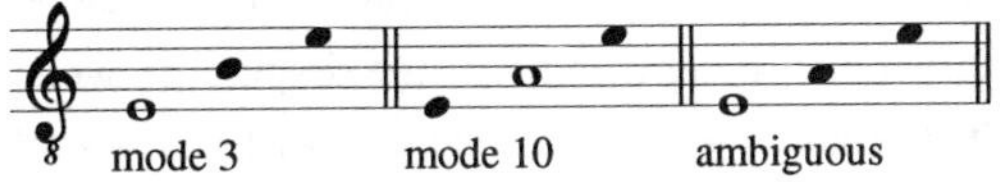

EXAMPLE 1B Rore, *Anchor che col partire*, tenor and bass (fragment, after CMM 14:4)

From the case described above, Zarlino concluded the mode of a composition can be judged in two ways,

> . . . prima dalla forma di tutta la cantilena; dipoi dal suo fine, cioè dalla sua chorda finale. La onde essendo la forma quella, che dà l'essere alla cosa; giudicarei, che fusse ragioneuole, che non dalla chorda finale semplicemente; come hanno voluto alcuni: ma dalla forma tutta contenuta nella cantilena, si hauesse da fare tal giuditio.

> . . . first by the form of the entire composition, and second, by its final note. Since it is form which gives being to a thing, I would consider it reasonable to determine the mode of a composition not merely by the final note, as some have wanted, but by the whole form contained in the composition.

Here Zarlino confronts the two methods for the determination of the mode in terms of two of the Aristotelian causes, formal and final. The formal cause is "the account of what the thing is," what earlier in the sixteenth century Pietro Aron called the "essence" of a thing. The final cause is the purpose of a thing, or simply "the end towards which something tends naturally to develop."[7] For Zarlino, the formal cause of a composition, that which makes it a unified whole rather than an arbitrary collection of consonances, is the mode, or, as he formulates it elsewhere, "modes or tones are the forms of musical compositions" ("Modi, o Tuoni: i quali sono le forme delle Compositioni Musicali").[8] The final cause, the final sonority, is not a sufficient indication of the mode; yet only when the final has been reached, the composition "is complete and has its true form" ("è perfetta, & hà la sua vera forma").[9]

For Zarlino the final can only provide a "working hypothesis" about the mode, which must be confirmed or refuted by a study of the form of the piece. Yet the phrase "as some have wanted" suggests that others may have thought differently. Indeed, the two methods are confronted in the dispute between Giovanni Maria Artusi and L'Ottuso Accademico, documented in the former's *Seconda parte dell'Artusi*. In his second letter to Artusi, L'Ottuso wrote:

> Alla dubitatione poi del Madrigale; Crud'Amarilli, io non sò come possa cadere nell'animo à V.S. che sia d'altro tuono, che del settimo, essendo ad ogn'uno notissimo, che dalle prime, & poscia dalle finale corde si deue dare giudicio del tuono, & non delle medie cadenze . . .

> Concerning the hesitation about the madrigal *Crud'Amarilli*, I do not know how the idea could have entered your honor's mind that it is in any tone other than the seventh, since everyone knows that one must determine the tone from the beginning and then from the ending notes, and not from the internal cadences.[10]

"Rule of how to determine the tone misunderstood" ("Regola di far giudicio del tuono mal inteso") is Artusi's dismissive comment in a marginal note, and he explains that to consider the first and last sonorities only is to take only musical matter but not musical form into account, a major sin against the teachings of Aristotle.

These sources thus give evidence of two contrasting approaches towards the final. The "internal view," to which Zarlino and Artusi adhere, sees it as the outcome of a musical development, dictated by the mode. L'Ottuso Accademico and the even more shady musicians Zarlino refers to consider the final as the fundamental criterion for modal determination; I will call their approach the "external" view. These views are not confined to only a few late-Renaissance sources, but reflect a widespread dichotomy, despite the apparent elusiveness of the adherents of the external view. That each view can be associated with a number of other features such as terminology, definition, and user group will help to clarify this proposition.[11]

Concerning terminology, the reader may have noted that L'Ottuso uses the term "tuono," tone, while Zarlino speaks of "modo," mode (as does Artusi most of the time). This distinction merits our attention. Already from Antiquity onwards, a number of synonyms, or better, near-synonyms, were used for "mode", as appears from Boethius's description of mode:

> Ex diapason igitur consonantiae speciebus existunt, qui appellantur modi, quos eosdem tropos vel tonos nominant.

> From the species of the consonance of the diapason arise what are called "mode." They are also called "tropes" or "tones."[12]

Often we find only "mode" and "tone" mentioned. This happens in the anonymous *Dialogus de musica* (c. 1000), in the oldest version of the most popular definition of mode of all times (which I henceforth will call the "*omnis cantus* definition"):

> Tonus vel modus est regula, quae de omni cantu in fine diiudicat.

> A tone or mode is a rule which distinguishes every chant in its final [scale degree].[13]

Through all ages, writers and musicians made some kind of distinction between the two terms. First, there is a "technical" one: Adriano Banchieri and Giovanni Maria Trabaci are two early seventeenth-century musicians who apply it. Banchieri's *Cartella* contains a chapter entitled "Breve narrativo della differenza da gl'otto tuoni, a gli dodeci modi" ("short account of the difference between the eight tones and the twelve modes"), concluding that the tones are used for liturgical polyphony, particularly for *alternatim* performance of psalmody, while the modes are for "ogni Cantilena discrepante al Canto Fermo" ("all composition not involving psalmody").[14] How modes and tones overlap is illustrated in the *Duo spartiti al contrapunto* in the same collection.[15] Trabaci makes a slightly different distinction between the twelve modes of the music of the "prima scuola," that is, strict composition (motets, madrigals, and ricercars), and the "toni," "toni ecclesiastici" or even "finali ecclesiastici" of other instrumental music (whether liturgical or not), to which no ambitus restrictions apply.[16]

There is also a status difference. Guido of Arezzo already called the use of "tonus" as a synonym of "modus" "abusive," improper,[17] and a number of authors followed him in this. Others pointed out that "tonus" simply was the commonly used term. In Renaissance Italy, we still find the same kind of comments being made. Vicentino wrote about the "modi detti uolgarmente toni" and the "modi, ouero toni (da prattici detti),"[18] and in *L'Artusi* the inquisitive character, Luca, asked the learned Vario:

> Di dove nasce, che tanti e tanti pratici, & quasi tutti, chiamano Tono, quella forma data alle Cantilene, & non Modo?
>
> Why do so many, indeed almost all practical musicians, call the form which is given to compositions, "tone", and not "mode"?[19]

An inspection of compositions with modal titles makes it abundantly clear that "tone" was indeed the preferred term of the practical musician. "Mode," by contrast, was the term of the speculative musicians or the practitioner with a sympathy for contemplative music.

This is related to the range of meanings both words have. The Latin "tonus" and its derivations in other languages are in the first place musical terms, meaning note or tone in general, and psalm tone in particular (as with Banchieri and Trabaci). There are non-musical connotations, but these are not so important as to influence the musical usage. "Modus," however, is a frequently used word in Latin; its original meaning is "measure." Other meanings like "manner," "style," and "rule" suggest connections with poetic theory; meanings like "moderation" and "norm" provide a link with philosophy. The Italian word "modo" has a very similar range of meanings. Note however that "modus" and "modo" hardly ever mean "psalmtone."[20]

Gaffurius made an explicit connection between terminology and "user group" in his *Theorica*, noting also that each group defined mode in a different manner. At the beginning of the chapter on modes he writes:

> Philosophi enim has septem diapason species modos dixerunt . . .
>
> Philosophers have called these seven species of the diapason "modes."

And at the end of the same chapter he writes:

> Eos . . . modos octonario depraehensos numero Ecclesiastici musici tonos nominant . . . quos quidem regulas esse dicunt quibus omnis modulatus concentus intentione atque remissione in fine cognoscitur discernitur & iudicatur.

> Churchmen call those modes . . . tones. These they call rules by which every melodious chant is recognized, classified, and judged by its end, by means of its ascent and descent.[21]

It appears that the philosophers' modes are species of the octave, like those of Boethius; the churchmen's tones are rules for classification of chant from its final and range, which is an instance of the *omnis cantus* definition.[22] An investigation of a considerable number of definitions of mode used in Italy shows that two sorts of definitions of mode were widely employed. One group of theorists, among whom are Tinctoris, Lanfranco, and Zacconi, present variants of the *omnis cantus* definition; these variants mention the final and usually the ambitus, and always employ the term "tone."[23] Another group of theorists, among which are Rossetti, Angelo da Picitono, Tigrini, and Bononcini, use the species definition or Zarlino's *forma* definition. None of their definitions mentions the final, and mode seems to be the preferred term, though tone (and even trope) occur a number of times.[24]

TABLE 1 Characteristics of the internal and external views

	Internal	External
term	modus, modo	tonus, t(u)ono
connotation	norm, rule	psalm-tones
judgment	entire composition	final
definition	species or form	omnis cantus
used by	"philosophers"	practical musicians

The internal and external views can now be summarized as in table 1. The internal view is a theoretical, even philosophical, view. It concerns the understanding of a musical composition, and the expression of mode through the entire piece. It employs the word "mode," and defines mode as interval species. The external view belongs to churchmen and practitioners. It is concerned with the classification of compositions, mainly by means of the final. It employs the word "tone," and defines it with a variant of the *omnis cantus* definition. Naturally, the internal and external view as shown in table 1 are abstractions that serve to stimulate the awareness of its variety, like the other dichotomies that have been proposed for modality.[25] What particular variety a musician developed depended not only on the tradition to which he belonged, but also on the purpose he had in mind for the modes.

USES OF THE MODES

Because the internal view of the modes may come close to a modern analytical view of music, we may be easily tempted to assume that composers held similar views. But there are many other uses of the modes than composition, and most of these do not require an internal view. I will investigate these first, and then try to extrapolate an image of the average musician's "modal background."

In discussions of the "modes of classical vocal polyphony" one tends to forget that at least until the Reformation, the most important application of the modes lay outside polyphony: in plainchant, especially in the connection of antiphons and psalm tones. This point is obvious enough to need no elaboration, though I would advise the reader to contemplate it from time to time.

In addition to psalmody, there are two more uses for the modes in plainchant: solmization and choice of pitch. The former use is documented in numerous Central European sources from the first half of the sixteenth century. Walter Werbeck explains this use as follows.[26] The western-ecclesiastical tradition, describing modes in terms of melodic patterns and function rather than of scales, was much more in evidence in Central Europe than elsewhere. As a consequence, one was allowed to use both B-natural and B-flat in any mode until the end of the fifteenth century. During the first half of the sixteenth century, this possibility disappeared for most modes. Werbeck contends that this happened under the influence of polyphony, but it seems also to be caused by the reception of the pseudoclassical, scalar tradition of modal theory transmitted through the writings of Gaffurius, among others.

The formerly "flexible" *B fa / mi* was now either interpreted as a B-flat or a B-natural, depending on the mode. Usually—the authors are not in complete agreement—the Phrygian and Mixolydian modes were given a B-natural, the Lydian a B-flat, and the Dorian modes kept both options. This means that in six out of eight modes only two hexachords are needed for solmization, which is thus made much simpler, assuming that one knows the mode of the song.

Choice of pitch is also well-documented as a use for the modes, both in Germany and elsewhere. The fifth of Ornithoparchus's ten rules for good singing was often quoted for this:

> . . . autentorum tonorum cantica, profunde subiugalium acute, neutralia vero mediocriter intonentur. Hec enim in profundum, illa in acutum, verum ista in vtrumque tendunt.

> The Songs of Authenticall Tones must be timed deepe, of the subiugall [plagal] Tones high, of the neutrall, meanly. For these goe deep, those high, the other both high and low.[27]

This rule can easily applied to polyphony. Martin Agricola quotes it in a context with many polyphonic examples.[28] Joachim Burmeister gives a similar rule:

> Ad mediocritatem sive medium in modulando tenendum accommodatae sunt inter septem diversas octavas diapason *C–c, D–d, E–e,* cuius gratia pro tenoris diapason omnibus omnium modorum, ut ut quilibet eorum proprio systemate sit comprehensus, ipsae erunt reputandae.

> To maintain moderation or a proper mean in music making, the diapasons on *c–c¹, d–d¹* and *e–e¹* are made to accommodate the seven different octave patterns. Those three diapasons should be assigned to the tenor in any mode, so that any mode can be contained within the proper system.[29]

Thus, each piece is sung at such a pitch that the octave species of the mode of the tenor fits one of the three given octaves. In polyphony the actual pitch depends on the ranges of the other voices, in monophonic song the octave should preferably be *d–d'*, or else *e–e'*.[30]

Calvisius's *Exercitationes Musicae Duae* (1600) contain a penetrating general account of the use of the modes by composers, singers, and instrumentalists. Composers should study the modes because

> Melopaei ex hac doctrina certò statuere possunt, non tantum in qua clave Cantilena quaelibet incipienda sit, & finienda: sed etiam vbi Clausulae ad affectum textui convenientem eliciendum appositae, sint formandae.

> From this doctrine composers can certainly determine not only upon which note each composition should begin and end, but also where cadences must be made in order to produce an affect that accords with the text.[31]

In other words, they must transform their external view of the modes into an internal one.

Singers in turn may learn through the modes better to understand what they are singing, and to choose the right pitch for a composition, so that they are no longer dependent on an instrumentalist (which is shameful). The exhaustive listings of Latin polyphonic compositions elsewhere in the treatise call the medieval tonaries to mind, and seem to serve as a tool for establishing performing pitch.

Organists must learn that there is more to modality than the final only, and their improvisations can gain much from this insight. Also, if in an *alternatim* performance the choir closes on the wrong note by accident, organists must have sufficient knowledge of modal cadences to lead the music back to the intended final. They ought to be able to play in all modes at all possible pitches, though Calvisius recognized that the unequal temperament of the organs would make this ideal impossible to realize.

As for instrumental music, Spanish collections of vihuela music abound with elementary modal theory, which, as Wolfgang Freis has demonstrated, was important in intabulation. Adrian Le Roy discussed the modes for the same reason.[32]

Lastly, Powers has described two important uses outside the field of performance or composing. The first is as a tool for ordering collections, as attested in the hundreds of surviving modal cycles,[33] and the second is as the musical dogma of the Roman Catholic Church, as seems for example the case in Palestrina's eight-mode cycles, the *Offertoria* in particular. By contrast, the twelve-mode system could express religious independence from Rome, as might be the case in Lutheran twelve-mode cycles or Claude le Jeune's *Dodecachorde* and *Octonaires*.[34]

The following uses of the modes have emerged so far:

- psalmody
- good singing, comprising
  1. pitch
  2. solmization
- ordering of musical collections
- intabulation
- transposition
- improvisation of preludes, verses, etc.
- composing
- judgment / explanation of composition
- "musical dogma" or other ideological use
- contemplation of music and the universe

If we relate the above to the education and experience of a practical musician from the Renaissance, his earliest contact with the modes would have been in psalmody and elementary theory. The term he would employ would be "tone" rather than "mode," and he would define it with a variant of the *omnis cantus* definition. Next comes the experience of polyphonic performance, which involves solmization and pitch determination. For a trained instrumentalist, new uses would be transposition and transcription of compositions, and the improvisation of preludes and verses.

For none of these tasks would an internal view have been necessary or even desirable.

How far the composer's view of the modes developed beyond the external one would depend on the extent of his specialist education, his experience, and his intentions. There is no reason to assume that the accepted masters of Renaissance polyphony came closest to an internal view, or even that their view was immutable.

EXAMPLES OF THE EXTERNAL VIEW

I now come to a series of vignettes illustrating the practical, external view. Some concern the final and its function; others exemplify negative judgments about music.

Simplification

If the final is used as the main or only criterion for judging mode, the distinction of authentic and plagal modes is likely to suffer. A textual source that documents such a simplification is Georg Rhau's *Enchiridion*:

> In eo enim cantu, claues affinales ad nutum sumuntur compositoris, iudicamusque tonos secundum has quatuor voces, re, mi, fa, sol . . . Haec de tonorum fine & agnitione sufficere arbitror, in quibus plus vsus spectari debet, quam tot praeceptiones pueriles, Nam inter tonum authenticum & plagalem non semper potest absoluta & exacta haberi cognitio & differentia, imo ex coniectura saepe cantus tono autentico vel plagali attribuitur.

> In this kind of song [polyphony], affinals are employed as the composer wishes, and we judge the tones according to these four syllables, *re, mi, fa sol* . . . I believe that this suffices concerning the ending and recognition of the tones, in which one should rather observe practice than so many puerile precepts. For one cannot always believe the knowledge and the difference between an authentic and plagal mode to be absolute and exact: indeed, a song is often classified in an authentic or plagal by guesswork.[35]

Two modal cycles that follow this model occur in the treatises of Martin Agricola, who was well acquainted with Rhau. But such cycles were also compiled elsewhere, for example in Spain, by Milán and Bermudo.[36]

Rhau's model is clearly related to Glarean's now well-known references to the three-mode system of practical musicians, for example in chapter ii,1 of the *Dodecachordon*.[37] The three modes were differentiated by the quality of the final only, which could be *ut*, *re*, or *mi*. Several musical sources indeed use such a method, though other finals than *ut*, *re*, and *mi* occur as well. The earliest examples I found are a *Praeambulum super re* and one over *fa* in the *Fundamentum Organisandi* (1452) by Conrad Paumann. The organ works by Hans Kotter (Strasbourg ca. 1485–Bern 1541), which carry titles like *Harmonia in sol*, are geographically and temporally quite close to Glarean.

In my opinion, such simplifications may be relics of the oldest layer of practical application of the modes to polyphony, before an adequate solution had been found to deal with the wide ranges of polyphonic composition.[38] It was an undercurrent with a long life span, emerging from time to time in curiously "anti-modal" sources like Valente's *Versi spirituali* over five of the six solmization syllables, and finally in "ecclesiastical tones" and "psalm-tone keys" of Banchieri, Trabaci and other seventeenth-century musicians. These are characterized by final and scale only, not by ambitus, although they are often described in the sources as variants of the modes or psalm tones.

Galilei's Classification by Final

The second edition of Vincenzo Galilei's lute handbook, *Fronimo*, contains a remarkable account of the twelve-mode system.[39] What appears at first sight as a résumé of Zarlino's theory, is actually a classification method that takes the final rather than the formal cause of the composition into account. The essence of this method lies in the "example of the final note of the tenor and bass for all the twelve modes" (ex. 2, omitting the similar examples for the transposed modes). The example shows the finals of the tenor and bass and their interval species. The regular final of a mode is the lowest note of the fifth species, and not only the tenor follows this rule precisely, as one would expect, but also the bass. For example, in the untransposed modes 3 and 4, the tenor ends on e. The bass of mode 3 is in mode 4, using the species B–e–b, and its final can only be (the same) e. In mode 4, however, the bass is in mode 3, an octave below tenor pitch: its octave species is thus E–B–e, and the final of the bass is therefore E, not e.

The twenty-five madrigals listed by Galilei as examples for the modes are said to illustrate this procedure. Table 2 shows their tonal types, including the octaves of the finals.

Two of these works do not follow the pattern, Striggio's *Herbosi prati* and Willaert's *Gentil coppia. Herbosi prati* is in mode 9 by Galilei's criteria. I assume that he mistook the c4-clef of the bass for an f4-clef; the final would then appear to be a d instead of an a. I see no reason why Galilei classified *Gentil coppia* in mode 3 rather than mode 4, unless it is that Galilei promised to give such examples as would "accidentally come to mind" ("che cosi all'improuiso mi souuerranno")[40] and that his "nobile sprezzatura" put him on the wrong track.

EXAMPLE 2 Galilei's finals (*Fronimo*, 90)

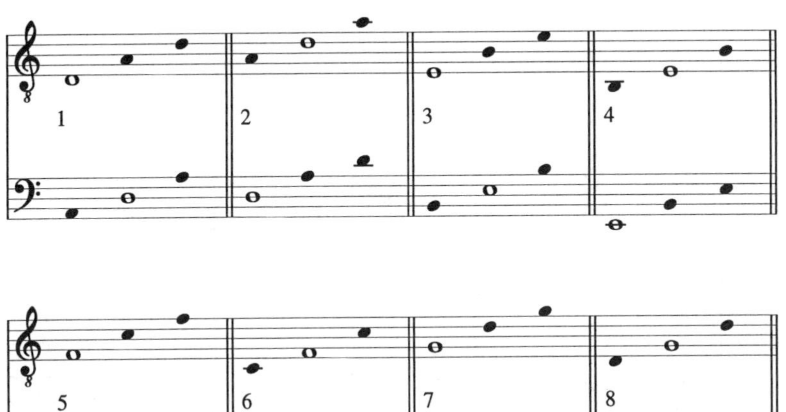

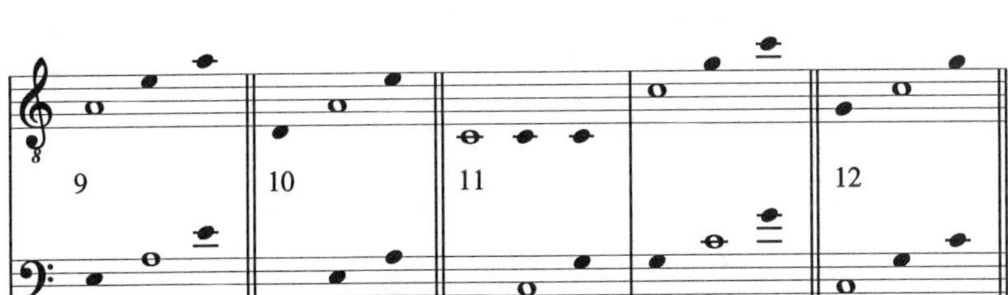

In some works, Galilei's procedure results in an evident misrepresentation of the internal mode, as in Rore's *Vergine chiara* which Galilei considers to be in transposed mode 7, while its melody and cadence disposition clearly suggest mode 12.[41] But this external view of the modes can be linked to a specific use. *Fronimo* is a handbook for lutenists, whose main use of the modes is not for strict composition, but the choice of a fitting prelude (or a similar piece) to a given composition. The "quality" of the final of the prelude is then the only thing that matters.[42]

Bad Music

Internal views of the modes, for example Zarlino's, relate many musical characteristics to the mode. Part of the intellectual stature of Zarlino is that he is well aware of the "idealized" nature of his constructions. While he is usually regarded as the archetypal prescriptive theorist, the reading of a random chapter from the *Istitutioni* will show that he concedes considerable liberty to the composer to depart from his

TABLE 2 Tonal types of Galilei's examples for the modes in *Fronimo*

Mode	Composer	Work	Tonal Type	Source
1	Cipriano de Rore	*Vergine bella*	$\natural-c_1-d$	RISM 1548^{10}
	Alessandro Striggio	*S'ogni mio bene havete*	$\flat-g_2-g$	Striggio, *Secondo libro a 6*
2	Alessandro Striggio	*Herbosi prati*	$\natural-g_2-a$	Striggio, *Secondo libro a 5*
	Cipriano de Rore	*Vergine, tale è terra*	$\flat-c_1-G$	RISM 1548^{10}
	Dominique Phinot	*Virgo prudentissima*[a]	$\natural-c_4-D$	RISM 1532^{10}
3	Cipriano de Rore	*Vergine sola*	$\natural-c_1-e$	RISM 1548^{10}
	Adrian Willaert	*Gentil coppia*[b]	$\flat-g_2-A$	RISM 1548^{10}
4	Alessandro Striggio	*Che deggio fare*	$\natural-c_2-E$	Striggio, *Primo libro a 6*
	Cipriano de Rore	*Vergine humana*	$\flat-c_1-A$	RISM 1548^{10}
5	Cipriano de Rore	*Donna, ch'ornata sete*	$\natural-g_2-f$	Rore 1550
	Alessandro Striggio	*Com'atra nube*[c]		
6	Alessandro Striggio	*Da queste altere soglie*	$\natural-c_1-F$	Striggio, *Secondo libro a 6*
	Cristofano Malvezzi[d]	*Torna sonno deh torna*	$\flat-g_2-B\flat$	RISM 1583^{16}
7	Alessandro Striggio	*Lascia deh Tirsi, mio*	$\natural-g_2-g$	Striggio, *Secondo libro a 5*
	Cipriano de Rore	*Vergine chiara*	$\flat-c_1-c$	RISM 1548^{10}
8	Cipriano de Rore	*Vergine saggia*	$\natural-c_1-G$	RISM 1548^{10}
	Adrian Willaert	*Ceda nata nel mare*[e]	$\flat-g_2-c$	RISM 1548^{10}

9	Alessandro Striggio	*Partirò dunque*	♮–g_2–*a*	RISM 1566^{23}
	Alessandro Striggio	*Ne perche'l mio desio*	♭–c_2–*d*	Striggio, *Secondo libro a 6*
10	Cipriano de Rore	*Vergine santa*	♮–c_1–*A*	RISM 1548^{10}
	Giovanni Domenico da Nola	*O verde amena apricia*[f]	♭–g_2–*d*	RISM 1561^{10}
11	Cipriano de Rore	*Vergine pura*	♮–c_1–*c*	RISM 1548^{10}
	Orlande de Lassus	*Pien d'un vago pensier*	♭–g_2–*f*	Lassus, *Primo libro a 5*
12	Alessandro Striggio	*L'aria s'oscura*	♮–g_2–*c*	Striggio, *Primo libro a 6*
	Cipriano de Rore	*Vergine quante lagrime*	♭–c_1–*F*	RISM 1548^{10}

[a] Ascribed in the source to "Domin." I would like to thank Bonnie Blackburn for her identification of the source.

[b] Part 2 of *Amor da che tu.*

[c] Title unknown; incipit of a second part?

[d] Galilei: "maestro nostro di capella."

[e] Part two of *Nelle amar e fredd'onde*.

[f] Galilei: "libro secondo delle Muse a 5;" actually book 3.

models, both with regard to counterpoint and to modality. Many other writers allow the same kind of liberties, though generally in a less articulate way.

Nevertheless, there is an unspecified but very perceptible line between liberty and transgression. Music that crosses this line is described in quite drastic language which is repeatedly reinforced with moral judgments, suggesting that taboos are being violated rather than that rules are being ignored.

For example, Ornithoparchus compared music that does not observe a mode to Horace's monster, with a head of a beautiful woman, a body composed of various animals, and an ugly fishtail.[43] Artusi uses a similar image in his condemnation of L'Ottuso, but since L'Ottuso claimed that beginning and end should be the same mode, Artusi invented a new monster with human feet that correspond with the head.[44]

Very lowly motives are sometimes attributed to inadequate musicians. Hermann Finck filled more than two pages with condemnations of the "idle ambition of certain recent instrumentalists, particularly organists," who prefer easy success among the vulgar to careful study of musical composition, especially of the modes.[45] Finck does not stand alone in this attitude towards organists: for example, Rossetti and Calvisius shared his judgment.[46]

Unfortunately, actual instances of bad music are never mentioned in sixteenth-century writings. This is different in the next century and I will discuss four seventeenth-century controversies about specific compositions, in which internal and external views of the modes seem to be juxtaposed.

We have already seen a great deal of the first of these in the dispute between Artusi and L'Ottuso.[47] In the terminology developed in this article, the issue seems to be that, according to Artusi, Monteverdi's madrigals observe the mode only externally, but not internally—from Zarlino and Artusi's viewpoint, they are formless. L'Ottuso is perfectly happy with an external view, but Giulio Cesare Monteverdi takes up Artusi's criticism as an invitation to an internal, "multimodal" view of the criticized works.[48]

The second concerns Mutio Effrem and Marco da Gagliano. Effrem republished Gagliano's sixth book of madrigals in his *Censure* of 1622, adding specific comments about the mistakes they contained. Several of these concern the modes.[49] From these it is evident that Effrem's general opinion of Gagliano's madrigals is similar to Artusi's of Monteverdi's works: their mode can be judged by external criteria, but is not maintained internally. But ironically, Effrem's understanding of mode itself seems to be rather external. One of his many criticisms of Gagliano's *La bella Pargoletta* is that its opening imitation displays ascending interval species, as if its mode is authentic, while the piece is in mode 12. However, both its ambitus and its melody formation show at once that it can only be in mode 11.[50] Effrem seems to have been misled by its unusual tonal type, $\flat$–c_1–F.

The third controversy concerned Cazzati's Mass opus 17. Its Kyrie was criticized in a number of documents, among other things for not using the notes and interval species of mode 1 to which it seemed to belong externally.[51] Arresti even composed a mass on the same subjects which he believed to be modally correct. Cazzati contended however that his mass was in a mixed mode, like Palestrina's *Missa L'homme armé*, and thus perfectly acceptable.

The controversy between Scacchi and Siefert, which took place in the 1640s, is a bit different from the previous ones, for here we find Scacchi, a defender of modern music, attacking someone of more traditional convictions, though with the same kind of arguments as in the previous examples. Scacchi's style consciousness plays a role,[52] for the essence of his criticism is that composing over a cantus firmus (the technique Siefert employed for his psalms) requires strict observation of the rules of composition. Liberties like Siefert's may be appropriate in other genres, but not here.

In his *Cribrum musicum* Scacchi examined Siefert's psalms according to (his own) rules of strict composition and found all of them deficient. Psalm 33, for example, displays two major errors in the treatment of mode—and numerous mistakes of other kinds. This psalm is in mode 1, which, like every other mode, is formed of a fourth and a fifth species, not of two fifth species, as Siefert's opening imitation displays. Scacchi's emendation is in example 3.[53]

This series of examples thus demonstrates the widespread use of simplified approaches to the modes over a period of more than two centuries. In some cases, abstract rules for the modes are rejected, other cases depend on particular uses of the modes, and again others document an informal practice which was usually accepted, but at times accused of transgressing musical propriety.

EXAMPLE 3A Paul Siefert, Psalm 33, beginning (Scacchi, *Cribrum*, 9)

EXAMPLE 3B Marco Scacchi, emendation of the same fragment (Scacchi, *Cribrum*, 2)

CONCLUSION

Let me return to the question I raised at the beginning of this study: how real was mode? My answer is that some version of mode was very real to all musicians over a considerable period, but only in a stripped-down version, the "external" view of the modes. The "internal" view, connecting species, scales, finals, cadences, melodies, affective qualities, and the like in an integrated whole—"real modality," so to speak—was an intellectual abstraction, perhaps even a Platonic ideal, that was never possible to realize fully in a composition, though it was repeatedly used as a measuring rod to judge existing compositions—and sometimes to beat the composer. The basic approach of Renaissance composers to modality was thus an informal one. Many composers seem to have drawn inspiration from the internal view for the organization of particular musical features: aspects of the intellectual, internal view could be, and often were, transferred from the realm of theory to that of composition at will. In this manner, composing became more difficult, but also more dignified.

This view has a consequence for those who wish to analyze music in historical terms. The full internal view of the modes cannot be the starting-point for such analysis, but the external view, however ill-defined this concept may still be, can. It must then be determined for each composition whether the internal plays a role, and if so, to what degree. In many cases the answers to these questions may be difficult or impossible to determine. In many other cases, it will be evident that, rather than a rigid, formal model, modality served as a source of inspiration and musical richness.

NOTES

1. Powers, "Tonal Types," 439.

2. *The Modes* is the most influential of his many publications.

3. Powers, "Is Mode Real?" 12; the earliest and fullest exposition of his argument is in his "Tonal Types."

4. All translations from the 1558 edition of the *Istitutioni* are after Cohen.

5. The examples he gives are Verdelot, *Si bona suscepimus* (mode 9, tonal type $\flat$–g_2–A) and Willaert, *O invidia* (mode 2, tonal type $\flat$–c_3–d). I always indicate the octave of the final in the tonal type.

6. Zacconi, *Prattica I*, 210^{v}: "fatti ad immitatione di essi aeri con che Salmeggia"; "si troua il quarto Tuono esser formato à somiglianza del aere da Salmeggiare." His judgment may derive from Lassus's *Magnificat* in tone 4 on Rore's madrigal (Zacconi sang under Lassus in Munich).

7. The descriptions of the causes are taken from *Dictionary of Philosophy*, 59, slightly adapted. Aron is quoted after the *Trattato*, chapter 1.

8. Zarlino, *Istitutioni*, ed. 1573, 359. Similarly, Zarlino regards the consonances as the matter of musical composition (see for example the "proemio" to the same edition). The division of the *Istitutioni* in four parts depends on the distinction of form and matter in both natural and artificial things (see my "Language of the Modes," chapter 8, and Fend's translation of parts 1 and 2, 5–6). A rather similar discussion of formal and final causes occurs in chapter 1 of Pietro Aron's *Trattato*, as Powers noted ("Is Mode Real?" 26). However, Aron discusses the causes of modes here; elsewhere, for example in chapter 3, Aron does use the term "forma" for a composition. For some older applications of Aristotelian form and/or matter to music see Bielitz, "Materia und Forma."

9. Zarlino, *Istitutioni*, chapter iv,30.

10. Artusi, *L'Artusi II*, 20–21.

11. In this article I will present only a selection of the evidence. For a comprehensive survey I refer to my "Language of the Modes," chapter 5.

12. Boethius, *De institutione musica*, chapter iv,15, Bower's translation.

13. *Dialogus*, chapter 8; translation Powers, "Mode," 377.

14. Banchieri, *Cartella*, 88.

15. Banchieri, *Cartella*, 112–135; see also Powers, "Mode," 414–16.

16. Trabaci, *Secondo libro*, 41, 70.

17. Guido, *Micrologus*, chap. 10.

18. Vicentino, *L'antica musica*, 5^{v}, 43^{r}.

19. Artusi, *L'Artusi I*, 49^{v}.

20. Glarean and Zarlino are exceptional in this respect.

21. Gaffurius, *Theorica*, k3^{v} and k5^{r}.

22. "Philosophers" and "churchmen" are generally used to indicate heathen and Christian authors; but Gaffurius certainly sees a place for the heathens' view in modern music.

23. Tinctoris, *Liber de natura*, chapter 1; Lanfranco, *Scintille*, 102; Zacconi, *Prattica II*, 38.

24. Rossetti, *Libellus*, e4r ; Angelo da Picitono, *Fior angelico*, chapter i,30; Tigrini, *Compendio*, 56; Bononcini, *Musico prattico*, chapter ii,15.

25. For example the pseudo-classical versus the western-ecclesiastical system (Meier, *The Modes*, 36–46), true Guidonian versus species theories (Powers, "Modality," 210), and mode as generalized tune versus mode as particularized scale (Powers, "Mode," 377).

26. Werbeck, *Studien*, 25–38, 99–111.

27. Ornithoparchus, *Musicae activae micrologus*, chapter iv,8; the translation is Dowland's. Among the Italian authors who cited this rule in the sixteenth and seventeenth century are Lanfranco (*Scintille*, 112) and Dionigi (*Li primi tuoni*, chapter i,39).

28. Agricola, *Musica choralis*, d7v–8r.

29. Burmeister, *Musica poetica*, chapter 8; translation after Rivera.

30. Thus Burmeister seems to return accidentally to Boethius's original purpose of the modes.

31. Calvisius, *Exercitationes*, 1.

32. Freis, "Perfecting the perfect instrument"; Le Roy, *Briefe and Plaine Instruction*.

33. Powers, "Tonal Types" and "Modal representation." Appendix C of my "Language of the Modes" lists 407 cycles, including Magnificat and psalm-tone cycles. Several more have come to light since its completion.

34. See Westendorf, "Glareanus' *Dodecachordon*," for a discussion of sixteenth- and early seventeenth-century German cycles of Gospel motets through the twelve modes.

35. Rhau, *Enchiridion*, f2v–3r.

36. Agricola, *Rudimenta*, c3v ("Fugae") and c5r ("Exempla"); Milán, *Libro*, g3v ("Pavanas"); Bermudo, *Declaración*, 114v ("Cantus").

37. Judd, "Modal Types," 437–38.

38. Wiering, "Language of the Modes," chapter 4.

39. Galilei, *Fronimo*, 79–92.

40. Galilei, *Fronimo*, 90.

41. See Meier, *The Modes* 360–61, for a description of the *exordium*; Meier of course considers this madrigal to be in mode 6 of the eight-mode system. Angela Lloyd compared all of Galilei's and Meier's modal assignments of Rore's *Vergine* madrigals ("Modal Representation," 31).

42. For a discussion of the 24 ricercars provided as illustrations of all transposed and untransposed modes, see my "Language of the Modes," pp. 138–39.

43. Ornithoparchus, *Musicae activae micrologus*, chapter iv,18. The description of the monster is in lines 1–4 of the *Ars poetica*.

44. Artusi, *L'Artusi II*, 21.

45. Finck, *Practica*, Oo2v-3v.

46. Rossetti, *Libellus*, n2v; Calvisius, *Exercitationes*, 3.

47. The classical account of this controversy is Palisca, "The Artusi-Monteverdi Controversy."

48. Powers, "Monteverdi's Model."

49. See Strainchamps, "Theory as Polemic," for a fuller survey of this controversy.

50. Strainchamps, "Theory as Polemic," 201, for a facsimile of the beginning of *La bella Pargoletta*.

51. For an account of this controversy, and an edition of the relevant texts and musical works, see Brett, *Music and Ideas*.

52. For this see, for example, Palisca, *Baroque Music*, 59–60.

53. Siefert attacked Scacchi in his *Anticribratio*. It is a point for point refutation of Scacchi's attacks, from which it is difficult to isolate a general line of argumentation.

Josquin's Gospel Motets and Chant-Based Tonality[*]

Cristle Collins Judd

Among the motets attributed to Josquin des Prez, those which set gospel texts have been accorded relatively little attention in the scholarly literature.[1] However two of these motets raise several issues that provide a starting point for reframing general questions of tonal organization in polyphony from the first quarter of the sixteenth century. Focusing on the intraopus style of these motets in relation to motet composition in general brings to the fore the complicated interplay of pre-existing musical material, liturgical associations, and generic conventions that determine tonal structure in sacred vocal polyphony from about 1500.[2] Although consideration of the use of pre-existent material has become almost a commonplace in studies of this repertory,[3] scholars have concentrated on the constructive, mensural, symbolic, allusive, and rhetorical significance of such borrowing rather than the relationship between pre-existent material and the "tonal coherence" of the resulting composition.[4]

From the outset I should acknowledge that terms like "tonal" and "coherence" represent analytical concepts that are both value-laden and increasingly decried in relation to analysis of early music.[5] Nevertheless, I invoke "tonal coherence" as a premise of this essay. I intend this not as an appeal to a concept overloaded with nineteenth-century baggage of functional tonality and organic unity. Rather, tonal coherence is identified in this instance according to narrowly situated criteria: the inseparability of musical and extramusical features engendered by liturgical (and sonic) associations of texts in gospel motets. Specifically, it is the gospel *tone* that, in the present context, gets converted into the adjective "tonal," and the "coherence" is in the amalgam of that kind of "tone / tonal" with the liturgical significance of the gospel. While Powers has demonstrated how fraught notions of polyphonic modality can be for the repertory at hand, the perspective of the present study questions to what degree we can speak meaningfully in any sort of universal terms of the "tonality" of polyphony from about 1500 apart from generic constraints, even if the specific vocabulary of modality is jettisoned.

***

This article begins by highlighting the significance of textual and musical associations in Josquin's *In principio erat verbum.*[6] The tonal template suggested by the analysis of this motet provides the basis for a comparative examination of another gospel motet attributed to Josquin: *In illo tempore assumpsit Jesus.*[7] A more general discussion of tonal and generic conventions of gospel motets focuses on a motet by one of Josquin's contemporaries, Ninot le Petit's *In illo tempore.*[8] Ninot's motet is particularly informative for the perspective advanced here in its manifestation of two coinciding tonalities—the tonality dictated by the tone and an *Ut (F)* tonality. The essay concludes with a discussion of the broader issues suggested by study of these gospel motets, arguing for a model of tonal coherences described as "chant-based tonalities" and suggesting that tonal structures in this period may best be understood in the context of specific generic conventions.

In principio erat verbum sets the first fourteen verses of the Gospel according to John in three *partes* in high clefs (g_2–c_3–c_3–f_3) with a flat signature. The final sonority of the motet is built on F, although the tenor concludes on A.[9] A brief summary of the literature on this motet reveals commentaries that are primarily modal in orientation. Helmut Osthoff's description of *In principio* may be taken as emblematic for discussions of its tonal features: he described it as "exceptional F-Ionian" on account of the emphasis on D at the close of the *prima* and *secunda partes* and the opening of the *tertia pars.*[10] The conclusions of all three *partes* of the motet are reproduced in example 1.

EXAMPLE 1 *In principio*, Conclusions of *partes*

A. Conclusion of *prima pars* (mm. 62–77).

EXAMPLE 1A (*cont.*)

B. Conclusion of *secunda pars* (mm. 200–10)

EXAMPLE 1B (*cont.*)

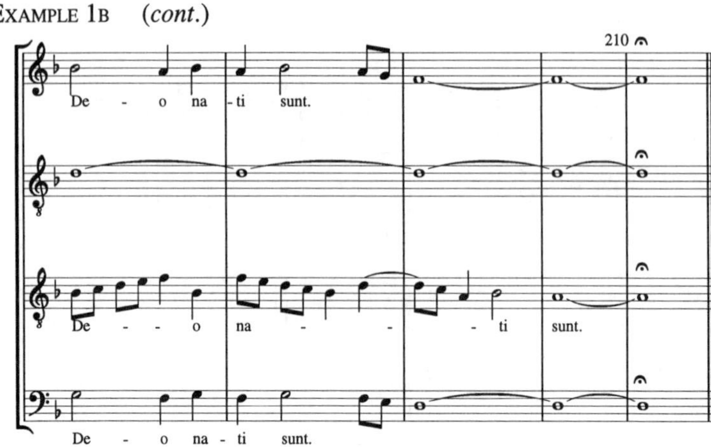

C. Conclusion of *tertia pars* (mm. 248–55)

Peter Urquhart grouped the motet with works which in his view evaded modal categorization, noting that it emphasized the third below the final cadentially and melodically and suggesting that this emphasis might support an assignment to the Phrygian mode (transposed to A by the flat signature of *In principio*).[11] Steven Krantz and Jeremy Noble both observed that the gospel tone associated with the text had structural significance for the motet.[12] Krantz went on to interpret the tone in relation to modal classification (assuming superius and tenor as mode-determining and thus "structural" voices):

> The tone consists primarily of recitation on c' with an inflection down to a. Imitation of this interval at the fifth below in the motet introduces f, which fills out the Lydian diapente and presumably accounts for the use of mode 5 on f for the overall setting.[13]

These comments hint at an array of contradictory modal labels—"Ionian," "Phrygian," and "Lydian"—suggesting the inappropriateness or, at the very least, problematic nature of such categories for describing this motet. [14] More importantly, such contradictory labels stem from the problems inherent in viewing motets like *In principio* apart from the liturgical (and thus musical) associations of their texts.[15] Further difficulties arise in the implicitly wide-ranging and universal definition of "modality" that underpins such attempted categorizations.

The text of *In principio* is prescribed for two places in the liturgy: it is the Gospel for the third mass of Christmas and the so-called "last Gospel," traditionally recited at the end of mass, following the *Ite Missa est* and *Deo Gratias*.[16] Josquin divides the text in three *partes*, shown in Figure 1. The division is straightforward: the *prima pars* is the so-called "logos hymn" (vv. 1–5); the *secunda pars* begins with the "testimony" of John (vv. 6–13); and the climactic "Et verbum caro factum est" (v. 14), traditionally marked by genuflection (and thus homophonic setting), opens the *tertia pars*.[17] The Latin text does not retain the chiastic structure of the Greek original, but it is nevertheless remarkable for its patterned organization. The repetitive character of the text is mirrored in Josquin's deployment of melodic material, a point which will be returned to below.

With two possible exceptions, the motet respects the syntactic structure of the text. The first is the solecism by which a new point of imitation begins on "quod factum est" and runs through "in ipso vita erat" (mm. 45–50). However, what might seem to be a grammatical misreading from a composer presumably well-versed in Latin actually reflects the standard version of the text circulated in the fifteenth and sixteenth centuries.[18] By contrast, the other text division (m. 126) which is only minimally observed may represent a deliberate compositional attempt to highlight the textual connection of two sentences: "Non erat ille lux . . . " / "Erat lux vera . . . " (mm. 114–38; see ex. 5). This interpretation is supported by the large-scale durational and tonal structure of the motet discussed below.

The primary characteristic of the gospel tone is the *re–mi–fa* third; Josquin's setting with a flat signature (*cantus mollis*) places this interval on the notated pitches D–E–F.[19] The tone occurs at this pitch level with F as reciting tone *not* in the supposedly "structural" tenor of a modal interpretation, but instead with clarity and consistency in the altus (labeled contratenor in some sources).[20] Although it is not apparent from the voice pairs of the opening of the motet (ex. 2) that the tone is being carried by the altus (at the pitch level of F) rather than the superius-tenor pair (on C), it is immediately obvious when reading the altus voice alone. Visually this is more striking in individual voices of the choirbook format in which the work was originally transmitted than in modern score notation, as illustrated by the opening of the *prima* and *secunda partes* of the altus in figure 2 (see especially "hic venit in testimonium," in fig. 2b).

FIGURE 1 *In principio erat Verbum*, Text and translation

In principio erat Verbum, et Verbum erat apud Deum, et Deus erat Verbum.	[1]	In the beginning was the Word, and the Word was with God, and the Word was God.
Hoc erat in principio apud Deum.	[2]	The same was in the beginning with God.
Omnia per ipsum facta sunt, et sine ipso factum est nihil. Quod factum est	[3]	All things were made by him; and without him was not anything made that was made.
in ipso vita erat, et vita erat lux hominum.	[4]	In him was life; and the life was the light of men.
Et lux in tenebris lucet, et tenebrae eam non comprehenderunt.	[5]	And the light shineth in darkness; and the darkness comprehended it not.

[*Secunda pars*]

Fuit homo missus a Deo, cui nomen erat Johannes.	[6]	There was a man sent from God whose name was John.
Hic venit in testimonium ut testimonium perhiberet de lumine, ut omnes crederent per illum.	[7]	The same came for a witness, to bear witness of the light, that all men through him might believe.
Non erat ille lux, sed ut testimonium perhiberet de lumine.	[8]	He was not the light, but was sent to bear witness of that light.
Erat lux vera: quae illuminat omnem hominem venientem in hunc mundum.	[9]	That was the true light, which lighteth every man that cometh into the world.
In mundo erat, et mundus per ipsum factus est, et mundus eum non cognovit.	[10]	He was in the world, and the world was made by him, but the world knew him not.
In propria venit et sui eum non receperunt.	[11]	He came unto his own, and his own received him not.
Quotquot autem receperunt eum, dedit eis potestatem filios Dei fieri, his qui credunt in nomine eius.	[12]	But as many as received him, to them gave he power to become the sons of God, even to them that believe on his name.
Qui non ex sanguinibus: neque ex voluntate carnis: neque ex voluntate viri, sed ex Deo nati sunt.	[13]	Which were born not of blood, nor of the will of the flesh, nor of the will of man, but of God.

[*Tertia pars*]

Et verbum caro factum est, et habitavit in nobis, et vidimus gloriam eius gloriam quasi unigeniti a Patre, plenum gratiae et veritatis.	[14]	And the Word was made flesh and dwelt among us, and we beheld his glory, the glory as of the only begotten of the Father, full of grace and truth.

John 1:1–14

EXAMPLE 2 *In principio*, Opening (mm. 1–21).

FIGURE 2 *In principio*, *MunBS 10*, contratenor
(By permission of the Bayerische Staatsbibliothek)

A. Opening of *prima pars* (f. 146r)

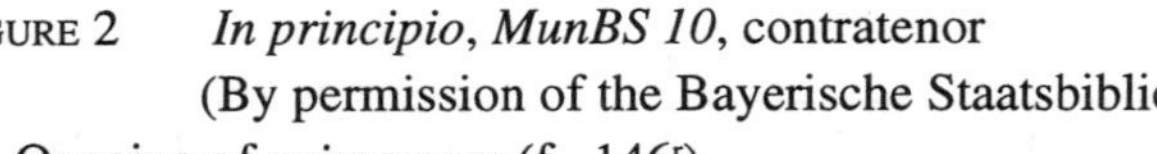

FIGURE 2 (*cont.*)
B. Opening of *secunda pars* (f. 150r)

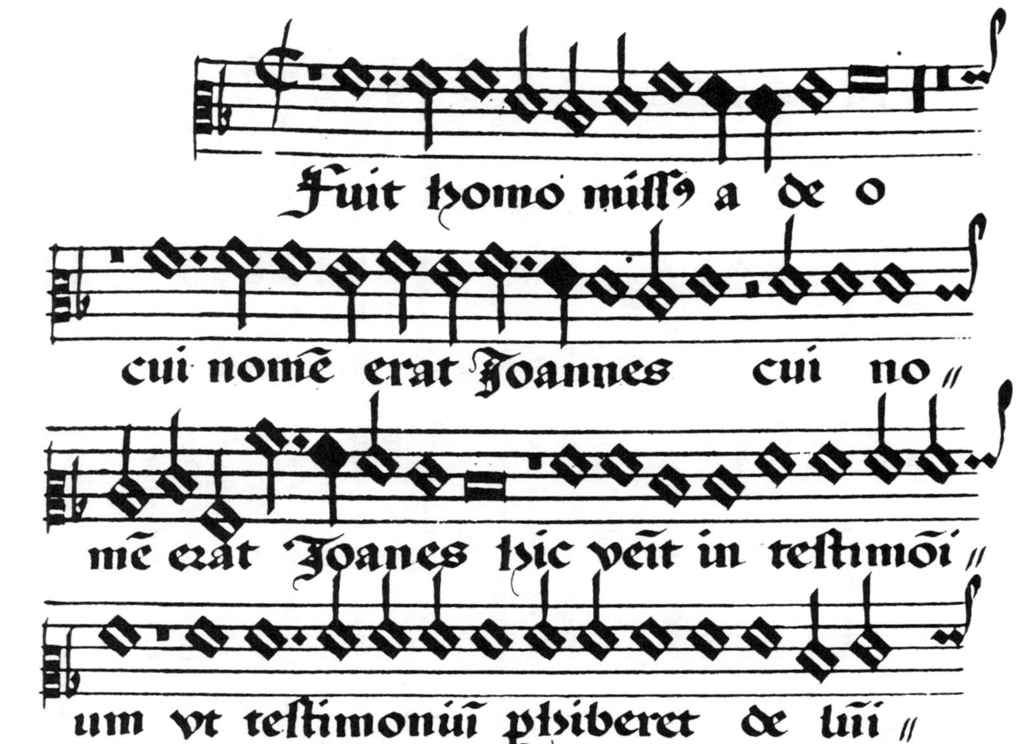

The characteristic features of this gospel tone are the half close (*metrum*), full close, and conclusion.[21] The recitation formula as incorporated in the altus of the motet includes the falling third characteristic of the tone (the *metrum* or half close), but it also modifies this with syncopated cadential patterning to F, usually associated with what I have described elsewhere as the *Ut* tonality.[22] (This is indicated on example 3 (pp. 120–21) by the divided column under "recitation"). The *fa–re* third is used consistently for full closes (both with and without a cadential syncope) and the chant concludes on the reciting tone. Although the chant is at times used imitatively throughout the texture (as in the opening shown in ex. 2) or repeated, other voices are indicated in example 3 only when the tone is absent from the altus, but present elsewhere in the texture. The tone dictates the cadential profile of the motet shown in figure 3: internal cadences on F, full stops on D, and the conclusion on F.

Contrasting tonal material characterizes sections which omit the tone entirely and establishes a series of alternations defined by the presence or absence of the gospel tone, creating an intricate interweaving of note-against-note and imitative textures, voice pairs and full texture, and varied mensuration.[23]

In principio reflects the association of the gospel text with its reciting tone on many levels: in the cadential profile (of the overall organization of its three *partes* as well as the interior arrangement of each *pars*); in its inclusion and embellishment of the tone; and in the pervasive use of the interval of a third as the melodic basis of points of imitation. But this setting is not simply a polyphonic "harmonization" of the gospel tone.[24] Rather textual, textural, and melodic features derived from that tone are used to establish connections among the motet's *partes*. These play an important part in shaping what may be described as "tonal coherence" and are best seen in the context of the motet as a whole. It is to these aspects I now turn.

By the term "tonal coherence" I wish to invoke the interrelationship of musical features of the motet, particularly the manipulation of pitch content, as it contributes to the organization of the motet as a whole.[25] Repetition of musical units underlies the structure of *In principio* at every level; the overall tonal organization of the motet, in its principles of construction, mirrors the strongly patterned gospel text and the inherently repetitive recitation tone associated with it. Immediate repetition in the motet includes repetition by voice pairs, as in the opening of the motet (see ex. 2 above), and at the near recurrence of a word or words, as in the phrases "in testimonium" / "ut testimonium" (mm. 98–102). Frequently, repetition of music (and text) provides emphasis and closure at the level of verse and *pars*. Immediate repetition with an added voice marks interior divisions of the text (as at the conclusion of the first verse, mm. 18–25). Similarly, musical and textual repetition marks the conclusion of each of the three *partes* of the motet, as indicated on the excerpts given in example 1.

FIGURE 3 *In principio erat Verbum*, Cadential Profile*

[Cadence Tones:	F		A		D]
In principio erat Verbum,	C/F				
et Verbum erat apud Deum,	C/F			et Deus erat Verbum.	D/D
		Hoc erat in principio apud Deum.	A		
Omnia per ipsum facta sunt,	F			et sine ipso factum est nihil	D
Quod factum est, in ipso vita erat,	F				
et vita erat lux hominum.	F			Et lux in tenebris lucet,	—
				et tenebrae eam non comprehenderunt.	D/D
Fuit homo missus a Deo,	F/C			cui nomen erat Johannes.	D/D
				Hic venit in testimonium	D
ut testimonium perhiberet de lumine,	F			ut omnes crederent per illum.	D
Non erat ille lux,	F/F	sed ut testimonium perhiberet de lumine.	(A)	Erat lux vera:	—
				quae illuminat omnem hominem	—
				venientem in hunc mundum.	D
In mundo erat,	F/F				
et mundus per ipsum factus est,	F			et mundus eum non cognovit.	D
In propria venit	F			et sui eum non receperunt.	D
Quotquot autem receperunt eum,	F			dedit eis potestatem filios Dei fieri,	(D)
his qui credunt in nomine eius.	F				
Qui non ex sanguinibus,	(F)				
neque ex voluntate carnis:	F				
neque ex voluntate viri,	F/F			sed ex Deo nati sunt.	D
Et verbum caro factum est,	F	et habitavit in nobis,	A/A		
et vidimus gloriam eius	F/F			gloriam quasi unigeniti a patre,	D
plenum gratiae	F/F				
et veritatis.	F/F				

* Text of the motet is distributed in order of appearance reading horizontally and down the page. Cadential pitches are indicated following text segments and by column. *Partes* are separated by double lines.

EXAMPLE 3 *In principio erat verbum*, Distribution of the Gospel tone

	Tone largely or entirely absent	Recitation a.	Recitation b.		Full Close	Conclusion
[Verse]						
[1]		In principio erat Verbum	et Verbum erat apud Deum		et Deus erat Verbum.	
[2]	[S/T] Hoc erat in principio apud Deum	[3]	Omnia per ipsum facta sunt			
	et sine ipso factum est nihil.		[4] Quod factum est in ipso vita erat			
[5]		et vita erat lux hominum		et lux in tenebris lucet		
				et tenebrae eam	non comprehenderunt.	
Secunda pars						
[6]			Fuit homo missus a Deo		cui nomen erat Joannes.	
[7]		Hic venit in testimonium	ut testimonium perhiberet de lumine		ut omnes crederent per illum.	
[8]			Non erat ille lux			
[9]	sed ut testimonium perhiberet de lumine. Erat lux vera quae illuminat omnem hominem venientem in hunc mundum.					

[10]
In mundo erat
et mundus per ipsum factus est
et mundus eum non cognovit.
[11] In propria venit
et sui eum non receperunt.
[12]
Quotquot autem receperunt eum
[13]
dedit eis potestatem filios Dei fieri his qui credunt in nomine ejus.
Qui non ex sanguinibus
neque ex voluntate carnis
neque ex voluntate viri
sed ex Deo nati sunt.
Tertia pars
[14]
Et Verbum caro factum est
et habitavit in nobis
et vidimus gloriam ejus
gloriam quasi unigenti a Patre
plenum gratiae
et veritatis.

The two most striking instances of repetition at the local level in the motet are characterized by motivic saturation, melodic units based on rising thirds, and the absence of literal reference to the gospel tone and its tonal influence.[26] The first, on the words "et sine ipso" might be construed as a direct response to the negative text. Even here, however, the influence of the tone is unmistakable in the overall contour of the melodic lines: C–A in superius and altus; F–D in tenor and bassus (ex. 4). The second instance of such repetition is an unusually extended section (ex. 5). It spans two verses of text with minimal demarcation, directly connecting the two contrasts: "non erat ille lux… " / "erat lux vera… ". This is the only place in the motet where textual punctuation of verses is so minimized, and each side is framed by imitative phrases and cadences to F. Like other such instances of literal repetition in motets with texts associated with a reciting tone, which on the face of it may seem to border on the banal, this section is strategically placed. It is built from repetition at the most immediate level—a three-note figure—and has consequences for the overall structure of the motet. These two verses of text, tied together musically, comprise the most extended section of the motet lacking literal reference to the gospel tone, and provide a graphic textural as well as tonal contrast to the material which frames them. This section occurs at the center of the motet and, I would suggest, reflects clear and careful compositional planning of the durational and tonal placement of events within the basic gospel tone scheme.[27]

EXAMPLE 4 *In principio*, mm. 35–45

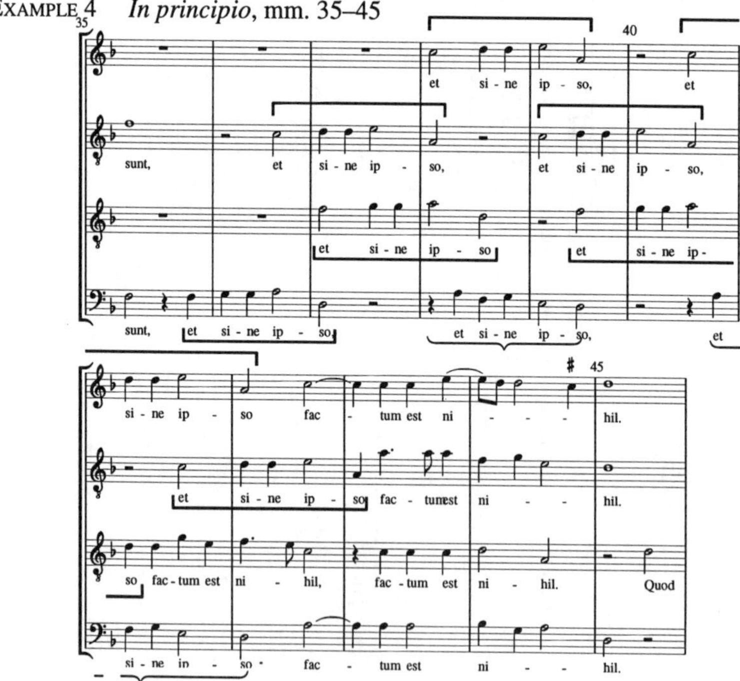

Example 5 *In principio*, mm. 111–44

Repetition on a larger scale cements formal relationships. Example 6 compares the opening of verses 10 and 11, illustrating temporal expansion (to accommodate the additional syllable of "in propria venit") and an exchange of tenor and altus. Each phrase concludes independently, but the next major text segment ("quotquot autem receperunt eum") opens with a varied musical repetition of the homophonic ending of verse 10. This series of partial repetitions sets up an alternation of textures and mensuration that prevails for the rest of the *secunda pars*, and builds to the homophonic opening of the *tertia pars* "Et Verbum caro factum est."

A similar principle establishes formal parallels on a large scale between the opening of the *prima* and *secunda partes* (for which the altus was given in facsimile in fig. 2 above).[28] Example 7 provides a common reduction between the two *partes* detailing the reordering and extension of shared underlying patterns.[29] The reduction suggests the patterning procedure on which the melodic construction of the motet depends—analogous to, but not directly parallel with, the patterned construction of the text itself. Just as the text constantly plays with reiteration and replacement of central words, so the musical form plays on the reiteration of small segments of polyphony. Barlines on the reduction mark the combinative paradigms, while notes enclosed in parentheses indicate variants between the *partes*. Registral ordering may be reversed (as in mm. 86–90) and repetitions inserted (as in mm. 100ff.) while the essential *tonal* order of the patterns remains constant.

Repetitive units organize the pitch materials of the motet on a several levels, as the reduction of the *prima pars* in example 8 illustrates. Five melodic paradigms, labeled A to E, which recur throughout the motet, are shown. The first (A) is directly connected with the gospel tone, but occurs as both a *fa–re* and *sol–mi* third. B is a subsidiary figure, subsumed in larger groupings. C is the rising third associated with sections of motivic saturation. D, a *fa supra la* figure, occurs only once at the local level in the *prima pars* but several times in other sections of the motet. E is the *ut–fa* fourth.[30]

Within this context of local and large-scale repetition, *In principio* uses the gospel tone regularly and literally, and the overall plan of the motet mirrors the structural features of the tone. Nevertheless, the tenor, *not* the primary carrier of the tone, provides—via its *A la mi re* termination—a crucial signpost to the modern observer for understanding how manipulation of the gospel tone coexists with generalized polyphonic tonal conventions associated with the framing pitches of its *re–fa* third. For a sixteenth-century theorist like Pietro Aron, a tenor termination on A could signal an irregular ending with a myriad of possibilities: Modes 1, 2, 3, 4, 5, or 6.[31] If one is determined to assign the work to a mode, the contradictory assignments by modern scholars cited earlier are therefore neither as surprising nor as disconcerting as they might first appear. Indeed, A is the termination

EXAMPLE 6 *In principio, secunda pars*, mm. 138–73

EXAMPLE 7 *In principio*, openings of *prima* and *secunda partes*

Prima pars [Verse 1]

Secunda pars

[Verse 6]

EXAMPLE 7 (*cont.*)

Prima pars

[Verse 1] (*cont.*)

et Deus erat Verbum.

[Verse 2]

Hoc erat in principio apud Deum.

Secunda pars

[Verse 6] (*cont.*)

[Verse 7]

nomen erat Johannes.

Hic venit in testimonium

ut testimonium perhiberet de lumine

ut omnes crederent per illum.

EXAMPLE 8 *In principio*, reduction of *prima pars*

A A’ A A’ A’ A’ A’ (B) C C+B C D C+B A’ A” A E + A A”+A E + Aext.

6 10 14 18 22 25 28 33 36 38 40 43 45 46 50 55 62 66 70 73

x A A A D x x

[ut re (mi) fa – re ut re (mi)]

point of the tenor in many cadences and at the conclusion of each of the *partes* of the motet. While tonal focus to A is infrequent, cadences to this pitch are strategically placed, occurring at the same durational point (at roughly the mid-point) in each of the three *partes* of the motet (see fig. 3, p. 119). Perhaps the most interesting of these is the internal demarcation of the repetition for the central textual elision of "non erat ille lux" / "erat lux vera" discussed above. The tenor breaks its repetition on the words "de lumine" (boxed on ex. 5, p. 123) and with the bassus articulates a *mi* cadence on A. A variation of the bassus pattern (indicated by the broken bracket on ex. 5) is also introduced as a means of textual demarcation.

While *A mi* does not function as the final of this motet,[32] it provides the means by which melodic paradigms associated with a *Re* or *Ut* tonality (as polyphonic realizations and extensions of the D and F of the reciting tone) are integrated. The two pitch levels at which paradigm A (the schematized reciting formula) occurs set up a primary tonal juxtaposition (see ex. 8). This juxtaposition is shown most clearly in measure 18 of example 8, and is of course suggested by the full close pattern of the gospel tone itself (from F reciting tone to D). The composite pattern labeled "x" (essentially a descent from f^2 to a^1) suggests a *fa–mi* pattern (that would be associated with *Mi* tonality in the flat system of this motet). It is divided variously at *la* or *sol*, as indicated in example 9. The superius frequently extends significant cadences with this melodic pattern (as shown on ex. 7), and the tenor employs it to mark the interior division of the central section of repetition discussed above. The *fa–mi* modal type associated with *A mi*, which occurs frequently throughout the motet, connects the *Re* and *Ut* types inherent in the gospel tone itself, as example 10 illustrates.

EXAMPLE 9 Division of *fa–mi* melodic pattern

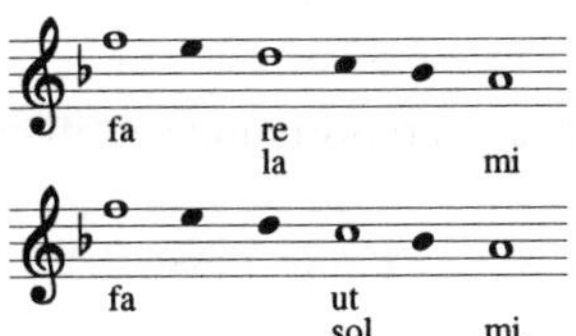

Such a mingling of *Re* and *Ut* types, with an ultimate prominence of the *Ut* tonality (especially in those sections where the gospel tone is not overtly present) represents a straightforward incorporation of the gospel tone in polyphony. This bears highlighting because it suggests that textual and musical associations are responsible for the way in which tonal materials generally common to sacred polyphonic composition in the period are ordered and incorporated in individual works. In other words, features that mark sub-genres of the motet provide the point of correlation between intra- and extraopus style. The conclusion of the *prima* and *secunda partes* on D may be out of the ordinary for the *Ut(F)* framework that melodic and internal cadential features seem to suggest, and it is indeed puzzling from a perspective that assumes tonally-closed modal structures. But it is hardly likely to have given a sixteenth-century musician aural pause since it follows exactly the full close formula of the gospel reciting tone.[33] The gospel tone, after all, represents a kind of musical commonplace and John 1:1–14 was without doubt the most well-known of the texts associated with it.

EXAMPLE 10 *fa–re* ←→ *fa–ut* via *fa–mi*

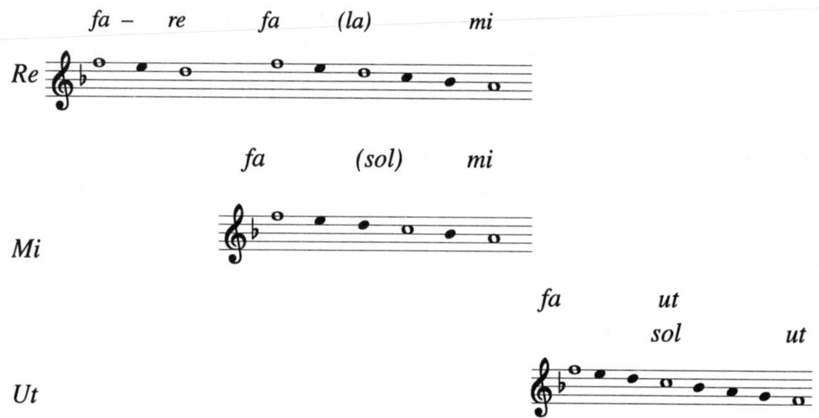

Josquin's setting of *In principio* provides a model of sorts of the ways in which a work that appears to bear all the hallmarks of "modal composition" (and encourages the tendency to describe it in terms of mode, as illustrated above) does indeed use tonal materials compatible to a modal or tonal interpretation, but in a distribution pre-determined independently of modal factors by a "non-modal" chant. The understanding of the gospel motet proposed here suggests a kind of understanding between composers and listeners which takes the gospel tone as a shared fundamental.[34] This in turn suggests an underlying premise of tonal organization that is best-described as "chant-based" tonality, and a specific version of this, determined according to generic expectations, as "gospel tone" tonality.

***

That such a category is meaningful in discussing this repertory may be illustrated by turning to *In illo tempore assumpsit Jesus duodecim discipulos suos.* Like discussions of *In principio, In illo tempore* has elicited its share of conflicting modal attributions. *In illo tempore assumpsit Jesus* sets three verses from the Gospel according to Matthew in a single *pars*, in roughly the same tonal space as *In principio*, but with the clef configuration g_2–c_3–c_3–f_4, no signature, and a final sonority on C. Like *In principio*, Osthoff characterized *In illo tempore* as "Ionian."[35] Saul Novack agreed with this classification, going on to criticize what he termed the "paucity" of harmonic motion in the motet, despite its being in the Ionian mode—the mode for which he postulated the greatest opportunity of harmonic motion of any mode.[36] Ellen Beebe's description of *In illo tempore* complements Osthoff's "exceptional" Ionian. She argued that the tonal center of the motet was F, pointing to a large number of cadences on F and A and few on C, and concluded that the motet represented the "archaic form of mode 5 on F" (i.e., lacking a B♭). She interpreted the motet's ending on C (which she described as "surprising") as the composer's expressive response to a change of affect in the last line of the text.[37] Urquhart, for his part, grouped the work with *In principio* as exhibiting Phrygian tendencies.

In light of the discussion of *In principio* and the perspective of "gospel-tone tonality," however, an interpretation of *In illo tempore* is more straightforward than these citations might suggest. The three verses from Matthew that comprise the text of the motet, given in figure 4, are proper to Quinquagesima and show the usual "in illo tempore" incipit. A description which invokes an "irregular" ending in service of text affect is, like an "ionian" categorization, an inadequate answer occasioned by an inappropriate question.[38] The tonal system of *In illo tempore* is the *cantus durus* counterpart to *In principio*.[39] The motet deals with only a short gospel text, set on a smaller scale, without the textural and mensural variety that characterizes *In principio*, yet the principle of tonal organization is the same. The reciting tone is C, imitated at various levels. Interior full closes are to A—figure 5 shows the reiterated cadences at the end of each verse—and the motet closes on C.

The gospel tone appears primarily in the superius and tenor, although it is occasionally present in other voices and imitated throughout (ex. 11). The use of the tone is less subtle and its deployment less consistent than in *In principio*: it is absent only in small sections of cadential extension and there are no contrasting sections like those of the larger *In principio*. Unlike *In principio*, the tone migrates among the voices, and is frequently stated by more than one voice. No single voice carries the tone throughout, although it is present in the tenor in all but a single phrase near the opening of the motet ("assumpsit Jesus duodecim discipulos suos secreto"), where it is divided between superius and altus.

FIGURE 4 *In illo tempore assumpsit Jesus*, text and translation

In illo tempore, assumpsit Jesus duodecim discipulos suos secreto et ait illis:	In that time Jesus took the twelve disciples apart in the way and said unto them:
Ecce ascendimus Jerosolimam et Filius hominis tradetur principibus sacerdotum et scribus, et condemnabunt eum morte,	Behold we go to Jerusalem; and the Son of man shall be betrayed unto the chief priests and scribes, and they shall condemn him to death,
et tradent eum gentibus, ad illudendum, et flagelandum, et crucifigendum, et tertia die resurget.	and shall deliver him to the Gentiles to mock, and to scourge, and to crucify him: and the third day he shall rise again.

Matthew 20:17–19

FIGURE 5 *In illo tempore assumpsit Jesus*, Cadential outline

Text	Cadences	
In illo tempore,	(C)	C
assumpsit Jesus	(C)	↓
duodecim discipulos suos secreto	F	
et ait illis:	A/A/A	A
Ecce ascendimus Jerosolimam	F/F	↓
et Filius hominis tradetur		
principibus sacerdotum et scribus,	(F)	
et condemnabunt eum morte,	A/A/A	A
et tradent eum gentibus,		
ad illudendum,		↓
et flagelandum,		
et crucifigendum,	(C)	
et tertia die resurget.	C/C/C	C

EXAMPLE 11 *In illo tempore*, Distribution of Gospel tone

In illo tempore sets up a contrasting framework of imitation which corresponds to the cadential emphasis on C and A, the boundary pitches of the reciting tone. The gospel tone is imitated at the fifth above in outer sections (ex. 12a) and at the fifth below in interior sections (ex. 12b). Varied repetition is used for closure so frequently as to be characteristic of the motet. Textual parallels provoke musical parallels at the level of word and adjacent phrase, as "ad illudendum" / "et flagelandum" / "et crucifigendum" (mm. 97–105).

EXAMPLE 12 *In illo tempore*

A. Imitation of tone at fifth above (mm. 1–9, 105–21)

EXAMPLE 12A (*cont.*)

Example 12 (*cont.*)

B. Imitation of tone at fifth below (mm. 25–50, 76–86)

Example 12b (*cont.*)

45
50
Ec - ce a scen - di- mus
mus Je - ro -lo - li - mam
Ec - ce a - scen - di - mus
Je - ro- so- li - - mam
76
80
et con - dem- na- bunt e -um mor - - - -te.
et condem na bunt e - um mor te.
et
85
et con-dem - na - - bunt e - um mor - te.
et con-dem - na - bunt e - um mor - - - te.
con-dem-na - bunt e - um mor - - - - - te.

EXAMPLE 13 *In illo tempore* (mm. 61–75)

On a larger scale, repetition is used for the adjacent phrases "et Filius hominis tradetur" / "principibus sacerdotum et scribus" (ex. 13). Here, as in *In principio*, the gospel tone is most remote and the melodic material relies on concentrated use of a third at the durational center of the motet. The sequential use of three thirds in the superius (bracketed on ex.13) leads to the stepwise rising third characteristic of the *Ut(C)* tonality, which is framed here by the reciting tone C.[40] Also as in *In principio*, a *mi* melodic type appears in cadential extension. The single *mi* cadence of the motet involves this pattern at the third and final extension of the cadence on A (resulting in a *mi* cadence on E in the superius and altus above the bassus A) for the text "et condemnabunt eum morte" (ex. 14).[41]

In principio erat verbum and *In illo tempore assumpsit Jesus* show the same approach to setting gospel texts in a motet format—one that resonates with the implication of the gospel tone associated with the texts. Indeed, it is an approach that suggests that the separation of such texts from their musico-liturgical associations was inconceivable to the composer, however foreign this way of viewing Biblical settings may seem to post-Reformation sensibilities.

These two texts represent different types of Gospels, however, both in textual style and liturgical significance.[42] *In principio*, with its prominent place in the Christmas liturgy and its ubiquitous position as Last Gospel, was an obvious candidate for motet composition, and indeed had a centuries-old tradition of polyphonic setting.[43] *In illo tempore assumpsit Jesus* had a more highly circumscribed place in the liturgy. As the proper Gospel for the *Missa in Honore Sancte Crucis*,[44] however, it had at least a loose connection with the "usual" subjects on which motets were based at the turn of the century, as may be seen by the title of one of Petrucci's early anthologies: *Motetti De passione De cruce De beata virgine et huius modi*.[45] In any case, none of the early published motet collections suggest the functional associations implied by the inclusion of an "in illo tempore" incipit.

Like psalm texts, traditions of setting gospel texts increased as the sixteenth century progressed.[46] *In principio* and *In illo tempore* stand as initial exemplars of what was to become a distinct sub-genre of motet: the gospel motet. As such, they are marked not only by the choice of text but by the overt faithfulness displayed to the gospel tone associated with that text.[47] A similar fidelity to the resonances of psalm tones is obvious in Josquin's securely attributed psalm motets and appears most characteristic of the initial compositions in the genre.[48] In other words, an adherence to chant associations of texts functions as a raison d'être of Josquin's motets and motet composition in general c. 1500. The distinctiveness of the resulting musical profiles engendered the possibility of recognizable sub-genres, often in liturgical and para-liturgical contexts other than those in which they originated.

EXAMPLE 14 *In illo tempore* (mm. 76–92)

***

A brief discussion of one final setting of a gospel text, Ninot le Petit's *In illo tempore*,[49] will lead to a broader evaluation of the relationship of genre and tonal convention in this repertory as the tradition is altered. Both Moser and Loge incorrectly connected this motet with Josquin's *In illo tempore*.[50] Although both texts share the standard gospel incipit followed by the words "assumpsit Jesus," Ninot sets different verses from the same chapter of Matthew (Matthew 17: 1–9). References to the reciting tone are prominent, especially at the opening of the motet, but occurrences of the tone, although unmistakable, are relatively infrequent in comparison to Josquin's motets. The tenor is the primary voice associated with citations of the tone, and the pitch level of the recitation is C, as illustrated by excerpts from the opening of the motet (ex. 15a), the conclusion of the *prima pars* (ex. 15b) and the end of the motet (ex. 15c).

EXAMPLE 15 Ninot le Petit, *In illo tempore*
A. mm. 1–14

Example 15 (*cont.*)
B. mm. 84–93

At first glance, this motet might seem a companion not so much to Josquin's *In illo tempore* as to his *In principio*. The primary cadential articulation is to F (some 16 of 24 cadences), the *prima pars* concludes on D (ex. 15b), and the motet is set in high clefs (g_2-c_1-c_3-f_3) with an overall range from B[♭] to f^2. Yet this motet differs from *In principio* in significant ways that are reflected in its varied transmission: two of its three sources transmit the work with no signature.[51] The conflicting signatures of the sources highlight two significant aspects of the way the gospel tone is incorporated in this motet that are of particular interest in light of the other motets discussed here. The relative priority accorded these aspects may be used to explain the presence or absence of the flat signature in the sources. First, unlike *In principio*, the reciting tone here is indeed C, as example 15 illustrates.

Example 15 (*cont.*)
C. mm. 238–47

The tone is never stated on F, even in imitation.[52] Such a tone properly uses the *re–fa* third A–C with its implicit *B mi* and no signature. But, second, unlike either of Josquin's motets, the gospel tone does not govern the overall tonal framework of this motet. Instead the tone has been incorporated within the framework of an *Ut (F)* tonality. All of the major articulations are to F, with C serving as the secondary cadence pitch of choice for internal articulations,[53] and the tonal focus of individual voices is to F. Thus, both melodically and contrapuntally the motet as a whole appears to suggest the B-flat signature found in the Florence source. The absence of a flat signature in two of the sources should not be construed to suggest that the motet is an example of a "true" lydian (or "archaic mode 5" as Beebe described it in reference to Josquin's *In illo tempore*). Rather, *B mi* is implicit in the pitch level at which the gospel tone occurs. By contrast, the Florence source overrides the *B mi* of the tone in favor of the "tonality" of the motet.[54] In effect, the conflicting signatures of the sources reflect not just the inherent tension between the pre-existent "tone" and the "tonality" to which it is accommodated but also suggest an awareness on the part of contemporary musicians and scribes of the significance of the C gospel tone and the contrapuntal and melodic realities by which the *B mi* of the tone is rendered *B fa* in polyphony.[55] Resonances of the gospel tone appear primarily in the tenor, secondarily in the superius, very occasionally in the altus, but never in the bassus. The few occasions on which the tone migrates to the altus appear motivated by a desire to have the tenor participate fully in cadences to F, as illustrated in example 15c, further strengthening the tonal focus of the motet and mitigating tonal features of the gospel tone. Thus this motet acknowledges the gospel tone associations of its text via obvious reference to the tone, without reflecting those associations in the overall tonal scheme of the polyphony.

***

In what remains an important study of sixteenth-century motet types, Oliver Strunk argued that specific formal relationships with chant types were a distinguishing feature of motets whose texts had chant associations.[56] The analyses presented here suggest an extension of Strunk's argument to include not only specific formal paradigms, but also tonal relationships. Recognizing the resonance of chant in motets with texts associated with a reciting tone (most notably psalms, gospels, and so forth) proves crucial not only to understanding the markers of sub-genres of the motet, but also for rethinking the terms in which tonality around 1500 is discussed.

One might be tempted to observe that the motets discussed in this chapter are fundamentally "uninteresting" from a tonal point of view. After all, these motets incorporate a reciting tone, rely on repetition of blocks of text and music, and make use of limited cadential material. However, the analysis of gospel motets presented here suggests that the notion of "free" composition as presently applied to sixteenth-century music is in need of revision and that a reconsideration of the ways in which pre-existing melodies may interact with tonal structure in polyphony is in order. This study has larger implications for situating analyses not only in relation to the historical context which informed the creation of the work (as so often argued for by analysts of early music), but equally and overtly within the historic-theoretic and reception tradition which frames the act of analysis.

While the emphasis in this essay has been on contextualizing "tonality" as manifest in *In principio* and other gospel motets in relation to the gospel tone with which the texts of these motets are associated, it is just as important to situate the impulse behind this analysis—the "search" for tonality—in its historical context, for the very nature of this endeavor is deeply implicated by its history.[57] Elsewhere, I have suggested that Josquin's motets might profitably be viewed from the perspective of three tonalities, which I identified as *Ut*, *Re*, and *Mi* tonalities.[58] The distribution of Josquin's securely attributed motets among those tonalities suggests a broad association of tonal conventions with text type.[59] The analyses presented in this article argue for a further nuancing via an interpretation of "chant-based" tonality. The motets I have discussed here share features of the *Ut* tonality, but *In principio* and Josquin's *In illo tempore* are no more representatives of that tonality than they are of the Ionian, Lydian, or Phrygian modes. Indeed, it is probably misleading to describe them as manifesting anything other than "gospel-tone" tonality: a pre-determined and closed chant-based classification. These works belong in a group of their own. Their tenor terminations on A and C are immediate indications that they are outside the normal scheme of Josquin's finals. This, together with their cadential hierarchy and freedom of movement between *Ut* and *Re* modal types by means of a *fa–mi* paradigm, marks these works as exceptional if viewed apart from the liturgical associations of their texts. The constant resonance of the gospel tone in *In principio erat verbum* has parallels in the tonal structure of the securely attributed psalm settings. Indeed, Josquin's motets bear witness to an extraordinarily creative faithfulness to the liturgical associations of their texts. The resulting tonal conventions embodied in what I have described as "chant-based" tonality, especially among motets based on a reciting tone, were clearly short-lived. They were neutralized, so to speak, as gospel and psalm motets were accommodated to and encompassed by more generic features of motet-writing and modal-tonal conventions,[60] as the glimpse at *In illo tempore* by Ninot le Petit demonstrated.

What I have attempted to do in these analyses is illuminate individual works. While the analytical method I have applied has "grown out" of the work, it has also overtly identified multiple contexts which impinge on our understanding of a motet like *In principio* and the way in which a group of works relates to it. Those contexts situate this analysis not only in relation to the conception of the work, but to its varied reception histories. By accepting the challenge these motets pose to traditional modal and tonal interpretations as well as to our understanding of the genre of motet, we may embrace a richer analytical perspective. "In the beginning was the Word . . . " and for Josquin, at least, that Word was inseparable from the resonance of its reciting tone.

AFTERWORD: STYLE AND ATTRIBUTION

Inevitably, perhaps, a discussion of motets attributed to Josquin (and Ninot) turns to questions of style and authenticity. There has been a strong tendency among Josquin scholars in recent years to see the primary function of analysis as the determination of such questions. Yet the two motets that are the primary focus of this article provide a cautionary tale in this regard.

Of the gospel motets I have examined, these two are most closely related in their tonal deployment of the gospel tone. The attribution of neither motet has been questioned in print, and Noble even described *In principio* as a "superb example of Josquin's late four-part style" which might serve as "the touchstone" by which to evaluate posthumously published works.[61] However, neither on the basis of their sources nor in purely stylistic terms is the position of these motets in the Josquin *oeuvre* unquestionable, and in each case Joshua Rifkin's admonitory words about accepting attributions at face value might well be invoked.[62] Like the early motet settings of psalm texts, these works became the basis of a German Protestant tradition. Like the psalm settings attributed to Josquin, this pair of motets appears to belong to the early part of that tradition, and indeed the two works share with several of the securely attributed psalms a common late source, *VatS 38*. The earliest sources of *In principio* date from the first third of the century (*ModD 9* and *ToleF 23*), and liturgical or at least para-liturgical use of this gospel setting is implied in the arrangement of *ToleF 23*.[63] It is also clear from later German sources that settings like Josquin's were used as the Gospel in "plenary" masses and formed the basis of a Protestant tradition of setting gospel texts in motet style.[64]

In illo tempore is transmitted only in relatively late sources and with conflicting attributions: *BerlGS 7* (1537–43) [Bruck]; *Tole BC 13* (1553–54) [anonymous]; and *VatS 38* (1563) [Josquin]. Only the bassus partbook of *BerlGS 7* (*olim GöttSA 7 olim KönSU 1740*), in which *In illo tempore* is transmitted anonymously, is extant. It is clear, however, that Moser's description (written before the other partbooks of this source were lost) of an *In illo tempore* which he attributes to Arnold von Bruck refers to this motet.[65] Indeed, Loge's dissertation on the manuscript confirms the Bruck attribution and concordances, although he gave priority to the Josquin attribution of *VatS 38*.[66] The concordance and Bruck attribution of *BerlGS 7* were "lost" and unknown to the editors of the *Werken* when *In illo tempore* appeared; neither was the Bruck attribution mentioned by Wessely.[67] Unlike the other gospel settings whose attribution to Josquin has gone unquestioned—*In principio* and the genealogies—the text of *In illo tempore* was not part of a polyphonic tradition and was not a repeatedly set text.[68] Its parallels with *In principio* and its gospel-tone tonality place it stylistically early in the sixteenth-century tradition of setting gospel texts. While this argues neither for nor against Josquin's authorship, the attribution to Bruck and the possibility that the motet was modeled closely on *In principio* deserves further consideration.

NOTES

*Portions of this material were first presented at Brandeis University (April 1991) at the invitation of Professor Jessie Ann Owens; I gratefully acknowledge her helpful input over the long course of the development of this essay. Subsequent versions were read at the University of Pennsylvania (December 1992), Princeton University (September 1993), the joint meeting of the American Musicological Society and the Society for Music Theory (Montreal, November 1993), and Oxford (January 1994) and portions appear in Judd, "Aspects of Tonal Coherence," 237–55. For helpful comments and criticisms on earlier drafts I am grateful to Professors Anthony M. Cummings, Christopher Hasty, Robert Judd, Jeffrey Kallberg, Patrick Macey, Harold Powers, and Gary Tomlinson. The perspective presented here is deeply indebted to the work of Harold Powers, especially his "Tonal Types," "Is Mode Real?" and "From Psalmody to Tonality" (this volume).

1. Six motets included in Josquin des Prez, *Werken*, fall into the category of "gospel motet," a generic classification discussed in more detail below: *In principio erat Verbum*, *In illo tempore assumpsit Jesus*, *Liber generationis*, *Factum est autem*, *In illo tempore stetit Jesus*, and *Missus est Gabriel Angelus a Deo*. Of these motets, the attribution of two is now doubted. On the six-voice "*satzfehler*" motet, *In illo tempore stetit Jesus*, see Sparks, "Problems of Authenticity." On the probable attribution of the five-voice *Missus est Gabriel Angelus a Deo* to Mouton, see Lowinsky, *The Medici Codex*, III, 219–28. Two other motets are settings of the genealogies—*Liber generationis* and *Factum est autem*—gospel texts which were accorded special treatment in chant and polyphonic traditions. For an extended discussion of these motets, see Just, "Josquins Vertonungen der Genealogien." On the genealogies, see also Noble, "The Function of Josquin's Motets," 21.

2. On intraopus and extraopus style structures, see especially Narmour, "Top-Down and Bottom-Up Systems," 21, and *Analysis and Cognition*, 47–48. Particularly relevant in the present context is Narmour's contention that musical style is to be understood as a cognitive dialogue between expectations created both from within and without a composition. In the simplest formulation of this theory, repetition of events within a piece defines "intraopus" style structures while replication of events from other compositions invokes "extraopus" stylistic contiguities. Using Narmour's terminology in the present context requires a subtle shift of focus from his original statement because I will be considering intraopus style in relation to generic (and essentially social) mediation of extraopus (musical) expectations.

3. E.g., Mattfeld, "Cantus Firmus"; Sparks, *Cantus Firmus in Mass and Motet*; Elders, "Plainchant in the Motets"; Bujic, "Josquin, Leonardo, and the Scala Peccatorum"; and Milsom, "The Eloquent Cantus Firmus."

4. The apparent lack of interest in such tonal relationships may be explained by the tacit assumption that tonal procedures are best studied in "free" compositions, since a preexisting melody naturally exerts some control on the tonal shape of the new composition.

5. Sarah Fuller's caveat about the dangers of imposing a modern analytical "unity" is important to bear in mind ("Exploring Tonal Structure," this volume), as is the concern I voiced in the introduction with the predilection of modern analytical studies to focus excessively on pitch ("Analyzing Early Music," this volume).

6. Josquin des Prez, *Werken*, 56.

7. Josquin des Prez, *Werken*, 79.

8. Ninot le Petit, *Opera Omnia*, CMM 87, 17.

9. The significance of the concluding pitch of the tenor is discussed in more detail below. The use of "high" clefs, relatively rare in Josquin's *oeuvre*, may be tied to the genre of gospel motets. See Judd, "Aspects of Tonal Coherence."

10. "Ungewöhnlich ist die tonale Struktur der in f-jonisch stehenden Motette insofern, als ihre beiden ersten Teile auf D schliessen, während der dritte Abschnitt auf D beginnt, dann aber die Grundtonart wider deutlich hervortreten lässt." Osthoff, *Josquin Desprez*, II:105.

11. Urquhart, "Cadence, Mode, and Structure," 56–59.

12. Krantz, "Rhetorical and Structural Functions of Mode," 294, and Reese and Noble, "Josquin Desprez," 38. Krebs also noted the use of the tone, but accepted Osthoff's modal classification, adding to it "commixture" of "d-mode" and "f-mode." He explained the features Osthoff described as "exceptional" through a textual metaphor (*Die Lateinische Evangelien-Motette*, 400–07). As discussed below (note 23), such a rhetorical interpretation becomes problematic when the tonal features of the gospel tone are taken into account.

13. Krantz, "Rhetorical and Structural Functions of Mode," 294. Bernhard Meier was the most eloquent proponent of the "tenor principle" of modal classification (as epitomized in *The Modes*) and Krantz's work was closely modeled on Meier's. However, an examination of *In principio* highlights problems inherent in assuming the structural function of the tenor-superius pair in compositions which do not use four distinct voice types (an important aspect of Meier's proposal often overlooked in applications of his work to repertories other than those he discussed). On voice-types in Josquin's motets, see Fallows, "Performing Ensembles," and Judd, "Aspects of Tonal Coherence," 256–81.

14. Krebs' "commixed mode 2" could also be added to the labels cited here (*Die Lateinische Evangelien-Motette*, 403).

15. See Cummings, "Sixteenth-Century Motet," and Noble, "The Function of Josquin's Motets," on the function of motets. The standard discussion of the tradition of polyphonic settings of gospels is Moser, *Die mehrstimmige Vertonung*; see also Göllner, *Die Mehrstimmigen Liturgischen Lesungen*. More recently, Krebs, *Die Lateinische Evangelien-Motette*, expands the material covered in Moser, surveying some 800 sixteenth-century motets which use texts from the Gospels and Acts of the Apostles.

16. I am grateful to Professor Patrick Macey for reminding me that this was the last Gospel. See the rubrics in the *Liber usualis*, 7, and Harper, *Forms and Orders*, 124 and 303. Although no archival references to performance of this text as a motet have come to light, this point in the liturgy is one of the places in which motets are known to have been incorporated in a para-liturgical context (see Cummings, "Sixteenth-Century Motet," 47 and 51). While motets often functioned as substitutes for the *Deo gratias*, it seems plausible that *In principio* may have followed it, either in place of, or simultaneously with, the priest's *sotto voce* recitation of the Last Gospel. The diary entries Cummings cited do not categorically suggest that a motet must function as a substitute *Deo gratias* at this point in the mass (e.g., "Cantore cantarunt missam cum motteto post ita missa est etc.," cited in Cummings, "Sixteenth-Century Motet," 51). Such para-liturgical use for *In principio* would be similar to that which Noble suggested for Josquin's other two large settings of texts from the Gospels, the genealogies, with respect to their place in the liturgy (Noble, "The Function of Josquin's Motets," 20-21).

17. Given the long-standing convention of marking genuflection with homophonic settings, Krebs may overstate the significance of this passage for Josquin's personal interpretation of the text when he argues that its setting represents a "classic example of a musical theology," *Die Lateinische Evangelien-Motette*, 402. The specific problem of this interpretation is discussed further below (note 23).

18. Punctuation following "quod factum est" occurs only in more recent versions of the Vulgate. See the *Missale Romanum*, I:20, for the usual fifteenth-century form.

19. I should stress that although gospel tones were most frequently notated with a C clef and C reciting tone, they also appear notated with an F clef and F reciting note. I am grateful to Professor David Crawford for providing facsimiles of gospel tones from several sixteenth-century *Cantorinus* books. Although Krebs remarks on the use of the tone in the motet, he seems to have considered it only in generalized terms as a source to be manipulated for melodic material. Thus he makes no mention of the specific pitch level at which the tone is used, nor does he discuss its distribution or structural significance (*Die Lateinische Evangelien-Motette*, 401).

20. There are several Josquin motets in which the consistent statement of chant in the altus (especially chant phrases which are apparently absent or transposed in other voices) has previously been overlooked. See Judd, "Aspects of Tonal Coherence."

21. While not an "exact" match with the tone used in *In principio*, these characteristic features may be seen in any of the "standard" tones, e.g., *Graduale Romanum*, 806–07. Mattfeld, "Cantus Firmus," 123 appears to have overlooked the use of the tone entirely when she grouped the motet with works in which "the text is provided with a simple reading tone in the liturgy. The tone is largely or totally disregarded by the composer, and no other cantus firmus is used."

22. Judd, "Modal Types" and "Aspects of Tonal Coherence," 177–205.

23. See Judd, "Aspects of Tonal Coherence," 244 for an outline of this alternation. Krebs, *Die Lateinische Evangelien-Motette*, 403–04, provides an overview of textural distribution for the entire motet. Although he cites the use of the gospel tone in the motet, he goes on to associate the cadential profile of the motet, not with the tone itself, but as an elaborate rhetorical realization of the theology of the text (following Meier on word-tone relationships). Thus he proposes that the shift from d to F which accompanies the text "Et verbum caro factum est" is a musical realization of the "Word" (represented by the "otherworldly" tonal area of d) which is transformed to incarnate "flesh" (the "worldly" or "grounded" f-mode of the motet as a whole). While the thrust of the present article is a recognition of the primacy of the musical associations of the text, Krebs' more literal textual interpretation is unsustainable here because the tonal shift to which he attributes theological significance is implicit in the full close formula of the gospel tone. The problematic nature of such a rhetorical interpretation is highlighted by the fact that *any* gospel motet built on the tone would have such an ending (see notes 33 and 38 below).

24. Given the function of the Gospel in the Latin rite, a polyphonic setting as a replacement for recitation is unlikely. Nevertheless, the recitation tone associated with the text allows an analogy along the polyphonic continuum associated with psalm tones ranging from "functional" *falsobordone* settings to motet-like settings of psalm texts (which could still potentially function as liturgical substitutions for monophonic recitation) to psalm motets proper (i.e., motets which happen to set a psalm text but are unlikely to have been used in a specific liturgical context). Much work remains to be done on the question of the psalm motet as a genre in the first half of the sixteenth century, but the groundwork has been laid by Nowacki, "The Latin Psalm Motet," and Steele, "The Latin Psalm Motet," 26–30 and *passim*.

25. For a more extended discussion of tonal coherence in this repertory, see my "Aspects of Tonal Coherence." Ironically perhaps, it is the undervaluing of the interrelationship of the musical, paramusical, and extramusical features (through which I am here identifying coherence) that fostered the problematic modal ascriptions cited above.

26. Such repetitive use of motivic thirds occurs in numerous other motets, and is particularly characteristic of psalm motets. See Judd, "Aspects of Tonal Coherence," 160 and *passim*. Macey, "Josquin as Classic," interprets these repeated figures differently, describing them as "drives to cadences." While this description is accurate in the specific cases Macey cites, it overlooks the consistent placement of such sections within the motet as a whole.

27. On "units" in this repertory, see Judd, "Aspects of Tonal Coherence," 68–92 and *passim*.

28. Josephson, "Formal Symmetry," 106–08, briefly highlighted what he describes as "formal symmetries" in the first two *partes* of *In principio*. However, like other commentators, he seems not to have recognized the use of the gospel tone (he makes a puzzling reference to "quasi-psalmodic intonations" in the melodic gesture he describes as a "minor

second" but makes no mention of the tone in those sections where it is most obviously present) nor does he recognize the syntactic associations (metrum, full close, etc.) that underlie the motivic parallels he highlights.

29. On the reduction techniques used in this example, see Judd, "Aspects of Tonal Coherence," 83–84.

30. It is instructive to note the differences between this analysis and table 2 in Josephson, "Formal Symmetries," 108. These differences result from the emphasis I have placed on syntactic divisions and the primacy of the gospel tone as primary (and contextual) agents of segmentation.

31. For a discussion of Aron's treatment of works ending on A, see Judd, "Reading Aron Reading Petrucci."

32. I believe it is important to maintain a distinction between "final" and "termination." The sonority on which a motet ends or the concluding pitch of its tenor need not represent a "final" in a "closed" tonal form. By "termination" I intend, as did sixteenth-century theorists, simply the place where a piece ends, which may or may not be the "final," the focus of tonal activity—theoretically the note on which a melody *should* end. The "final" of the polyphonic complex is determined by a timeless pitch hierarchy of tonal focus generally on a *vox* and specifically on a *littera*; other factors, most notably liturgical associations of the text, may determine where a motet ends, which may or may not coincide with the primary focus of tonal activity responsible for the "tonality" of the motet. See Judd, "Aspects of Tonal Coherence," 162–63.

33. The theological and rhetorical reading imputed to Josquin by an interpretation like that of Krebs (*Die Lateinische Evangelien-Motette*, 401–08) thus becomes plausible only if one assumes a listener unaware of the Gospel tone and listening within a framework that presumes closed modal structures. The nature of closure (by tonal and other means) in this repertory is beyond the scope of the present discussion, but deserves more attention than has previously been accorded it. See Judd, "Aspects of Tonal Coherence."

34. This idea of genre as a social phenomenon is eloquently argued in Kallberg, *Chopin at the Boundaries*, 4ff.

35. Osthoff, *Josquin Desprez*, II:103.

36. Novack, "Fusion of Design and Tonal Order," 198.

37. Beebe, "Tonal Type and Octo-Modal Classification." I am grateful to Dr. Beebe for a typescript of this paper.

38. Thus Beebe ("Tonal Type and Octo-Modal Classification") and Krebs (*Die Lateinische Evangelien-Motette*), both closely following Meier's lead, independently advanced text-based arguments for the "surprising" tonal frame of these motets. Yet, while the motets share a near-identical tonal framework, the detailed musical theology of the incarnation Krebs proposed for *In principio* contrasts markedly with the crucifixion / resurrection close of *In illo tempore*.

39. Novack, "Fusion of Design and Tonal Order," 196-98, noted the significance of the third in this motet, and its gospel tone resonance, but in a very different frame of reference from that suggested here.

40. For several examples of third-based motives in this motet, see Novack, "Fusion of Design and Tonal Order," 198, example 4. The larger-scale stepwise third noted in my example 13 and its strategic placement were not observed by Novack.

41. This cadence is not mentioned in other commentaries, but would certainly weaken Beebe's classification of the work as Mode 5 on F.

42. See the "Afterword" to this article on questions of style and attribution in these motets.

43. Göllner, *Die Mehrstimmigen Liturgischen Lesungen*, cites several polyphonic settings from the twelfth century on.

44. *Missale Romanum*, I, 453.

45. *RISM 1503*^{1}. On the changing choices of texts for motets, see the succinct summary in Brown, "The Mirror of Man's Salvation."

46. Moser, *Die Mehrstimmige Vertonung* and Lowinsky, *The Medici Codex*, I,220 note the increasing frequency with which gospel texts are used for motets. Untangling the relationship of this tendency with the changing nature of motet composition and liturgical upheaval is beyond the scope of the present study, but the appropriation of gospel settings in German publications is noteworthy. The trend culminates in the six-volume cyclically organized series of gospel settings published in mid-century by Berg and Neuber under the title *Evengelia dominicorum et festorum* for four, five, and six voices (*RISM 1554*^{10}, *1555*^{10}, *1555*^{11}, *1555*^{12}, *1556*^{8}, and *1556*^{9}). A year earlier Susato began a fourteen-volume series of settings of New Testament texts which included a number of gospel texts, but lacks the calendrical ordering of the Berg and Neuber series. *RISM 1553*^{8} is the first volume in Susato's series. Such text choices and ordering for motet collections reflects entirely different priorities from the earlier Italian collections. Petreius' ordered psalm motet compilations (*RISM 1538*^{6} and *1539*^{9}) stand at the head of this trend. On the sources of *In principio* and *In illo tempore* see the "Afterword" to this article. For a listing of polyphonic settings of Gospel texts in the sixteenth century, see Krebs, *Die Lateinische Evangelien-Motette*.

47. See Kallberg, *Chopin at the Boundaries*, 7–11 for an illuminating discussion of "first" works in a genre. While Krebs, *Die Lateinische Evangelien-Motette* provides a useful overview of motets setting gospel texts, the generic perspective suggested here is unaddressed.

48. See Judd, "Aspects of Tonal Coherence."

49. Ninot le Petit, *Opera Omnia*, CMM 87, 17.

50. Moser, *Die Mehrstimmige Vertonung*, 41 and Loge, *Eine Messen- und Motettenhandschrift*, 56. Krebs briefly discussed this motet (*Die Lateinische Evangelien-Motette*, 41–42), but was concerned primarily with questions of date and provenance.

51. *CorBC 95-6/Paris BNN 1817* and *VatS 42* have no signature; *FlorBN II.I.232* has a flat signature in all voices. For a discussion of the Florence source, see Cummings, "A Florentine Sacred Repertory." Hudson's edition opts for a conflation of sources, but primarily follows *FlorBN II.I.232* in his introduction of flats throughout (although not by means of a signature). See the critical commentary, CMM 87, 17, xxiv. Example 15 follows Hudson's edition.

52. In two instances of voice-pairing, the bassus enters a fifth below the tenor on F (mm. 36 and 192), but in neither instance does it appear to be an obvious statement of the tone.

53. Indeed the only exceptions to these cadential pitches are the cadences to D in the *prima pars* already cited, and a series of cadences moving in descending fifths (G–C–F–B♭, mm. 173–204) in the *tertia pars* before a caesura on A and return to F for the conclusion of the motet.

54. Yet in spite of the signature, numerous flats are individually, if somewhat inconsistently signed, suggesting an original exemplar which lacked the signature flat.

55. This is not to say that there is not still enormous and telling flexibility in choosing *B mi* or *B fa* in specific instances. When the tone is overtly stated, *B mi* is not only a possibility, but preferable in that voice in the reading of *VatS 42* (e.g. mm 36–41; 51–3; 74–9; 83–9; 165–68; 238–47). The editorial accidentals in Hudson's edition effectively illustrate the implicit performance of the Florence source via the "strong default" of contrapuntal procedures. Yet, a strikingly different performance is possible from the same source if the Gospel tone is read as the "strong default." (See Bent, "Diatonic Ficta Revisited" for the concept of strong default in rendering performance choices.) The bracketed question marks following editorial accidentals in Example 15c highlight three places where the tone implies B♮.

56. Strunk, "Some Motet-Types." There remains a vast amount of work to be done on motet types of the first half of the sixteenth century and the way in which the genre has been defined. The association of tonal and generic conventions outlined here suggests rethinking not only the way in which the genre "motet" is understood, but also how narrowly defined such associations may be.

57. There is an extended tradition, of which much of my own work partakes, of analyzing selected motets by Josquin des Prez as demonstrations of "early" tonality (especially my earlier work; see Judd, "Some Problems of Pre-Baroque Analysis"). A more recent parallel trend, claiming for itself the authenticating power of contemporaneous theory, views certain of Josquin's motets as paradigms of polyphonic modality. These approaches to analysis are discussed more fully in the introduction to this volume. The contrast between the modal descriptions of *In principio* and the analysis which followed illustrated just how impoverished such modal descriptions can be.

58. Judd, "Modal Types," and "Aspects of Tonal Coherence."

59. For a detailed discussion of these associations, see Judd, "Aspects of Tonal Coherence." While the examples presented in this article represent the closest connections of text-types and tonal conventions, they also suggest rethinking the terms by which tonal conventions for this repertory have been described, whether in terms of modality or functional tonality. Although I can only assert the association of text-type and tonal convention in Josquin's motets with any degree of confidence, my preliminary work with a wider repertory suggests that such associations are not composer specific. See the discussion of chansons and motets ending on A in Judd, "Reading Aron Reading Petrucci."

60. I borrow the term "neutralized" from Strunk. He used it in a formal context, but I think an argument for tonal conventions may be made as well. It is unclear as yet to what extent the approach to chant-based tonality described here may be composer-specific. On "psalm-tone tonalities" see Powers, "From Psalmody to Tonality," this volume.

61. Reese and Noble, "Josquin Desprez," 38.

62. Rifkin, "Problems of Authorship."

63. *In principio* is in the "Christmas" section of the manuscript, which orders compositions according to the liturgical calendar. See Snow, "Toledo Cathedral MS 'Reservado 23'," 274.

64. In one such collection, *RISM 1545*[5], Balthasar Resinarus supplied three of the Gospel motets—on the same three texts for which settings are attributed to Josquin: the "special" gospels *In principio* and the genealogies. Josquin's setting of *In principio* and one by Valentin Soir appear in ordered Gospel cycle, *RISM 1554*[10], cited above. Later (mostly German) settings of *In principio* make much less obvious reference to the gospel tone than Josquin's setting, although the tone is clearly incorporated in the tenor of Mathias Werrecore's 8-voice motet. For a more detailed discussion of later settings of *In principio*, see Krebs, *Die Lateinische Evangelien-Motette.*

65. Moser, *Die Mehrstimmige Vertonung*, 22.

66. Loge, *Eine Messen- und Motetten handschrift*, 59, n 26.

67. Wessely, "Bruck, Arnold von," 351–52.

68. For early polyphonic settings of these texts in chant notation, see Moser, *Die mehrstimmige Vertonung* and Göllner, *Die Mehrstimmigen Liturgischen Lesungen.*

Tonal Coherence and the Cycle of Thirds in Josquin's *Memor esto verbi tui*[*]

Timothy H. Steele

The tonal structure of Josquin's *Memor esto verbi tui* has been discussed by several scholars in recent years, largely because of the modal ambiguity created by a lack of agreement among its internal and concluding cadence pitches.[1] The main point at issue is that the motet fails to achieve tonal closure, and thus lacks the tonal consistency we would expect based on the behavior of most early sixteenth-century motets, including those of Josquin himself. Although D is clearly established as a tonal center at the beginning, and although the majority of cadences throughout the work are on D, the motet comes to an "inconclusive" close on a 10–8–5 sonority with A as the lowest pitch.[2] The issue is further complicated by the fact that the *prima pars* also concludes on a 10–8–5 sonority, this time with E as the lowest pitch.

How are we to comprehend this tonal structure? Some have argued that Josquin had good rhetorical reasons for leaving the motet open-ended, basing their arguments on the account of the motet's origin related by Heinrich Glarean in the *Dodecachordon*.[3] Yet it must also be acknowledged that the tonal structure represented by *Memor esto verbi tui* is not exclusively a rhetorical phenomenon, but seems to be a common feature of compositions that end on A while alternately emphasizing D or E throughout.[4] It should be noted at the outset that D, A, and E are tones that form special relationships with one another because of the structure of the diatonic system. Both D and A may be sung as *re* in the natural and hard hexachords, respectively, and A and E likewise may be sung as *la*, or *mi*, depending on the context. Moreover, two-voice counterpoint between adjacent voices with real imitation at the fifth predominates throughout *Memor esto verbi tui*, thus bringing the fifths D–A and A–E into frequent contrapuntal alignment. The tonal structure of *Memor esto verbi tui* is a product of the relationships that are created when these two first-species fifths, D–A and A–E, are arranged conjunctly. D is the foundation for this structure of conjunct fifths, and it quite naturally assumes the role of primary tonal center throughout much of the motet. A is ambiguous since it is subject to constant reinterpretation depending on whether the fifth above or the fifth below is used. It thus acts as a pivot between areas of tonal focus on D and on E.[5] E is tonally remote from D; and when coupled with its fifth, B, it tends to push the boundary of tonal coherence, an effect that is clearly audible during several passages in the motet. The tonal space created by these conjunct fifths is filled in motivically by thirds throughout *Memor esto verbi tui*, creating a single, coherent tonal structure that links together all of the pitch classes from the diatonic system in a meaningful relationship.

This analysis of *Memor esto verbi tui* will begin with the text and overall formal structure of the work, followed by a discussion of its tonal content. The second part of the analysis will focus primarily on the ways motivic material, contrapuntal relationships, and cadential goals are related to one another. These relationships show the influence of a diatonic cycle of thirds, which provides a key to the tonal coherence of the motet.

I

In addition to its remarkable tonal structure, *Memor esto verbi tui* also has a novel formal structure, consisting in the reprise of words and music from the *exordium* (in this case the first verse of the psalm text), which are brought back at the end to provide a conclusion for the motet. There is as yet no completely satisfying explanation for this unusual formal structure, though it bears a clear resemblance to the practice of singing the first verse of a psalm as its antiphon, which was common enough in liturgical psalmody.[6] Although it is possible that Josquin's use of reprise structure in *Memor esto verbi tui* is related to a specific rhetorical occasion, such as was described by Glarean, the present discussion will focus on consideration of Josquin's role as a reader of the text apart from any specific occasion.[7]

Table 1 gives the complete text of the motet, with a tabulation of cadence pitches that occur at the cola and periods of the psalm's sixteen verses, together with the abbreviated Gloria Patri and the reprise of the first verse at the end.[8] Nearly all verses end with cadences on D, the only exceptions being verses six, eight (the conclusion of the *prima pars*), and the final cadence of the *secunda pars*. Internal cadences are made on F, A, and E. Although not included in table 1, additional cadences on C occur within the members of some verses, along with melodic motion that implies cadences to G in verse sixteen.[9] The important structural role played by D gives it the status of a goal pitch throughout the motet.

The strongest cadences in the *prima pars*, those that appear to mark major divisions of the form, are found in measures 39 and 66, as shown in figure 1. Both cadences are made on D, but the second cadence is the stronger of the two by virtue of its four-voice scoring and the manner in which Josquin builds up to the cadence by motivic concentration and repetition. The cadence is immediately extended to a homorhythmic resolution on an A sonority accompanied by a brief melodic flourish in the tenor. Verses four through eight are linked by a chain of duets, all but the last beginning with tenor and bassus, answered by superius and altus. The texture of the second half of verse eight builds from two voices (tenor and superius) to three and then four before the cadence. The unique structure of this verse is doubtless the result of Josquin's desire to create a satisfying rhetorical conclusion to the *prima pars*.

As summarized in figure 1, the linkage among verses established by contrapuntal design and cadential structure is reflective of the development of ideas in the psalm. Sections Ia and Ib describe the situation suffered by the psalmist, while section II supplies the remedy. Moreover, sections I and II begin with similar text constructions: "Memor esto verbi tui ..." and "Memor fui iudiciorum tuorum ...." Thus it appears that Josquin based his formal design of the *prima pars* on a reading of the psalm that focused on the concept of "remembering," in the first place on the part of God, and, secondly, on the part of the psalmist.

The *secunda pars* does not divide into subsections as clearly as the *prima pars*. Figure 2 shows a diagram of the *pars* indicating a possible parsing of Josquin's linkage of verses. Except for verses thirteen through fifteen, Josquin is careful to articulate each verse by at least a two-voice cadence; yet the strongest impression is of a continuous stream of duets punctuated by major structural events that give the *pars* a sense of shape and direction. Rhetorically significant climaxes occur in verses ten and twelve on "miserere mei" and "mandata tua," and a passage of nearly strict canon between tenor and bassus serves to link verses thirteen to fifteen.[10] The strongest cadence is made on D at the end of the abbreviated Gloria Patri (labeled "Dox" on the diagram), which is followed by a varied reprise of verse one. The lack of a four-voice cadence at the end of verse sixteen, the absence of the second portion of the Gloria Patri ("Sicut erat in principio," etc.), and the tonally inconclusive *mi* cadence on A at the end of the reprise all suggest a deliberate avoidance of closure at the end of the motet.

As summarized in figure 2, the *secunda pars* divides roughly into four sections. This division reveals an emphasis within each section on particular ideas that have rhetorical and/or musical significance: (1) a petition for mercy (*miserere mei*); (2) a promise to keep God's commandments (*mandata tua*); (3) a musical allegory for the concepts of "cords wound about me" (*circumplexi sunt*) and being a "companion" (*particeps*); and (4) the concluding appeal in the last verse of the psalm, doxology, and reprise of verse one.

TABLE 1 Cadences at cola and periods

Verse	Text	Translation*	Cadential pitch mm.	Cola	Periods	Comments
Prima pars						
1	Memor esto verbi tui servo tuo:	Remember thy word to thy servant:	—	—		no cadence
	in quo mihi spem dedisti.	in which thou hast given me hope.	21		D	S/A
2	Haec me consolata est in humilitate mea:	This was my comfort in my affliction:	30	F		S/A with D in bassus
	quia eloquium tuum vivificavit me.	for thy word enlivened me.	39		D	S/A/B
3	Superbi inique agebant usquequaque:	The arrogant were always persecuting me unjustly:	54	(A-F)		S/A evaded cadence
	a lege autem tua non declinavi.	yet from thy law I have not turned aside.	66		D	S/A/T/B
4	Memor fui iudiciorum tuorum a seculo domine:	I remembered thy judgments of old, O Lord:	—	—		no cadence
	et consolatus sum.	and was comforted.	82		D	S/A
5	Defectio tenuit me pro peccatoribus:	Dejection possessed me before the wicked:	—	—		no cadence
	derelinquentibus legem tuam.	those who forsake thy law.	96		D	S/A
6	Cantabiles mihi erant iustificationes tuae:	Thy precepts were my songs:	112	A		S/A with F in tenor
	in loco peregrinationis meae.	in the place of my wandering.	123		E	S/A with A in tenor
7	Memor fui nocte nominis tui Domine:	I remembered thy name in the night, O Lord:	136	E		S/A
	et custodivi legem tuam.	and I kept thy law.	144		D	S/A with *B-mi* in tenor
8	Haec facta est mihi:	This has been done to me:	—	—		no cadence
	quia iustificationes tuas exquisivi.	because I sought out thy precepts.	164		E	S/A/T/B

Secunda pars

9	Portio mea Domine:	Thou art my portion, O Lord:	—	—		no cadence
	dixi custodire legem tuam.	I have said I will keep thy law.	174		D	S/T
10	Deprecatus sum faciem tuam in toto corde meo:	I entreated thy face with my whole heart:	184	E		S/A/T/B
	miserere mei secundum eloquium tuum.	be merciful to me according to thy word.	192		D	S/T
11	Cogitavi vias meas:	I considered my ways:	197	A		T/B
	et converti pedes meos in testimonia tua.	and turned my feet to thy testimonies.	211		D	S/A with *B-mi* in tenor
12	Paratus sum et non sum turbatus:	I was ready, and not disconcerted:	218	F		S/A
	ut custodiam mandata tua.	to keep thy commandments	228		D	S/A/T
13	Funes peccatorum circumplexi sunt me:	The cords of the wicked were wound about me:	—	—		no cadence
	et legem tuam non sum oblitus.	but I did not forget thy law.	240		(D)	T/B close on D-A
14	Media nocte surgebam ad confitendum tibi:	At midnight I always rise to give thanks to thee:	—	—		no cadence
	super iudicia iustificationis tuae.	concerning thy just precepts.	259		(D)	T/B
15	Particeps ego sum omnium timentium te:	I am a companion of all who fear thee:	268	E		S/A/T/B
	et custodientium mandata tua.	and those who keep thy commandments.	279		D	S/A/T/B
16	Misericordia tua Domine plena est terra:	The earth is full of thy mercy, O Lord:	291	F		S/A
	iustificationes tuas doce me.	teach me thy precepts.	296		D	S/A
[Dox]	Gloria Patri et filio,		304	F		S/A
	et spiritui sancto.		310		D	S/A/T/B
[1]	Memor esto verbi tui servo tuo:		—	—		no cadence
	in quo mihi spem dedisti.		325		A	S/A/T/B

* Translation adapted from the Authorized Version (Psalm 119: 49–64).

FIGURE 1 Formal Diagram of the *prima pars*

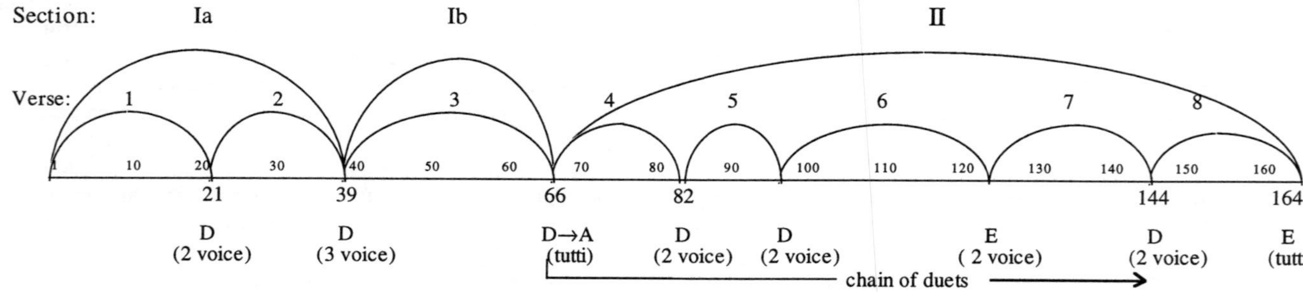

Section Ia, verses 1–2: The Word of God is the psalmist's comfort in affliction;

Section Ib, verse 3: the affliction involved persecution by "the arrogant";

Section II, verses 4–8: the psalmist remembered God's Word and was comforted.

FIGURE 2 Formal diagram of the *secunda pars*

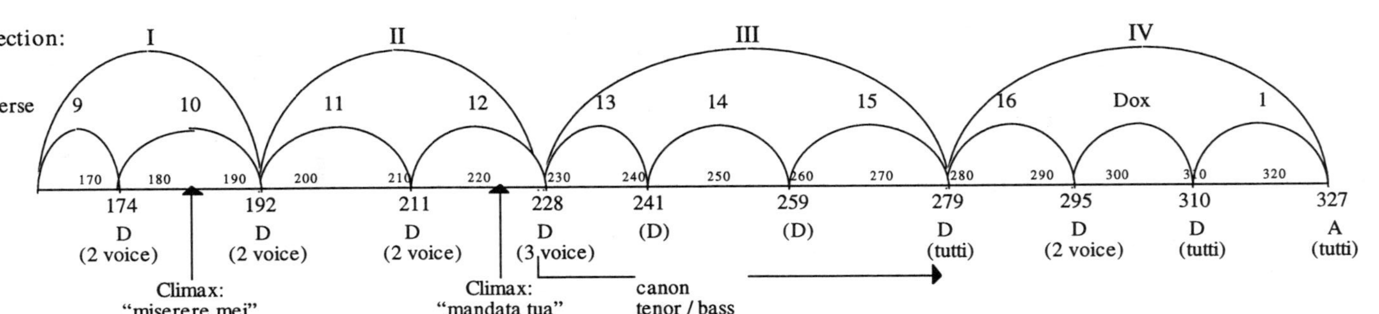

Section I, verses 9–10: climax at "miserere mei," set in four voices in homorhythmic style, motion to A.

Section II, verses 11–12: climax at "mandata tua," ostinato figure in tenor and bass, rushing scales in superius and altus.

Section III, verses 13–15: canon in tenor and bassus, possibly motivated by references to "circumplexi sunt" (wound about) and "particeps" (companion).

Section IV, verse 16, abbreviated Gloria Patri, and reprise of verse 1.

Considered from the point of view of oratory, the reprise technique Josquin employed in this motet works to heighten the expectation of closure and thus render more emphatic its denial. The acceleration of rhythm; the close, stretto imitation in which the voice pairs, separated at the beginning of the motet, are joined at the conclusion in a frantic exchange of high and low duos; the entrance of tenor and bassus in measure 321 at the extreme high end of their respective ranges—all point to a rhetorical climax, as would be expected in a *peroration.* As may be seen in example 1, the promise of a conclusive arrival on D, maintained up to the point of a D cadence in the superius and altus in measure 321 that parallels strong D cadences at the beginning of the work, is frustrated by the weak close on A with which the motet ends. This denial of tonal closure is all the more effective in that the cadential formula that concludes the superius/altus duo in measure 321 is altered in the final cadence just enough to leave the voices suspended, as it were, on the third, A–C.[11]

EXAMPLE 1 *Memor esto verbi tui*, mm. 311–27

EXAMPLE 1 (*cont.*)

Listening to *Memor esto verbi tui,* our intuitive response is to hear D as the center of tonal focus, in relation to which emphases on E and A represent areas of tonal contrast. This analysis of Josquin's rhetorical plan suggests that he intended for the ending on A to be heard as inconclusive. Tonal shifts within the *prima pars* indicate a similar correlation between tonal structure and rhetorical plan. For example, the departure from tonal focus on D that occurs in verse six, which closes on E, may conceivably have been motivated by the mention of "the place of my wandering" (*in loco peregrinationis meae*).[12] Already in verse four the motet takes a turn toward A and E that coincides with the text "Memor fui iudiciorum" and the start of the second section of the *prima pars*.

In *Memor esto verbi tui*, Josquin composed a reading of the psalm text that makes full use of the tonal potential of the diatonic system. Within this system both vertical and linear intervallic relationships are set up within conventional norms of melodic/motivic style, voice ranges, and contrapuntal technique. The predominance of motivic patterns involving the intervals of the third and fifth, and the technique of real imitation at the fifth between paired voices in the extensive duos (especially tenor and bassus), when coupled with principal tonal focus on D and secondary tonal focus on A and E, create a tonal space of extraordinary potential which Josquin exploits for rhetorical purposes.[13] The relationship between Josquin's motivic material, the cycle of thirds, and the opening up of areas of tonal contrast are the matters to be explored in the remainder of this article.

II

The motivic material of the exordium of *Memor esto verbi tui* and its varied reprise at the end of the motet may be analyzed as diatonic chains of thirds beginning on D. It has been pointed out by several scholars that tertian chains are a relatively common feature in medieval melodic style, from Gregorian chant to the songs of the troubadours and trouvères.[14] The cycle of thirds provides a useful representation of certain tonal relationships within the diatonic system that constitute a foundation on which the surface level of melodic behavior rests. Expanded to take in contrapuntal relationships, the cycle of thirds can be seen to operate on many levels of a work, and it offers a means of describing the way in which a piece remains tonally consistent, while accounting for the possibility of significant contrast.

The tonal content of *Memor esto verbi tui* is shown in figure 3, represented as a cycle of thirds from *B–fa* to *B–mi*, with the main series running from D to E.[15] D, F, A, and E are the primary structural tones, as is clear from their use as cadential pitches, while C occurs less frequently as a cadence pitch, but more often as the upper step in a *re–fa* third on A–C. G, B, and B♭ are secondary tones, serving primarily to complete thirds or fifths above E or below F. The five main tones include the two fifths, D–A and A–E, as well as the thirds, D–F, F–A, A–C, and C–E. The *re–fa* third on D–F and A–C is prominent throughout the motet.[16] The F–C fifth, which is given structural significance in the *exordium*, is formed from the tones that mediate the two first-species fifths.

The role of B in the course of *Memor esto verbi tui* requires some special explanation. As the variable *recta* pitch in the untransposed gamut (*cantus durus*), B must be sung as *B–fa* or *B–mi*, depending on the context.[17] In the case of *Memor esto verbi tui*, B♭ occurs frequently as an upper neighbor to A, and is solmized as *fa* above *la* in the natural hexachord. In such cases, B♭ does not significantly affect the tonal structure of the motet. A more significant situation occurs when B♭ appears as the fifth below F and the third below D.[18] The use of B♭ in such functional units opens up the possibility of a shift toward the more "flat" side of the cycle of thirds. B♮, on the other hand, most often occurs in a functional relationship with G or E, well to the "sharp" side of the cycle of thirds, where it would be sung as *B-mi*. *B-fa* and *B-mi*, when found in functional units in conjunction with main tones, thus occupy opposite ends of the tonal spectrum.[19]

FIGURE 3 The Tonal Content of *Memor esto verbi tui*

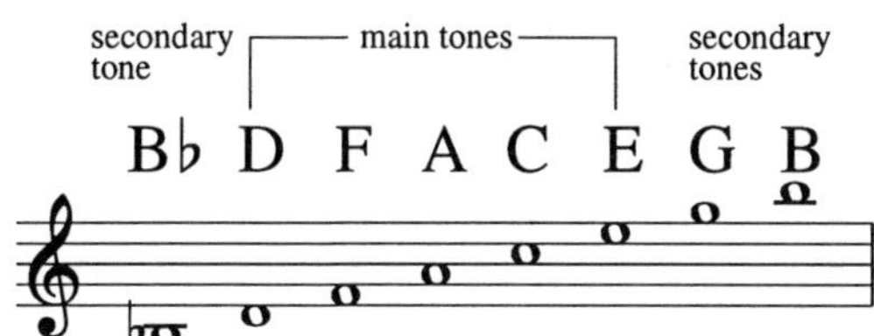

The most important tonal event in the *prima pars* of *Memor esto verbi tui* is the shift in tonal focus from D to A and E, culminating in a cadence on E at the end of the *pars*. The first indication of this shift occurs at the end of verse three, where, just after the important formal cadence on D in m. 66, Josquin repeats the text "non declinavi" in homorhythmic texture, moving from D to A. Prior to this, verses one and two remain within the lower main tones D–F–A–C, forming cadences on F, C, and D. The tonal structure of these verses is representative of the processes at work throughout the motet, and we shall examine them in detail.

As shown in example 2, the motet begins with a tenor ascent through the tertian series d–f–a–c^1–e^1 before closing with a cadence on d^1. The superius and altus then repeat the same imitative duo an octave higher. During the duo, the bassus ascends in imitation with the tenor until arriving on c^1, then it reverses course and descends back from c^1 to d, passing through the thirds c^1–a, a–f, and f–d. Throughout the duo, e, g, and b are used as secondary tones in contrast to the main series. Josquin arranges the ascending tertian chains in imitation at the semibreve, resulting in an overlapping stretto pattern that emphasizes the structural tones of the fifths D–A and F–C. Theoretically the sequential pattern of ascending thirds and overlapping fifths could continue for one or two more statements, leading into the upper main tones of the third cycle represented by the fifth A–E and the thirds A–C and C–E. This potential is realized later in the *prima pars*.

Significantly, when Josquin repeats the first verse at the end of the motet, the motivic pattern is varied in such a way that the third chain is emphasized, and the structure of the ascent clearly outlines the third A–C before continuing to C–E and the cadence in measure 321 (see ex. 1). Following the cadence in measure 321, the final measures of the superius restate the tertian pattern in compressed form, so that the A–C third and the C–E third are heard immediately after one another in the same voice. Because of this carefully constructed motivic/contrapuntal design, the arrival on C and A in the superius and altus in measure 325 seems completely

EXAMPLE 2 *Memor esto verbi tui*, mm. 1–14

natural. It could be argued that the avoidance of a conventionally constructed cadence at the end of the motet creates a greater sense of inconclusiveness than the fact that the final sonority is not on D.

At the beginning of verse two (ex. 3) the two fifths D–A and F–C overlap in a tenor and bassus duo that recalls the tonal structure of the first verse. The *re–fa* thirds on D–F and A–C sung at the imitative distance of a fifth are also strongly reminiscent of the opening tertian structure of the first verse. Internal cadences are formed on F (m. 30, foreshadowed in m. 28), and on C (m. 35). The verse concludes with a formally significant cadence on D at measure 39. As we have seen, verses one and two form a single thought in Josquin's rhetorical structure, and it is evident that they form a single tonal unit as well, centered in the lower portion of the cycle of thirds D–F–A and C.

EXAMPLE 3 *Memor esto verbi tui*, mm. 23–41

EXAMPLE 3 (*cont.*)

Verse three opens with another duo for tenor and bassus that outlines the D–A fifth. The superius and altus imitate the tenor/bassus duo, concluding in measure 54 on an F–A third. The tenor and bassus begin the second half of the verse with a new duo that moves to a cadence on C in measure 58 (ex. 4, mm. 54–58). As in verse two, the tonal shape of the verse is designed around the main tones, D–F–A–C. Josquin builds up energy toward the end of the verse through a series of repetitions of a two-voice contrapuntal unit on the text "non declinavi" (mm. 58–66). The superius and altus exchange the chief element of the unit, moving down by thirds from C to A, then from A to F, and finally from F to D, the last statement being repeated by the tenor at the point of the cadence (mm. 64–66). Thus the D–F–A–C tertian structure is stated as a descent in the second half of this verse, balancing the ascending statements of verses one and two and the first half of verse three.

EXAMPLE 4 *Memor esto verbi tui*, mm. 53–72

EXAMPLE 4 (*cont.*)

The tonal shift that occurs at the end of verse 3, which is coincident with the major division of thought in the *prima pars*, can be described as a shift from the lower main tones of the cycle of thirds, centered particularly around the fifth D–A, to the upper main tones, A–C–E. This shift in tonal focus occurs as the entire ensemble repeats the text "non declinavi" a final time after a dramatic grand pause (ex. 4, mm. 66–68), concluding with a 10–8–5 sonority on A that looks forward to the conclusions of the *prima* and *secunda partes*. Embedded within this repetition, the tenor voice ascends through the main tones D, F, and A in a leaping manner that recalls the opening motive of the motet (mm. 66–70). It continues up to C, now with stepwise motion, and closes by moving stepwise downward to E. This close on E may be described as a statement of the *mi–la* second-species fourth, but by implication it also represents the fifth above A, filling out the full ascent through the third cycle from D to E.

This brief tenor extension at the end of verse three provides a paradigm for the tonal structure of the entire *prima pars*, showing how D and E are related by their connection through A, which is the pivotal tone in the series and the center of the cycle of thirds. Likewise, the structure of verse eight (ex. 5), the conclusion of the *prima pars*, demonstrates the connection of D and E through A, and the role of the cycle of thirds in mediating this connection. In the second half of the verse, beginning in measure 148, each voice sings a recitation formula that strongly suggests a psalm tone. The tone is passed from tenor on D (mm. 148–54) to superius on A (mm. 150–56), followed by the bassus on A (mm. 156–62) and the altus on E (mm. 158–64). The tone contains a *re–fa* leap that occurs in the first two statements on D–F and A–C, while the bassus repeats the A–C third down an octave, followed by the altus with the *mi–sol* third E–G. Meanwhile, in measures 156 and following the tenor sings a melody related to the leaping figure from the end of verse three, this time spanning the thirds A–C and C–E, and concludes with a recitation on E. The close of the section on E seems inevitable because the recitation tone concludes with a stepwise descending sixth, first ending on A, then E, then, finally, B, which is harmonized by the lower fifth, E.

Example 5 *Memor esto verbi tui*, mm. 148–65

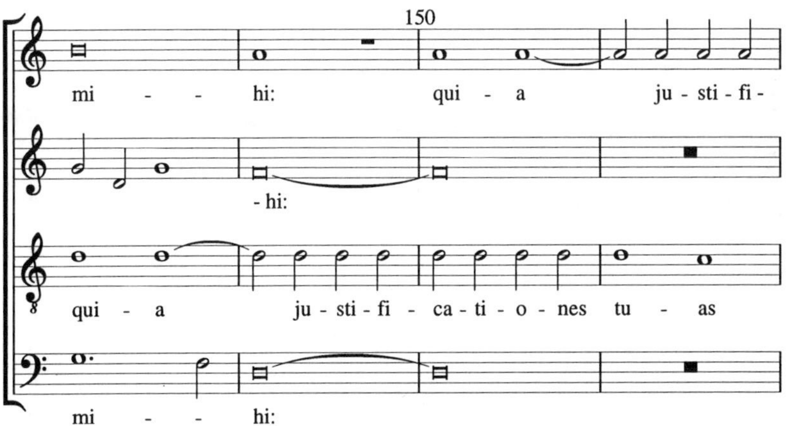

EXAMPLE 5 *(cont.)*

Figure 4 graphically summarizes the tonal shift from D to E through A as it occurs in the *prima pars*. Figure 4a provides a reduction of the tenor in measures 66–70, at the end of verse three; 4b gives a reduction of the exchange of recitation tone from tenor to superius, then bassus to altus that concludes the *prima pars*. Disregarding the change in melodic direction in the tenor (4a) and the octave shift of the recitation tone in verse eight from superius to bassus (4b), both examples illustrate a coherent, interlocking structure of thirds and fifths.[20] These examples are not circle of fifths progressions; rather, they are changes in tonal focus along the axis of the cycle of thirds. Verse eight is most extensive, traveling through virtually the entire cycle: first d^1–f^1–a^1–c^2, then a–c^1–e^1–g^1–b, following the pattern of the *re–fa* thirds as the recitation tone is passed from one voice to another.

FIGURE 4 Tonal shift from D to E through A in the *prima pars*

a)

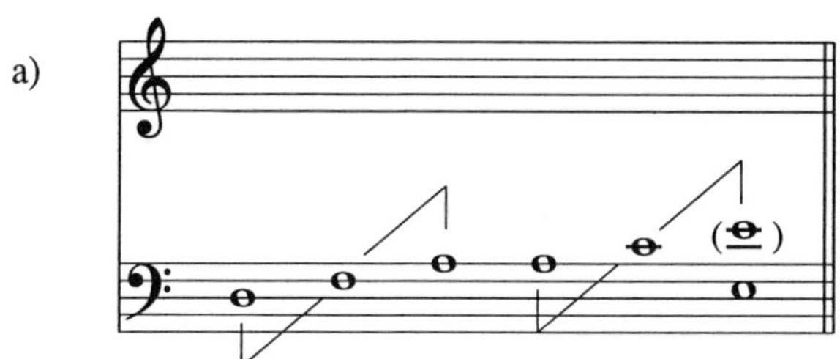

b)

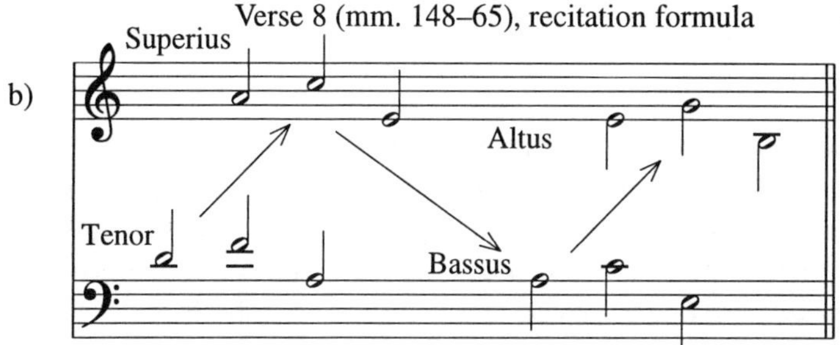

The shifts from lower to upper tones of the cycle of thirds are paralleled by shifts in the overall range of the vocal ensemble. As figure 5 shows, the entire ensemble shifts ambitus at the beginning of verse four (m. 67), from the span of a seventeenth from d to f^2 to the seventeenth from A to c^2 (the note d^2 occurring occasionally as an upper neighbor to c^2 when the ensemble is in its low range). Apart from a momentary contraction to a fifteenth (d to d^2) in the first half of verse eight, the shift in ambitus remains until the repetition of verse one at the conclusion of the motet, where, once again, the ensemble fills the seventeenth from d to f^2.[21] While the ensemble is in its low ambitus, the focus is largely on the upper tones of the third cycle, A–C–E–G–B, and the conclusion of the *prima pars* is a 10–8–5 sonority on E. When the ambitus shifts back up at the end of the *secunda pars*, the focus is once again D–F–A–C–E, and the concluding sonority is a 10–8–5 on A. This systematic shifting of ambitus and its correlation with tonal areas a fifth apart illustrates the degree to which *Memor esto verbi tui* exhibits a unified, consistent tonality, despite its lack of a strong, affirmative conclusion on D. The only place, in fact, where this tonal coherence begins to break down is in the setting of the last verse of the psalm.

FIGURE 5 Shift of ambitus and final sonority

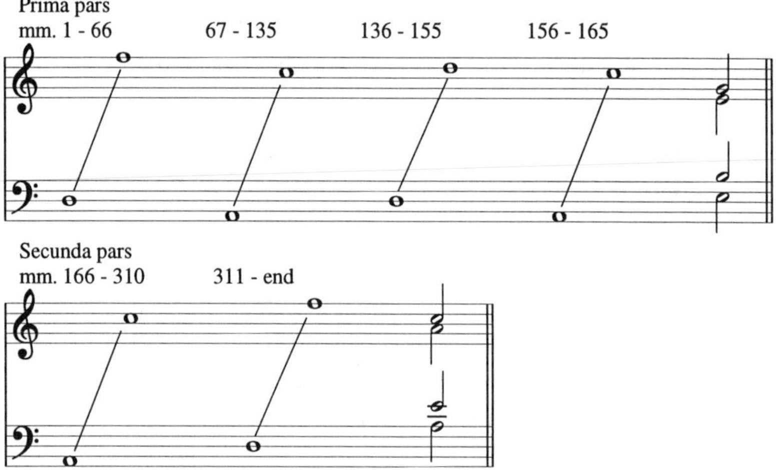

Verse sixteen is unique in several ways. First, it is the only verse that is completely dominated by a duo for superius and altus. Second, it concludes without a strong cadence, and, instead, overlaps with the Gloria Patri, which begins with the more typical bassus/tenor duo. The expected cadence in measure 296 has only one element (the *cantizans* figure with ornamented suspension in the altus voice) to mark the end of the psalm text (see ex. 6). Clearly Josquin intended to drive on through to the Gloria Patri and the reprise of verse one. The verse is also unusual in its tonal structure, placing greater emphasis on G than anywhere else in the motet and thus opening up a tonal area that exceeds the main tertian series from D to E. The result is that for a few measures the prominence of G and B undermines the tonal stability of the previous fifteen verses, achieves maximum contrast, and reinvigorates the music in preparation for the final rhetorical gesture that is to come with the repetition of verse one.

Verse sixteen follows immediately after the long canon for tenor and bassus that provides linkage in verses thirteen through fifteen, and which finishes after

EXAMPLE 6 *Memor esto verbi tui*, mm. 280–97

EXAMPLE 6 (*cont.*)

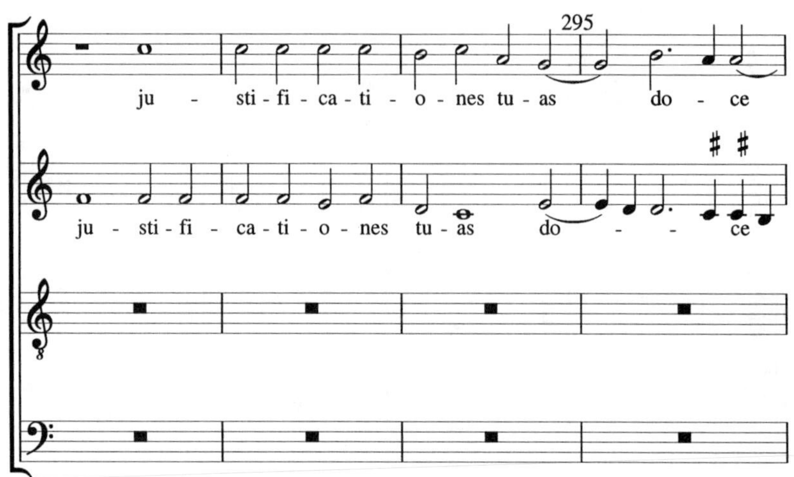

several changes in mensuration and a tutti close on D in measure 279. The tenor, melodically extending the D cadence, begins with a reference to the *re–fa* third (D–F) in a similar rhythm to the opening motive of verse one, while foreshadowing the rhythmic variation of the motive at its return at the end of the motet (ex. 6, mm. 280–83). It then suddenly leaps the octave and descends to G. This motion is answered in the bassus where the tertian motive with its characteristic dotted rhythm is transposed to fill the third from G to B, followed by a stepwise ascent and descent through the fourth-species fifth G–D (mm. 283–85). The use of *tenorizans* figures in the tenor and bassus combines with octaves on G to create for a few moments the sense of a new tonal center, far removed from the previous emphasis on D and the main tones of the cycle of thirds.

Meanwhile, the superius and altus sing a rising motive spanning the first-species fourths on D–G and A–D, in stepwise motion. The superius melody between measures 282 and 291 is characterized by ambiguity as it first rises to D, falls back to B, then twice runs stepwise through the fifth F–C. Although seemingly a simple repetition, the two statements of the descending fifth from C to F move first through *B-mi* (harmonized by E in the altus), then *B-fa* (harmonized by F in the altus). When the superius and altus duo reaches a cadence on F in measure 291 it seems forced. The tonal distance that separates the first part of the phrase (mm. 280–86) from the cadence and continuation to the end of the verse (mm. 287–96) is so great, and is traversed so quickly, that the sense of tonal stability is strongly disturbed. This is in fact the point where tonal coherence is most severely threatened in the motet.

***

To return to the question posed at the beginning of this study, how are we to comprehend the tonal structure of *Memor esto verbi tui*? It is impossible to speak of Josquin's intentions with certainty, but it seems reasonable to believe that Josquin's chief motivation in composing the motet was rhetorical: to deliver a meaningful and persuasive reading of the text. As he worked out each segment of the motet, motivic ideas and contrapuntal combinations were conceived that fit the rhetorical purpose at hand. The tonality of the resulting work unfolds as a network of intervallic relationships that arise quite naturally from the diatonic system. The affinity of D and A with respect to ascent and descent, and the tonal space created by the contrapuntal combination of first-species fifths mediated by thirds, constitute a tonal foundation on which both the motivic details and overall coherence of the motet depend. The diatonic cycle of thirds provides a paradigmatic, descriptive resource that schematically represents this tonal foundation, while also taking account of the interactions and relationships among all of the pitch classes that are used in the motet. By reference to the cycle of thirds it is possible to demonstrate how areas of the motet that are tonally remote relate to those that are fundamentally central to its tonality, and to account for the means by which changes in local tonal focus are carried out.

Although not dependent on the terminology of sixteenth-century theory, the methodology applied here to *Memor esto verbi tui* is not in conflict with it. On the contrary, the cycle of thirds is a means of conceptualizing the diatonic system that can also be viewed through the prism of modal theory and the deductions of the hexachords. The observations presented here arise from consideration of the internal musical evidence of one motet, but they may apply equally well to other motets by Josquin and his contemporaries. Further use of the cycle of thirds as an analytical tool has the potential to reveal much about the nature of tonal coherence in early sixteenth-century music.

NOTES

* Much of the work on which this chapter is based was carried out and first presented at a National Endowment for the Humanities summer seminar at Brandeis University in 1995. I would like to thank Professors Jessie Ann Owens, Cristle Collins Judd, and Richard Hoffman for their valuable comments on early drafts of this article.

1. The best recent study of the sources, style, and influence of *Memor esto verbi tui* is Macey, "Josquin as Classic," 28–41. See also Osthoff, *Josquin*, 2: 115–49. The motet is edited in Josquin, *Werken*, Motetten 2, no. 31. The Smijers edition relies upon the readings in 15141 (Petrucci's *Motetti de la Corona*, vol. 1), which is inferior to the version in I-Fn II.I.232, from which the musical examples for this study were transcribed. The tonal organization of the motet is discussed by Meier, *Modes*, 347, and Dahlhaus, *Studies*, 263. More complete analyses are provided by Krantz, "Rhetorical and Structural Functions," 226–33, and Judd, "Aspects of Tonal Coherence," 161–64.

2. The final cadence apparently seemed inconclusive to the editor of RISM 1559[2], who extended the motet by adding a close on D. Although this addition may reflect the editor's desire to preserve modal purity, its existence suggests that our interpretation of the final cadence as interrupted or inconclusive is not merely anachronistic, though it must be conceded that this print was issued more than fifty years after the likely date of composition of *Memor esto verbi tui*, and in a completely different cultural context.

3. Both Meier, *Modes*, 347, and Krantz, "Rhetorical and Structural Functions," 226–33, are inclined to accept Glarean's word regarding the original purpose of the motet, attributing irregularities in its modality to text expressiveness. According to Glarean, Josquin composed *Memor esto verbi tui* as a reminder to Louis XII of a promise that had gone unfulfilled. Upon hearing the motet, Louis was "filled with shame" and "discharged the favor which he had promised" (*Regem suffuso pudore promissionem diutius differre non ausum, beneficium quod promiserat* . . . . Glareanus, *Dodecachordon*, 2: 271–72. Latin text from the Basel, 1547 edition; facsimile reprint, Hildesheim, 1969, fol. 441v). Nevertheless, the anecdote is of questionable reliability on several accounts. What little we know of Josquin's association with the French court during the reign of Louis XII comes from reports of a few important contacts during the years immediately prior to his employment as *maestro di cappella* in Ferrara, beginning in April of 1503. See Lockwood, "Josquin at Ferrara," 107–18, and *Music in Renaissance Ferrara*, 202–07. It is, of course, possible that Josquin was in contact with the French court after he returned north to become provost of the collegiate church of Condé-sur-Escaut. On the date of Josquin's arrival in Condé and

the evidence for his subsequent contacts with the French and Burgundian courts, see Kellman, "Josquin and the Courts," 206–07. On the general issue of Josquin's relationship to the French monarchy, see Macey, "Josquin's *Misericordias Domini*," 163–77, Osthoff, *Josquin*, 1: 41–49, and Reese and Noble, "Josquin," 7–9. One important manuscript source for *Memor esto verbi tui*, GB-Lcm 1070, was probably written during the later years of Louis's reign (about 1510 to 1515), and thus provides some evidence that the motet was known at his court (see Nowacki, "Psalm Motet," 164). The motet also appears together with a setting of the next sixteen verses of the same psalm, *Bonitatem fecisti*, in Petrucci's *Motetti de la Corona*, where it is attributed to Carpentras, and in I-Fn 232. The Petrucci volume may have been intended to honor the French king (Gehrenbeck, "Motetti de la Corona," 333–41). In his anecdote, Glarean infers that *Bonitatem fecisti* was written by Josquin as a grateful response to the king's favor, about which he is certainly in error. A more detailed discussion of the anecdote and its reliability is given in my dissertation, "The Latin Psalm Motet," 220–36.

4. A good overview of this phenomenon in a very different context is Powers, "The Modality of 'Vestiva i colli'." The tonal structure of Palestrina's madrigal, *Vestiva i colli* resembles that of *Memor esto verbi tui* in its use of first species fifths on D and A and its "modal indecisiveness" (see especially pp. 38–40 of Powers's article).

5. Judd notes the special role of A in this and other *re* motets by Josquin ("Aspects of Tonal Coherence," 162–63). On the characteristics of *re* tonality in general, see Judd, "Aspects of Tonal Coherence," 93–176, and "Modal Types," 437–38.

6. The relationship of the reprise technique to the antiphon with psalm *ipsum* was suggested by Harrison, *Music in Medieval England*, 345. The practice was common in the Roman liturgy (Steele, "The Latin Psalm Motet," 66–68). The use of reprise technique is relatively rare among early psalm motets, however, and it is not clear why certain motets observe the practice while others do not. Its use by Josquin in *Qui habitat* (à 4), a psalm motet that resembles *Memor esto verbi tui* closely, may represent the composer's reuse of a successful strategy—both formal and tonal. On the text and function of *Qui habitat*, see Macey, "Josquin as Classic," 8–11. Judd discusses the tonal relationship between these two motets in "Aspects of Tonal Coherence," 161–67.

7. On the general issues faced by composers in their reading of and response to the psalms, see my discussion of composers as "readers" of psalm texts in Steele, "The Latin Psalm Motet," 135–202. The concept of a musical work as a reading of a text has been explored in Randel, "Dufay the Reader," and Owens, "Palestrina as Reader."

8. Most cadences involve at least two voices in the standard formula of major sixth to octave. Exceptions are noted in the comments section of the table. Typical cadential structures in Josquin's motets are described in Judd, "*Salve Regina*," 119–21.

9. Two-voice cadences on C are found in measures 35 and 58. In measures 283 and 285 the tenor and bassus, in imitation, sing melodic figures that are recognizable as *tenorizans* functions. Coupled with arrivals on the octave in another voice, these figures strongly im-

ply cadential motions to G. These partial G cadences play a significant role in the unfolding tonal structure of the motet, as will be discussed below.

10. The relationship of *dux* and *comes* between bassus and tenor is reversed in measures 254–59; otherwise the canon is exact. Several changes of mensuration from *tempus imperfectum diminutum* to *proportio sesquialtera* are embedded in the canon between measures 264 and 279.

11. This deflection away from D leaves the listener in a state of anticipation, more or less as if the final verse were to end with a question mark or ellipse. It suggests an interpretation of the final verse: the psalmist stands ready to receive judgment on his appeal, but he has reason to be hopeful and is consequently anticipating an immediate response. Meier writes that later musicians "took over the device expressing 'hope' that Josquin used here perhaps for the first time, and incorporated it into their musical vocabulary as a typical formula, available as needed" (*Modes*, 347). Krantz interprets the ending similarly ("Rhetorical and Structural Functions," 232).

12. Judd, "Aspects of Tonal Coherence," 164.

13. On the structure of Renaissance tonal space, see David Schulenberg, "Modes, Prolongations, and Analysis," 308.

14. Smits van Waesberghe called attention to the prominent role of thirds and fifths in establishing functional units within diatonic, modal melodies (*Textbook of Melody*, 23–59), and Hansen has found that the third is the most frequent leap in the repertory of Gregorian chant contained in the Montpellier Codex H 159, and that the tertian series d–f–a–c^1 and d–f–a–c^1–e^1–g^1 account for the main tones most frequently encountered ("Tonality in Gregorian Chant," 425–31). Hansen's complete study was published in 1979 as *The Grammar of Gregorian Tonality*. Hansen points out that the Alleluia chants, the most modern in the repertory, often exhibit a tonality marked by contrasting sonorities made up of overlapping tertian chains, representing alternate poles of tonal stability and tension. See also Mathiassen, *The Style of the Early Motet*, 56–70, who suggests that the harmony of the early thirteenth century rests on the principle of contrasting sonorities, and Sachs, *The Rise of Music*, 295–311, who found that melodies based on third chains are common throughout the world. On the presence of tertian chains and the use of contrasting sonorities in troubadour and trouvère song, see Van der Werf, *Chansons*, 50–53.

15. Cf. Dahlhaus, *Studies*, 249–50. According to Dahlhaus, B♭ may be accidental, it may indicate transposition of the diatonic system, and it may operate as an eighth degree in an octatonic collection generated by the circle of fifths, B♭–F–C–G–D–A–E–B[♮]. In an earlier passage in his *Studies*, Dahlhaus discusses the principle of contrasting sonorities and the cycle of thirds beginning on D, but his discussion is limited to an assessment of the work of Smits van Waesberghe (*Textbook of Melody*) as it is applied to interval succession in fourteenth-century counterpoint (71–74).

16. The importance of this *re–fa* third is a significant factor in Judd's assignment of this motet to the modal type, *Re (D): re–fa* ("Aspects of Tonal Coherence," 164–67, and

"Modal Types," 442, 445). The prominence of this third suggests a close relationship to the recitation formulas of psalmody—a connection that seems to be borne out by veiled references to psalm-tone formulas in verse 8 and other places (see Judd, "Aspects of Tonal Coherence," 165).

17. Bent, "Diatonic *Ficta*," 3-7.

18. Such is the case in measures 304–5 where B must be sung as *fa* in order to avoid a diminished fifth with F in the altus. The altus melody at this point seems to be a termination formula for the second psalm tone (F–E–C–D), and Josquin harmonizes it twice in immediate succession: once in quasi-fauxbourdon (mm. 304-6), and once in quasi-falsobordone (mm. 306–310).

19. Cf. Dahlhaus's "octatonic" interpretation of B♭ in his *Studies*, 250. The cycle of thirds provides a means of interpreting B♮ that suggests a merging of Dahlhaus's catagories of "accidence" and "octatonicism."

20. I do not mean to imply that one should ignore the specific pitches involved in these passages. There is no question that the second species fourth (e–a) and the first species fifth (a–e^1) are completely dissimilar in their function and position with respect to the theory of hexachords and modes. Taken as pitch classes, however, the relationship of these passages to the cycle of thirds is significant and telling with regard to the overall tonal shape of *Memor esto verbi tui*.

21. The bassus does not descend below d between measures 136 and 155. Since the superius does not ascend to f^2 here, I do not consider this contraction of range to be a return to the d to f^2 ambitus of measures 1–66.

Concepts of Pitch in English Music Theory, c. 1560–1640*

Jessie Ann Owens

for Harold Powers

> There is nothing doth trouble, and disgrace our Traditionall Musition more, than the ambiguity of the termes of Musicke, if he cannot rightly distinguish them for they make him uncapable of any rationall discourse in the art hee professeth.
>
> Thomas Campion,
> *A New Way of Making Fowre Parts in Counter-point* (c. 1613)[1]

Tonality casts a large shadow over the scholarship concerned with English music and English music theory of the sixteenth and seventeenth centuries. The critical approaches to the music most frequently employed are either unabashedly tonal or invoke a version of modality closely related to tonality. At the same time, investigations of English music theory seem to be concerned primarily with identifying elements of emerging tonality. Titles such as Wienpahl's "English Theorists and *Evolving Tonality*," or Lewis's "*Incipient Tonal Thought* in Seventeenth-Century English Theory," or Johnson's "Solmization in English Treatises Around the Turn of the Seventeenth Century: *A Break from Modal Theory*" (italics added for emphasis) reveal the underlying assumption of progress towards tonality.

This focus on tonality is readily understandable: English music *sounds* tonal and English music theory uses concepts associated with tonality well before either happens on the continent. The consequence, however, of a preoccupation with tonality is that analyses of both music and theory can be anachronistic and dominated by teleological concerns. There is surprisingly little engagement of critical approach as a valid scholarly concern, nor have there been consistent attempts to derive a critical language from contemporary theory.

My goal is to focus on concepts associated with pitch. One constellation of concepts might be characterized by what William Bathe calls "naming" (the title of the first chapter in his *Briefe Introduction to the Skill of Song*). It includes basic notions such as solmization, key signature, scale (in the sixteenth-century sense as defined by key signatures rather than in the modern sense, as, for example, "major scale"), and some aspects of key. These topics are concerned at root with being able to read notation ("naming" deals with pitch, "time" and "quantity" with meter and duration) and to produce sounds ("tuning").[2] A second group includes terms used to describe the pitch content of actual compositions, such as tone, air, and other aspects of key. In effect, these two groups of concepts are on two different levels, one dealing with basic elements of music, and the other with higher-order concepts associated with organization of pitch in actual music. It is helpful to keep the two levels separate: an understanding of the first is crucial for interpreting the far more complex second level.

Because of limitations of space, I will attempt a thorough elaboration only of the first set of concepts, while offering a preliminary sketch of the second. I will leave to a later time the task of developing a new critical approach based on the close reading of the theorists.

* * *

Let me begin by illustrating characteristic critical approaches to English music and considering some of the problems they present. By way of example I consider a sampling of the scholarship devoted to the music of William Byrd.[3]

Writers from the first half of this century generally invoke the language of tonality. Thus, Edmund Fellowes, the great editor and biographer of Byrd, describes *Emendemus in melius*:

> Its beauty lies mainly in a wonderful succession of simple chords. The opening of the second section in E flat after the close in G major agrees exactly with the spirit of the words, which changes at this point from penitence to pleading: Adiuva nos, Deus; with a sure hope of salvation: Deus, salutaris noster. And here Byrd has a splendidly strong cadence in C major to express this confidence.[4]

The description of *Ave verum corpus* by Frank Howes, the author of the first monograph on Byrd, is even more explicit in its use of tonal vocabulary:

> To the modern listener homophonic music inevitably sounds like so much harmony; the harmony of *Ave Verum Corpus* he will notice sounds queer; the reason for this is the repeated juxtaposition of the chords of D major and F major. The motet is in G minor (taking the liberty for convenience sake to assign keys to this

> modal and transitional music); the chord of D major is the dominant of the key, while D minor has F as its relative major. The two chords are therefore quite nearly related—brother-in-law in fact, but like brothers-in-law they differ profoundly in temperament. When Byrd begins [g min, D, F] he plunges the ear into an unstable world in which the ground, as it were dissolves beneath it and leaves the poor bewildered organ to ask: 'Are you talking flats or sharp?—you can't talk both at once, you know.'[5]

Nearly all of the early writers on Byrd draw attention to his harmonic innovations, particularly his use of false relations. While acknowledging the "transitional" nature of his music, they nonetheless adopt the vocabulary of tonality: chords, keys, harmonic functions.

Since the 1950s the prevailing critical language has been that of modality, which at least has a veneer of authenticity. Within this broad framework I would distinguish two approaches. One is that employed by Bernhard Meier, who, in his 1974 book on modality in sixteenth-century polyphonic music, provided a synthesis of theoretical writings about mode and illustrated how the system worked with music by Rore, Clemens, Lasso, Palestrina, and others.[6] It is a system consisting of eight elements in its traditional formulation, and twelve in the expansion proposed by Glarean. Meier's particular contribution was to demonstrate the validity, both in theory and in practice, of the distinction between authentic and plagal modes in polyphonic compositions.

Meier makes modal assignments for ten compositions by Byrd: *Emendemus in melius* is in mode 1, three motets from the 1575 *Cantiones sacrae* are in mode 2 transposed, five compositions are in modes 5 or 6. He discusses only one piece in any detail, the *Gloria patri*, which he identifies as a plagal a-mode piece with no flat in the signature. He argues that Byrd had committed a modal monstrosity—namely shifting to C at the end—for purposes of text expression:

> That is, the mode that Byrd introduces shortly before the end instead of the one used and constantly observed until then is Mode 12 in Glarean's numbering—hence, the "last" mode. However, if this mode appears precisely at the words "from eternity to eternity," it can only mean that the word "eternity," which means a "last" thing, is to be represented in music by introducing the "last" mode.[7]

Meier uses this piece as evidence that Byrd was "an adherent of Glarean's modal theory and [. . .] a master who is not afraid even of an extreme method of word expression." Unfortunately (and uncharacteristically) he does not realize that the edition employs a transposition up a step or that *Gloria patri* is the third part of *Tribue Domine*, a large votive antiphon.[8] As a result, Meier's interpretation of a closing on C as an example of text-painting and as an affirmation of Byrd's adherence to a twelve-mode system is untenable.

Apart from the problems with this example stands the basic issue of whether Byrd's harmonic practices are analogous to Palestrina's or Lasso's. Many composers whose music fits securely within the theoretical framework of modality described by Meier made their modal assignments explicit by publishing modally-ordered sets.[9] Byrd, with exclusive control over the publication of his music, organized his prints by number of voices or type of text, never by modal order with clear distinctions between authentic and plagal in eight or twelve categories. Scholars have tried to find other patterns—grouping by final, palindromic organization, circle of fifths—but in my view none shows the consistency necessary for an air-tight case.[10]

The other modal approach, by far the most common critical language in use today, I call "neo-modal," for want of a better term. It is a modern hybrid that reduces Glarean's twelve modes to five transposable scale-types: Dorian, Phrygian, Mixolydian, Aeolian, and Ionian (ex. 1).

EXAMPLE 1 "Neo-Modal" system

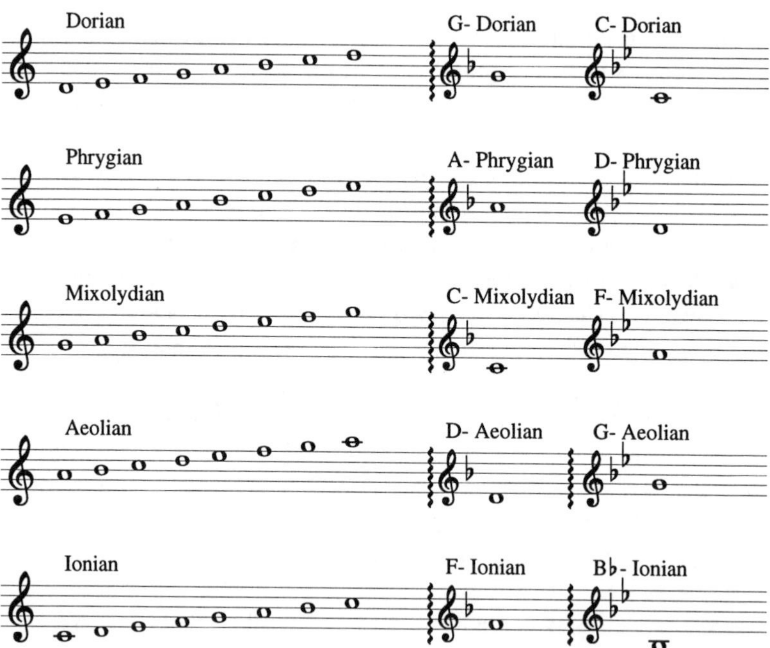

It eliminates the Lydian, which in practice is nearly always found with a B♭ and thus duplicates the Ionian; in some formulations, it eliminates a distinction between authentic and plagal.[11] H. K. Andrews provides the most thoroughgoing application of this approach to the music of Byrd.[12] He lists the number of occurrences of each "mode" (scale-type) in Byrd's publications.[13] Essential to his approach is the notion that each scale-type can exist in several transpositions (his terminology is "transposed Aeolian with one flat in the signature" or "D-Aeolian"). Andrews' book continues to be influential: nearly all of the most respected critics of Byrd's music employ this "neo-modal" approach.[14]

The absence of these concepts in English theory of the time means that scholars have had to identify characteristics that differentiate one scale-type or "mode" from another by studying the music.[15] For example, Neighbour, Kerman, and Andrews all arrive at somewhat different ideas about the distinctions between Dorian and Aeolian. Thus, Neighbour focuses on the lack of emphasis of the sixth degree in Dorian in contrast with Aeolian.[16] Kerman's view of the distinction between Aeolian and Dorian also concerns the sixth degree, focusing on whether or not it is altered. As I understand his argument, an important melodic characteristic of Dorian pieces is the fluidity in the treatment of the sixth degree (B♭ / B♮), while true Aeolian pieces make little use of the sharpened sixth degree.[17] Andrews, in contrast, relies to a great extent on characteristic species of fourth and fifth, as well as on cadence distribution and melodic formulae.[18]

Kerman changes his mind about the modal assignment of *Emendemus in melius*. In a path-breaking analysis published in 1963 and still rightly regarded as one of the best examples of critical writing about Renaissance music, Kerman describes the piece: "Byrd's Aeolian mode is G minor, somehow or other biassed."[19] By his 1981 volume on the masses and motets, he believes that *Emendemus in melius* should be thought of as Dorian.[20] He writes:

> The point is worth making [i.e., about the character of the Dorian mode discussed above] if we wish to employ the concept of mode as a means of distinguishing between the actual sound of certain groups of compositions, rather than as a purely taxonomic device. *Libera me Domine de morte aeterna* and *Emendemus in melius* must be aligned with Dorian compositions such as *Libera me Domine et pone me juxta te*, not with Aeolian ones ending on A[. . . .] It is a secondary question whether Byrd assented to Glarean's analysis and terminology and would actually have called this music 'Aeolian'. Whatever he called it, the essential point is that in the early and middle years there is a real difference between his motets in A on the one hand, and those in G with signatures of (generally) two flats on the other. Motets in A exhibit none of the flexibility with regard to the sixth degree that characterizes motets in G.[21]

The fact that a critic as perceptive as Kerman can change his mind about the assignment should raise questions about the validity of the approach.[22]

All of the writers who employ neo-modal terminology also use tonal terminology as well: tonics and dominants, modulations to the flat side of the circle of fifths, Roman numerals, etc.[23] Thus, for example, Kerman identifies the cadences in *Emendemus in melius* as I, V, III, IV. In a sense, they are continuing the early tradition of writing about Byrd, inherited from Fellowes, Howes, and others. By calling a piece ending on G with two flats in the signature G-Aeolian instead of G minor they are claiming authenticity through a supposed proximity to Byrd that the terminology does not possess.

Carl Dahlhaus offers brief but telling arguments against both modal and tonal approaches in a little-known passage from his *Studies on the Origin of Harmonic Tonality*.[24] He notices that the C pieces and G pieces in the 1588 print of *Psalmes, Sonnets and Songs* cadence on the same four degrees: C, D, G, and A. "A harmonically tonal interpretation" of the cadence degrees would mean that in "C major" Byrd could modulate to VI but not to IV, while in "G major" he could do only the reverse (IV but not VI).[25]

Dahlhaus uses the same print to argue against a traditional modal interpretation. He notes Byrd's practice of cadencing on D in pieces ending on C, a choice at odds with the prevailing modal practices on the continent. In traditional modal theory, D would be foreign to the mode, to be used only fleetingly and for specific reasons such as word-painting. Instead, Dahlhaus finds D to be a regular feature, not associated with any distinctive texts.

> In Byrd's c-mode, the d-clausula does not appear where the text speaks of mistakes and troubles, nor does the disposition of the clausulas allow one to conclude that Byrd perceived those clausulas which modal theory would classify as "*impropriae*" as deviations toward what is exceptional and remote. In his c-mode, the d-clausula stands with equal rank alongside the c- and g-clausulas.[26]

Dahlhaus concludes that a traditional modal interpretation is out of the question and instead advocates an idiosyncratic approach—neither modal nor tonal—that employs the idea of "component keys" or "component modes" (*Teiltonarten*), in which cadence degrees are "related primarily to each other and not to a fixed center."[27] The possibilities of this approach, standing as it does well outside the mainstream of Byrd criticism, have yet to be explored.

The problem, as I see it, is that none of these approaches employs concepts derived from theoretical writings that originated at approximately the same time and in the same geographical area as the music itself. Byrd surely did not employ the kind of modality we associate with Lasso or Palestrina, and still less either the modern version—"neo-modality"—or tonality. I believe that close reading of contemporary English theory can provide some of the elements on which a historically grounded critical approach could be based.

The theoretical evidence falls into three main categories. The first, and most important for this study, consists of published—or manuscript—treatises about "practicall musicke," whose aim is to teach the art of singing (the notes and their names, notation of pitch and rhythm, solmization) and elementary counterpoint (often referred to as "descant").[28] A second category consists of psalm books, published in large numbers from 1561 on.[29] Some of them contain brief anonymous prefaces or instructions to aid the musically illiterate reader; many employ a system of notation in which the solmization syllable is attached to the note on the staff. A third category, which like the second was directed toward musical amateurs, consists of instrumental tutors.[30] (See table 1.)

All of the writers listed in table 1 assumed education as their purpose and goal—either explicitly or implicitly; their aim was to teach beginners. And so their writing needs to be viewed in the larger context of the transformation of English educational practices during this tumultuous time of religious strife.[31] It is no accident that all of the sources under consideration here date from the reign of Elizabeth or later: their very existence was due to changes in musical education that created "a new kind of market [. . .] for a new kind of musical source, the comprehensive book, such as Morley's *Plain and Easy Introduction.*"[32]

The major figures—in chronological order, according to date of publication—are William Bathe; the anonymous author of *The Pathway to Musicke*; Thomas Morley; Thomas Ravenscroft; Thomas Campion; and Charles Butler. The five whose names we know reflect a curious cross-section of musical interests.[33] Only Thomas Morley (1557 or 1558–1602) and Thomas Ravenscroft (by 1590–1638)—both composers and performers—had careers as professional musicians. Thomas Campion (1567–1630) was a poet and composer who made his living as a physician.[34] William Bathe (1564–1614) was an Irish gentleman-scholar interested in music both as an intellectual and as a performer; his two treatises date from his early years (the first published when he was only twenty years old and a student at Oxford, the second probably not much later). He would later leave England and become a Jesuit. Charles Butler (c. 1560–1647) was a parish priest and author of a treatise on bee-keeping (*The Feminine Monarchie, or a Treatise Concerning Bees*, 1609) as well as a grammar advocating reform of English orthography (*English Grammar*, 1633).

Despite the more than five decades—1584 to 1636—that separate Bathe's and Butler's publications, four of the five writers were born within a decade of one another (Ravenscroft was of a younger generation), and may have traveled in some of the same circles. Three were at Oxford in the 1580s: Morley, the oldest of the five, received his B.Mus. in 1588; Bathe was certainly there in 1584 until as late as 1586, probably at St. John's College;[35] Butler (who described himself as "Magd. *Master of Arts*") was at Magdalen Hall from 1579 until 1593 (he received his B.A.

Table 1 Selected Writings on Elementary Music Theory Written or Published in England c. 1560–1640

Author	Title	Date
anonymous	"A Shorte Introduction into the Science of Musicke," in *The Whole Book of Psalms*	1561 and subsequent editions
anonymous	"To the Reader," in *The Whole Books of Psalms*	1569 and subsequent editions
Adrian Le Roy	*A Briefe and Plaine Instruction to Set All Musicke of Eight Divers Tunes in Tableture for the Lute*	Brown 1574$_2$
P. Delamotte	*A Brief Introduction to Music*	1574; lost
William Bathe	*A Brief Introduction to the True Art of Music*	1584; preserved in ms
William Bathe	*A Briefe Introduction to the Skill of Singing*	extant print is undated but may date from 1592 or later (see Appendix)
anonymous	*The Pathway to Musicke*	1596
Thomas Morley	*A Plaine and Easie Introduction to Practicall Musicke*	1597
John Dowland, trans.	*Andreas Ornithoparcus his Micrologus, or Introduction, containing the Art of Singing...*	1609
Thomas Ravenscroft	"Treatise of Musicke"	c. 1610, unpublished; London, British Library, Add. 19758
John Coperario	"Rules How to Compose"	c. 1610, unpublished; San Marino, Huntington Library
Thomas Campion	*A New Way of Making Fowre Parts in Counterpoint*	c. 1613
Thomas Ravenscroft	*A Brief Discourse of the true (but neglected) use of charactering the Degrees*	1614
Charles Butler	*The Principles of Musick*	publ. 1636; written earlier?

in 1583 and M.A. in 1587).[36] Another connection was Gray's Inn, one of the inns of court in London where gentlemen's sons studied law and the finer aspects of the courtier's life: Campion, after three years at Peterhouse, Cambridge, went to Gray's Inn in 1586, when he was nineteen, and stayed until 1591;[37] Bathe registered in 1589.[38] The Inns of Court in some ways resembled intellectual academies and served as well as venues for musical and theatrical performances, especially masques.[39] These connections may or may not be significant. But given what I see as the common threads that run through most of the treatises it makes sense to read their texts in light of one another, both for what they share and for what is distinctive.

In the following sections of this study, I will first consider the concepts associated with "naming": basic topics such as the gamut, clefs and signatures, scales and solmization. I will then address higher order concepts such as tone, key, and air. Within each, I discuss the theoretical evidence in chronological order, while trying at the same time to bring out the distinctive characteristics of English theory.

* * *

"NAMING"

"Naming," Bathe's title for the first chapter of his primer, is the most fundamental and basic aspect of any theoretical system. English theorists resemble their counterparts on the continent (particularly Italy and Germany) in presenting the tonal system as the traditional gamut: a combination of the first seven letters of the alphabet (differentiated by octave through the use of capital, lowercase or double lowercase letters—from Γ to ee) and six hexachord syllables (*ut, re, mi, fa, sol, la*). They invariably use both *littera* and *vox* (for example, *C sol fa ut*) to refer to pitches in the texts of their treatises. Beneath this apparent similarity, however, lie striking differences in solmization and in pitch collections as defined by the presence or absence of one or more flats at the beginning of each staff—what we now call key signatures (Morley refers to them as "flat cliffes").[40]

On the continent, writers generally explain that the gamut is a "universal" scale, built from all three hexachords and thus containing both B *fa* (♭) and B *mi* (♮). They divide the universal scale into two "particular" scales. The scale with no key signature, based on the C and G hexachords, is usually referred to as *cantus durus* or *scala duralis*. The one with a B♭ signature, based on the C and F hexachords, is called *cantus mollis* or *scala mollaris*. Theorists sometimes recognize a third scale, with two flats, called *cantus fictus*, but its status is clearly inferior to the two main scales, *cantus durus* and *cantus mollis*.[41] Note that "scale" in this sense means the collection of pitches defined by the hexachords and by the "key" signature.[42]

In contrast, many of the English writers routinely set forth three scales, usually as the by-product of their rules for teaching students how to solmize. (See table 2a.) The rules for—and indeed the practice of—solmization differ somewhat from theorist to theorist, but the underlying concept of scale is remarkably similar. In contrast to continental practices, which give rules for mutating between hexachords (for example, notes are sung differently depending on whether the line is ascending or descending), in England the key signature usually determines the solmization, and in fact affixes particular syllables to particular pitches.[43] The decision about how many syllables to use—only four, usually four but with occasional additions of a fifth and sixth syllable, six, or seven—occurs within the context of the near-universal adoption of a system employing three scales (no flat, one flat, two flats), in practice if not always in theory.

To see in greater detail how the English theoretical system presents the concepts associated with naming, we can begin with the earliest and in many ways clearest of the writers, William Bathe. As we shall see, his ideas—or at least the ideas he expresses—resonate during the entire period.[44]

Bathe sets forth the tonal system ("the Scale of Musick, which is called Gamut") with its "letters and sillables" at the beginning of his treatise (fig. 1).[45] The beginner must "know, wherein every key standeth, whether in rule or in space: and how many Cliefes, how many Notes is contayned in every Key." Bathe's gamut differs from others frequently encountered. For example, Morley (fig. 2) sets forth seven "deductiones," hexachords arrayed on the system in order from low to high.[46] Bathe distributes the syllables ("notes") into three columns, making it easy to see which syllables are associated with each letter ("key"), and whether the letter has one, two or three syllables, but hard to see the hexachords.

Bathe does not use the word hexachord.[47] He simply states: "There bee sixe names, Ut, Re, Mi, Fa, Sol, La." He refers neither to the three different kinds of hexachords (i.e., on C, G, or F) nor to mutation; in fact, in this part of the discussion the syllables are not tied to any pitches. His illustration shows a scale with eight syllables: *ut re mi fa sol la fa ut* (see fig. 1).The repetition of *fa* as the seventh syllable comes close to creating a seven-syllable solmization system, and the use of *ut* to show octave duplication implies nearly a one-to-one relationship between *littera* and *vox*. If we assume a c2 clef, then both *ut*s are G, and all the remaining syllables except for *fa* have their own letter (*re*=A, etc.).

Bathe uses what he calls the "rule of *ut*" to teach solmization.

> There be three places, in one of which the *ut* must alwaies be: that is to say, [1] in *G* which is *Gamut* and *G sol re ut*, when there is no flat [2] in *C*, which is *C fa ut*, *C sol fa ut*, and *C sol fa*, when there is a flat in *b mi*, or *b fa b mi*. [3] In *F* which is

TABLE 2A Terminology for "Scales"

Author, Title	Name (general)	Name (no flats)	Name (one flat)	Name (two flats)
Bathe, ... *Skill of Song*	[key]	ut in G	ut in C	ut in F
anon, *The Pathway*	scales	sharpe [C, G hex]	flat [F, C hex]	—
Morley	property	sharp	flat	[no name]
Ravenscroft, "Treatise"	property	# quare	properchant	b molle
Campion	—	sharpe in Bemi	flat Gamut	flat in Elami
Coperario	—	—	flatt in Bfabmi	—
Butler	scala	scala duralis (MI=B)	scala naturalis	scala mollaris

TABLE 2B Terminology for "Hexachords"

Author, Title	Name (general)	G	C	F
anon., "A Shorte Introduction"	vii deductions	ut in G	ut in C	ut in fa, sing fa in bfa#mi
anon, *The Pathway to Musicke*	songs	sharp	naturall	flat
Morley	property; deductio ("prima sex vocum deductio")	b quarre	properchant	b molle
Ravenscroft (text and figure)	property	# quare	properchant	b molle
(figure only)	—	sharp	naturall	flat

FIGURE 1 Bathe, *A Briefe Introduction to the Skill of Song*, sig.Aiv[v] (by permission of the Houghton Library, Harvard University)

Rules of Song.

The Scale of Muſick, which is called Gam-vt, conteineth 10 rules, and as many ſpaces; and is ſet downe in letters and ſillables, in which you muſt beegin at the loweſt word, Gam-vt, and ſo go vpwards to the end ſtill aſcending, and learne it perfectly without booke, to ſay it forwards and backewards: to know, wherein euery key ſtandeth, whether in rule or in ſpace: and how many Cliefes, how many Notes is contayned in euery Key.

Hie. Middeſt. Low.

ee	la			1 Note	
dd	la	ſol		2 Notes	
cc	ſol	fa		2 Notes	
bb	fa	b-mi		2 Notes	2 Cliffes
aa	la	mi	re	3 Notes	
g	ſol	re	vt	3 Notes	
f	fa	Vt		2 Notes	
e	la	mi		2 Notes	
d	la	ſol	re	3 Notes	
c	ſol	fa	vt	3 Notes	
b	fa	b-mi		2 Notes	2 Cliffes
a	la	mi	re	3 Notes	
G	ſol	re	vt	3 Notes	
F	fa	vt		2 Notes	
E	la	mi		2 Notes	
D	ſol	re		2 Notes	
C	fa	vt		2 Notes	
B	mi			1 Note	
A	re			1 Note	
Γ	vt			1 Note	

For Naming. Cap. primo.

There bee ſixe names, Vt, Re, Mi, Fa, Sol, La.
The order of aſcention & deſcention with them is thus.

vt re mi fa sol fa fa vt fa fa sol fa mi re vt.

Exceptions

FIGURE 2 Morley, *A Plaine and Easie Introduction*, 2
(by permission of the Houghton Library, Harvard University)

Keyes	Key				Notes
Double or Treble keyes.	ee	*la*		*la*	1 note.
	dd	*la ſol*		*ſol la*	2 notes.
	cc	*ſol fa*		*fa ſol*	2 notes.
	bb	*fa*♮*mi*		*mi fa*	2 notes, 2 cliffes.
	aa	*la mi re*		*re mi la*	3 notes.
	g	*ſol re vt*	Septima vt prima.	*vt re ſol*	3 notes.
	f	*fa vt*	Sexta vt tertia.	*vt fa*	2 notes.
	e	*la mi*		*mi la*	2 notes.
Meane keyes.	d	*la ſol re*		*re ſol la*	3 notes.
	c	*ſol fa vt*	Quinta vt ſecunda.	*vt fa ſol*	3 notes.
	b	*fa*♮*mi*		*mi fa*	2 notes, 2 cliffes.
	a	*la mi re*		*re mi la*	3 notes.
Graue or Baſe keyes.	G	*ſol re vt*	Quarta vt prima.	*vt re ſol*	3 notes.
	F	*fa vt*	Tertia deductio.	*vt fa*	2 notes.
	E	*la mi*		*mi la*	2 notes.
	D	*ſol re*		*re ſol*	2 notes.
	C	*fa vt*	Secunda deductio.	*vt fa*	2 notes.
	♮	*mi*		*mi*	1 note.
	A	*re*		*re*	1 note.
	Γ	*vt*	Prima ſex vocum deductio.	*vt*	1 note.

Phi.

> *F fa ut*, when there are two flats, one in *b mi* or *b fa b mi*, the other in *E la mi*, or *E la* (sig. Avi^r^).[48]

His example (ex. 2) shows three seven-note scales, which I supply with solmization syllables in accordance with his earlier explanation. The position of the *ut* (and thus of the other syllables) is determined by the key signature, and of course by the clef as well (I will skip over his explanation of the clefs). When there is no flat, the *ut* is G, one flat C, two flats F, or in his words:

> No b flat, the (*ut*) in G. The b flat in b onely, the (*ut*) in C. The b flat in b and E, the (*ut*) in F.

This explanation makes clear that Bathe conceives of three scales—no flat, one flat, and two flat—even though he does not employ any term to refer to what I am calling scale (see table 2a). He includes a fourth scale in an example, though not in his prose explanation. In the eighth and final rule for determining the placement of *ut,* Bathe allows for *ut* on B♭: "if there commeth two b.b. being a second a sunder, the upper taketh place [i.e., is *ut*], which chanceth very rare" (sig. Avi^v^). The example has signature flats on B, E, and A.

EXAMPLE 2 Bathe, *A Briefe Introduction to the Skill of Song*, sig.Avi^r^, three scales as determined by placement of *ut*

Bathe's scales (ex. 2) are identical in terms of the configuration of half-steps and whole-steps, but otherwise have no other properties that we associate with key or mode. *Ut* is not the tonic or final, nor is the scale represented here meant to explain the pitch content of a composition. The point rather is that in a given scale (that is, as defined by key signature) only one note can be *ut.*[49]

My interpretation contrasts sharply with that of Johnson, who sees Bathe's decision to label as *ut* the syllable an octave above *ut*, rather than as the *sol* of what he calls "Renaissance" theory (I would call it continental) as innovative:

> Bathe's modification of the solmization system reveals his remarkably advanced perception of the concept of key. [. . .] Bathe interprets each of the signatures as definitively indicating a key. A signature of no flats denotes the key of G, one flat the key of C, and two flats the key of F.[50]

The problem is that Johnson links the solmization system to keys: "his addition of a seventh syllable to the hexachord completing the scale and his use of the solmization system for the recognition of keys and modulation display a clear break from hexachordal theory and point to a developing concept of tonality."[51] But *ut* need not be the tonic; it is simply a way to associate syllables with pitches in a particular environment.[52]

Bathe emphasizes the defining function of *ut* only in the opening pages of his textbook in order to teach "naming" (and to illustrate for us the three scales), but once he has finished with the basics, he introduces three "exceptions."[53] He explains that *ut* and *re* are changed to *sol* and *la euphoniae gratiae* ("for the sake of euphony"). On sig. Avi^{v} he allows *ut* for the "base or lowest part in the first place" (presumably the bottom of the staff), but at the end of the volume he provides a comprehensive "A Table of the comparisons of Cliffe, how one followeth another for the naming of Notes: changing (Ut) into (Sol) and (Re) into (La)" that does not use *ut* or *re* at all.[54] Bathe's goal is to show the appropriate syllables on every space and line of the staff—eleven in all—for all possible clefs and for all three kinds of scale. The examples, three of which I present as example 3, employ the four-syllable system generally credited to Campion, not Bathe's earlier sequence *ut re mi fa sol la fa ut*.[55]

Example 3 Bathe, *A Briefe Introduction to the Skill of Song*, sig.D^{r} (fold-out sheet), three scales showing a fixed four-syllable solmization scheme

a. no-flat scale

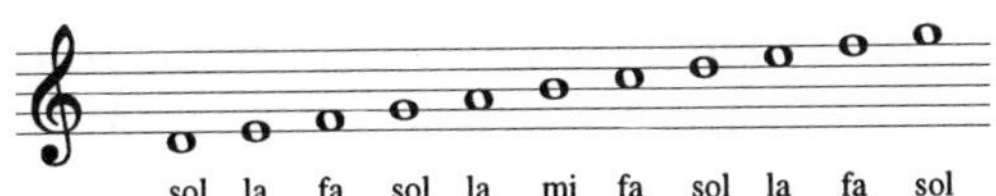

b. one-flat scale

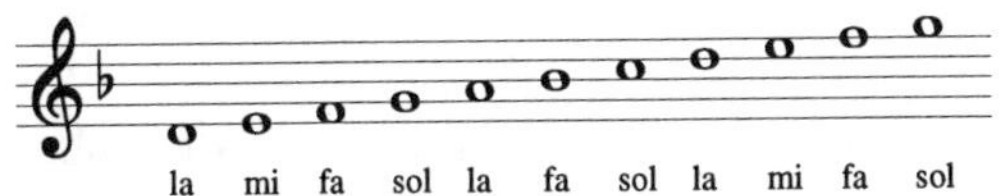

c. two-flat scale

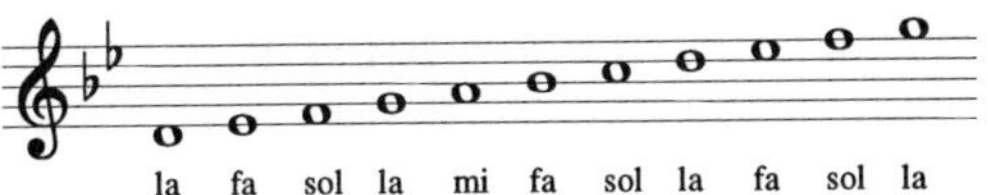

The solmization is "fixed" in that within a given environment (i.e., scale as defined by key signature) particular syllables are always associated with particular pitches: in a no-flat scale all Ds are *sol*, though all *sol*s are not D.

The third exception involves "intermingled" (i.e., added) sharps and flats, which Bathe discusses both in the first section of his treatise ("naming") and the fourth and final section ("tune"). Karnes makes the important observation that flats and sharps behave differently in Bathe's theory.[56] Flats change the *ut* or name (solmization), while sharps change the tune (pitch) without affecting the solmization. In effect the singer is asked to do a kind of mental gymnastics in dealing with sharps: the sharp alters the *ut* by moving it to a position a third below the sharp: F♯ makes the *ut* D, C♯ the *ut* A, G♯ the *ut* E.[57]

Of particular interest in this context is Bathe's notion "the Ut of the Song," that is, the collection of pitches initially determined by the key signature. An intermingled flat alters the *ut* of the song, and in this context Bathe introduces the term "key" not in its meaning of pitch or letter but as pitch collection: changing the *ut* alters the key. He explains by setting up a problem, which I translate into staff notation in example 4:

> Let us suppose, that in the middle of a song which had *fa* in *C sol fa ut* [in other words, the *ut* is G], there came two notes, one in *C sol fa ut*, & another in *B fa b mi*, having a flat before it, then if the latter note in *B fa b mi*, having a flat before it, be not called *fa* it is against the order of the *ut*, which by the solutions should most be kept, if it be named *fa*, then commeth the absurditie proved in the last example: that is, that two places together should have one name [. . .] (sig. Aviii[r]).

EXAMPLE 4 Bathe, *A Briefe Introduction to the Skill of Song*, sig.Aviii[r], hypothetical example of solmization with consecutive *fas*

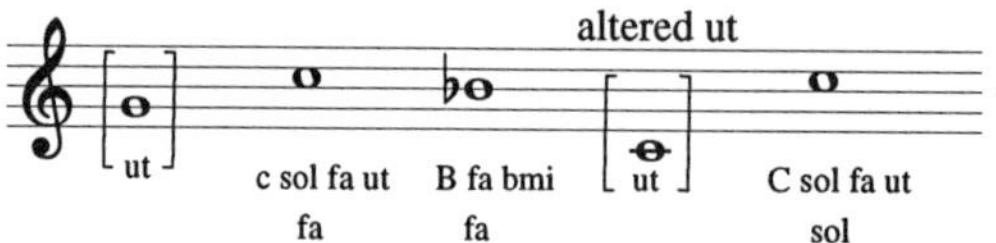

Bathe concludes that it is a necessary absurdity, as he puts it, to have two notes next to one another with the same name. The flat alters the *ut*, causing subsequent Cs to be called *sol*. He continues:

> It is graunted by the last solution, that the flat so comming should alter the *ut*, but to alter the *ut*, doth alter the key (which is in musick a great absurditie) therefore by the last solution, there is a great absurditie graunted.

> [. . .] It is graunted conditionally, that is to say, if the like happened (as in the argument obiected) though sometimes in the middest of a song, to change the key, and come into it againe, is allowed (sig. Aviii^{v}).

Key in this sense has nothing to do with final. A piece begins in one key (scale), goes into another because of the addition of a flat, and then returns to the first key. Bathe provides four examples on sig. Biii^{v}–Biiii^{r} (ex. 5) that include solmization syllables and illustrate the notion of a changing pitch collection.[58]

EXAMPLE 5 Bathe, *A Briefe Introduction to the Skill of Song*, sig.Biii^{v}–Biiii^{r}, examples showing solmization with intermingled flats (possible identification of *ut* added, not in original)

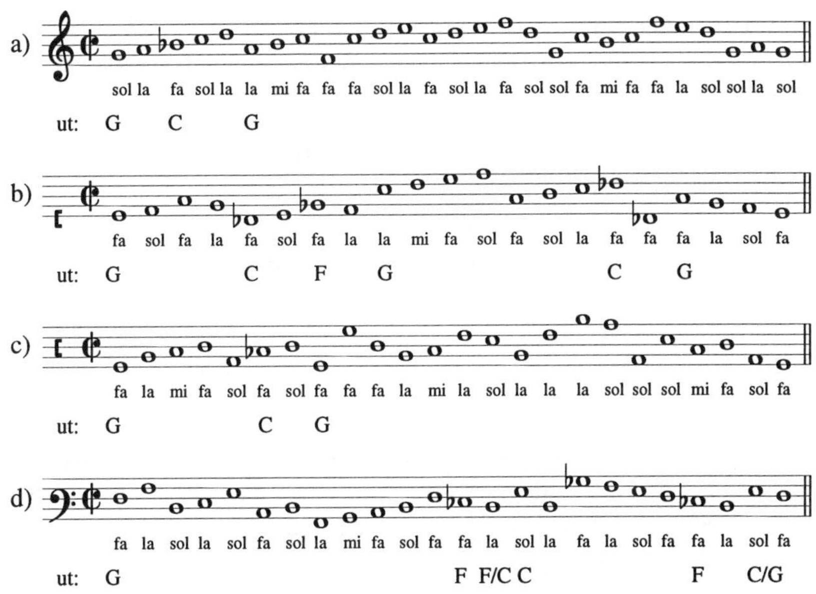

We will see that the concepts explained by Bathe recur in most of the other English writers. Ironically, however, the next surviving treatise published in England, the anonymous *Pathway to Musicke*, published in 1596, presents a continental viewpoint.[59]

The first illustration of the "Gamma-ut" in *The Pathway to Musicke* (sig. Aii^{v}) shows the seven hexachords looking like truncated organ pipes; the hexachords are not named.[60] The second (sig. Aiii^{r}), "the common Scale like the Ladder," is virtually identical to Bathe's gamut, given above.[61] The third (sig. Aiiii^{r}), which could have been taken from Beurhusius, shows the "universal scale," the full gamut with the hexachords labeled “Sharp, Naturall and Flat songs.”[62] The next two figures illustrate the two “particular” scales—also in Beurhusius—the “Sharpe Scale” (consisting of C and G “songs” on sig. Bi^{r}) and the “Flat Scale” (consisting of C and F “songs” on sig. Bi^{v}). He also adopts labels found in German theory that identify the six syllables as pairs: the lower two (*ut* and *re*) “flat,” the middle two (*mi* and *fa*) “meane,” the higher (*sol* and *la*) “sharp” in sound.

The author of *The Pathway*, like Bathe, includes a section on “tune keeping,” which he defines as “a lifting up or letting downe of the voice” (sig. Bii^{v}). His examples (the fourth, from sig. Biii^{r}, is given in ex. 6) of how to tune, that is, how to sing and solmize the various intervals, suggest that he is using the continental system of two scales—*cantus durus* and *cantus mollis*—each employing two overlapping hexachords with mutations between them.

EXAMPLE 6 Anonymous, *The Pathway to Musicke*, sig.Biii^{r}

a. Illustration (sig.Biii^{r}) of the fourth using solmization syllables (labels indicating hexachords added)

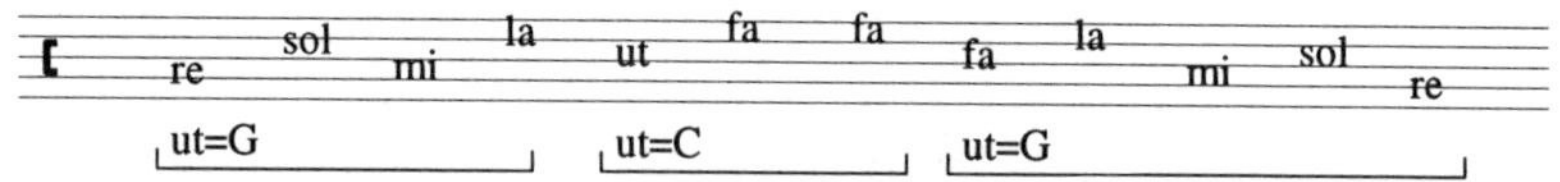

b. Same example, arranged in ascending order

G:	re	mi	fa	sol	la	
C:			ut			fa

All of the other English writers whose treatises are extant employ versions of the concepts explained by Bathe. The best known and most widely disseminated is Thomas Morley’s *A Plaine and Easie Introduction to Practicall Musicke*, published 1597, a year after *The Pathway to Musicke*.[63]

Morley begins with an explanation of the gamut that appears to be drawn nearly word for word from Bathe’s:[64]

Bathe	**Morley**
The Scale of Musick, which is called Gam-ut, conteineth 10 rules, and as many spaces; and is set downe in letters and sillables,	*Master*. I will do so, and therefore behold, here is the Scale of Musicke, which wee terme the *Gam*. *Philomathes*. In deede I see letters and syllables written here, but I doe not understand them nor their order.

in which you must beegin at the lowest word, Gam-ut, and so go upwards to the end still ascending,

and learne it perfectly without booke, to say it forwards and backewards: to know, wherein every key standeth, whether in rule or in space: and how many Cliefes, how many Notes is contayned in every Key (sig. Aiv^{v}).

Ma. For the understanding of this Table, *You must begin at the lowest word* Gam-ut, *and so go upwards to the end still ascending.*[65]
Phi. That I do understand. What is next?
Ma. Then must you get it perfectly without booke, to saie it forwards and backwards. Secondly, *You must learne to knowe, wherein every Key standeth,* that is, whether in rule or in space. And thirdly, *How manie cliefes and how manie notes every Key containeth.*[66]

But that is as far as the overlap with Bathe extends.[67] Morley's explanation of the hexachords, which he calls "the three natures or properties of singing" and "deductio sex vocum," seems to have more in common with the author of *The Pathway* than with Bathe; he identifies the three kinds of hexachord as "*b quarre*, *Properchant*, and *b molle*" (p.4).[68] (See table 2b.)

> *Phi.* What is *b quarre*?
> *Ma.* It is a propertie of singing, wherein *mi* is alwaies song in *b fa ♮ mi*, and is alwayes when you sing *ut* in *Gam ut.*
> *Phi.* What is *Properchant*?
> *Ma.* It is a propertie of singing, wherin you may sing either *fa* or *mi* in *b fa ♮ mi* according as it shalbe marked *b* or thus ♮ and is when the *ut* is in *C fa ut.*
> *Phi.* What *if there be no marke.*
> *Ma. There it is supposed to be sharpe.* ♮
> *Phi.* What is *b molle*?
> *Ma.* It is a propertie of singing, wherein *fa* must alwaies be song in *b fa ♮ mi*, and is when the *ut* is in *F fa ut* (pp. 4–5).

The example (ex. 7, from p. 4) shows three hexachords: G (no signature), C (one flat), and F (also one flat).

Example 7 Morley, *A Plaine and Easie Introduction*, 4, three properties (labels below the staff are not in the original but are taken from Morley's text)

But it soon becomes clear that Morley conflates hexachord and scale, and furthermore that he is uncertain about whether there are two or three scales. (See table 2a.) In the annotations he qualifies his explanation of properties:

> But though, as I said, these three properties be found in plainsong, yet in pricktsong they be but two: that is, either sharp or flat, for where nature is, there no b. is touched (sig. ¶4ʳ).

This passage suggests that Morley is not only shifting the meaning of property from hexachord to system, but in effect employing the *durus-mollis* dichotomy of continental theory in much the way *The Pathway* does.

In fact, the two-flat scale does make several appearances in Morley's treatise.[69] In the final part, he recognizes its usefulness for organists but condemns its use in vocal music:

> but some have brought it from the Organe, and have gone about to bring it in common use of singing with bad successe if they respect their credit, for take me any of their songes, so set downe and you shall not find a musicion (how perfect soever hee be) able to *solfa* it right, because he shall either sing a note in such a key as it is not naturally as *la* in *C sol fa ut*, *sol* in *b fa b my*, *fa* in *a la mi re*, or then hee shall be compelled to sing one note in two several keyes in continual deduction as *fa* in *b fa b mi*, and *fa* in *A la mi re* immediatlie one after another, which is against our very first rule of the singing our sixe notes or tuninges, and as for them who have not practised that kind of songes, the verie sight of those flat cliffes (which stande at the beginning of the verse or line like a paire of staires, with great offence to the eie, but more to the amasing of the yong singer) make them mistearme their notes and so go out of tune (p. 156).

At least in this instance, Morley seems to practice what he preaches: unlike most of his English colleagues, he never uses the two-flat scale in his own music, just the *durus* and *mollis* systems.[70]

The ambivalence about the status of the two-flat scale finds a counterpart in Morley's approach to solmization, which could be characterized as a blend of English and continental approaches. His gamut has the traditional seven hexachords each beginning on *ut*; in practice he recommends that *ut* be used only at the lowest position on the staff ("*except it be in the lowest note of the part wee never use ut*" [p.4]). In Morley's explanation of solmization, the Master wants Philomathes to sing the notes given in ex. 8. Philomathes has no trouble with the first six syllables. At the seventh, *F fa ut*, he must choose between *ut* and *fa*, but the prohibition of *ut* means the choice will be *fa*. This seems a peculiarly English explanation: no continental musician would consider singing *ut* on F in a *cantus durus* context. At the tenth note, *b fa ♮ mi*, the problem is *mi* or *fa*; the absence of a flat in the signature dictates *mi*. Morley has thus constructed a recurring four-syllable pattern (*mi fa sol la fa sol la*) where *mi* occurs only on B and *ut* and *re* are only at the low end of the scale.

EXAMPLE 8 Morley, *A Plaine and Easie Introduction*, 5, solmization of pitches starting from *Gamma ut*, in the sharp (no-flat) scale

On the next page (p. 6) Morley provides three examples of the flat scale. The first (ex. 9) is quite straightforward: C is *ut*, E is *mi*, and the solmization is virtually identical to a typical English four-syllable scheme (for example, Bathe's in ex. 3b). In the second (ex. 10), the identity of the *ut* and of the *mi* is not as clear. As Philomathes first solmized it, the *ut* was on F and there were *mi*s on both A and E.

EXAMPLE 9 Morley, *A Plaine and Easie Introduction*, 6, solmization of pitches starting from *C fa ut* in the flat (one-flat) scale

ut re mi fa sol la fa sol la mi fa

EXAMPLE 10 Morley, *A Plaine and Easie Introduction*, 6, solmization of pitches starting from *F fa ut* in the flat (one-flat) scale.

ut re mi fa sol la mi fa sol la
fa sol la

In response to prompting from the Master, Philomathes recognized that he could change the names of the first three notes (and their "eyghtes") from *ut re mi* to *fa sol la*, which results in a scale identical to the one in example 9 (implied *ut*=C and *mi*=E). The third example (ex. 11) addresses the problem of solmizing notes not in the gamut. The first pitch, *F fa ut*, is below the lowest note of the gamut, *Γ ut.* It can be *ut* or *fa*, since it is an octave below the *fa* that is the lowest note of example 10. Morley's willingness to solmize *F fa ut* as either *ut* or *fa* shows, it seems to me, a continental rather than English approach. Continuing upwards in example 11, the next note is *Γ re*, a syllable not associated with Γ in the gamut, but made possible because the *re* occurs with the G an octave higher. The next problem is how to handle the flat before *E la mi*, which does not regularly have the *fa* required by the flat. The "intermingled" flat changes the normal alternation of whole steps and half steps, in effect changing the *ut* from C to F (to use Bathe's terminology).[71]

EXAMPLE 11 Morley, *A Plaine and Easie Introduction*, 6–7, solmization of pitches starting from FF in the flat (one-flat) scale with intermingled E♭ (labels below the staff derived from Morley's text)

ut re mi fa sol la fa
fa sol la
F fa ut Γ ut A re B mi C fa ut D re sol E la mi

On pages 8 and 9, instead of simple scalar patterns Morley provides melodic exercises that use a variety of clefs and three different signatures. From these examples, it is possible to derive composite scales that resemble those in the table at the end of Bathe's treatise. None of the examples uses *ut*, but instead substitutes other syllables so that in effect Morley uses the four-syllable solmization.[72] The composites of the sharp scale (no flats) and the flat scale (one flat), given in example 12, are identical to Bathe's: each has a singular, unique *mi* (though neither Bathe nor Morley ever says so) and thus a defining *ut* (which Morley uses only in his initial explanation and not in these practice exercises).

EXAMPLE 12 Morley, *A Plaine and Easie Introduction*, 8, composite scales drawn from examples of solmization

a. no-flat scale

b. one-flat scale

The confusion comes in the example of a two-flat scale, shown in example 13. Example 13a shows the notes and syllables in Morley's example; above the staff are my assignments to a scale, either one flat (*ut*=C) or two flats (*ut*=F), in both cases temporarily extended by an intermingled flat (first the E♭, then the A♭, both sung as *fa* outside the prevailing scale).[73] Example 13b reorders the pitches and their syllables from low to high. Below the staff I show the standard fixed solmization scheme found in Bathe and other English writers. Notice Morley solmizes *G sol re ut* as both *sol* and *la*; in other words, despite the two-flat signature, he is alternating in a rather unpredictable way between the one-flat and two-flat scales.

Example 13 Morley, *A Plaine and Easie Introduction*, 9, example of solmization with a two-flat signature

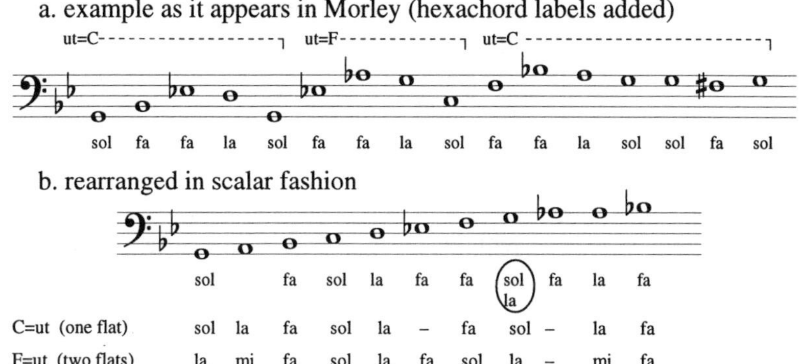

In contrast, there is no ambiguity about either the existence of the two-flat scale or the notion of a fixed solmization scheme in the treatises of Thomas Ravenscroft and Thomas Campion written perhaps a decade or so after *A Plaine and Easie Introduction.*

Ravenscroft's brief "Treatise of Music" is an introduction to music (the gamut, solmization, the intervals, etc.).[74] At first he seems to be following *The Pathway* by showing a gamut with the hexachords labeled "sharp," "naturall" and "flat"; but he also uses Morley's names, "♮quare," "Properchant," and "b Molle."[75] (See table 2b.) Ravenscroft associates "property" with the pitches *F fa ut, C sol fa ut,* and *G sol re ut,* and with the "3 chiefe clifes" (F, c, g). But both from the key signatures he uses (two flats, one flat, no flats) and from his verbal descriptions—

> b Molle signifieth ut in f faut and a b:flat in bfabmi and a flat in E lami. [example has two B♭s and an E♭ in the signature]
>
> Properchant is that which carrieth ut in [C] solfaut: mi in Elami with a b flat in bfabmi. [example has a B♭ in the signature]
>
> ♮quare is called our naturall or chant songe and is knowne by ut in g solreut: mi in bfabmi and la in E lami. [example has no flats in the signature]—

it is clear that property also means scale.[76]

One of the most interesting passages in the treatise is his comparison of English practices of solmization and the "Belgian" practices that he read about in Calvisius.[77] He notes that the Netherlanders have seven names (syllables), while the English have but six or four. Ravenscroft's example of English solmization (ex. 14) uses four syllables, and shows a C–C octave scale with nothing in the signature (*mi*=B).[78]

EXAMPLE 14 Ravenscroft, "Treatise of Musick," f.5r, "English names" (solmization)

Ascendinge

fa sol la fa sol la mi

Descendinge

fa mi la sol fa la sol la

He then presents *his* version of the scales found in Calvisius (ex. 15; the scales as they actually appear in Calvisius are shown in ex. 16). The first of Calvisius' scales (ex. 16a) shows a fixed solmization, one syllable for each pitch class, identical going up or down. Ravenscroft's version (ex. 15a) is virtually identical—he (mistakenly?) uses *mi* instead of *ni* for the seventh syllable, and he only extends his scale for an octave. The second of Calvisius' scales (ex. 16b) is the same as the first except that it is transposed up a fourth and has a flat in the signature; Calvisius is thus employing continental *cantus durus* and *cantus mollis* systems ("regular" and "transposed" in his terminology). His second pair of scales (ex. 16c–d), likewise at both the regular and transposed levels, has a flatted seventh degree, *pa*.

Ravenscroft introduces his second and third scales (ex. 15b–c) as follows:

> Also they have another denominated, which is from E lami (or E la) flat to B mi (or Bfa ♮mi) flat or when either of them cometh on the soddaine or by the property of b Molle.

The second scale (ex. 15b) shows the "soddaine" use of flat (the flat before B means that it is solmized *pa*, while descending without a flat it is *mi*). The third scale (ex. 15c) shows Ravenscroft's version (I would even say, the *English* version) of *b molle*: he has changed Calvisius' *cantus mollis* (with one flat) into a two-flat scale. One could hardly ask for a clearer illustration of the difference between continental and English practices.[79]

One curiosity that seems to have escaped notice is what appears to be a carelessly written draft of a melody found on f. 19v and bearing Ravenscroft's name

Example 15 Ravenscroft, "Treatise of Musick," f. 5v, "Belgiol names" (solmization)

a. no-flat scale

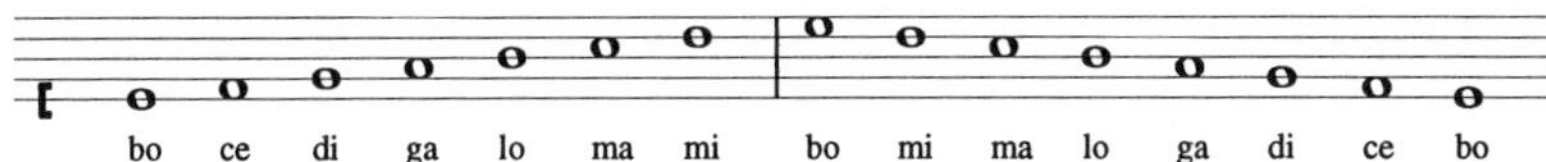

b. scale with intermingled flat ascending, natural descending

c. two-flat scale

Example 16 Calvisius, *Exercitationes musicae duae*, 122–23, "Belgian" solmization

a. *cantus durus*

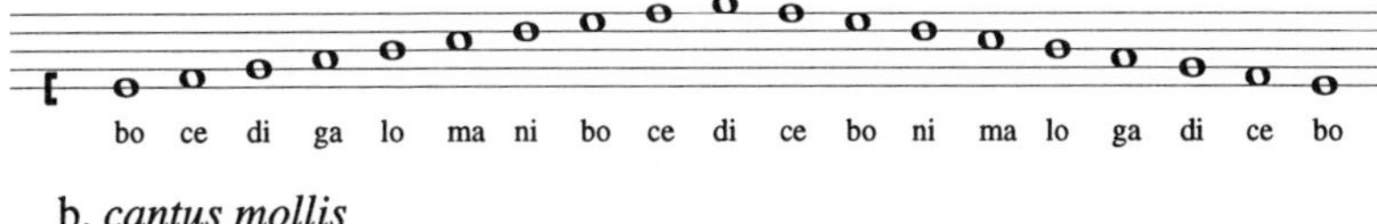

b. *cantus mollis*

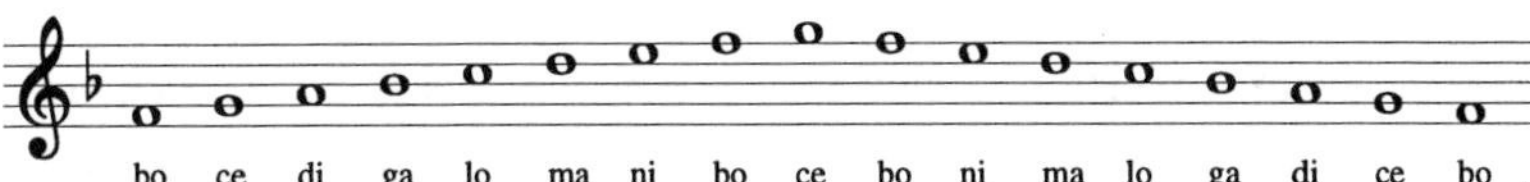

c. *cantus durus* ("in regulari") with added flat

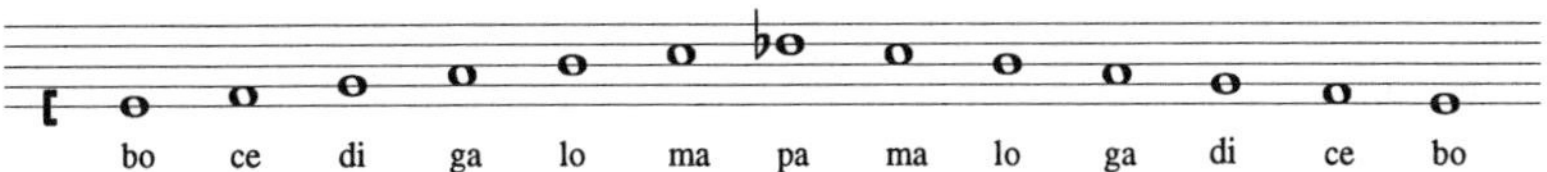

d. *cantus mollis* ("aut in transposito") with added flat

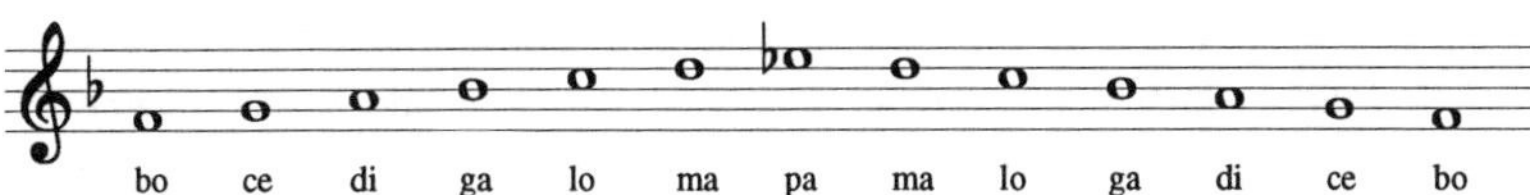

("Thomas Ravζ"). (See fig. 3 and ex. 17.) The tune, which I did not find among Ravenscroft's published music, employs four solmization syllables, usually abbreviated to the first letter, instead of a text (there may be a "hay how" in measure 2). This draft may prove to be a rare instance of a composer autograph that contains solmization syllables.[80] Ravenscroft's description of English solmization (given in ex. 14) and this tune are both in the same (no-flat) scale and thus employ the same solmization scheme. Example 14 goes from c to cc, while example 17 from g to ff; a juxtaposition of the two points out the independence of the system of naming (solmization derived from one of the three scales, in the sixteenth-century sense) from modern concepts of key or scale.

EXAMPLE 17 London, British Library, Add. 19758, f. 19v, Ravenscroft, autograph (?) draft of a melody with solmization syllables

Thomas Campion, whose treatise dates from approximately the same time as Ravenscroft's, describes the same three scales as Ravenscroft and Bathe, but gives them different names. Campion is usually credited with inventing a way of solmizing that uses just four syllables, but we now know that this practice was in use at least since the time of Bathe, and probably a decade earlier, to judge from the early psalm books.[81] Campion himself makes no such claim: his focus, as his title suggests, is on *A New Way of Making Fowre Parts in Counter-point, by a Most Familiar, and Infallible Rule*. In fact, he places his brief comments about scales and solmization in the preface:

> In like manner there can be no greater hinderance to him that desires to become a Musition, then the want of the true understanding of the Scale, which proceeds from the errour of the common Teacher, who can doe nothing without the old *Gam-ut* in which there is but one Cliffe, and one Note, and yet in the same Cliffe he will sing *re* and *sol*. It is most true that the first invention of the *gam-ut* was a

FIGURE 3 London, British Library, Add. 19758, f. 19v, Ravenscroft, autograph(?) draft of a melody with solmization syllables (by permission of The British Library)

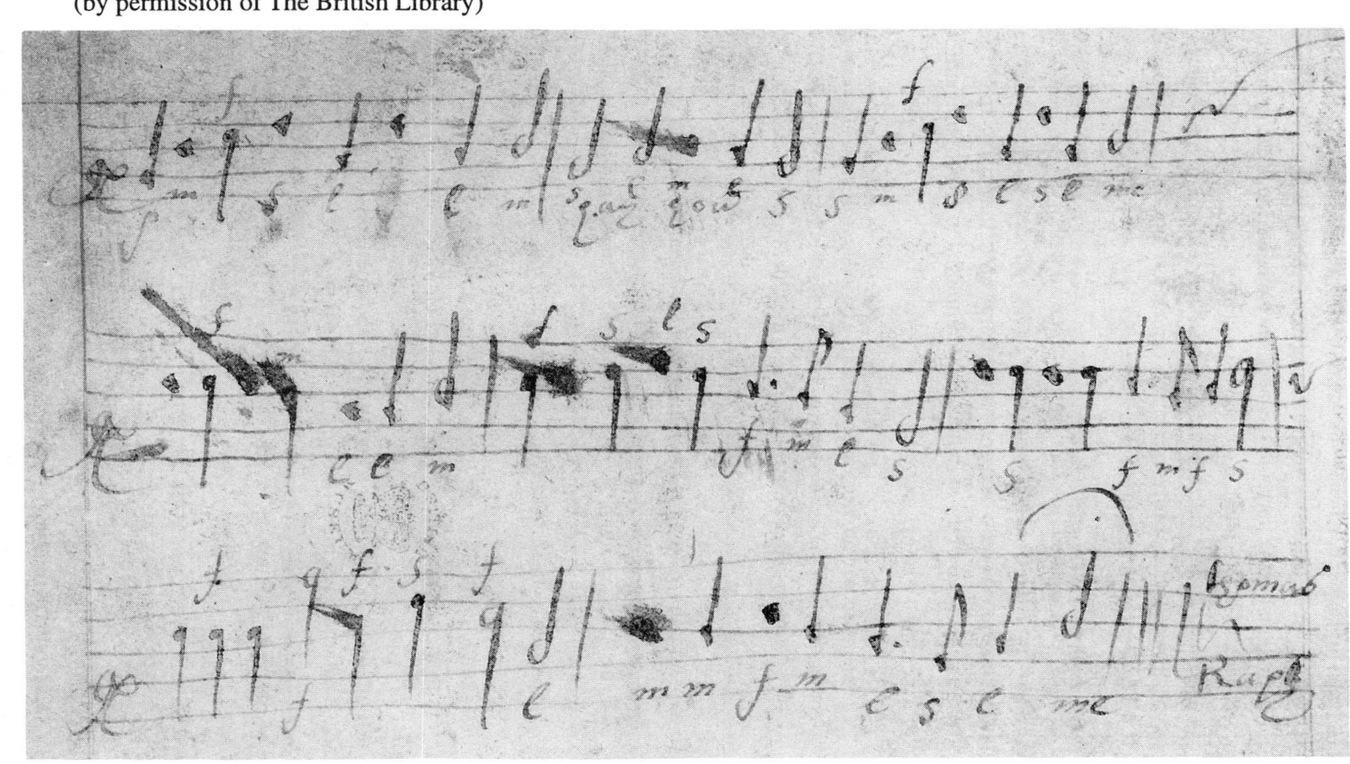

> good invention; but then the distance of Musicke was cancelled within the number of twenty Notes, so were the sixe Notes properly invented to help youth in vowelling; but the liberty of the latter age hath given Musicke more space both above and below, altering thereby the former naming of the Notes, the curious observing whereof hath bred much unnecessary difficultie to the learner, for the Scale may be more easily and plainely exprest by foure Notes, then by sixe, which is done by leaving out *Ut* and *Re*.[82]

The old gamut worked fine for music that stayed within the range of twenty pitches, but the expansion of tonal space made it a good idea to find a different way for naming the notes, one which does not employ more than one syllable per note, and dispenses with two of the syllables. For Campion, the crux of the naming system is the half-step:

> The substance of all Musicke, and the true knowledge of the scale, consists in the observations of the halfe note, which is expressed either by *Mi Fa*, or *La Fa*, and they being knowne in their right places, the other Notes are easily applyed unto them.

To explain solmization he gives three different scales:

> To illustrate this I will take the common key which we call *Gam-ut*, both sharpe in *Bemi* and flat, as also flat in *Elami*, and shew how with ease they may be expressed by these foure Notes, which are *Sol, La, Mi, Fa*.

His example consists of the three scales that are by now familiar to us (ex. 18). He refers to them as "in the sharpe," "the flat *Gam-ut*," and "this Key as it is flat in *Elami*."[83] (See table 2a.) Coperario, whose manuscript treatise has many passages in common with Campion's and may be dependent on it, follows Campion's practice of naming the scale by the quality of the B or E: "if the song be flatt in Bfabmi."[84]

EXAMPLE 18 Campion, *A New Way*, 325–26, three scales

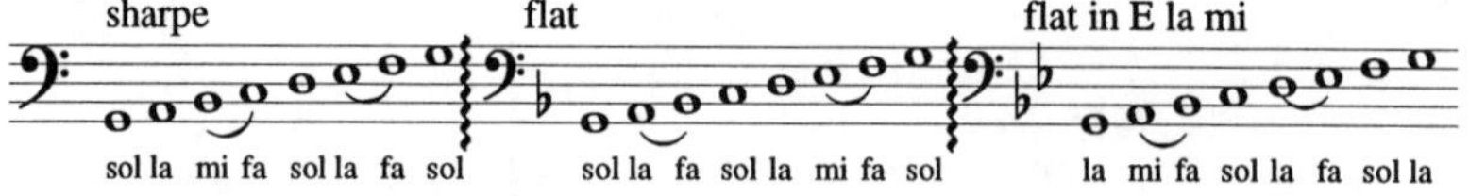

Campion, even more clearly than Bathe, uses key as a synonym of scale. In the passage just cited he writes of the two-flat scale "let us examine this Key as it is flat in *Elami*." Later in the treatise he refers to an example with two flats in the signature, then continues by imagining the same example notated with no flats. His words are: "But if the same Base had beene set in the sharpe key" (p. 336).

Campion's solmization, in contrast to Bathe's and Morley's, completely eliminates *ut* and *re*. He offers short-cuts that teach the beginner how to use the four-syllable system, for example, "if the lowest [halfe Note] be *Mi Fa*, the upper halfe Note is *La Fa*" (and vice versa) or "above *Fa*, ever to sing *Sol*, and to sing *Sol* ever under *La*" (p. 325). In effect, they illustrate important properties of the tonal system.

The final witness in this survey, Charles Butler, though a contemporary of Bathe's and Campion's, published his *Principles of Musik* in 1636, when he was in his seventies. He employs an odd and idiosyncratic solmization that in many ways hearkens back to Bathe.[85] He acknowledges that "vulgar" musicians use a four-syllable solmization—

> These Names though they be still taught in Schooles, (according to the first institution,) among other Principles of the Art; yet the modern vulgar practice doth commonly change *ut* and *re*, the one into *sol*, the other into *la*: so that, for the 7 several Notes, they use but 4 several Names[86]—

but he prefers to employ six:

> For the 7 Notes, there are but six several Names: [*Ut*, *re*, *MI*, *fa*, *sol*, *la*.] The seventh Note, because it is but a half-tone above *la*, as the fourth is above *MI*; (whereas the rest are all wholetones) is fitly called by the same Name: the which being added, the next Note will be an Eight or Diapason to the first; and consequently placed in the same Letter or Clief, and called by the same Name (p. 12).

While he says that he uses *six* syllables, his scale and diagram both show a seventh, spelled *pha*, which he explains in his endnotes (ex. 19):

> But because (as is above said) this seventh Note is but a *Semitonium* from his inferior *La*, as the fourth is from his inferior *MI*; questionless it is best, and most easy for the Learners, to call them both (as the manner now is) by the same Name: although the second halfe-note may, for difference from the first, be written *pha*: which is the first syllable of *Pharos*, the name of an high tower, and of an upper garment; as this second *Hemitonium* is the uppermost and highest of all the seven Notes (p. 15).

Butler thus accomplishes something that Bathe was unable to, namely distinguishing (at least by spelling if not by pronunciation) between the fourth and seventh notes and creating a system with a one-to-one relationship between letter and syllable, at least within a given scale (thus in ex. 19, in the scale with no flats in the signature all Gs are *ut* and only G is *ut*).[87] Like Bathe, he too lays out three scales, but unlike Bathe, who lets the *ut* determine the scale, he relies on *MI*:

> [. . .] there are also in the Scale to be noted 3 MI-cliefs: [B, E, and A:] so called, because in one of these 3, is placed the Master-note MI, by which the names of all other Notes (as before is shewed) are known.
>
> To know which of these 3 Cliefs hath the *MI* in the present song, First, by the Signed clief, looke out the next *B*: where, if you find not a Flat, is his place: if the Flat put him out thence; looke him in *E:* where you shall have him; unless the Flat likewise (which happeneth seldom) do remove him: and then his place is certainly in *A* (p. 14).

MI, the "Master-note" that often appears in capital letters, functions as his way of defining the scale.

EXAMPLE 19 Butler, *The Principles of Musik*, 12, solmization

ut re MI fa sol la pha ut re MI fa etc.

Butler explains further in the annotations (see fig. 4, and ex. 20, which realizes the lower portion of the gamut in staff notation):

> Of the 3 *MI-cliefs*, the Scale is threefold.
>
> *Scala* — *Duralis*
> *Naturalis*
> *Mollaris.*
>
> The Dural, or sharp, hath no Flat marked: and his *Ut* is in *G*. The Natural hath one Flat: and his *Ut* in *C*. The Mollar or Flat hath 2 Flats and his *Ut* in *F*. As it is in the olde Verse:
>
> *In G Dural, in C Natural, F quoque Mollar* (pp. 21–22).[88]

Bathe is using the familiar names for the hexachords (duralis in Latin, dural or sharp in English) but now representing the three scales. He defines the scales by the key signature, the placement of the *ut,* and the placement of the *MI.* He even admits a fourth scale (when the *MI* is on D); as we saw with Bathe, the *ut* is B♭ and the signature has three flats.[89]

EXAMPLE 20 Butler, *The Principles of Musik*, 19, three scales

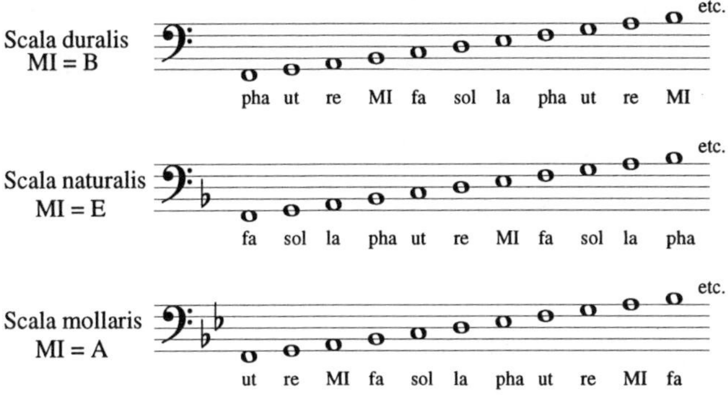

English music theory from the end of the sixteenth and beginning of the seventeenth centuries presents a remarkably consistent profile. With the exception of the anonymous author of *The Pathway*, whom Morley criticized for "filching" from German theory texts, and the other translations of continental theory, all of the writers recognize the existence of three scales, each with its own "key signature": no flats, one flat, two flats. While Morley condemns the practice of using more than one "flat cliffe," his comments suggest that the practice was in fact prevalent in England, though not on the continent.

The scales are defined by several different methods: for example, the position of *ut* (Bathe); the signature (Ravenscroft); the position of *MI* (Butler); the quality of the B and E (Campion, Ravenscroft); or some combination of these features And they are called by several names: ♯quarre, properchant, flat; duralis, naturalis, mollaris; sharp, naturall, flat; and the kind of B and E. But regardless of definition or name, the basic content is identical.

Each scale is associated with one of several possible systems of solmization, shown in example 21. While the number of syllables employed can vary from four to six or seven, the fundamental principles of solmization remain constant.[90] Solmization is fixed, with a complete or near-complete congruence between syllable and pitch class. There is no need to think in terms of hexachords or to invoke the principle of mutation. Syllables keep the same name whether the line ascends or descends. All of the systems employ octave duplication.

At root, these three scales with their fixed solmization schemes are ways of naming pitches. They are independent of the finals (i.e., lowest sounding pitch of the final sonority) of compositions. Thus, the scale with *ut*=G/no flat in the signature/*mi*=B can be used for compositions ending on G, D, C, etc.

Scholars have often been struck by the use of the octave to illustrate the scales, which seems to suggest a version of our own scale (for example, a major scale). In

FIGURE 4 Butler, *The Principles of Musik*, 19
(by permission of the Houghton Library, Harvard University)

Cap. II. §II. *Of* de *Nam's of Not's.* 19

But if de rigt Nam's of de Not's wer' affixed to deir Keyz in deir natural order, as dey follow *Mi* in every of his 3 Cliefs, [*B*, *E*, and *A*;] den wold' dis bee de tru' form of de Scal'.

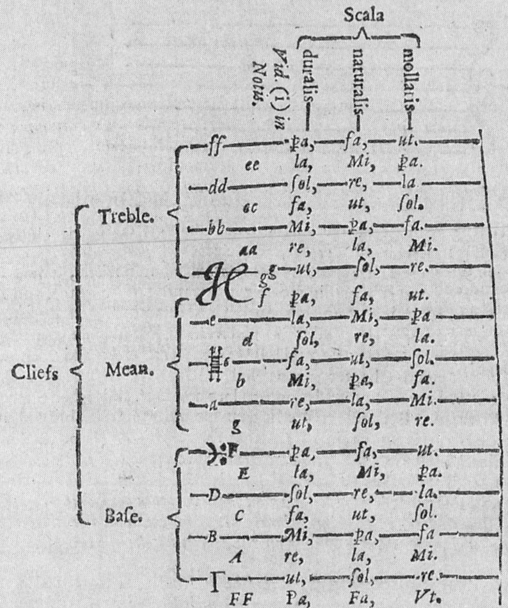

In wie you may not', dat wat nam' de Not' of any Clief hat, de sam' nam' (8) properly hat his Eigt: *Fa* in de Mean *C*, and *Fa* bot' in de Treble and Bas' *C*: *Re* in de Bas' *A*, and *Re* in de oder two. (8)

Vnto dis Scal' of a Trisdiapason, may bee added (for de * *Virginal* and *Organ*) de rest of de 4 † *Hypobolæan*, or dubble Bas'-cliefs, [*EE La Mi*, *DD sol Re*, and *CC fa Vt*;] wit de 4 * *Hyperbolæan*, or Hig Treble-Cliefs [*G*, *A*, *B*, *C*,] wie mak' up a Tetrakisdiapason: and (for de Organ) *D*. For de *Organ* hat but dis on' Key, mor' dan de *Virginal*: all de oder transcendent Not's, [bot' Grav' and Acut'] even unto Pentakisdiapason, Hexakisd. and Heptakisd. ar mad' by de Stops.

* *Vid.* (b) in §1.
† Of ὑποβάλλω *subiicio.*
* Of ὑπερβάλλω *superiniicio.*

Not's upon de Not' (f.)

(1) *Hypate* (2) *Nete*. ὕπατος of ὑπέρτατος, de Superlativ' of "ὑπὲρ *supra*: * as ὕπατον ὄρος *altissimus mons*, † ὕπατος Ζεὺς *supremus* "*Iupiter*:

* *Homer Epigr.*
† *Iliad* T, Ἴστω νῦν Ζεὺς πρῶτα θεῶν ὕπατος καὶ ἄριστος.

fact, there are several different ways of illustrating the scales with musical examples. For example, Bathe shifts the beginning note from G to C and then to F, adding a flat each time. Campion, on the other hand, keeps the same pitches—a G octave—but changes the key signature. It is unwise to draw conclusions about the significance of the octave in these illustrations. Scales tell us the names of the pitches, but not how to think about their use in a musical composition. But knowing their names will help us to understand the concepts associated with the actual pitches of musical compositions.

EXAMPLE 21 Comparison of solmization schemes by scale

a. no-flat scale

Bathe 1.text	ut	re	mi	fa	sol	la	fa	ut	re	mi
(ut=G) 2. exx.	sol	la	mi	fa	sol	la	fa	sol	la	mi
Morley (p. 5)	ut	re	mi	fa	sol	la	fa	sol	la	mi
(p. 8)	sol	la	mi	fa	sol	la	fa	sol	la	mi
Ravenscroft (♮ quare)				fa	sol	la	fa	sol	la	mi
Campion (sharpe)	sol	la	mi	fa	sol	la	fa	sol		
Butler (scala duralis) (MI=B)	ut	re	MI	fa	sol	la	pha	ut	re	mi

b. one-flat scale

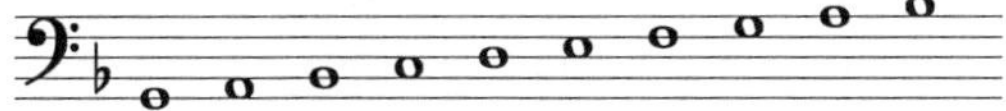

Bathe 1. text	sol	la	fa	ut	re	mi	fa	sol	la	fa
2. exx.	sol	la	fa	sol	la	mi	fa	sol	la	fa
Morley (p. 8)	sol	[la]	fa	sol	la	mi	fa	sol	la	fa
Campion (flat)	sol	la	fa	sol	la	mi	fa	sol		
Butler (scala naturalis) (MI=E)	sol	la	pha	ut	re	MI	fa	sol	la	pha

c. two-flat scale

Bathe 1. text	re	mi	fa	sol	la	fa	ut	re	mi	fa
(ut=F) 2. exx.	la	mi	fa	sol	la	fa	sol	la	mi	fa
Campion (flat in *E la mi*)	la	mi	fa	sol	la	fa	sol	la		
Butler (scala mollaris) (MI=A)	re	MI	fa	sol	la	pha	ut	re	mi	fa

* * *

KEY, TONE, AND AIR

The terms associated with the pitch content of actual music are in some ways far more difficult to define and understand, in part because they can have multiple meanings.[91] There are also fewer witnesses: Bathe's comments about changing the key do not go beyond issues of naming and tuning (what note to call *ut*) and neither Ravenscroft nor the author of *The Pathway* have anything at all to contribute on the subject. The three writers on whom we must rely are Morley, Campion, and Butler.[92]

Morley brings up the issue of what we might call "tonal organization" only in the third section of treatise, "treating of composing or setting of songs," and then in a casual rather than systematic way; his handling of these topics does not inspire confidence. For example, when the pupil asks, "Have you no generall rule to be given for an instruction for keeping of the key?" the master can only respond "No, for it must proceede only of the iudgement of the composer" (p. 147).

Morley explains "key" by giving examples that have mistakes.[93]

> *Ma.* Yes, for you have in the closing gone out of your key, which is one of the grosest faults which may be committed.
>
> *Phi.* What do you call going out of the key?
>
> *Ma.* The leaving of that key wherein you did begin, and ending in an other.
>
> *Phi.* What fault is in that?
>
> *Ma.* A great fault, for every key hath a peculiar ayre proper unto it selfe, so that if you goe into another then that wherein you begun, you change the aire of the song, which is as much as to wrest a thing out of his nature, making the asse leape upon his maister and the Spaniell beare the loade. The perfect knowledge of these aires (which the antiquity termed *Modi*) was in such estimation amongst the learned, as therein they placed the perfection of musicke, as you may perceive at large in the fourth booke of *Severinus Boetius* his musick, and *Glareanus* hath written a learned booke which he tooke in hand onely for the explanation of those moodes; and though the ayre of everie key be different one from the other, yet some love (by a wonder of nature) to be ioined to others so that if you begin your song in *Gam ut*, you may conclude it either in *C fa ut* or *D sol re*, and from thence come againe to *Gam ut*: likewise if you begin your song in *D sol re*, you may end in aire and come againe to *D sol re*, &. (pp. 146–47).[94]

The passage (ex. 22) is out of key because it begins on G but ends on F.[95] It is curious that Morley does not comment on the "intermingled" sharp and especially the flat, which according to Bathe changes the *ut* and thus the key.

The explanation allows us to extract several properties implicit in Morley's understanding both of key and of the closely related "aire" (or "ayre").[96] Key, in

EXAMPLE 22 Morley, *A Plaine and Easie Introduction*, 146, example of going out of key

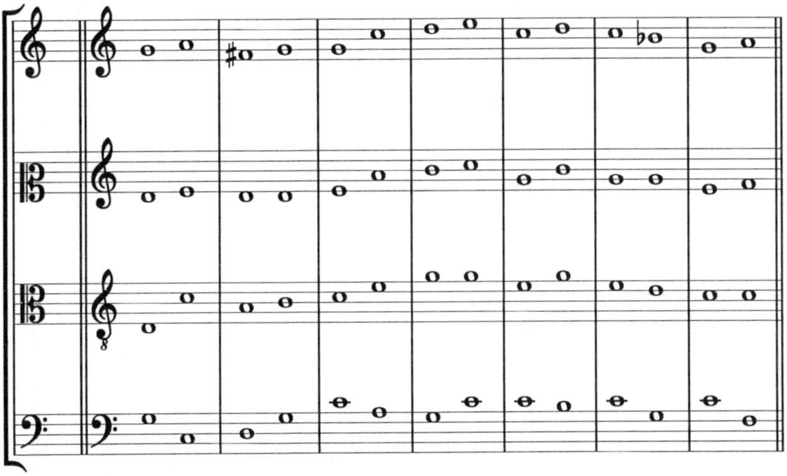

addition to its basic meaning of pitch, seems to have the sense of an aggregate of pitches, something that one can be in or out of, something that one can leave. He invokes "aire" / "ayre"—which I understand to mean character or sound—to help explain key: a key has a "peculiar ayre proper unto it selfe"; going out of key changes the "air of the song"; "aire" is what antiquity called "Modi" (Morley then refers to the books by Boethius and Glarean on the "moodes"). The "ayre of everie key" is distinct, yet some [keys] like to be joined. Here he returns to his starting point: you can begin in *Gam ut* and end in *C fa ut* or *D sol re*, and return to *Gam ut*, or you can begin in *D sol re* and end "in aire" *D sol re*; what you cannot do, according to the example, is begin on G and end on F. A feature of this passage that makes its interpretation difficult is Morley's use of "in" with a pitch name ("when you begin your song in *Gam ut*"). I think he means "with" or "on" and that "in" has an unfortunate connotation for us of being "in a key" in the modern sense of a closed pitch collection.

The second example (ex. 23), in a section that teaches how to "make foure parts of mingled notes," concerns pitches that can be used for imitative entries as well as for the final cadence:

> . . . and lastlie the base is brought in out of ye key which faulte is committed because of not causing the base answere to the counter in the eight, or at least to the tenor, but because the tenor is in the lowe key, it were too lowe to cause the base answere it in the eight, and therefore it had beene better in this place to have

> brought in the base in *D sol re*, for by bringing it in *C fa ut*, the counter being in *D la sol re*, you have changed the aire and made it quite unformall, for you must cause your fuge answere your leading parte either in the fifth, in the fourth, or in the eight . . . (p. 155).

The bass is out of key; it has changed the air.

EXAMPLE 23 Morley, *A Plaine and Easie Introduction*, 155, example of bass brought in out of key

The fault in both cases is in handling the key incorrectly; Morley's word is "unformall." Cadence points must be wondrously related, as C and D are to G. Imitative entries must be at the interval of the fourth, fifth or octave, rarely the third or sixth; the second and seventh are not even mentioned. We can lament that Morley chose this method for explaining key and air—giving examples of mistakes—but his explanation, as far as it goes, is internally consistent and fairly clear.

The same cannot be said for his discussion of tune and moode (*Modi* and mode). On page 147, at the end of the discussion of example 22, Morley continues, with the exchange quoted earlier:

> *Phi*. Have you no generall rule to be given for an instruction for keeping of the key?
>
> *Ma*. No, for it must proceede only of the iudgement of the composer, yet the church men for keeping their keyes have devised certaine notes commonlie called the eight tunes, so that according to the tune which is to be observed, at that time if it beginne in such a key, it may end in such and such others, as you shall immediately know. And these be (although not the true substance yet)

> some shadowe of the ancient *modi* whereof *Boethius* and *Glareanus* have writtten so much.
>
> *Phi.* I pray you set downe those eight tunes, for the ancient *modi*, I mean by the grace of God to study hereafter.
>
> *Ma.* Here they be in foure partes, the tenor stil keeping the plainesong (p. 147).[97]

Morley's confusion is evident. The eight "church tunes" are not the modes used on the continent by composers such as Palestrina or Lasso, still less even a shadow of the ancient modes he had tried to understand by reading Boethius and Glarean, but rather settings of psalm tones. (See Powers's essay in this volume.)

Morley's choice of psalm tones to illustrate mode suggests a surprising lack of understanding both of earlier theoretical traditions and of contemporary continental practices. As long ago as 1952, Robert Stevenson drew attention to the marginality of mode in Morley's discussion—"the small and obscure place Morley gives the subject"—but the point bears repeating.[98] Readers accustomed to using the modern edition may not realize just how marginal the comments are. After Morley had completed the volume (and in fact it would seem after all the gatherings in the main text had been printed), he gave it to colleagues to read, and they suggested that he make some additions.

> When I had ended my booke, and showne it (to be perused) to some of better skill in letters then my selfe, I was by them requested, to give some contentment to the learned, both by setting down a reason why I had disagreed from the opinions of others, as also to explaine something, which in the booke it selfe might seeme obscure (sig. ¶ 1r).

And so he added the Annotations in three unpaginated gatherings at the end, signed ¶, *, (∴).

The only annotations to the third part are in fact two full pages devoted to mode. Morley first presents the traditional eight-mode system and then a condensed version of Glarean's twelve-mode theory.[99] He thus contradicts what he had written in the main part of his book:

> It is also to be understood that those examples which I have in my booke set downe for the eight tunes, bee not the true and essentiall formes of the eight tunes or usuall moodes, but the formes of giving the tunes to their psalmes in the Churches (sig.(∴)2r).

A second passage in the main text employs the same numbering system that he had used for the eight Church tunes ("first tune," etc.):

> and above all thinges keepe the ayre of your key (be it in the first tune, second tune, or other) except you bee by the wordes forced to beare it, for the Dittie (as you shall know hereafter) will compell the author many times to admit great absurdities in his musicke, altering both time, tune, cullour ayre and what soever else, which is commendable so hee can cunninglie come into his former ayre againe (p. 166).

My guess is that he is using "tune" as he had earlier, confusing psalm tone and mode. Although there is no qualification of this particular passage in the Annotations, his repudiation of the earlier passage can probably be assumed to refer to this one as well.

Morley is not alone in his unfamiliarity with continental modal practices: there is remarkably little written about mode by English writers of the period under consideration. The only treatises published in England that discuss mode at all are translations of continental theorists, Le Roy and Ornithoparcus.[100] The presence of these two pages in Morley's Annotations does not convince me that mode in the continental sense had much meaning for Morley or for most of his readers.[101] The most important notions are key and air, terms that he uses in much the same way as Campion.

Campion, in contrast to Morley, devotes the entire second section of his brief treatise to "the tones of musicke." In the first section, "Of Counterpoint," he had signaled the importance of the bass, not only for his approach to counterpoint, but also because "the Base containes in it both the Aire and true judgement of the Key."[102] And in the preface, as part of a statement about the difficulties posed by the multiple meanings of terms such as tone or note, he had offered the following definition: "But if wee aske in what Tone is this or that song made, then by Tone we intend the key which guides and ends the whole song" (p. 324). In the section "Of the Tones of Musicke" he provides a systematic explanation. He begins:

> Of all things that belong to the making up of a Musition, the most necessary and usefull for him is the true knowledge of the Key, or Moode, or Tone, for all signifie the same thing, with the closes belonging unto it; for there is no tune that can have any grace or sweetnesse, unlesse it be bounded within a proper key, without running into strange keys which have no affinity with the aire of the song (p. 343).

His terminology is strikingly similar to Morley's: key as an aggregate of some sort as well as individual pitches, with a sense of inclusion (proper key) and exclusion (strange keys), and having a particular character (aire).

Campion next introduces a definition of the terms *Modus authentus* and *Modus plagalii* [sic] that will be crucial to his definition of key and of the cadences or closes associated with each key. He uses the terms to differentiate two divisions of the octave into its constituent fourth and fifth; the lower note of the fifth is the key-note (ex. 24).[103] He then explains which cadences or closes are proper to each key, making a broad distinction between keys which have a greater or sharp (i.e., major) third above the bass key-note and those which have a lesser or flat (i.e., minor) third.

> The maine and fundamentall close is in the key it self, the second is in the upper Note of the fift, the third is in the upper Note of the lowest third, if it be the less third; as for example, if the key be in *G.* with *B.* flat, you may close in these three places [the example shows cadences on G, D, and B♭]. The first close is that which maintaines the aire of the key, and may be used often, the second is next to be preferd, and the last, last (p. 344).

EXAMPLE 24 Campion, *A New Way*, 343, division of the octave

modus authentus modus plagalii

Campion continues with a series of examples that have been frequently discussed and need not be rehearsed here.[104] For our purposes, it is his terminology that seems particularly significant, for example, "if the key should be *G.* with *B.* sharpe"; he gives both the bass of the final sonority and the kind of scale.

Campion concludes the section on "tones" with a discussion of a faulty handling of a well-known tune:

> There is a tune ordinarily used, or rather abused, in our Churches, which is begun in one key and ended in another, quite contrary to nature; which errour crept in first through the ignorance of some parish Clarks, who understood better how to use the keyes of their Church-doores, then the keyes of Musicke, at which I doe not much mervaile; but that the same should passe in the booke of Psalmes set forth in foure parts, and authorised by so many Musitions, makes mee much amazed. This is the tune (p. 346). (See ex. 25.)

EXAMPLE 25 Campion, *A New Way*, 347, tune (OXFORD)

The tune is one of four that Thomas East described as used "in most churches of this realme" for singing psalms.[105] Nicholas Temperley has unearthed much of its fascinating history.[106] First published in a 1564 Scottish prayerbook, and later known as OXFORD and sometimes as OLD COMMON, it appeared "in almost every psalmody collection from England, Scotland, or America between 1590 and 1720."[107] Campion describes the tune as beginning in one key (F) and ending in another (G). Its structure is in fact unusual: Temperley notes that it is the only tune in a database of over 18,000 that begins on the seventh degree.[108]

Campion composes a bass line to go with this tune (ex. 26):

> If one should request me to make a Base to the first halfe of his aire, I am perswaded [sic] that I ought to make it in this manner:

EXAMPLE 26 Campion, *A New Way*, 347, proposed bass line

> Now if this be the right Base (as without doubt it is), what a strange unaireable change must the key then make from *F*. with the first third sharp to *G*. with *B*. flat (p. 347).

He does not like the "unaireable change" the key must make. I am not certain how to interpret his remarks: does he mean the contrasting kinds of thirds in the melodic contour F–G–A as opposed to [F]–G–A–B♭ or the different sounds of the F "major" opening sonority compared to the G "minor" final sonority (not in this example)?

He continues with a criticism of one of the many four-voice settings of this melody, which he neither names nor provides as an example, though he does mention that it comes from "the booke of Psalmes set forth in foure parts"; it seems to be the setting composed by George Kirby and published in East's *Whole Booke of Psalmes*, 1592 (the source for ex. 27).[109]

> But they have found a shift for it, and beginne the tune upon the upper Note of the fift, making the third to it flat; which is as absurd as the other. For first they erre in

> rising from a flat third into the unison, or eight, which is condemned by the best Musitions; next the third to the fift is the third which makes the cadence of the key, and therefore affects to be sharpe by nature, as indeed the authour of the aire at the first intended it should be.

EXAMPLE 27 Kirby, Psalm 10 (East, *Whole Book of Psalms*, 1592)

He criticizes Kirby's harmonization because the minor third of the opening sonority goes to an octave and because F, which makes the cadence to the key (i.e., in our terms, functions as the leading tone), must be sharp. He then provides his own setting, using F♯s throughout (ex. 28):

> I will therefore so set it downe in foure parts according to the former Rule of Counterpoint.

> This was the Authors meaning, and thus it is lawfull to beginne a song in the fift, so that you maintaine the aire of the song, joyning to it the proper parts (pp. 347–48).

It thus also serves as an example of a piece that begins on the fifth. I can't explain the curious signature—two flats for the upper three voices, one flat for the bass—especially since there is only one E in the entire setting (top line, measure 10). Kirby's setting, which uses only one flat in the signature, is much flatter in its frequent use of "intermingled" E♭s.

There seems to be a kind of progression in the terminology employed by our three witnesses. Campion follows Morley in describing key as something that has

EXAMPLE 28 Campion, *A New Way*, 348, alternative setting

its own particular air or character, but he uses tone as well, as a synonym for key and moode (Morley does not use tone in this sense). Campion entitles the whole section about keys and airs "Of the Tones of Musick" and even offers the explanation quoted above ("But if wee ask in what Tone is this or that song made, then by Tone we intend the key which guides and ends the whole song"). But like Morley, his focus seems to be on the concepts of key and air.

Butler, in contrast, equates air and tone, while using key to mean pitch:

> The last and chiefest Ornament is Formality: which is the mainteining of the Air, or Tone of the Song, in his Parts.[110]

His definition of tone is virtually identical to Campion's:

> The proper Tone of each Song, is the Close-note of the Base in his Final Key.

But he extends the meaning of tone in an interesting and I think significant way, making a distinction between key and tone. Butler believes that there are six tones and he names them according to his own solmization system.

> Of Tones there are six several Sortes, defined and distinguished by the six Servil notes [*Ut*, *Re*, *Fa*, *Sol*, *La*, and *Pha*], the Seventh (which is the Master-note) will not be subject to his Subjects, nor, in that low place, agree with them (p. 82).

A tone or air is an ordered collection of pitches, with a unique placement of half-steps and whole-steps. We might say that it has a characteristic sound (ex. 29). The six tones are not all used with the same frequency:

> Of these Six Airs, the Third, Second, Fourth, and First [*Fa*, *Re*, *Sol*, and *Ut]* are frequent: *Pha* is rare, and *La* more rare.

An important aspect of Butler's understanding of tone or air is that each can occur at three different pitch levels, according to the scale (no flats, one flat, two flats—or *scala duralis*, *naturalis*, and *mollaris* in his terminology). (See table 2a.) He recognizes that simply providing the "close-note of the bass in his final key" is insufficient to describe the air or tone.

> (d) *Ut, Re, Fa, Sol*, &c. The distinction of the Airs by the Keys, (which *Calvis.* seemeth to allow) is uncertain; because in the same Key are many different Tones: as in *D*, may be *La*, or *Sol*, or *Re*: in *C*, may be *Sol*, or *Fa*, or *Ut*: &c. So that, if we say the Tone is in *Dla sol re*, *Csol fa ut*, or *Gsol re ut,* &c; we are yet to seeke which of the three Notes, in any of these Keys, to take for the Tone. But the distinction of the Airs by the Notes, is certain and constant, in what Keys so ever they stand. It is true, that every of the six Tones, hath three several Keys, (according to the number of the *Mi*-cliefs) in which it may indifferently be set: but wheresoever it be set, all cometh to one. For example: If *Re* be the Tone or Aire-note; whether it stand in *Are* (the *Mi-clief* being *B*) or in *Dsol re*, (the *Mi-clief* being *E*) or in *Gamut*, (the *Mi-clief* being *A*) there is no difference at all, either in the Song, or in any Part of the Song, or in any Note of a Part (p. 86).

A pitch has a different solmization syllable (and function) in each of the three scales. D can be *la*, *sol*, or *re*, depending on the scale. Instead of linking the final

EXAMPLE 29 Butler, *The Principles of Musik*, 81–88, six tones or airs (slur shows the half-steps)

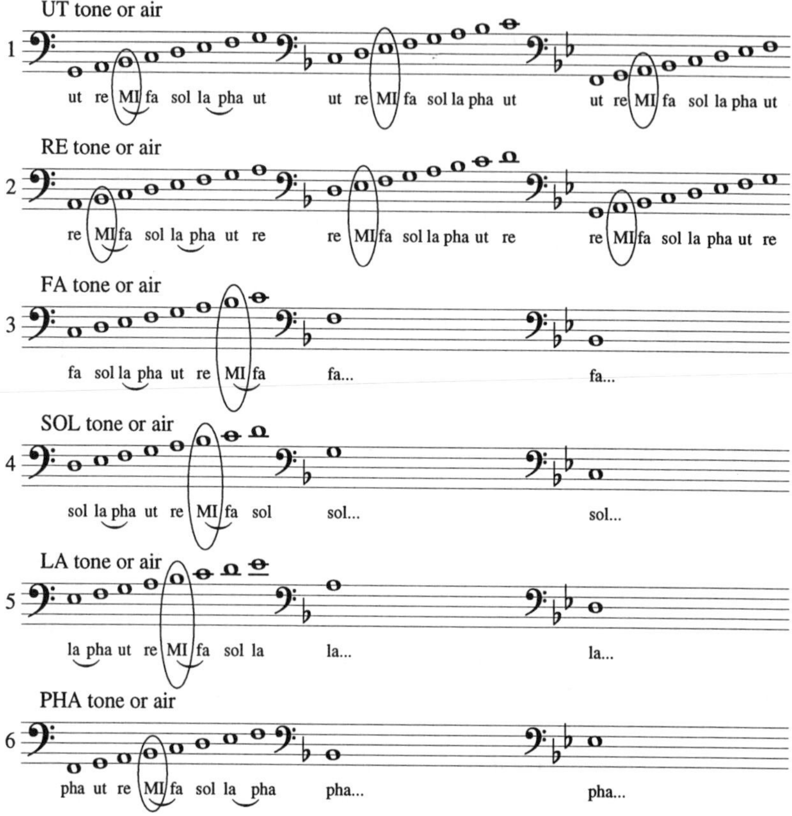

pitch (key) directly to scale as Campion did ("if the key be in G. with B. flat"), Butler links it to solmization syllables. He uses his solmization system both to describe and to define the six airs or tones; each is identified by the solmization syllable that bounds the octave. To identify the "tonality" (there is no term in the treatises for the aggregate of scale/solmization and key) therefore requires two kinds of information: close-note of the bass (Campion's key) and solmization syllable denoting the tone or air. The information is similar to what Campion provides; the difference is that Butler's concept of tone or air permits the observation that three keys can share the same characteristic sound. G in the *ut* tone (*duralis*) shares characteristic sounds with C in the *ut* tone (*naturalis*) and F in the *ut* tone (*mollaris*); they are in effect transpositions at three different pitch levels. The three different scales mean that pieces ending on G in *duralis* (no flats), *naturalis* (one flat) and *mollaris* (two flats) will have different sounds, and in fact they belong to different tones or airs: *ut*, *sol*, and *re*.

There are precedents in earlier writers for Butler's concept of transposition. Campion, in his explanation of the three scales, shows that his example of the "flat in *Elami*" scale (G–G octave with two flats in the signature) can be sung on A, with no flats in the signature (ex. 30):[111]

> but next let us examine this Key as it is flat in *Elami*, which being properly to be set in *Are*, so is it to be sung with ease, *La*, instead of *Re*, being the right limits of this eight.

EXAMPLE 30 Campion, *A New Way*, 326, two-flat scale transposed to no-flat scale

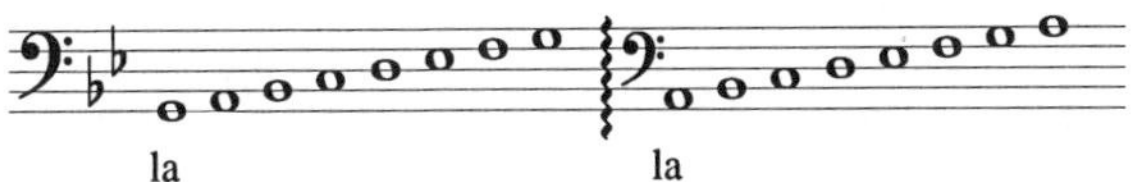

In other words, the scale ("key") notated beginning on G with two flats can be notated starting on A *re* (i.e., the name of the pitch) and sung *la* (the name of the solmization syllable for A in the "sharpe" scale).

Morley provides an example notated in two different scales and pitch levels (keys) (ex. 31a –b). The master criticizes the version that uses a signature with E♭ and B♭ (ex. 31a):

> The musick is in deed true, but you have set it in such a key as no man would have done, except it had beene to have plaide it on the Organes with a quier of singing men, for in deede such shiftes the Organistes are many times compelled to make for ease of the singers . . . [112]

In a passage already cited above, Morley expounds on the difficulties singers have with the "flat cliffes" and asks

> what can they possiblie do with such a number of flat *bb* which I coulde not as well bring to passe by pricking the song a note higher? (p. 156).[113]

He shows the same piece "altered in nothing but in the Cadences and key," notated to end on D with one flat in the signature (ex. 31b). Morley's example is a little tricky. In its flat version, ending on C, it should have three flats in the signature: a glance at the music shows that the sixth degree, A, is always flat, while the third and seventh can be raised or lowered as the situation demands. In the version ending on D, the flat governing the sixth degree is notated in the signature.

Example 31 Morley, *A Plaine and Easie Introduction*, 155–56

a. example notated in two [*recte* three] flats

b. same example notated in one flat

By chance, Morley's and Campion's examples both come from the same "tone"—to use Butler's term—the *re* tone. In both cases "pricking" the music in another key, up one step, removes two flats from the signature. G with two flats in the signature can be notated as A with no flats, C with three flats as D with one flat see ex. 32). The difference between Campion and Morley on the one hand and Butler on the other is that Campion and Morley invoke transposition as a way of avoiding signature flats while Butler uses it as a way of drawing connections between collections of pitches that are similar in sound, and of defining the idea of distinct tones or airs.

EXAMPLE 32 Transpositions of the *re* tone

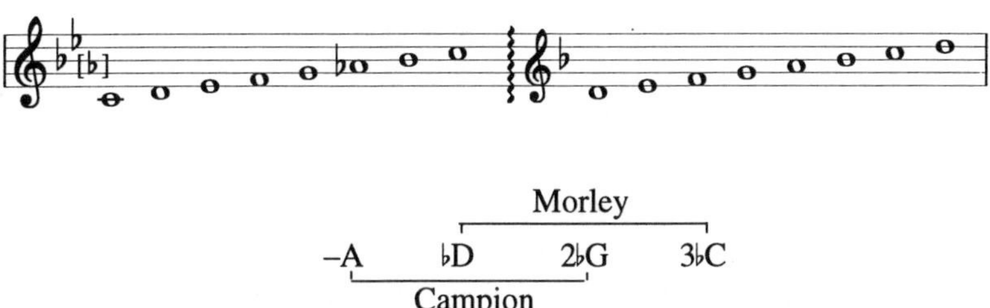

It is striking that only Morley has any discussion of continental modal theory as practiced by composers such as Lasso and Palestrina and described by theorists such as Zarlino or Calvisius; his comments appear as an afterthought in the annotations as a response to a reader. This near total lack of interest in mode should warn us against trying to impose continental modal theory on this repertory. Nor is there any evidence in the treatises to justify "neo-modal" terminology in common use today.

All three of the principal witnesses have a great deal to say about the pitch content of music. They share common assumptions about the existence of three scales, defined by the key signature (no flats, one flat, two flats), and all of them accept—in one way or another—the idea of transposition from one key (that is, pitch level) to another. Rather than mode, they use the terms key, tone, and air. While Morley is in some ways unclear, his use of key and air, in particular, agrees with that of Campion. And Campion's usage in turn has much in common with Butler. Butler assigns a particular significance to tone (which he usually combines with air).

By combining the evidence about key and air in Morley and Campion with Butler's idea of distinct tones, it is possible to suggest a kind of amalgam for which there is no good word in any of the treatises. For want of a better term, I use "tonalities" to describe this combination of key (final or close-note) with the six tones or airs (in reality an ordered pitch collection) and the three scales (no flats, one flat, and two flats). Example 33 is a schematic representation of these "tonalities." Campion might describe a piece that ends on G and has two flats in the signature as being "in the key of G with flat in *E la mi*" while Butler might call it "G in the second (*Re*) tone or air."

Example 33 "Tonalities" of English music

	[3♭]		[E♭	B♭	F	C]		
	2♭	E♭	B♭	F	C	G	D	A
	♭	B♭	F	C	G	D	A	E
	—	F	C	G	D	A	E	B
Butler's tone / air:		pha	fa	ut	sol	re	la	mi
frequency		rare	⇐	frequent		⇒	more rare	
Byrd (1575, 1589, 1591)		—	14	7	2	28	2	—

All three writers address other topics associated with the pitch content of music; for example, where cadences are allowed, how they are made, what notes are allowed in a particular key, etc. But a more extended consideration of these topics will have to await another occasion.

* * *

This examination of a group of English treatises from approximately 1560 to 1640 suggests two related conclusions. The first is that English theoretical concepts are remarkably consistent and coherent over the entire period under consideration. The second is that English theory is significantly different from continental theory.

The second conclusion leads to a question. In earlier times, English and continental theory seem to have been much closer. Why should English practices be idiosyncratic for this period and not for earlier ones?

I can suggest at present only a tentative answer. I suspect that the upheaval caused by the waves of reformation, restoration, and then reformation that dominated England during most of the sixteenth century will prove crucial.[114] For example, Jane Flynn has documented major changes in music education during the course of the sixteenth century. She characterized the early period:

> During the pre-Reformation, all school students learned to chant the psalms in Latin, not least partly because they chanted them in services every day, or heard them chanted. [. . .] The older choristers learned to read polyphonic music and also to build on their knowledge of plainsong by improvising on it in a number of ways [. . .]. These vocal techniques were transferred to the organ by the most

> skillful choristers and secondaries and practised on paper as written compositions.[115]

In contrast, after Elizabeth's accession, "the whole approach to music education became more 'academic' than practical, with an emphasis on written rather than oral (improvised) exercises."[116]

> However, after Elizabeth had been on the throne about seven years, none of the choristers at any given song school would have experienced singing Latin chant. They still learned Latin grammar and moralistic songs, but now had only a small amount of music to learn for services. Music reading had a higher priority than before, since improvisation was no longer necessary to provide musical items during a service. Moreover, choristers spent more of their time in the classroom writing and studying compositional exercises than in the choir. They also spent more time learning secular music, including instrumental music, and they performed many more increasingly secular plays each year.[117]

This dramatic change in music education mirrors profound changes in the institutions that supported musical performance, composition, and training. The composer and performer Thomas Whythorne drew a vivid contrast in his autobiography between the state of music before and after the reformation.

> In time past music was chiefly maintained by Cathedral churches, abbeys, colleges, parish churches, chauntries, guilds, and fraternities &c. But when the abbeys and colleges without the universities, with guilds, and fraternities, &c. were suppressed, then went music to decay.
>
> [. . .] Now I will speak of the use of music in this time present. First for the Church, ye do and shall see it so slenderly maintained in the cathedral churches and colleges and parish churches, that when the old store of the musicians be worn out the which were bred when the music of the church was maintained (which is like to be in short time), ye shall have few or none remaining except it be a few singing men, and players on musical instruments. Of the which ye shall find a very few or none that can make a good lesson of descant.[118]

Whythorne's account can be read as a kind of "cultural revolution" in which the old learning, based on continental models, after a time was supplanted by a home-grown version, tied more closely, perhaps, to the practices of composers and performers. The continental versions of the gamut employing hexachords and mutation and the continental explanations of mode—whether eight- or twelve-mode—had little meaning or value in the new culture. Clearly, the causes of and explanations for this distinctive voice of English music theory deserve further investigation.

The notion of a distinctive English theory of music provides a valuable set of concepts and terms that we should consider adopting for our discussions of this music. Skeptics will point to the fact that the "neo-modal" terminology in common use today is not unlike Butler's tones or airs. Why bother to refer to a piece as in the "re tone on G with two flats in the signature" instead of the more familiar "G-Aeolian"? My answer is that the lack of any theoretical underpinning for the "neo-modal" terminology means that scholars inevitably rely on the inherently circular reasoning of using the music to define the properties of the various modes (Aeolian, Dorian, etc.), and then work from their understanding of these modes backward to assign the music to modal categories. And the very word "mode" has connotations that can interfere with an understanding of these peculiarly English "tonalities" that are not modes, not keys (in the later sense), but something distinctive.

An advantage of taking a theoretically grounded understanding of this music as a point of departure is that it opens new avenues for approaching a study of the music itself. Composers choose which "tonalities" they write in, and in fact, I suspect that each composer will prove to have a distinctive profile when his output is considered as a whole. Morley never uses the scale with two flats; Campion, in contrast, often uses scales with three flats. Byrd, in the three volumes of *Cantiones sacrae* from 1575, 1589, and 1591, composes in eleven of the twelve tonalities that Butler described as "frequent" (ex. 33); he did not use *♭♭ C sol*, but did the "more rare" *♭A la*. The distribution is striking. The *re* tone represents nearly half of the pieces. Is this distribution characteristic of Byrd? Is it related to the date of composition, or possibly the genre?

Working with concepts articulated by a broad spectrum of theorists over the period of more than half a century should provide of a way of examining both individual compositions and groups of similar compositions. How much variation is possible within Byrd's *re* tone compositions, and is the variation a function of time or genre? How do Morley's *re* tone pieces differ from Byrd's or Campion's? Within each tone or air, can we see an explanation for the choice of one key rather than one of its transpositions? Freeing the investigation from concepts associated with mode or key will make it possible to look more closely at how composers realize a particular tonality, and may eventually help us to understand the distinctive sounds of English music from this period.

APPENDIX

1. Bathe

William Bathe (1564–1614), best known today as for his method of teaching language, was born in Dublin.[119] According to an autobiographical statement written when he entered the Jesuit order, he studied humane letters in Ireland, philosophy at Oxford, and theology in Louvain. His earliest treatise on music, *A Brief Introduction to the True Art of Music*, was published in 1584 but survives now only in a seventeenth-century manuscript copy.[120] In the preface Bathe identifies himself as a student of Oxenford. He lived in London probably in the late 1580s, where he was known for his skill as a musician (he presented a harp to Queen Elizabeth). His second treatise, *A Briefe Introduction to the Skill of Song*, exists only in an undated print. Thomas Whythorne included him in a scrawled list of "the most famous musicians of this time," probably written in 1592.[121] In 1591 Bathe left England and went to Spain; he would spend the rest of his life in exile on the continent, as a valued member of the Society of Jesus. Scholars generally regard the second treatise as a "wholesale revision" of the first.[122] I would be more inclined to view them as two separate treatises, with some overlap in content. *The Brief Introduction to the True Art of Music* considers quite briefly in Book I the four main topics of *The Briefe Introduction to the Skill of Song*—naming, quantity, time, and tune—and concludes "sic finit ars cantandi." Book II is a counterpoint treatise that concludes with the recommendation that students imitate "guid authors, as M. Talis, M. Byrd, M. Tailor and others." *The Briefe Introduction to the Skill of Song* offers a more thorough *ars cantandi* or introduction to the elements of music and concludes with a series of separate items that relate to counterpoint, but seem more like appendices than a coherent exposition.[123] In short, the titles seem to me to indicate accurately the main subjects of the two treatises.

Various dates have been suggested for *A Briefe Introduction to the Skill of Song*. Rainbow proposed c. 1587–1591 on biographical grounds.[124] However, according to Fenlon and Milsom, Thomas East began printing music only in 1588.[125] Brown listed the volume as $158?_2$.[126] Others have suggested 1596, perhaps because East registered it that year in the Stationers' Company along with nine other volumes.[127] Registration need not indicate publication, however; Krummel explained that

> books issued under the royal patents did not fall under the administration of the Company and were usually not entered in the registers. Byrd's patent was now no longer in force to protect East's music book, and East apparently thought highly enough of these to seek the protection of the Company. He may also have issued reprints (i.e., new editions) at the same time as he registered the titles.[128]

Krummel himself described it simply as "an undated book which is thought to be among Thomas East's earliest music publications."[129]

It is possible that typographical evidence may help date the treatise. Krummel identified its music type face as Granjon, but the volume actually uses two different types: Granjon for the larger musical examples, and Van den Keere for the smaller examples, including two psalm settings (*O God that art my righteousnesse*, sig. Biiii^{r} and *O Lord in thee is all my trust*, sig. Cv^{v}–vi^{r}) and the table at the end of the volume.[130] According to Krummel, East first used the small Van den Keere type in 1592 for his book of four-voice psalm settings (Krummel's fig. 11).[131] Nicholas Temperley confirmed that the two psalm settings in Bathe's treatise are typographically identical to the settings in East's 1592 volume.[132] I wonder if the presence of these two settings in this edition of Bathe's treatise implies that the print can date from no earlier than 1592.

2. Anonymous, *Pathway to Musicke*

In 1596, William Barley, a "publisher & seller of Bookes," as he styled himself, paid ("to my great cost and charges") to have "sundry sorts of lessons to be collected together out of some of the best Authors professing this excellent science of musicque, and have put them in print." These words are drawn from his dedicatory letter to *A New Booke of Tabliture, Containing sundrie easie and familiar Instructions, shewing howe to attain to the knowledge, to guide and dispose thy hand to play on sundry Instruments, as the Lute, Orpharion, and Bandora: Together with divers new Lessons to each of these Instruments* which he published in 1596.[133] Its title page continues: *Whereunto is added an introduction to Prickesong, and certaine familliar rules of Descant, with other necessarie Tables plainely shewing the true use of the Scale or Gamut, and also how to set any Lesson higher or lower at your pleasure.* This "introduction to Prickesong" is a slim volume that survives separately and in only one copy, entitled *The Pathway to Musicke contayning sundrie familiar and easie Rules for the readie and true understanding of the Scale, or Gamma ut: wherein is exactlie shewed by plaine deffinitions, the principles of this Arte, brieflie laide open by way of questions and answers, for the better instruction of the learner. Whereunto is annexed a treatise of Descant, & certaine Tables, which doth teach how to move any song higher, or lower from one Key to another, never heretofore published.* Although the treatise is sometimes attributed to Barley, it is clear from the dedication that he commissioned someone to write it. Possible candidates might be either Francis Cutting or Philip Rossiter, thought by John Ward and Thurston Dart to have served as music editors for *A New Booke of Tabliture.*[134]

NOTES

*This article began as a seminar on "mode" in the vocal music of William Byrd at the Eastman School of Music, an extension of my own studies on mode in sixteenth-century German and Italian music with Harold Powers; it evolved in subsequent seminars on the history of theory at Eastman and Brandeis University. Parts of it were presented in two papers, "Charles Butler: A Key to the Music of William Byrd," American Musicological Society, Philadelphia, 1984, and "Toward a Critical Language for English Music ca. 1600" at Yale University (1991) and the University of Pennsylvania (1994). I am grateful to many colleagues who read and commented on my work, including Linda Austern, Jane Bestor, Philip Brett, Elizabeth Crownfield, Ellen Harris, Kevin Karnes, John Milsom, Craig Monson, Oliver Neighbour, Christopher Reynolds, David Schulenberg, Nicholas Temperley, members of my 1995 NEH Summer Seminar "Analyzing Early Music 1300–1600" (especially Candace Bailey, Jane Flynn, and Jeff Meyer), and, of course, Harry Powers. Special thanks to Cristle Collins Judd for her thoughtful reading of this study at several different stages in its preparation and for her skillful editing of the final version.

1. Campion, *Works*, 323.

2. "Tune" is a complicated word with several different meanings, as the following quotations from Bathe, *A Brief Introduction to the Skill of Song*, make clear: (1) "There be eight notes, whose ascention, and descention doe comprehend all tunes" (sig. Bi^{v}); (2) "Tune the first Note of any song as it serveth best for the voyce" (sig. Bi^{v}); (3) "Some learne to Tune only by the Voice of another: some use helpe of an Instrument, which is the better way" (sig. Bvii^{v}; cf. "A Short Introduction," Rainbow, *English Psalmody Prefaces*, 32); (4) "by the knowledge of this [i.e., compt from any cleve], men may give their tunes to the parts without knowledge of the Gamut" (sig. Bvii^{v}). See also the definitions offered by Strahle, *An Early Music Dictionary*, 396–99.

3. See Turbot, *William Byrd*, for a listing in chronological order.

4. Fellowes, *William Byrd*, 62–63.

5. Howes, *William Byrd*, 72.

6. Meier, *The Modes*.

7. Meier, *The Modes*, 381.

8. Kerman, *Masses and Motets*, 109–11. *Gloria patri* is notated in the Byrd-Tallis *Cantiones sacrae* of 1575 ending on B♭ with two flats in the signature. In both the Fellowes and Monson editions it ends on C with no flat in the signature.

9. Wiering, "Language of the Modes," provides an exhaustive survey of modal cycles in treatises and musical sources.

10. This is a point that needs more space to be presented properly. For now, let me simply say that I find some ordering by system, clef, and final (the parameters of Powers's "tonal types") in 1575, 1588, all three 1589 volumes, 1591, and 1611; but other factors are also important (the pattern of alternating groups of three in 1575; the type of text in 1588;

the number of voices in the 1589 *Songs*, 1591 and 1611; and the number of voices and liturgical order in 1605 and 1607). For full titles of the prints, see Turbot, *William Byrd*, 3ff. Wiering, "Language of the Modes," does not include any of Byrd's collections among the 410 modal cycles he lists in Appendix C; the only English music to be included are psalm tone settings by Morley (no. 259) and Tallis (no. 368).

11. This is the usage, for example, of Gustave Reese, who writes in *Music in the Renaissance,* 186: "In any event, it is plain that in polyphony only five modes mattered for practical purposes. Glareanus himself emphasizes that the Lydian pair, as modified into Ionian and Hypoionian, has almost completely supplanted the unmodified pair. Moreover, the distinction between an authentic mode and its plagal is, in polyphony, an academic one. This leaves, as the really fundamental modes of Late Renaissance polyphony, the Dorian, Phrygian, Mixolydian, Aeolian, and Ionian."

12. Andrews, *Byrd's Vocal Polyphony*, ch. II, "Modes and Tonality." The theorists whom Andrews cites in his explanation of "the ecclesiastical modal system" are continental, not English.

13. Andrews, *Byrd's Vocal Polyphony*, 19. Andrews includes Lydian as the sixth scale-type, though it constitutes only 0.5% of Byrd's output.

14. For a critical assessment of this approach, see Perkins, Review.

15. The terms are never associated with modes in English theory, but with genres. Thus, Butler, *The Principles of Musik*, 1–2, writes: "The Dorick Mood consisteth of sober slow-timed Notes, generally in Counter-point, set to a Psalm or other pious Canticle, in Meter or Rhythmical verse." [I translate his imaginative orthography into the normal alphabet.] For a number of similar definitions of "Dorick" see Strahle, *An Early Music Dictionary*, 123–24. See also Cooper, "Englische Musiktheorie," 200–01.

16. Neighbour, *Consort and Keyboard Music*, 180: "In his keyboard pavans and galliards Byrd adopts the Dorian form of C, D, and G minor, never allowing the chord of the sixth degree in any prominent position, whereas in Aeolian (except in the Earl of Salisbury pieces) he constantly uses F major as the starting point for a new strain or a new phase within a strain—a feature which contributes more to the individual flavour of the mode in these pieces than the choice of secondary cadence degrees." He qualifies these remarks in a footnote: "In certain, mostly later works these distinctions become harder to draw. In g3 [=BK 4], an out-and-out Dorian work, the persistent sharp sixths rule out any opening or cadence on the third degree, whereas g2 [=BK 3] makes great play with it, as do d1 [=BK 52] and d2 (in which strain II' even opens on the Aeolian sixth)."

17. Kerman, *Masses and Motets*, 68–69.

18. Because of these features, he considers *Domine tu iurasti*, despite its Aeolian ending on A, to be "an almost text-book instance of a Dorian work." Andrews, *Byrd's Vocal Polyphony*, 22.

19. Kerman, "On William Byrd's *Emendemus in Melius*," 439.

20. Kerman, *Masses and Motets*, 68, argues that Byrd's use of partial signatures (in *Emendemus in melius*, the second tenor has only one flat in the signature, and the altus and first tenor drop the second flat from m. 44 of the second part to the end of the piece) "should warn us against placing too much reliance on signatures as a criterion for determining a composition's mode. H. K. Andrews did so when he assigned both *Libera me* and *Emendemus in melius* to the transposed Aeolian mode, while settling *Libera me Domine et pone me juxta te* [. . .] in the transposed Dorian." In a revised version of "On William Byrd's *Emendemus in Melius*" (1997), Kerman writes: "*Emendemus in melius* is in the Dorian mode on G." It is interesting to read the two versions of his opening statements about tonality side by side.

21. Kerman, *Masses and Motets*, 69: "Byrd most probably regarded them all [i.e., *Emendemus in melius*, *Libera me Domine de morte aeterna* and *Libera me Domine et pone me juxta te*] as Dorian; they all exhibit about the same amount of fluctuation between the raised and lowered forms of the sixth degree of the scale."

22. Ironically, Perkins (review of Kerman, *Masses and Motets* and Neighbour, *Consort and Keyboard Music*) takes Kerman and Neighbour to task for not adopting a sufficiently rigorous modal approach; Perkins favors traditional continental modal theory, a description of which Morley added to the Annotations to his treatise. My thanks to John Milsom for drawing my attention to this review.

23. A point brought out by Perkins, Review.

24. It is not included, for example, in Turbot's useful bibliography, *William Byrd*.

25. Dahlhaus, *Studies*, 244. He was reacting to points made by Zimmerman, "Advanced Tonal Design," 323–24: "Byrd frequently used the submediant, supertonic, dominant, and tonic degrees, more or less in that order. [. . .] In each, Byrd has formulated a logical harmonic structure based on a very modern concept of harmonic functions."

26. Dahlhaus, *Studies*, 244.

27. Dahlhaus, *Studies*, 245.

28. A detailed list of English treatises is given in Atcherson, "Symposium"; a bibliography of printed Tudor and Jacobean music and music treatises (in alphabetical order) is given in Boyd, *Elizabethan Music*, 323–42 (discussion in ch. 9). Studies of English theory include in addition Cooper, "Englische Musiktheorie"; Apfel, *Geschichte der Kompositionslehre*, Teil III, Kap. 4; Johnson, "Solmization"; Lewis, "Incipient Tonal Thought"; Wienpahl, "English Theorists." See also the recent overviews now available by Bray, "Music and Musicians," and McGuinness, "Writings about Music."

29. Two sixteenth-century prefaces are included in Rainbow, *English Psalmody Prefaces*. See Stainer, "Music Introductions"; Illing, *The English Metrical Psalter 1562*; Frost, *Psalm and Hymn Tunes*; Temperley, *English Parish Church*; and Weaver, *'Goostly Psalmes'*. This vast territory could profitably be explored for evidence of English solmization practices; scholars will soon be able to consult *The Hymn Tune Index*, compiled by Nicholas Temperley.

30. For a list of the tutors and a brief discussion, see Boyd, *Elizabethan Music*, 153–61. See also Adrian Le Roy, *Les instructions pour le luth*; Casey, "Lute Instruction Books"; Harwood, "Adrian Le Roy's Lute Instructions"; Simpson, "A Short-title List."

31. Flynn's richly-documented study of music education in sixteenth-century England, "A Reconsideration," a portion of which is now published as "The Education of Choristers," demonstrates the dramatic changes in musical culture, and provides an invaluable context for this article.

32. Flynn, "A Reconsideration," 116.

33. The biographical dates given here are taken from *Grove*, except for Ravenscroft's, which are from Austern, *Music in English Children's Drama*, 20. Secondary literature concerning the careers of these writers and their treatises is cited below.

34. Boyd, *Elizabethan Music*, 277: "But of all the musicians Campion astonishes us most, through both the extraordinary variety of his accomplishments and his proficiency in each. He studied law, and wrote both poetry and music of outstanding excellence, together with technical treatises dealing with the latter two subjects, also a considerable quantity of Latin verse; yet medicine was his profession, and he achieved contemporary recognition in that field as well as in music and poetry."

35. Ó Mathúna, *William Bathe*, 37–39.

36. Pruett, "Charles Butler." On Oxford, see Carpenter, "The Study of Music" and *Music in Medieval and Renaissance Universities*; and Caldwell, "Music in the Faculty of Arts."

37. Lowbury, Salter, and Young, *Thomas Campion*, 16–22.

38. Ó Mathúna, *William Bathe*, 43, 70n.

39. Campion was one of the actors in a comedy performed before the Earl of Leicester in 1588. See Wienpahl, *Music at the Inns of Court*, 221 and ch. 10. See Flynn, "A Reconsideration," 70–115, concerning another musician who entered Gray's Inn in 1589: Thomas Molyneux, who she argues may be the Thomas Mulliner who wrote the Mulliner Book (British Library, Add. MS. 30513).

40. Morley, *A Plaine and Easie Introduction*, 156. See below, p. 200.

41. See Urquhart, "Canon, Partial Signatures," 144–170, for a discussion of the evolution from a three-hexachord to a two-hexachord scale. See also Preußner, "Solmisationsmethoden."

42. I am using "scale" to describe what Powers refers to as "system" because I want to be able to use "system" in a more generic, less technical sense. Powers, "Tonal Types," 436.

43. Atcherson, "Symposium," 8, noticed the three kinds of scales in Ravenscroft, Butler, and Playford, but thought them to be a garbling of traditional Guidonian hexachords; Bathe's version he thought showed "evidence of even greater confusion." On English solmization, see the brief but perceptive account of four-syllable systems in Henderson, "Solmization Syllables," ch. 10; Boyd, *Elizabethan Music*, "Sight-singing," 248–54; Cooper, "Englische Musiktheorie," 183–86; Johnson, "Solmization." See also Hughes,

"Solmization," *Grove*, (including citations for the older literature that has mostly not been superseded); and for the German context, Preußner, "Solmisationsmethoden."

44. The most extended descriptions of Bathe's writings are found in Boyd, *Elizabethan Music*, 250–51; Johnson, "Solmization"; Henderson, "Solmization Syllables," 271–80; Ó Mathúna, *William Bathe*, 173–83; the introduction by Hill to *A Brief Introduction to the True Art of Music*, and by Rainbow to *A Briefe Introduction to the Skill of Song c. 1587* (also as "Bathe and his Introductions to Musicke"). See the Appendix for notes on his two treatises. Bathe has had a remarkably poor reputation, to my mind unjustified. Cooper, "Englische Musiktheorie," 158, dismisses *A Briefe Introduction to the Skill of Song* as more elementary than the anonymous *Pathway to Musicke* (1596) and intended only for singers. Even his most recent biographer, Ó Mathúna, *William Bathe*, 183, concludes "that Bathe's influence on singing was not great." Perhaps Hawkins (*A General History*, ch. 101, 497–99) is partly to blame for Bathe's low reputation. I think that Johnson, "Solmization," was correct to include him as one of his four main witnesses. Kevin Karnes (Brandeis University) is currently preparing a detailed interpretation of the sections of Bathe's treatise concerned with "naming" and "tuning" for publication. I include only those points essential to Bathe's conception of pitch.

45. Bathe, *A Briefe Introduction to the Skill of Song*, sig. Aiv^{v}. I do not supply citations for subsequent passages on the same page or folio.

46. Morley, *A Plaine and Easie Introduction*, 2.

47. Cooper, "Englische Musiktheorie," 184, correctly notes that none of the writers use the term "hexachord," but conflates their terms for scale with those for hexachord.

48. I supply the numbers in brackets to make the passage easier to understand.

49. Johnson emphasizes that Bathe presents the solmization syllables in terms of an octave scale, which he takes to be a "scale with a fixed series of syllables and a clearly defined tonal center," in other words, a scale in the modern sense. He calls it a mixolydian scale (as do Henderson, "Solmization Syllables," 274, and Rainbow) and realizes it as a musical example on C with one flat in the signature. Rainbow describes it as "a complete, recurring octave of the Mixolydian scale" (introduction to Bathe, *A Briefe Introduction to the Skill of Song*, p. 12). Cooper ("Englische Musiktheorie," 184–86) finds the "minor seventh" used in English solmization "extraordinarily meaningful because it leads to the implication that the entire hexachord system is now oriented toward the dominant rather than toward the tonic, and that in turn creates further particularities of English music theory." Of course the notion of "seventh" enters only when one introduces the notion of tonic.

50. Johnson, "Solmization," 46.

51. Johnson, "Solmization," 49. Note that Bathe does not add a new seventh syllable but repeats one of the original six. See also Atcherson, "Symposium," 10. The distinction is worth noting, given the experimentation on the continent with newly invented seventh syllables (*sy*, *ho*, *ni*, etc.).

52. One consequence of Johnson's reading is that he interprets example 2 to mean: "These signatures have one flat too many compared with our modern signatures." There is one flat too many only if we think of the three as G major, C major, and F major.

53. Boyd, *Elizabethan Music*, 250–51, describes Bathe's system accurately, and characterizes it: "So far, excellent; like a modern sol-faist he has discarded hexachords in favor of an eight-note system, and *ut* always refers to the same note while the key remains the same; he was tending toward the Curwens' *movable do* system, not the awkward *fixed ut* of the French. But then he unfortunately allows exceptions to creep in . . . ". Boyd concludes, "Bathe was courageous enough to think out a new idea. He then took a fatal look backward at his contemporaries, hesitated, and was lost." For a more sympathetic interpretation, see Karnes, "William Bathe's *A Briefe Introduction to the Skill of Song*: A Lesson in Practical Solmization," forthcoming.

54. Bathe, *A Briefe Introduction to the Skill of Song*, foldout page, sig. D.

55. The 1569 edition of the *Whole Book of Psalms* uses fonts with conjoined solmization syllables to show two scales (no flats and one flat), with a four-syllable solmization (*ut* and *re* are used only at the bottom of the staff or for the final). See Temperley, *English Parish Church*, fig. 2 and p. 65.

56. Karnes, "William Bathe's *A Briefe Introduction to the Skill of Song*: A Lesson in Practical Solmization," forthcoming.

57. Bathe, *A Briefe Introduction to the Skill of Song*, sig. Bii^{r}. See Henderson, "Solmization Syllables," 271–80. An unrealized implication of these new *uts* is to create three additional scales in the sharp direction.

58. My thanks to Kevin Karnes for the solmization of example 5d. Sig. Biiii^{r} also contains a four-voice setting of the Sternhold translation of Psalm 4, *O God that art my righteousnesse*, with the "Church tune" in the tenor. This tune was one of four in common use, according to the 1594 edition of East's *Whole Book of Psalms* (1592). See Temperley, *English Parish Church*, fig. 3. I wonder if it was added by the printer (East) to fill up space: it has no obvious connection to Bathe's argument.

59. Morley attacks the author for stealing from the German theorists Lossius and Beurhusius, authors of *musica poetica* treatises, and from an unnamed descant treatise (*A Plaine and Easie Introduction*, sig. *3^{v} in the Annotations): " . . . one part of his booke he stole out of *Beurhusius*, another out of *Lossius*, perverting the sence of *Lossius* his wordes, and giving examples flatte to the contrary, of that which *Lossius* saith. And the last part of his booke treating of *Descant*, he tooke *verbatim* out of an old written booke which I have. But it should seeme, that whatsoever or whosoever he was, that gave it to the presse, was not the Author of it himselfe, else would he have set his name to it, or then hee was ashamed of his labour." Concerning *The Pathway*, see Cooper, "Englische Musiktheorie," 158–59, and the Appendix.

60. A facsimile of the treatise is readily available on reel 1149 of the microfilm set Early English Printed Books (STC I). This gamut bears some resemblance to the one in the

anonymous "A Short Introduction," Rainbow, *English Psalmody Prefaces*, 29, as well as to Dowland's 1609 translation of *Andreas Ornithoparcus His Micrologus*, 8.

61. The author or the printer did not quite grasp the significance of the columns and so ♯ *mi* takes up too much space and is partly in the third column.

62. Morley, *A Plaine and Easie Introduction*, sig. *3ᵛ: "Take away two or three scales which are filched out of *Beurhusius*, and fill up the three first pages of the booke, you shal not finde one side in all the booke without some grosse errour or other."

63. The full title reads: *A Plaine and Easie Introduction to Practicall Musicke, Set down in forme of a dialogue: Devided into three partes, The first teacheth to sing with all things necessary for the knowledge of pricksong. The second treateth of descante and to sing two parts in one upon a plainsong or ground, with other things necessary for a descanter. The third and last part entreateth of composition of three foure five or more parts with many profitable rules to that effect.* Morley's is by far the best known of any of the English music treatises, due in part perhaps to its availability in a modern paperback edition (I nonetheless recommend using one of the facsimile editions instead because the editor has occasionally changed wording without comment). For bibliography concerning Morley, see Damschroder and Williams, *Music Theory*, 210–11; Cooper, "Englische Musiktheorie," 159–60; Boyd, *Elizabethan Music*, 225–42; Henderson, "Solmization Syllables," 281–84.

64. I include for purposes of comparison a similar statement using different wording from the brief anonymous treatise in the 1562 *The Whole Book of Psalmes* (Rainbow, *English Psalmody Prefaces*): "In this table, or *gamma ut*, is conteyned all, what is necessari to the knoweledge of singing wherefore it must be diligentlie waid [sic] & muste also bee perfectly committed to memory, so that ye can redely and distinctly say it without boke, both forwarde and backward: that is, upward and downward And this is the greatest pain that ye nede to take in this travayle."

65. The italics are found in the 1597 edition. I wonder if in this instance they indicate Morley's indebtedness to another source.

66. Morley, *A Plaine and Easie Introduction,* 2–3. Johnson, "Solmization," 27, is incorrect in asserting that Morley was the only theorist of this time to encourage memorizing the gamut.

67. This chance observation underlines the need for a critical (and somewhat less hagiographic) assessment of Morley's treatise—in particular, a consideration of his sources.

68. Henderson, "Solmization Syllables," 281, notes that Morley's terms had been used by Leonel Power more than a century earlier.

69. He actually calls it "three-flat" but the absence of the notion of octave duplication means that either the B♭ or the E♭ is notated twice, depending on the clef.

70. I am indebted to Daniel Page for this observation, presented in a seminar report at Brandeis; see his forthcoming "Tonal Types and Designs in Thomas Morley's Published Collections."

71. *fa sol la fa sol la fa*[=E♭] *sol la mi fa sol* instead of the usual *fa sol la fa sol la mi* [E♮] *fa sol la.*

72. A point made by Johnson, "Solmization," 51. While Johnson and I make some of the same observations, our terminology and conclusions are quite different. For example, he focuses on the issue of mutation (how Morley's practice differs from "Renaissance" practice) and does not consider scales at all; I would not invoke the idea of mutation given what I see as an emphasis on fixed scales.

73. Henderson, "Solmization Syllables," 287, describes this example as "a riddle seemingly made to demonstrate the exception to the rules." I cannot explain why Morley supplied the apparently superfluous intermingled E♭s when the flat was already in the signature.

74. The treatise, thought to date from ca. 1610, was never published; it survives in a single manuscript, London, British Library Add. MS 19758. See Cooper, "Englische Musiktheorie," 160–61, where the treatise is characterized as being partly taken from *The Pathway*; Damschroder and Williams, *Music Theory*, 260. The *explicit* reads "Thomas Ravenscroft Bacheler of Musicke And one of ye children of poules." According to Austern, *Music in English Children's Drama*, 20 and 213, Ravenscroft was a member of St. Paul's Cathedral choir ca. 1597–ca. 1604.

75. Ravenscroft, "Treatise," f. 2^{v}. Boyd, *Elizabethan Music*, 242, cites a passage from Ravenscroft's published treatise on notation, *A Briefe Discourse*, in which he compares Morley to "the Sunne in the Firmament of our Art, and did give light to our understanding with his Praecepts."

76. Ravenscroft, "Treatise," f. 4^{r}–4^{v}; transcription based in part on Ruff, "The 17th Century English Music Theorists," 411 (my thanks to Timothy Johnson for providing a xerox of Ruff's transcription; I have not yet been able to consult the entire dissertation), who describes Ravenscroft's information as incorrect because his description of the three scales does not match traditional definitions of the hexachord. Johnson, "Solmization," 51, commented on the E♭ in the soft hexachord, not realizing that Ravenscroft was describing scales (in the sense that I have been using the word); he explained the result as the same mixolydian scale Bathe had used. He concludes: "Thus, his reliance on a new device for pitch organization, the scale, when attempting to describe a traditional device, the hexachord, suggests that Ravenscroft's treatise breaks from modal theory."

77. Ravenscroft, "Treatise," f. 5^{r}–5^{v}. His citation "Setho Calviso Li: 2, fo: 121" refers to *Exercitationes musicae duae* of 1600, "Exercitatio altera De initio et progressu musices," 121–23. I discuss this form of solmization in my forthcoming "Waelrant and Bocedization: Reflections on Solmization Reform."

78. On Ravenscroft's solmization, see Atcherson, "Symposium," 10, and Johnson, "Solmization," 52, both of whom emphasize the fact that Ravenscroft used a major scale.

79. It is worth noting that Ravenscroft is interested in the two different names for the "seventh degree"—*B mi* and *B pa*—but he does not comment on the resulting difference in

"scale-type" (in the sense of a pitch collection with a particular configuration of half and whole steps).

80. Composers frequently played on solmization syllables that occur in the text. There are several such examples in Ravenscroft's *Pammelia* (1609), pp. 29, 33, 41, 43, some of which use the traditional six-syllable gamut. Three of them are transcribed and discussed by Flynn, "A Reconsideration," 176. Concerning composers' autographs, see Owens, *Composers at Work.*

81. On Campion, see Cooper, "Englische Musiktheorie," 162–63; Damschroder and Williams, *Music Theory*, 49–50; Wilson, *Words and Notes*, ch. 6; Lowbury, Salter, and Young, *Thomas Campion*; Johnson, "Solmization in English Treatises," 53–55; Henderson, "Solmization Syllables," 284–86.

82. Campion, *Works*, 324–25.

83. A handwritten addition to John Amner, *Sacred Hymns* (1615; copy in Sibley Music Library, Rochester, New York), cantus secundus, sig. B contains a solmization for the "flat Gam-ut" that is identical to Campion's; the staff, with a soprano clef and one flat signature, has the lines annotated from bottom to top C s[ol] E m G s B f D l, and the spaces D l F f A l C s E ł m [*sic*], a seventeenth-century version of Every Good Boy Does Fine! David Greer pointed out the existence of a handwritten addition to this print in his "Manuscript Additions in 'Parthenia'," 181. I am grateful to Prof. Patrick Macey for sending me a transcription of the manuscript addition.

84. Coperario, *Rules How to Compose*, 3. On the relationship between the two treatises, see Bukofzer's introduction and Wilson, *Words and Notes*, 254–57.

85. On Butler, see Boyd, *Elizabethan Music*, 245–48; Cooper, "Englische Musiktheorie," 165–67; Damschroder and Williams, *Music Theory*, 42–43; Pruett, "Charles Butler"; introduction to the facsimile edition of *The Principles of Musik.*

86. Butler, *Principles of Musik*, 13, with further comments on 15–16.

87. The notes make clear that he was aware of some of the continental experiments with seven-note systems, including those of Puteanus and Waelrant.

88. I do not know the source of the "olde Verse"; for once Butler supplies no citation.

89. Butler points out (*The Principles of Musik*, 22) that adding the flats does not make the song flatter: "the song would prove no more flat with all these flats, than with none of them."

90. It follows that I disagree with Johnson's conclusions, for example, "The four-syllable system of Ravenscroft and Campion, based on Morley's adaptation of hexachordal theory, is fundamentally different from Bathe's system" ("Solmization," 55) and "As in Bathe's system the four-syllable system makes the concept of octave equivalence, which was absent from the hexachordal system, explicit in the solmization syllables. The inclusion of octave equivalence in the syllables and the arrangement of the scale in two tetrachords show that the four-syllable system constitutes a break from hexachordal theory. The correspondence between these aspects and contemporary musical practice suggests that

Ravenscroft and Campion may have had an implicit recognition of the developing concept of tonality" (56–57).

91. To cite but one example, the root meaning of key as derived from the Latin *clavis* is what you open a door with. A key is a note—A, B, C, D, etc.—that stands on a line or space of the staff. Some of the keys are "signed"; they are called clefs in English. Morley also uses key to mean the clefs in a composition, translating the Italian *chiave* and *chiavette* as low key and high key, what we today refer to as low clefs and high clefs (Morley, *A Plaine and Easie Introduction*, 195–96). We have seen that key can mean scale, and we will encounter still other meanings in the ensuing discussion. I disagree with Cooper's assertion ("Englische Musiktheorie," 199) "'Moode', 'Mood', 'Tone', 'Tune', 'Key', und 'Air'—aller dieser Wörter wurden mit Bezug auf Tonalität gebraucht und hatten ungefähr dieselbe Bedeutung."

92. The extensive literature on this subject includes: Lewis, "Incipient Tonal Thought"; Cooper, "Englische Musiktheorie," especially the section entitled "Tonalität"; Atcherson, "Key and Mode" and "Symposium"; Wienpahl, "English Theorists"; Zimmerman, "Air, A Catchword."

93. This comes from a section, referred to on p. 149 as "counterpoint," that consists entirely of chordal four-voice passages.

94. Harman, 248f. Members of my seminar at Brandeis advanced the interesting possibility that "aire" in the final line of this quotation could be "*A re*."

95. This example is transcribed and discussed by Cooper, "Englische Musiktheorie," 201–02, among others.

96. On air as it is used during the entire seventeenth century but especially the second half, see Zimmerman, "Air, A Catchword."

97. Modern editions of the eight "tunes" are given in Morley, *A Plain & Easy Introduction*, ed. Harman, 250–52; Stevenson, "Thomas Morley's 'Plaine and Easie' Introduction," 181.

98. Stevenson, "Thomas Morley's 'Plaine and Easie' Introduction," 180. See also Perkins, Review, 136–37.

99. Morley, *A Plaine and Easie Introduction*, sig. (∴) 1^v–2^r. He refers the reader to Glarean, Zacconi, and Zarlino. I suspect that it may be possible to find his source because on the final page of the volume he lists some 51 "practicioners, the moste part of whose works we have diligently perused, for finding the true use of the Moods." The names from the beginning of the list probably come from Glarean.

100. Both use "tune," translations, respectively, of the French *ton* and the Latin *tonus*. Dowland, trans. *Andreas Ornithoparcus His Micrologus*; "F.Ke.," trans. Le Roy, *A Briefe and Plaine Instruction*.

101. It is of course curious, in light of the nearly complete absence of continental modal theory from English treatises of the time, that the readers to whom Morley gave his almost finished book missed having such a discussion and recommended that he include one.

102. Campion, *Works*, 327.

103. Wiering, "The Language of the Modes," 267, notes that Campion "describes Zarlino's double division of the octave, probably after Calvisius 1600," that is, *Exercitationes Musicae Duae*.

104. In the key of G with B sharp, Campion does not allow a cadence on B (the greater or sharpe third), but permits A and C, as well as D; in F [with B sharp!]: C, A, F; in A [with B flat]: A, E, C; in G [with B flat] G, D, B♭. He also writes (Campion, *Works*, 346): "To make the key knowne is most necessary in the beginning of a song, and is best exprest by the often using of his proper fift, and fourth, and thirds, rising or falling." See, among others, Wilson, *Words and Notes*, 250–85; Apfel, *Geschichte der Kompositionslehre*, 1446–56; Cooper, "Englische Musiktheorie," 202–03.

105. Temperley, *English Parish Church*, 68, and fig. 28, where is it listed as the first of eight tunes in East's *Psalms*, 1594 edition. Davis (in Campion, *Works*, 346n.) identified it as "the second of ten traditional psalm tones" in East's *Psalms*, 1592 edition. I am extremely grateful to Professor Temperley for identifying the tune, explaining its history, and providing me with an annotated list of sources where it appears as listed in the Hymn Tune Index.

106. Temperley, "Adventures of a Hymn Tune—2," 488–89; Temperley, "The Old Way of Singing," 520–23, 530–31; Temperley, *English Parish Church*, I, 69–70, 74; II, exx. 10 (a, b), 14.

107. Temperley, "The Old Way of Singing," 521.

108. Personal communication, 20 February 1992.

109. Davis, in Campion, *Works*, 346n.

110. Butler, *Principles of Musik,* 81. On Butler, see Cooper, "Englische Musiktheorie," 203–04. I disagree with his view that "Butlers Anschauung von Tonart und Modus, die hauptsächtlich auf umgearbeitetem Gedankengut aus Calvisius beruht, ist konservativ und höchst subjektiv, wenn auch nicht ohne einsichtiget Beobachtung."

111. Campion, *Works*, 326, discussed earlier.

112. Morley, *A Plaine and Easie Introduction*, 156. The continuation of this passage is cited earlier, note 40.

113. He makes a further objection to the voice-leading in measure 4 of both versions: "But here you must note that your song beeing governed with flats [ex. 31a] it is unformall to touch a sharpe eight in *E la mi,* as in this key [ex. 31b] to touch it in *F fa ut*, and in both places the sixth would have been much better."

114. For a revisionist view of a very neglected chapter in this saga, see Page, "Uniform and Catholic."

115. Flynn, "A Reconsideration," 277.

116. Flynn, "A Reconsideration," iii.

117. Flynn, "A Reconsideration," 277–78.

118. Whythorne, *Autobiography*, 1962 ed., 203–04.

119. The following biography is based on Ó Mathúna, *William Bathe*, 33–75. See also the introduction by Hill to the edition of *A Brief Introduction to the True Art of Music* and by Rainbow to the facsimile edition of *A Briefe Introduction to the Skill of Song.*

120. The 1584 volume was known to Hawkins (*A General History*, ch. 101, 497–99).

121. Whythorne, *Autobiography*, 1961 ed., 302.

122. For example, Ó Mathúna, *William Bathe*, 174.

123. "A generall Table comprehending two parts in one, of all kindes upon all plaine Songs" (with three pages of explanation); a representation of a sword as a mnemonic device, also explicating the table; the names of the consonances and dissonances; four *sententiae* "De inventione"; a four–voice psalm-setting by "G.K," *O Lord in thee is all my trust*; and *10 sundry waies of 2. parts in one upon the plain song.*

124. Rainbow, introduction to Bathe, *A Briefe Introduction to the Skill of Song.*

125. Fenlon and Milsom, "'Ruled Paper Imprinted'," 148–52.

126. *Instrumental Music Printed Before 1600*, 359.

127. Bathe, *A Brief Introduction to the True Art of Music*, ed. Hill, i ; Cooper, "Englische Musiktheorie," 158–59; Ó Mathúna, *William Bathe*, 175–76.

128. Krummel, *English Music Printing*, 21–22. East registered both of Bathe's treatises in 1596.

129. Krummel, *English Music Printing*, 56–57. Kevin Karnes pointed out to me that Krummel included a facsimile from Steele (fig. 31, from Bathe's treatise) in his list of printers who used the Van den Keere type face (Appendix, 175).

130. Krummel, *English Music Printing*, 56–57.

131. Krummel, *English Music Printing*, 20 and 60–61.

132. Personal communication. I am grateful to Prof. Temperley for his prompt and helpful responses to several queries during my work on this project.

133. On Barley, see Lavin, "William Barley." Barley was not himself a printer but engaged the services of various printers for his ventures. According to both Lavin and the *STC*, the printer of the volumes under consideration was J. Danter. See also Krummel, *English Music Printing*, 21.

134. Ward, "Barley's Songs," 22; for a scathing assessment of *A New Booke*, see Dart's review of *Lute Music of Shakespeare's Time*. On *The Pathway*, see Cooper, "Englische Musiktheorie," 158–59.

Concepts of Key in Seventeenth-Century English Keyboard Music*

Candace Bailey

A variety of signatures for a single keynote exists in English keyboard music throughout the seventeenth century. The consistency of varied signatures is remarkable and implies an understanding of key—not mode—that differs significantly from later ones. As suggested by Jessie Ann Owens in "Concepts of Pitch in English Music Theory" (this volume), Charles Butler allows the possibility of various signatures in his *Principles of Music* (1636). The following analyses will show that the application of Butler's ideas concerning "Tone" (or "Air") to English keyboard music c. 1640-1707 yields some distinguishing characteristics in tonal structure as indicated by key signatures and keynote. MS 1179 in the library of Christ Church, Oxford, provides a unique starting point for an investigation into the reasoning behind these signatures, for its copyist labeled ten pieces, using such classifications as "In G♭," "In G♭♭," "In G♯," and "G♮." These labels roughly coincide with the "keys" defined by Christopher Simpson in his *Compendium of Practical Music* (1667). No other English keyboard source from the seventeenth century contains labels that so closely match those described by theorists.[1] These labels, which I believe reveal something about the tonal structure of the inscribed works, are given in Table 1.

Three copyists entered pieces into the manuscript. The hand that concerns us here is the second, responsible for pages 18–41; the copyist of the section remains unknown and shall be refered to as "Copyist B." Since Copyist B referred to Blow as "Dr." and included a concordance with Nicolas Lebègue's *2nd Livre d'Orgue*, published in 1678/79, his contributions to MS 1179 must not predate 1679 (Blow received his doctorate in 1677).[2] George Luellyn added the final contribution to MS 1179, an inscription on page 42: "George Luellyn Anno Domi 1690."[3] Luellyn's date of 1690 provides the *terminus ante quem*, and the middle section must date c. 1680–1690.[4]

TABLE 1 Contents of MS 1179 in the hand of Copyist B

Page	Title	Designation	Keynote	Signature	Attribution
18			C	—	Dr. Blow
19			F	♭	
20			C	—	
20			C	—	Dr. Blow
21			C	—	H. Purcel
22	Saraband		C	—	Dr. Blow
22	Almand		C	—	Dr. Blow
23	Almand		C	—	Dr. Blow
24	Corant	In C	C	—	Dr. Blow
24		in D♭	D	♭	Dr. Blow
25		in G♭	G	♭	
26		in G♭♭	G	♭♭	Dr. Blow
27	Chiacone		G	♭	Dr. Blow
28	Ground in Cfaut	Cfaut	C	—	Dr. Blow
33	A Ground in G♯	G♯	G	♯	Dr. Blow
35	Prelude	G natural	G	—	Dr. Bull
36	In E		A/E	—	H. Purcel [Lebègue]
36			A	—	Dr. Blow
37	Prelude	G♯	G	♯	Dr. Blow
38		In C	C	—	H. Purcel
39		In A	A	—	Dr. Gibbons
40	Prelude		A	—	
41	Hunting Almond (inc.)		G	♯	

Copyist B labeled only ten pieces, and all compositions between pages 25 and 39 are thus designated except two. No evidence exists to pinpoint the exact sources from which Copyist B copied MS 1179; no other sources survive with remotely similar labels, suggesting that he probably decided upon the titles himself.[5] After he had completed page 39, Copyist B added the two compositions between pages 25 and 39 without labels.[6]

Of the other pieces without labels in Copyist B's hand, all are on C with no signature or F with one flat. A logical explanation of why Copyist B chose certain pieces to label, then, is that the first time he entered works into MS 1179, he copied pieces of no special concern—they followed "regular" conventions. With the next bit of copying, he noticed a difference between signatures on the same keynote and pointed these differences out by labeling the keys. The last set of copying, the final pieces, again followed contemporary practice as far as Copyist B was concerned. Copyist B did not worry with labels for the additions to pages 27 and 36.

Most curious is the diversity of signatures for G, for it challenges us to explore the concept of "key" during the seventeenth century; the variety cannot be simply explained by major / minor tonality nor by mode. Jessie Ann Owens convincingly demonstrated that "mode" is an inappropriate term for describing seventeenth-century English music.[7] MS 1179 provides a venue for applying the critical language Owens suggests.[8]

* * *

Copyist B's key designations bear some relation to contemporary theoretical writings (e.g., Simpson) in his use of "flat" to denote a minor third above the keynote and "sharp" for a major one.[9] In his *Compendium*, Simpson noted that

> in our modern music, we acknowledge no such thing as Properchant [i.e., the natural hexachord], every song being of its own nature either flat or sharp, and that determined not by B's flat or [natural] but by the greater or lesser third being joined next to the key in which any song is set.[10]

Therefore, if the keynote is G and there is a minor third above it, the "key" is "G♭." The "key" prescribes neither the sixth nor the seventh scale degree, and Simpson did not give any details concerning the treatment of $\hat{6}$.

Because Copyist B's labels describe the quality of both third and sixth, "G♭" must differ from "G♭♭." The flat is not simply missing from the signature in "G♭." Copyist B, at least, felt obligated to notate which "system" was being used—minor third with either major or minor sixth. These two signatures for G are not to be thought of as Dorian and Aeolian, as contemporary discussions of mode clearly show;[11] indeed, Simpson's explanation of "mode" leaves one questioning just how familiar he was with the term:

> Before we treat of Figurate Discant, I must not omit to say something concerning the Modes or Tones. Not so much for any great use we have of them as to let you know what is meant by them and that I may not appear singular, for you shall scarce meet with any author that has writ of music but you will read something concerning them.[12]

Simpson followed these comments by discussing the eight plainsong tunes of the "Latins," which appeared in the tenor. He criticized Morley because Morley left the "business . . . imperfect or obscure as to any certain rule for regulating the key and air of the music though one of the *greatest concerns of musical composition*."[13]

Thus, "key" existed as a concept, but its definition was far from clear.[14] "Mode" was of little concern to English composers during the most of the seventeenth century.[15] The two "keys," flat and sharp, are not the equivalent of minor and major keys in the modern sense, for if more than one signature can denote a "flat key," then more than one possibility exists for that collection of pitches associated with a minor third above the keynote. The task at hand, then, is to suggest what the guiding principles for tonal structure were during the mid-seventeenth century as they relate to the titles in MS 1179. "Key" provides a starting point for this inquiry, being a word familiar both to contemporary and modern authors. As a general concept, key cannot be divorced from vertical sonority: "the bass is the foundation of the harmony, upon which the key solely depends."[16] As for key as a harmonic concept, not only did Simpson name the key by the quality of its third, but he also stated that one can expect certain cadences in flat keys and others in sharp ones.[17] By noting which scale degrees should be accessed as cadential degrees, Simpson pointed to tonal structure as indicated by the key—key is associated with function.

Slightly later than Simpson's initial publications, two writers limit the keys, and apparently the signatures available, to two: Francis North (Baron Guilford) and Henry Purcell.[18] North, writing only ten years after Simpson, states that

> Hereby it appears that any Note may be the Key Note, as to pitch: As to species or sorts of Keys, they are two, *viz.* Flat and Sharp . . . When the third is Flat or Sharp, the sixth must be so likewise . . . .[19]

While the existence of two keys, flat and sharp, does not necessarily limit the possibility of signatures, making the quality of third and sixth follow each other (as North asserts) does.[20]

The central question, then, is the difference between the two pieces on G with a minor third above them in MS 1179. Is the "missing flat" a mere coincidence or copyist's (or composer's) oversight, or do the signatures signal a true difference in tonal structures? The multiplicity of signatures throughout the seventeenth century clearly suggests that the signatures for pieces with a minor third above the keynote were *choices*, not mistakes. Table 2 illustrates the variety of signatures in two seventeenth-century English keyboard sources. It only includes those pieces for which keynotes have more than one signature in the source.

A seventeenth-century method distinguishing between the two possible "minor" keys exists in Charles Butler's *Principles of Music* (1636).[21] In his description of "Airs," Butler showed that several systems organizing tonal structures were common in England. Using the terms "Air" and "Tone" interchangeably, he listed six. They correspond to the six "servile" notes: *ut*, *re*, *fa*, *sol*, *la*, and *pha* (his name for the seventh degree, a half-step above *la*); *mi*, the "master note," does not function as a "Tone." Butler fixed the notes according to the three types of hexachords, indicated by no signature, one flat, or two flats. (No sharp signatures are given.) The place of the given note, or "key," within the hexachord indicated by the signature defines the Tone or Air. Of the six Tones, *fa*, *re*, *sol*, and *ut* are frequent, *pha* is rare and *la* even rarer.[22] Table 3 illustrates Butler's Tones and Airs per his narrative.

Perhaps the logical term for Butler's "Tone" is, indeed, "tone." However, several seventeenth-century English writers use that word in varying contexts, making its precise meaning somewhat confusing for the modern reader. A more appropriate appellation might be "tonal type." Borrowing from terminology made familiar in several articles by Harold Powers, Alexander Silbiger described the tonal type of Frescobaldi's keyboard compositions as "defined solely by the . . . tonic center and key signature."[23] This definition may also be applied to Butler's tone plus keynote. Thus, there are eighteen tonal types, twelve of which are commonly used. (Butler noted the rarity of *la* and *pha* pieces.) A signature of one flat with G as the keynote is tonal type *G sol*; G with two flats is tonal type *G re*. That these are indeed distinct groups is clear in Butler's description of the cadences to be used in the different Tones.

> Of Secondary Cadences the Fifth is chief, as most pleasing and best maintaining the Air . . . . But because, in true Cadences, the binding half-note must ever be sharp; therefore in the first and third Tone (Ut and Fa) the Third is excluded: and in the second and fifth Tone (Re and La) the Fifth is excluded: because their Binding half-notes are neither sharp, nor apt to be sharped.[24]

Here, Butler described the half-step motion necessary at cadences, and his rules on where to cadence (or not) were echoed by Simpson and later writers. In practical terms, if one is composing in the Tone *ut* with G as the keynote, one does not cadence to the third degree, B, because that would necessitate an A♯, and A is "not apt to be sharped."

Recognizing the potential confusion, Butler noted that one cannot simply distinguish the Airs (Tones) by the *keys*—that is, names of the notes—"because in the same Key are many different Tones." He listed several of these overlapping keys and Tones: "as in D, may be La, or Sol, or Re . . . so that if we say the Tone is D *la sol re* . . . we are yet to seeketh which of the three Notes, in any of these Keys, to taketh for the Tone." But to Butler "the distinction of the Airs by the Notes is certain and constant, in what Keys so ever they stand." Furthermore, in a statement acknowledging transposition, Butler noted that "If Re be the Tone or Air-note; whether it stand in *A re* (the Mi-clef being B [no signature]) or in *D sol re*, (the Mi-clef being E [B♭ in signature]) or in *Gamut* (the Mi-clef being A [B♭ and E♭ in

TABLE 2 Signatures in seventeenth-century English keyboard sources

A. *GB-Och* 1236, copied by William Ellis, c. 1650–1660

Composer	Title	Source	Keynote	Signature
Tresure	[Corant]	p.3	D	–
Tresure	Ayre	p.7	D	–
Tresure	Corant	p.8	D	♭
	Sarabrand	p.8	D	♭
La Barre	Corant	p.10	D	–
	Courant	p.11	D	–
	Tole Tole	p.14	G	–
	Coranto	p.14	D	♭
	Almaine	p.20	D	♭
	Corant	p.22	D	♭
	Sarabrand	p.22	D	♭
	Ayre	p.24	D	♭
Roberts		p.25	D	♭
Roberts	Coranto	p.26	D	♭
Noue	Corant	p.30	G	–
J. Ferrabosco	Almond	p.33	D	♯♯
J. Ferrabosco	Corant	p.34	D	♯♯
J. Ferrabosco	Sarabrand	f.34	D	♯♯
	Courant	f.35v	D (?M/m)	–
	Sarabrand	f.36	D	–
Rogers	Corant	f.36v	G	♯
Ellis	Almaine	f.37	D	♭
Dufaut	Corant	f.42v	E	♯
La Barre	Corant	f.46	D	♭
	Madgana Cree	f.1v	G	–
	Midsomer	f.2	G	♭
	Parson of ye Parrish	f.2	D	–
	Pretty fancy	f.4v	G	–
	Corant	f.5v	D	–
	Hedge or Haycork	f.6	D	–
	Corant	f.7	D	♯♯
	Mask	f.7v	D	–
	Mayds delight	f.8	G	–
Ellis	Almaine	f.8v	D	–
fragment		f.9	D	–
Ellis	Corant	f.9v	D	♭
Ellis	Corant	f.10	D	–
Ellis	Almaine	f.10v	A	♯♯♯

TABLE 2 (*cont.*)

Composer	Title	Source	Keynote	Signature
Ellis	Almond Mariae	f.13^v	D	♭
Ellis	Corant	f.14	D	♭
Moulin/Ellis	Sarabrand	f.15^v	D	♭
	Vulcan e Venus	f.16^v	G	♯
Moulin/Ellis	Corant	f.18	D	–
	Thomas you Cannott	f.18^v	G	–
	Sarabrand	f.18^v	D	–
	Irish Way	f.19	G	–

B. *Melothesia*, published 1674 by Matthew Locke

Composer	Title	Piece #	Keynote	Signature
Preston	Prelude	22	G	♯
Preston	Almain	23	G	♯
Preston	Corant	24	G	♯
Preston	Saraband	25	G	♯
Roberts	Prelude	26	E	♯
Roberts	Almain	27	E	–
Roberts	Corant	28	E	–
Roberts	Corant	29	E	–
Roberts	Saraband	30	E	–
Gregory	Almain	31	D	♭
Gregory	Corant	32	D	♭
Gregory	Saraband	33	D	♭
Gregory	Horne Pipe	34	D	♭
Hall	Corant	42	G	♯
Smith		43	G	♯
Smith	[Digby's Farewell]	44	G	♯
Smith	[Holle's Farewell]	45	G	♯
[Thatcher, arr.]		49	D	–
[Thatcher, arr.]		50	D	♭
[Thatcher, arr.]	Charity	51	D	♭
[Thatcher, arr.]		52	D	♭
Preston	Horn Pipe	60	D	–
Locke	For the Organ	62	E	–
Locke	For the Organ	65	D	–
Locke	For the Organ	66	G	–
Locke	For a Double Organ	68	D	–

TABLE 3 Butler's airs and tones (in the order listed by Butler)

	FA	RE	SOL	UT	PHA	LA
no signature	C	A	D	G	F	E
one flat	F	D	G	C	B♭	A
two flats	B♭	G	C	F	E♭	D

signature]) *there is no difference at all.*"[25] (Emphasis mine.) That is, *D la sol re* does not differentiate among *D la, D sol,* or *D re,* which, according to Butler, are different entities with different signatures. Furthermore, *D re* and *G re* are to his way of thinking manifestations of the same thing with different starting pitches.

Butler's exposition of the Tones or Airs makes it clear that signatures of nothing, one flat, and two flats were possible for G. Moreover, his explanations show that there were differences among these—they are distinct tonal types. The signatures suggest discreet tonal structures.

The pieces labeled "In G♭♭" and "In G♭" in MS 1179 (exx. 1a and b) illustrate this concept.[26] "In G♭♭" is an Almaine by Blow, published in *The Second Book of the Harpsichord Master* (1700); "In G♭" is a slightly altered version of Frescobaldi's setting of the "La Monica" tune.[27] A comparison of the use of E♭ and E♮ in these two compositions yields a difference between the two tonal structures. In Blow's Almaine ("In G♭♭"), E♭ takes a prominent role in the cadences concluding each half, particularly the first, where the half-cadence (as defined by Roger North) highlights the move from D to E♭ in the bass.[28] The half-cadence makes good use of the half-step between E♭ and D, as indeed other pieces with similar indications in the signature do (i.e., pieces on D with one flat and A with nothing in the signature.) At the other major cadence in this composition, the cadence at the end, Blow wrote a Cm–D–Gm progression. The final cadence in the other work, "In G♭," is very different: CM–D–GM.

The chords used in each signature vary. In "G♭♭," chords occur on $\hat{1}$, $\hat{4}$, and $\hat{5}$. Those on $\hat{4}$ are usually in first inversion—stressing the D–E♭ half-step described above. In "G♭," chords also appear on $\hat{1}$, $\hat{4}$, and $\hat{5}$; however, all root-position chords on $\hat{4}$ are major (except one in m. 9). I believe these compositions illustrate Butler's Tones *sol* (G♭) and *re* (G♭♭). The different labels indicate that Copyist B also distinguished between the two. G with one flat was not as common as it had been earlier, but composers such as Blow continued to use both signatures for G (and two for D, as well).

EXAMPLE 1A "In G♭♭"

EXAMPLE 1A (*cont.*)

The ambiguity of the E♭ / E♮ between these two pieces accounts for a very different sound. Undoubtedly, "In G ♭" sounds antiquated next to Blow's almain, and rightly so for "In G ♭" is a tune that was popular almost one hundred years before "In G ♭ ♭" appeared.[29] Nonetheless, it was copied and labeled in the 1680s, providing a valid comparison. Furthermore, as will be shown below, differences between these tonal types (specifically *G re* and *G sol*, and *D re* and *D sol*) existed throughout the seventeenth century.

Characteristics of *re* pieces include a *melodic* emphasis on $\hat{3}$, a considerable amount of time on $\hat{4}$, a tendency to employ the half-cadence (or modern "Phrygian cadence") at important points, and melodic significance given to the interval of a fourth from $\hat{5}\smile\hat{8}$ ($\hat{1}$) . Attributes of *sol* compositions involve a melodic stress on $\hat{5}$, a *harmonic* stress on $\hat{3}$, and emphasis on the fifth interval from $\hat{3}\smile\hat{7}$. Finally, the structural significance of $\hat{6}$, its quality, and a tendency to move either to the "sharp" or "flat" side of the tonal center differs between the two systems.[30]

EXAMPLE 1 B "In G♭"

Two voluntaries by John Lugge (appearing in an autograph manuscript, *GB-Och* 49) embody the distinctions between *re* and *sol* pieces.[31] The first of these (ex. 2, p. 233 in MS) is on D with one flat in the signature—a *re* piece. The opening clearly illustrates how *re* pieces utilize the fourth scale degree, for each of the three parts begins with the interval D–G, and most cadences in the composition are to G—an example of how $\hat{4}$ may be highlighted. I have included only the first 5 measures in the example, but the remainder of the piece emulates the patterns seen here.

EXAMPLE 2 Lugge Voluntary, *GB-Och* 49, p. 233, mm. 1–5

In comparison, Lugge's Voluntary on p. 240 (ex. 3) also has D as the keynote but is a *sol* composition (D with nothing in the signature). Of particular significance is Lugge's tendency to avoid G in this work, placing more emphasis on $\hat{5}$ (A), which is not used as a secondary cadential degree in the *re* piece. The *sol* work inclines more to the sharp side, as noted with the cadences on A (necessitating a G♯) and E (using D♯); see table 4.

EXAMPLE 3 Lugge Voluntary, *GB-Och* 49, p. 240, mm. 1–10

TABLE 4 Major chords appearing in Lugge voluntaries with D as keynote

Voluntary #1 (*re*)	A♭	E♭	B♭	F	C	G	D	A		
Voluntary #3 (*sol*)			B♭	F	C	G	D	A	E	B

The conclusions of each Lugge voluntary (ex. 4) also illustrate the tonal structures dictated by the systems of *re* and *sol*. The first maintains a minor third above D until the final chord, while the second work introduces D major in m. 71 and preserves it to the conclusion. The second voluntary cadences to E major (via B major) at a crucial place: just before beginning the final imitative point. In contrast, the first never ventures to cadence even to *A major*; no G♯s appear in the entire composition. The tonal structures contrast profoundly in these two voluntaries, echoing the distinctions noted in the MS 1179 examples.[32]

EXAMPLE 4A Lugge Voluntary, p. 233, final nine measures

Example 4a (*cont.*)

Example 4b Lugge Voluntary (p. 240), final fourteen measures

EXAMPLE 4B (*cont.*)

Perhaps not surprisingly, the distinction between the two minor systems, *re* and *sol*, continued longer in voluntaries, verses, preludes, and fantasias than in dance music.[33] The final two works I shall present here offer several opportunities to examine late manifestations of *re* and *sol*. The first is a verse, tonal type *G re*, found in *GB-Lbl* MS Add. 31403 and *J-Tn* MS N-3/35, possibly by John Blow (ex. 5).[34] The opening point clearly features the descending fourth, D–G, and the next entrance (top voice) answers with the interval G–B♭, highlighting $\hat{3}$. The entire verse is given in example 5. Its tendency to flatten cadences and a pronounced use of $\hat{6}$ are two of the characteristics associated with *re* pieces.

EXAMPLE 5 Verse in *G re*

EXAMPLE 5 (*cont.*)

The second piece (ex. 6) is tonal type *D sol*. The initial statement outlines the D–A fifth characteristic of *sol* pieces. The chords utilizing $\hat{4}$ are predominantly major, notwithstanding the final B (m. 20), which is flat. It is in comparing the concordances of this composition that the crucial differences between *re* and *sol* may be determined. This verse occurs in two sources, *GB-Lbl* MS Add. 34695 and *GB-Cfm* MS 652; it is one of the few pieces with concordances that differ in the signature.[35] The Cambridge manuscript has a flat in the signature; the London source does not. While this may seem to undermine the tonal distinctions I am suggesting for this repertory, in fact, it is the exception that proves the rule. Example 6 shows that the two versions differ not only in signature, but in the quality of $\hat{6}$ as well. I have marked the Cambridge version below the staff: it incorporates the flats of Add. 34695, and adds several new ones of its own. The differing qualities of B cause a pivotal change in the sound of the piece, and hence its tonal structure.

EXAMPLE 6 Verse in *D sol* with *D re* version underneath

EXAMPLE 6 (*cont.*)

A few composers maintained the use of varied signatures for minor keys in harpsichord music. Giovanni Battista Draghi, an Italian emigré popular in England, employed both *re* and *sol* systems in his works. Significantly, some of the sources containing these pieces may be autograph. Draghi's use of *sol* signatures appears not to have occurred before c. 1690, even though he was in England in the 1660s.[36] Only those pieces with *re* signatures incorporate the "half-cadence" described by North at the close of the A section, and only *sol* pieces delay the prominent use of a melodic $\flat\hat{6}$ scale degree until into the B section. Another characteristic of Draghi's interpretation of the two systems is that *re* pieces tend to be much more chromatic than *sol* pieces (a tendency that exists throughout the period).

TABLE 5 Draghi's use of *re* and *sol* on D and G (numbering from the Klakowich edition)

Piece #	Signa.	A section	A section	A section	♭6 until B section
55	G♭	V/V–V			yes
57	G♭		V/III–III		no
62	D	V/V–V			no
63	D	V/V–V			yes
14	G♭♭			iv_6–V	no
15	G♭♭			iv_6–V	no
16	G♭♭	i–V			no
17	G♭♭			iv_6–V	no
18	G♭♭	V/V–V			delay ♭6 in A sect.
26	D♭		V/III–III		no
27	D♭		V/III–III		no
28	D♭			iv_6–V	no
29	D♭			iv_6–V	no
30	D♭	V/V–V			no
31	D♭	V/V–V			no
42	D♭	V/V–V			no
43	D♭	V/V–V			no
44	D♭			iv_6–V	no
56	G♭♭			iv_6–V	no
58	G♭♭		V/III–III		no
64	D♭			iv_6–V	no

* * *

Just as we assume certain things about the harmonic structure of a work written c. 1800, we may be able to predict structural sonorities in seventeenth-century music. Notably, the patterns differ from later ones and should not be viewed as "evolving" into the later tonality or still belonging to a putative sixteenth-century modal system.[37] We cannot take for granted that seventeenth-century composers did not notice the flat sixth degree missing from the signature and simply "correct" it.[38] A critical language derived from Butler's, as Owens suggests, provides a viable alternative to the inappropriate "Tone 2" or "transposed Dorian/Hypodorian," which clearly does not account for all seventeenth-century usage of compositions on G with a minor third: "G flat." Acknowledging *re* and *sol* pieces in this repertory begins to account for idiosyncrasies much more adequately than terms borrowed from distant times or locales.[39]

I do not wish to imply that Copyist B read Butler, only that he noticed the different signatures and noted them in his manuscript. He did not "correct" them—perhaps he was vaguely familiar with an outdated concept of key and documented such in MS 1179. His labels closely match those of Simpson, except that Simpson did not distinguish among all four used by Copyist B. Butler does describe such systems (at least three of them) in 1636; he most likely did not invent these ideas, but chronicled a current practice in his elementary tutor. How long this lasted remains to be determined; but I suspect it is present in the works of Byrd.[40] Certainly, pieces composed c. 1640 (e.g., the Lugge examples) appear to subscribe to Butler's classifications. As with many aspects of English keyboard music, patterns become difficult to follow around midcentury. Vestiges of different tonal types remain until at least 1707, but I do not feel comfortable saying they are the norm at that time.

The freedom inherent in seventeenth-century music reflects the detail in signature examined in this paper.[41] The difficulties perhaps explain why scholars have been relatively reluctant to explore harmony in the seventeenth century, beyond seeking "incipient" or "evolving" tonality. As scholars scrutinize other repertories, England's strikingly different approach to key may be placed in perspective.[42] It is in such a manner that the enigmatic harmonic idiom of seventeenth-century English music must be explored in order to understand better its unexpected twists and delights.

NOTES

*This work was supported in part by a grant from the National Endowment for the Humanities, as part of its Summer Seminars for College Teachers ("Analyzing Early Music, 1300–1600," Brandeis University, 1995). The author graciously acknowledges Jessie Ann Owens, director of the seminar, for her assistance in its development and preparation.

1. Occasionally, one finds such titles as "Saraband to the lesson before in A re" or "Ground in D sol re," but most of these are on A and C, which yield little in the exploration of differing signatures. A few collections, such as *US-NYp* Drexel 5612, are organized by the "keynote" (usually defined by contemporary writers as the final note in the bass) but do not follow patterns involving major or minor third above the keynote. The only other title relating to those in MS 1179 is "in g sol re ♯" in *GB-Och* 1003.

2. Copyist A might be associated with Martha and Sarah Long, whose names appear on the front cover of the manuscript. Lebègue's piece in MS 1179 (on p. 36) is entitled "Trio de 4e. Tu solus" in *2nd Livre d'Orgue*. Regarding the Lebègue attribution, see Williams, "Spurious Purcell," 371.

3. George Luellyn is discussed in Foster's *Alumni Oxoniensis*, 921. Luellyn invited some very distinguished musicians to his rooms while chaplain at Christ Church (1693–1703), and kept up with royal musicians, whom he might have met while a page-boy at the court of Charles II (Thompson, "Francis Withie," 11). Charles Burney refers to a Rev. George Luellyn's possible contributions to the second edition of *Orpheus Britannicus*; I doubt, however, that this is the same person, for Burney describes him as residing in London, becoming acquainted with Henry Purcell while at court, then moving to Shrewsbury for the rest of his life (Burney, *A General History*, 396n).

4. On MS 1179, see Cooper, *English Solo Keyboard*, 53; Cox, *Organ Music*, 82 and 512-13, and Bailey, "English Keyboard Music," 335–41.

5. Some of the pieces occur in printed editions, and others are found in contemporary keyboard books from Oxford. Publications with concordances include Matthew Locke's *The Present Practice of Music Vindicated* (1673), Lebègue's *2nd Livre d'Orgue* (1678/79), *Parthenia* (1612/13), *Second Book of the Harpsichord Master* (1700), *The First Part of Musick's Hand-maid* (1678), etc. Manuscript concordances of particular interest because of their provenance include the Bauyn MS (*F-Pn* Rés. Vm7 674 and 675) and *GB-Ob* MS Mus.Sch. D.219.

6. The nib size is clearly different on page 27 (much smaller), and both of these pieces have been crowded onto the last lines of their respective pages: Copyist B had to add lines to the ends of the staves to accommodate these short works. As all the ruled pages in MS 1179 contain music, it is reasonable to assume that Copyist B added these two Blow compositions after the rest of the book had been filled. Presumably he did not bother with key labels at this time.

7. Owens, "Concepts of Pitch." I am grateful to Professor Owens for a typescript of an earlier version of this article. Powers comments on the "English innocence of Continental modal theory" in "From Psalmody to Tonality," this volume.

8. Atcherson's examples show G with one flat as the "normal" tone/mode 2. Per Atcherson, "pitch-key mode" accounts for those uses of quasi-modal signatures given in seventeenth-century theory books that seem to appear most often in keyboard music. In such use, mode 2 is usually described as a mode on G with a flat in the signature—not as a transposition at all. These examples may fit specific repertories and certainly have foundations in contemporary theory; it should be noted, however, that the seventeenth-century examples of pitch-key modes in Atcherson's article are not English, and the application of "pitch-key modes" to English keyboard music is difficult. Atcherson, "Key and Mode," 204–33.

9. "Ev'ry composition . . . is . . . designed to some one key or tone in which the bass doth always conclude. The key is said to be either Flat or Sharp, not in respect of itself, but in relation to the ♭ or ♯ third which is joined to it. To distinguish this you are first to consider its 5th which consists always of a lesser and a greater 3rd, as you see in these two instances, the key being in G. [An example follows of a G-minor and a G-major triad.] If the lesser 3rd

be in the lower place next to the key, then is the music said to be set in a flat key. But if the greater 3rd stand next to the key as it doth in the second instance, then the key is called sharpe." Simpson, *Compendium*, 22.

10. Simpson, *Compendium*, 58. English theorists described uses of scale, hexachord, etc. that differ from contemporary Continental theorists, as has been detailed in Owens, "Concepts of Pitch," which provides an illuminating discussion not only of the primary sources, but also modern writings. Other authors on the subject include Wienpahl, "English Theorists"; Atcherson, "Symposium" and "Key and Mode"; Johnson, "Solmization"; Cooper, "Englische Musiktheorie"; Lewis, "Incipient Tonal Thought"; and Zimmerman, "*Air*, a Catchword." Only Owens takes Butler's notion of key ("Tone") seriously.

11. See Owens's perceptive review of analyses of Byrd's music by Kerman, Neighbour, and others in "Concepts of Pitch," 184ff.

12. Simpson continued, "That which the Grecians called Mode or Mood the Latins termed Tone or Tune. The design of either was to show in what key a song was set and which keys had affinity one with another. The Greeks distinguished their Modes by the names of their provinces, as Doric, Lydian, Ionic, Phrygian, etc." Simpson, *Compendium*, 57.

13. Ibid., 59. Emphasis mine. Simpson chastised Morley's explanation of "keeping the key" because Morley used a plainsong tenor, "And no marvel they could give no certain rule so long as they took their sight from the tenor, in which case it must be of necessity . . . what bass he will apply unto it." Since Simpson considered the bass the foundation of the music, "upon which the key solely depends," he began with the bass.

14. Owens notes the difficulties involved in looking at seventeenth-century uses of "key" in "Concepts of Pitch," this volume.

15. Playford's consideration of mode in his 1654 edition of *An Introduction to the Skill of Music* is similar to Simpson's quoted above:

> That which the Grecians called Mode or Mood, the Latins termed Tone or Tune: The design of either, was to shew in what Key the Song was set, and how each Musical Key had relation one to another. . . The Latins reduced theirs to Eight Tones or Tunes, and were by Churchmen termed Plain-songs. These exceeded not the compass of six Notes, and was to direct how to begin and end in the proper Keys. (Playford, *Introduction*, 57–59)

Playford then described the modes (Dorick, Lydian, Aeolick, Phrygian, and Ionick) as Butler had done in 1636 (in *The Principles of Music*, 1–9) as having certain aesthetic qualities. Half-steps and the like have no part of this discussion. Playford dropped the discussion of mode from editions of the *Introduction* printed between 1662 and 1670; in the 1672 edition, he used the same prefatory comments as Simpson concerning mode. By the 1683 edition, all discussion of mode vanished.

16. "as also the other keys which have an affinity therewith . . ." Simpson, *Compendium*, 58.

17. "*Of the Closes or Cadences belonging to the Key.* Having spoken of the key or tone it follows in order that we speak of the closes or cadences which belong unto it and here we must recourse to our forementioned fifth [above the keynote] and its two thirds [major or minor above the key note], for upon them depends the air of ev'ry composition, they serving as binds or limits which keep the music in a due decorum" (Ibid., 23). Skillful composers can make closes on any note, but beginners should conclude on scale degrees 1, 5, and 3 in flat keys and 1, 5, 4, and 2 in sharp ones. Simpson noted the particularly difficult close on $\hat{3}$ in a sharp key and cautions the reader to avoid that chord. Interestingly, cadences to scale degree 3 in "sharp" keys are common in the music of Locke and Blow. I should note that Simpson's description of key, and "air" for that matter, differed from those of some of his contemporaries. For example, North's essay "What is Ayre?" contains a slightly different concept of key from Simpson's (North, *Memoirs*, 67–92). Nonetheless, the latter's resembles that attributed to Henry Purcell in the 1694 edition of Playford's *Introduction*, 105.

18. Purcell clarifies that the only two "keys" appropriate for beginners are "the two Natural Keys, which are in A re and C fa ut, the first the lesser and the last the greater *Third.* From these all others are formed by adding either *Flats* or *Sharpes*: . . . . These examples are placed in the two open *Keys* to make it plainer, but transpose them into any other, they have the same effect" (Playford, *Introduction*, 12th ed., 105). Lewis has taken Purcell's words to prove "a complete realization of a fully transposable major-minor dualism" (Lewis, "Incipient Tonal Thought," 37). I will not undertake here whether or not Purcell describes major / minor tonality of the Common Practice Period, but how one deals with the repertory containing differing signatures for the same keynote, and Purcell's comments help define that body of music to pieces composed primarily between c. 1590 and 1690. Indeed, in manuscripts copied in the early eighteenth century a few signatures such as "G ♭" remain (e.g., *GB-Lbl* Add. 31403); however, the percentage of these pieces decreases significantly from c. 1675 on.

19. [Francis North] *A Philosophical Essay of Musick*, 23.

20. Clearly, "mode" is not the answer to the questions posed by "G♭♭," "G♭," and other such signatures. Neither is major / minor tonality. Burney thought Dr. [William] Boyce's approval of Blow's music unusual, since Boyce was "so excellent a judge of correct and pure harmony." Burney obviously prefered the harmonic style we define as "tonality" and he hints that this was not the guiding principle in Blow's works. Burney recognized the "pure" harmony of Boyce—one might say narrow or confined—and harshly judged the freedom in Blow's choice of notes. Apparently, a noticeable difference marked the harmonic language of the seventeenth century (Burney, *A General History*, 351–52). The pertinence of Burney as a judge in seventeenth-century music has been discussed by Shaw in "Tradition and Convention,"136–45; and by Silbiger in "Music and the Crisis," 35–44.

21. Owens ("Concepts of Pitch") has argued in favor of Butler's treatise for determining a critical language to describe English music and opens the door for a closer investigation of his ideas. In particular, she noted Butler's recognition that one must look at more than the final bass note (keynote) in order to determine the tone, that three keys can share characteristic sounds, his concept of transposition, and his manner of naming tones.

22. "The Air or Tone being thus deduced from the subject, or otherwise (without a Subject) chosen and constituted by the Author, is to be maintained in all places [Entrance, Progress, and Close,] of the Song" (Butler, *Principles*, 82).

23. "Il tipo tonale di una composizione è determinato solamente dal tono centrale (determinabile empiricamente) e dalla armatura di chiave" (Silbiger, "Tipi Tonali," 304). He adds that "later generations would exchange the diversity of tonal types for the diversity of keys . . . " ["Le generazioni successive poi scambiarono la diversità dei tipi tonali con la diversità delle tonalità . . . "] (Silbiger, "Tipi Tonali," 310). See also Powers, "Tonal Types," 428–70.

24. Butler, *Principles*, 83.

25. Ibid., 86.

26. The almain also occurs in *GB-Cfm* MS 653, p. 24 and *F-Pn* Rés. 1186bis1, f. 43v, and the version in MS 1179 is the least satisfactory of all. Howard Ferguson edited the version of "In G ♭♭" from the *Choice Collection* in *Six Suites * John Blow*, 14, and the version from MS 653 in *Early English Keyboard Music*, 2:44. The only modern edition of "In G ♭" as presented in MS 1179 is in Fuller-Maitland's *Contemporaries of Purcell*, 7:3. Fuller-Maitland "corrects" the signature by adding another flat. In my transcriptions, I have preserved such elements as beam groups and stem direction as much as possible. Incorrect details have been corrected based on the *Choice Collection* version, without editorial comment. Accidentals follow modern practice, and editorial accidentals are in brackets, cautionary ones in parentheses.

27. I wish to thank Prof. Silbiger for bringing my attention to this tune. The version in MS 1179 differs from Frescobaldi's published arrangement in the use of some E♭s and the lead-in to the second half in MS 1179 (missing from the Frescobaldi setting).

28. Incidentally, this particular cadential structure, Cm_6–DM, was pointed out by Roger North as the "most harmonious" cadence—and he suggested performers should hold onto the notes longer than the meter allowed, in order to emphasize its beauty (North, *Memoirs*, 83).

29. Blow wrote a small treatise entitled "Rules for playing on a Thorough Bass upon Organ & Harpsicon"; it exists in autograph in the British Library, MS Add. 34072, ff. 1–5. In his examples in "G flat" and "D flat," one flat appears in the signature. In his list of keys, the signatures of "flat" keys are with one sharp, E and A; with nothing, D; with three flats, C; with four flats, F, with two sharps, B; with three sharps, C♯ and F♯. The explication closes with "Finis Dr. Blow," dating it post-1678. The treatise is found in Arnold's *Art of Accompaniment*, 163–72.

30. These attributes have also been noticed by Jeff Meyer, who has examined the use of Butler's "airs" in the songs of John Dowland and found conspicuous differences in Dowland's use of the two "minor" airs, *re* and *sol.* I would add that in many bipartite *sol* works from 1650 on, composers often delay the appearance of a melodically significant $\flat\hat{6}$ until somewhere in the B section, and highlight that moment with registral accent. Meyer's research into the tonal structures of Dowland's lute songs will be presented in his forthcoming dissertation, "Tonality in John Dowland's Lutesongs: English Theory and the Constructive Use of Airs" (University of Minnesota). I am grateful to Mr. Meyer for a copy of a paper he presented at Brandeis University in August 1995. Among the several examples of the motion $\hat{4}$–$\hat{5}$–$\flat\hat{6}$, see the Roberts almain in *US-NYp* Drexel 5611 (*D sol*). This example also illustrates the harmonic emphasis on $\hat{3}$ (Bailey, "English Keyboard Music," 96).

31. John Lugge was organist at Exeter from at least 1602 until 1645 or later. Both voluntaries are printed in an edition of three voluntaries, edited by Jeans and Steele (*Three Voluntaries*).

32. Although there is not enough extant music by Christopher Gibbons to investigate truly the two minor "airs" in his *oeuvre*, one curious incident deserves mention. In a "Verse for the Double Organn [*sic*]," one of the sources adds a substantial conclusion that does not appear in the other three concordances of the work. This particular copyist added two versions of the piece to *GB-Lbl* Add. 34695. In the second, the conclusion cancels the flat in the signature (D is the keynote) for the remainder of the composition. The tonal structure shifts drastically to the sharp side and has extended sections on C as well. Meyer also noted similar correlations between different *airs* and tendencies to sharper or flatter internal cadences, relative to the final in Dowland's songs.

33. Circa 1670, the distinctions between *re* and *sol* pieces begin to blur. Composers, such as John Roberts, who used both systems during the 1650s and 1660s, discarded the *sol* system in favor of *re*. Dance music utilizing *sol* signatures becomes increasingly difficult to find during the last quarter of the seventeenth century.

34. MS Add. 31403 was copied by Daniel Henstridge, probably in the early eighteenth century. The Tokyo source dates from the late seventeenth or early eighteenth century. See Cox, *Organ Music*, 516.

35. MS Add. 34695 is in the hand of Nicholas Harrison. The part of MS 652 containing this verse is in the hand of John Harris (d. 1743), son of the organ builder Renatus Harris. See Cox, *Organ Music*, 485 and 498.

36. I have found only two instances of Draghi's pieces having a different signature in two sources, and in both cases, the *sol* signature may be autograph, while the *re* signature is definitely not.

37. Thus, Gerald Hendrie's grouping of all Gibbons's keyboard pieces into "Tones" (and similar uses of "neo-modal theory") must be called into question (*Keyboard Music of Orlando Gibbons*). Owens, "Concepts of Pitch," coined the term "neo-modal" and defines it as "a modern hybrid that reduces Glarean's twelve modes to five scale-types: Dorian,

Phrygian, Mixolydian, Aeolian, and Ionian" (186). Seventeenth-century composers were well aware of what the signature implied and did not overlook the "missing flat."

38. Editors in the past have often "corrected" seventeenth-century key signatures. Lord, in his edition of Simpson's *Compendium*, wrote "This example is lacking a sharp in the signature . . . The use of sharp key signatures did not appear until the middle of the seventeenth century and those key signatures then used are frequently misleading. Flat keys usually had one flat less than those of to-day" (Lord in Simpson, *Compendium*, 24 n. 13). A similar view regarding a signature of A with three sharps was taken by Shaw: "What may be regarded as a 'transitional' use of the modern key-signature of A major, by copyists who still thought of key A as the mixolydian mode of D with a sharpened leading note, gives rise to a certain amount of doubt here and there as to the correct inflexion of the Gs in this piece" (Shaw, *Blow Complete Organ Works*, 68).

39. This approach suggests revising certain editiorial practices, such as making all chords on $\hat{4}$ major at the end of minor pieces, and may have implications of other practical sorts as well. See, for example, the numerous "corrections" made in Raynor's edition of Christopher Gibbons keyboard works (*Keyboard Compositions*, ed. Raynor). Several questions remain: how does the practice of using flats (or sharps) for *all* flatted notes in the signature (e.g., all Bs in the bass clef) relate to the concept of "key?" What was Richard Goodson's reasoning for canceling the flats in only the bass for three measures of a composition in *GB-Och* MS 1177 (f. 35^{v})? How far does the perception of *re* and *sol* pieces depend on a composer's personal interpretation? The "sharp" side opens up other avenues of investigation, for "E flat" (E with a minor third) frequently appears with signatures of either one sharp or nothing.

40. Meyer also sees it in Dowland ("Tonality in John Dowland's Lutesongs").

41. This freedom extends to such idiosyncracies as "when the bass doth fall a 5th or rise a 4th, that note from which it so rises or falls doth commonly require the sharp or greater 3rd to be joined to it" (Simpson). Lord takes "this wavering between use of the flattened or sharpened leading note" as a "feeling for modality," noting that a sharped leading tone was more common in the fourteenth century than the sixteenth (Simpson, *Compendium*, 26 and n. 19). Such generalizations are precisely the source of inspiration for this paper.

42. England's approach may be placed in perspective to the "crisis" evaluated by Silbiger and others (Silbiger, "Music and the Crisis," 35–44).

From Psalmody to Tonality*

Harold Powers

At a certain point in my article on "Mode" for *The New Grove*, I wrote the following:

> By a circuitous but traceable route through French- and German-speaking Catholic countries, what had begun as Banchieri's eight "psalm-tone keys" were finally incorporated into the system of 24 Major and minor keys in Mattheson's *Das neu-eröffnete Orchestre*.[1]

Since I had not the space to do so then, I propose to trace the circuitous route from Banchieri to Mattheson now, or at least to point to some landmarks along the way.

The route "from psalmody to tonality" goes by way of seventeenth-century Continental organ practice and modal theory, but it is only one of several by which our forebears arrived at a practice and theory of what we now call "tonal music." There is, for instance, the one taken by English theory, which was never seriously infected with Continental doctrines of polyphonic modality, neither octenary nor dodecachordal.[2] But the route under consideration here is particularly instructive on several counts. For one thing, it is a fine demonstration of the genetic fallacy: the fact that the central tonalities in Mattheson's system of 24 originated in psalmodic liturgies, above all Vespers, a hundred years in the past and a thousand kilometers to the south, is irrelevant to the fact of the tonalities themselves, as Mattheson understood them; he knew only the most recent phases of the development. And more than that, the evolution of Mattheson's scheme of tonalities out of polyphonic psalmody exemplifies one of the ways in which one conceptual model of tonal space and tonal relations was gradually uprooted and replaced by a radically different conceptual model. In the bringing together of organ and choir in *alternatim* rendition of psalm verses in succession, and of psalm and antiphon, two radically incompatible conceptual models, one vocal and one instrumental, were brought into intimate contact and instructive conflict.

In the first part of this essay is described the replacement of the older model of tonal space by the newer one as it is illustrated in the route "from psalmody to tonality," beginning with an explication of the endpoint of the route, the system of tonalities presented in Johann Mattheson's *Das neu-eröffnete Orchestre* (1713). In the second part of the essay, the all too often neglected distinction between the eightfold system of theoretical modes and the eight psalm tones of church practice is insisted upon and the beginning of the route in polyphonic psalmody, as illustrated by Pietro Pontio and Adriano Banchieri, is elucidated. In the third part is demonstrated the gradual transformation of the tonalities of polyphonic and organ psalmody in Pontio and Banchieri to the major and minor keys of Mattheson's scheme, by way of theoretical and musical works from French- and German-speaking Catholic Europe.[3]

I

The earlier of the two conceptual models of tonal space is of purely vocal origin; it crystallized in the eleventh and twelfth centuries, as a control on singers' perceptions of intervallic relationships and tonal functions; with some changes in emphasis but never in principle, it continued to function that way for half a millennium, as the didactic substratum for making music (both performing and composing) and contemplating music. Elsewhere I have called this conceptual model the "Guidonian diatonic."[4] Margaret Bent has called it "*musica recta*"; in a particularly vivid metaphor, she pointed out that

> *musica recta* is not an arsenal of fixed pitches but denotes a set of relationships to a notional norm of pitch stability that is more like a flotilla at anchor than a Procrustean bed or a pre-tuned keyboard.[5]

By the sixteenth century the most common visual model for the Guidonian diatonic was a *scala*, a ladder, whose rungs and spaces—they were called *claves*—were labelled with the dual nomenclature of *litterae* and *voces*, letters of the alphabet and hexachord syllables. The role of the *litterae* was to fix order position (the first seven letters of the Roman alphabet in the abstract) along with relative register (their concrete forms, e.g., A, a, aa). The role of a *vox* was to indicate the melodic role of a particular *littera* in its immediate intervallic environment. The dual nomenclature for pitch and pitch relationships was obligatory, since order position and relative register in the whole system of the Guidonian diatonic were independent of tonal function and local intervallic context of any individual *littera*.

Extensions of the basic Guidonian diatonic by manipulation of *vox / littera* combinations were already becoming familiar in the fourteenth century. The so-called "Berkeley treatise" provides for ten *coniunctae* in addition to the basic system of six *litterae* C, D, E, F, G, A, plus B-*mi* and B-*fa*. Each of the *coniunctae* is said to come between *litterae* a whole step apart, is denoted either *fa* or *mi*, and is said to be properly situated within a hexachord of its own. For example, if c^1 is signed with a diesis sign it becomes *mi* in a hexachord where a is *ut*: a–b–$c\sharp^1$–d^1–e^1–$f\sharp^1$. For all but the two highest *coniunctae*, moreover, the anonymous author of the Berkeley treatise cited and notated a phrase of plainchant.[6] A century and a half later, similar extensions were laboriously spelled out by Pietro Aron in three different writings: in Chapters 26–45 of his *Trattato della natura et cognitione di tutti gli tuoni di canto figurato* (Venice 1525); in a clarification published as a supplement to the *Trattato* (Venice 1531); and in an *Aggiunta* to his *Toscanello in musica*, in which he cites a number of examples from polyphony. In this way, as Margaret Bent has observed,

> He thus joins those early sixteenth-century theorists whose nomenclature begins to reflect the keyboard as an instrument of reference for theoretical discusssion.[7]

But as Bent further observes,

> Circumlocution in the *Aggiunta*, as Aron gropes toward the idea of a notation fixed with respect to the signs of b molle and diesis, show that his training did not fully embrace such fixity, and that he may not have thought through the implication for, for example, his notation-bound modal theory.[8]

Indeed, modal theory never did take account of "musica ficta," and it was another century and a half or more before theories of tonality caught up with a practice ever more dominated by the keyboard. The change from "modal" nomenclature, be it octenary or dodecachordal, to "tonal" nomenclature is a function of the concomitant developments in the organization and control of pitch relationships conceived in terms of the vocally-based model, ultimately derived from chant theory, to the gradually intruding keyboard-based model. Only by the second quarter of the eighteenth century was the vocally based scheme of reference for a purely aural control of pitch relationships and tonal function, as represented in the Guidonian diatonic and its epicyclic extensions, completely replaced by a pre-compositional and pre-theoretical background scheme whose conceptual referential base was physically tied to the keyboard as visual model. Positions on the keyboard were also *claves*, like the Guidonian *litterae*, but they were always fixed relative one to another, and they had single names.[9]

TABLE 1 Johann Mattheson's scheme of the 24 tonalities along with their affects and effects, *Das neu-eröffnete orchestre*

> Those who think the whole secret rests in the minor versus the Major third, and want to suppose that all the minor tonalities generally speaking, are necessarily sad, but to the contrary, that all the Major tonalities have a cheerful quality in common, are indeed not too far wrong, but they have not yet looked far enough into the matter. Much less close to the mark are those who are of the opinion that if a piece has a flat signature it must inevitably sound soft and tender, but if it is provided with one or more sharps its nature must thus be hard, fresh, and cheerful. (232–33)

> The Italians and present-day composers are accustomed to differentiate their tonalities in a way different [from the twelve pseudo-Greek modes of Glarean and his followers]. (60)

The tonalities are listed on pp. 60–62, and again on pp. 236–53, along with affects for the first seventeen; in both lists pseudo-Greek equivalent names are given for tonalities 1–6, 8, and 11. The tonalities are listed below, with key words from their affects. Tonality numbers in the far left margin are from Falck's *Idea boni cantoris* (Nuremberg, 1688); see table 6d. Numbers in the right margin below suggest a transpositional rationale for Mattheson's ordering.

(Falck)	Mattheson		Affect		
{(1)	1	d minor	rather devotional, calm … agreeable and satisfying …		
(2)}	2	g minor	tender as well as enlivening, yearning as well as contenting		
{(3)	3	a minor	rather mournful … patient…		
(4)}	4	e minor	pensive … troubled … sad		
{(5)	5	C Major	rugged and bold quality …		
(6)}	6	F Major	generosity, steadfastness, love …		
{(7)	7	D Major	rather sharp and self-willed …		
(8)}	8	G Major	insinuating and eloquent …		
			"Although the foregoing eight tonalities are the best known … the following are no less useful and agreeable." (61–62)		
{(12)	9	c minor	extremely lovely yet sad …	1	} ↓T
(15)}	10	f minor	mild and pathetic … anxiety … despair …	2	} ↓T
{(10)	11	B♭ Major	diverting and magnificent …	5	} ↓T
(13)}	12	E♭ Major	only serious and plaintive things …	6	} ↓T
{(9)	13	A Major	affecting, though brilliant as well …	8	} ↑T
(14)}	14	E Major	morbid sadness … helpless and hopeless matters …	7	} ↑T
{(11)	15	b minor	bizarre, joyless and melancholy …	3	} ↑T
(16)}	16	f♯ minor	affliction … but more languishing …	4	} ↑T

TABLE 1 (*cont.*)

"Whoever is eager to know *all* must add the following …" (64! sc 62)

17	B Major	contradictory … hard … unpleasant … desperate …
18	F♯ Major	"The effect that the remaining tonalities make is still little known, and must be left to posterity … except for B Major." (251)
19	g♯ minor	
20	b♭ minor	
21	A♭ Major	
22	c♯ minor	
23	C♯ Major	
24	d♯ minor	

After Johann David Heinichen, *Neu erfundene und gründliche Anweisung … des General-Basses*, 261.

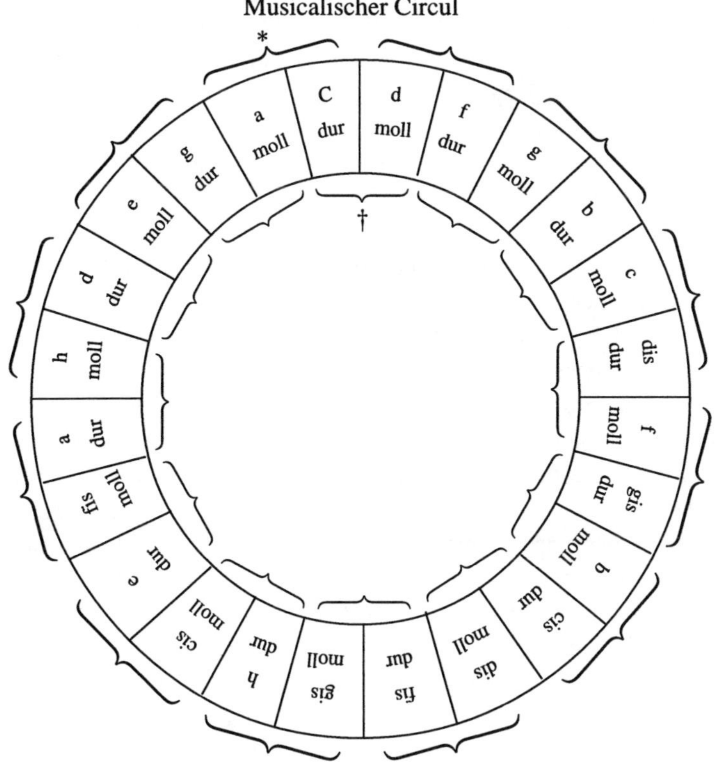

*brackets in the outer circle: minor / Major pairings

†brackets in inner circle: *ut–mi–sol* / *re–fa-la*

The replacement of the one conceptual model by the other is neatly epitomized in the way the separate components of the obligatory dual nomenclature of the Guidonian diatonic have separately survived in the now single nomenclatures for the *claves*—the "keys" in both of the modern English senses of the word as a musical term—in the different European languages. The *litterae* became the basis of the Germanic-language names for pitches and tonalities—including the curious survival of the square B (for b-*mi*) as "H" and the rounded B (for b-*fa*) as "B" in German itself—while in the Latin languages it was the *voces* that survived as names, with the addition of "*si*" and the substitution in Italy of "*do*" for "*ut*", both changes having taken place in the seventeenth century. The dual nomenclature with its *vox-littera* coupling was no longer needed; for the time being the *claves* alone, the keys on the keyboard, were enough.[10]

* * *

With these two conceptual models at the beginning and the end of all the intertwined routes to the twelve major and twelve minor tonalities, we can proceed to our particular route, beginning with an overview of its particular endpoint in Mattheson's *Das neu-eröffnete Orchestre*, as shown in table 1.[11] Three features stand out, one of them less obviously than the other two. The first feature is the grouping into sets of eight. In an important essay first published in 1978 Joel Lester pointed out that Mattheson's list of tonalities belongs with several analogously structured earlier lists, all with less than 24 entries; he started his account with Adriano Banchieri.[12] The second obvious feature, the list of affects, has played a role in two comprehensive studies published simultaneously and independently by Rita Steblin and Wolfgang Auhagen, on persisting beliefs in key characteristics in seventeenth to nineteenth-century music.[13]

The third feature of Mattheson's scheme is less obvious. The grouping and ordering of tonalities into sets of eight in table 1 is his; mine is the grouping of the sixteen tonalities in his first two sets two by two. Considering them thus in pairs brings out the fact that the tonal centers in each pair in the first two sets are systematically always a fourth apart. This binary feature reminds one almost as suggestively of a similar binary feature of the "church modes," their authentic-plagal pairing, except that in authentic versus plagal in chant theory it is the *ambitus* that are a fourth apart, whereas in these pairs it is the *finales*—or better here, the tonics—that are a fourth apart. And though Mattheson himself had no notion of the connections, it is indeed the case that his first set of eight evolved, as a system, from an octenary set—but it was not the set of eight Gregorian modes but rather the corresponding set of eight Gregorian psalm tones. Nonetheless, the pairing with tonics a fourth apart does indeed reflect, in a curiously indirect way developed below, the modal distinction of authentic and plagal—as valid for modal representation in polyphony as for modal classification in chant, as Bernhard Meier conclusively demonstrated.[14]

Once the tonalities in Mattheson's second set of eight have been similarly grouped in pairs, several systematic relations both among and within the paired tonalities emerge. First, every tonality in the second set is one degree higher or one degree lower than a tonality in the first set, as shown by the arrows to the right of the second set. The first two pairs of tonalities in the second set (9–10 and 11–12) are one degree lower than the first and third pairs in the first set (1–2 and 5–6). Similarly, the last two pairs of tonalities in the second set (13–14 and 15–16) are one degree higher than the fourth and the second pairs in the first set (8–7 and 4–3).

Second, though there are sixteen tonalities there are only ten tonics, because six of those ten have two varieties, one with the minor third, one with the major third. Within the first set of eight the D-major / G-major pair (7–8) shares tonics with the D-minor / G-minor pair (1–2); so too the C-minor / F-minor pair in the second set (9–10) shares tonics with the C-major / F-major pair (5–6) in the first.

Third, one notes an anomaly in the third pair of tonalities in the second set: the order of tonics a fourth apart is reversed: 13–14 corresponds with 8–7. This is a consequence of their major-third / minor-third correspondence with the A-minor / E-minor pair of the first set (3-4). The anomalous disposition of tonics within the A-minor / E-minor pair itself—the tonic E of the second (4) is a fourth lower than the tonic A of the first (3) where in the other three pairs the second tonic is a fourth higher than the first—is a fossilized remnant of the ultimate origin of Mattheson's *Neu-eröffnete Orchestre* scheme in the Gregorian psalm tones.

II

The principal roadblocks to mapping the route from polyphonic psalmody to Major / minor tonalities have been failures to make distinctions both logical and substantive. On the logical side, one should distinguish between an *inherent* property and an *ascribed* characteristic. Similar to that is the distinction between actually *being* something and merely *representing* something. On the substantive side, dealing with the distinction of authentic and plagal in polyphony should by this time no longer be a problem, thanks to Bernhard Meier; but one should still make the distinction between octenary and dodecachordal modal schemes, and avoid using dodecachordal names in inappropriate contexts. But most important of all for present purposes is the distinction between modes and psalm tones.

By the beginning of the seventeenth century in Counter-Reformation Italy the psalmodic liturgy of the Office, especially Vespers with its Mariolatric Magnificat, had become very sumptuous, with polyphonic settings and/or organ versets used for some or all of its verses.[15] Initially the *soggetti* for polyphony or organ versets were supposed to be the initials, medials, and terminations of the recitation melodies for the psalms, including their *differentia*, their variable terminations; this meant that the "finals" often did not correspond with the finals of the corresponding chant-theory modes of their antiphons. As time went on, polyphonic settings of the psalms were more and more composed with freely invented *soggetti*, but the tonalities established by the terminations of *differentiae*, generally standardized for polyphony as one for each psalm tone, continued in force because of their liturgical uses. Psalm-tone tonalities come in a set of eight, like the eight modes of chant theory, but the tonalities for polyphonic psalmody and organ versets, with their particular formulae and their *differentia*-terminations, do not necessarily correspond with the tonalities ascribable to their antiphons (and to all other kinds of polyphony), with their particular species of the fifth and fourth and their finals. In short, psalm-tone tonalities and the corresponding tonalities of the octenary modal system are not necessarily going to be the same.

Table 2 is a conspectus of the tonal types that appear in three sixteenth-century collections where a series of tonal types is being used to represent the eight modes of the traditional octenary theory in numerical order. The tonal types are symbolized in a tabular shorthand for what I have called the three "minimal markers" of a tonal type.[16] The first marker identifies the subsystem within the Guidonian diatonic: the flat sign denotes *cantus mollis*, requiring a B-flat in the signature marking B-*fa* as the essential variety of that scale degree for that subsystem; the natural sign denotes *cantus durus*, with no signature, making B-*mi* the essential variety of that degree for the subsystem. The second marker signifies the *ambitus* of the highest voice, for whose general compass and tessitura the cleffing, cutting out eleven-degree segments of the Guidonian diatonic, is usually indication enough. The third marker identifies the concluding tonal focus, signalled by the pitch class of the lowest sounding voice in the final sonority.

In the Pontio duos summarized on table 2a, for instance, all except the duo representing mode 6 are in *cantus durus*, and the pitch classes of the final octaves are those of the four regular finals of traditional octenary modal theory. For the duos representing modes 1 and 2 and modes 5 and 6, moreover, the contrast between authentic and plagal is also represented in the traditional way, as a contrast between higher and lower *ambitus*, as marked by the contrasted cleffings. The use of a single tonal type to represent both authentic mode 3 and plagal mode 4 is common in polyphony of the period; one sees it also, for example, in the Lasso motet collection whose tonal types are listed in table 2b-1562. Pontio claimed that there was no need for a separate duo to represent mode 4 since its principal cadences were the same as those for mode 3; Example 1a is his exemplary duo representing both mode 3 and mode 4.

TABLE 2 Tonal Types in collections representing the octenary modal system

A. Pontio, *Ragionamento* (1588), 99–121

Duos exemplifying "cadenze de' Motetti …"

	Mode	System	Ambitus	Finals	
	1	♮	$c_1\ c_3$	d^1/d	
	2	♮	$c_2\ F_3$	d^1/d	
	3	♮	$c_2\ c_4$	e^1/e	Ex. 1a
	4				
	5	♮!	$c_1\ c_3$	f^1/f	
	6	♭	$c_4\ F_4$	f/F	
	7	♮	$g_2\ c_2$	g^1/g	Ex. 3a
	8	♮	$g_2\ c_3$	g^1/g	Ex. 2a
"… trasportati …"					
↑4	1	♭	$g_2\ c_3$	g^1/g	
↑4	2	♭	$c_1\ c_4$	g^1/g	
↑8	2	♮	g_2		discussed, but without exemplary duos
	3*				
	4	♭	g_2		
(↑4)	5				
↑5	6	(♮)			
(↑4)	7	(♭)			
	8*				

*quasi sempre si lascia in { sua propria qualità (3) / suo proprio essere (8) }

B. Lasso*

Penitential Psalms (c. 1560)

	Mode	System	Ambitus†	Final‡
	1	♮	$c_1\ c_4$	D
↑4	2	♭	$c_1\ c_4$	G
	3	♮	$c_1\ c_4$	E
	4	♮	$c_2\ F_3$	E
	5	♭	$g_2\ c_3$	F
	6	♭	$c_1\ c_4$	F
	7	♮	$g_2\ c_3$	G
	8	♮	$c_1\ c_4$	G

Sacrae cantiones…a5 (1562)

	Mode	System	Ambitus†	Final‡
↑4	1	♭	$g_2\ c_3$	G
↑4	2	♭	$c_1\ c_4$	G
	3	♮	$c_1\ c_4$	E
	4			
	5	♭	$g_2\ c_3$	F
↑5	6	♮	$g_2\ c_3$	C
	7	♮	$g_2\ c_3$	G
	8	♮	$c_1\ c_4$	G

* After Powers, "Tonal Types," Tables 3 and 8-A.

† Clefs shown for cantus and tenor parts only.

‡ Pitch class in the bass of concluding triads.

EXAMPLE 1 Pietro Pontio, *Ragionamento di musica* (1588): Mode 3 and tone 3

A. Essempio dell cadenze de/ Motetti del terzo Tuono … del Quarto tono …saranno le istesse

7 – 6 – 8

2–3–1

7– 6 – 8

7– 6 – 8

4– 3–

3

2 –3 –3

7– 6 – 8

B. Essempio della imitatione, cadenze, mediatå, & fine de' Salmi del terzo Tuono

EXAMPLE 1B (*cont.*)

Pontio's duos for modes 7 and 8 have contrasted clefs only in their lower voices (*ambitus* g-a^1 and g-f^1 respectively); the respective upper voices have the same clef (*ambitus* $f(\sharp)^1$-f^2 in both). This is unusual: in modally ordered collections known to me, a real distinction in *ambitus* between representations of the authentic and plagal G modes, such as may be seen in the conspectus of the two Lasso collections in table 2b, is always made. Here Pontio supplied two different duos; as he had done for modes 3 and 4, he claimed that the the cadences were the same, but he then modified the claim.

> Musicians . . . make the same principal and final cadences [in mode 8] as in mode 7, in making a motet or madrigal or any other such composition. It is true that the diligent composer will take the degree C sol fa ut as principal cadence, so that this mode [*tuono*] may be the better recognized and distinct from mode 7, in that it is the degree that makes the reciting-tone [*medietà*] of the psalmtone [*salmo*] for the mode in question.[17]

And indeed, Pontio's duo for mode 8 (ex. 2a) has a full 7–6–8 cadence in C just halfway through, as opposed to the weak 4-3-3 cadence to C that comes first in the duo for mode 7 (ex. 3a). Conversely, the duo for mode 7 (ex. 3a) has a full 7-6-8 cadence to D as its second cadence, while the 11–10–0 cadence to D that comes first in the mode 8 duo (ex. 2a) is very weak harmonically. This kind of contrast between two different G tonalities both with the major third—two kinds of "G major"—is found in a number of sets of compositions throughout the seventeenth century.[18]

EXAMPLE 2 Pietro Pontio, *Ragionamento di musica* (1588): Mode 8 and tone 8

A. Mode 8

B. Tone 8

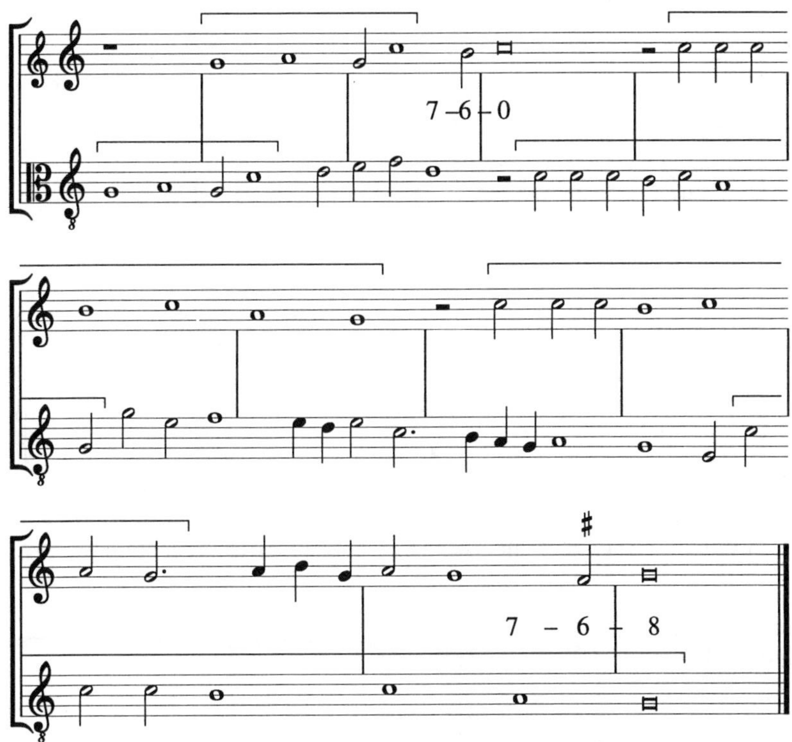

EXAMPLE 3 Pietro Pontio, *Ragionamento di musica* (1588): Mode 7 and tone 7 (116–17)

A. Essempio della cadenze de motetti dek settimo tuono

EXAMPLE 3A (*cont.*)

B. Essempio della imitatione, cadenze, medietá, & fine del settimo tuono

To say that there is an influence on one or another mode from the corresponding psalm tone, however, is not to say that that psalm tone embodies the mode in question. Quite to the contrary, they are completely separate as musical entities—indeed they stand on completely different ontological planes. A "mode" is an abstract theoretical category, while a "psalm tone" is a concrete musical entity. So while Pontio felt that authentic and plagal modes with the same final might overlap in varying degrees, as we have just seen for his duos representing modes 3 and 4 (ex. 1a) and modes 7 and 8 (exx. 2a and 3a), and while in a specific piece ascribed to a particular modal category there might be some reflection of the corresponding psalm tone, the generic polyphonic modes to which any number of motets and madrigal and other such compositions might be ascribed are not the same as the polyphonic tonalities with which psalms were sung. So Pontio supplied a separate set of eight duos for the eight regular psalm tones; table 3a is a conspectus of their tonal types.

Pontio's two sets of duos, one for psalmody and one for everything else, succinctly illustrate the distinction between *inherent* and *ascribed* properties.[19] Consider for instance examples 3a and 3b, Pontio's duos for mode 7 and psalm tone 7. The *soggetti* for the polyphonic psalm tone, bracketed on Example 3b, are taken from the intonation formula, the recitation pitch, and the conclusion of the psalm tone (they may be seen in their plainchant forms in line 7 of table 4a below). The principal *differentia*—variable ending formula—for psalm tone 7 is a descending first species of the fifth, from e^1 down to a, *la–sol–fa–mi–re* in the hard hexachord, and the final cadence of the psalm-tone duo is therefore to pitch class A. But the termination at A and the descent from the fifth above it in no way constitute a warrant for ascribing the Aeolian mode, or mode 9, or indeed any mode at all, to polyphonic psalm tone 7. That polyphonic psalm tone 7 is liturgically, and in consequence of that, musically linked in performance with G-tonality antiphons in mode 7, is an inescapable metonymic association. And just as Pontio brought in the psalmodic recitation on pitch class C to distinguish his duo in mode 8 cadentially from the duo in mode 7, so also one might well perceive a thematic hint of the *differentia* from psalm tone 7 in the penultimate *soggetto* of the duo for mode 7, the descending line of a fifth from pitch class E down to pitch class A, from the 7–6–8 cadence on E to the 7–6–8 cadence on A (which is followed by a sequential shift down to the cadence on pitch class G proper to mode 7 to conclude the duo). But a metonymic association of psalm tone 7 and antiphons in mode 7 in liturgical practice obviously does not constitute a paradigmatic equivalence in modal theory. It is an instance of the distinction between *being* and *representing*. Example 3b *is* a form of psalm tone 7, by virtue of its concrete thematic content. Example 3a, to the contrary, *represents* mode 7, which is ascribable to any number of "motets, masses, madrigals, and other similar compositions," as Pontio put it, that can be

TABLE 3 Tonal types for polyphonic psalmody

A. Pontio, *Ragionamento* (1588), 99–121
Duos exemplifying "imitazione, cadenze, principio, medietà, et fine de' Salmi"

	Tone	System	Ambitus	"Finals"*	
	1	♮	$c_1\ c_3$	d^1 / d	
↑4	2	♭	$c_1\ c_4$	g^1 / g	
	3	♮	$c_1\ c_3$	a^1 / a*	Ex. 1b
	4	♮	$c_1\ c_4$	e^1 / e	
	5	♮	$c_1\ c_3$	a^1 / a*	
	6	♭	$c_1\ c_4$	f^1 /f	
	7	♮	$g_2\ c_2$	a^1 / a*	Ex. 3b
	8	♮	$g_2\ c_3$	g^1 / g	Ex. 2b

* Every "final" pitch class in fact represents the principal (or the only) *differentia* of the respective psalm tone, though those for tones 1, 2, 4, 6, and 8 coincide with the finals of the corresponding modes (transposed in the case of tone 2).

Psalm tones 3, 5, and 7, however, have no *differentia* as low as the finals of the corresponding modes.

B. Banchieri, *Cartella musicale* (1614), 72–83
Duos exemplifying "termine [dell' Ottava] … fugare … cadenze …" etc., in "tutto gl' Otto Tuoni [ecclesiastici]"

	Tone	System	Ambitus	"Finals"	
	1	♮	$c_1\ c_4$	d^1 / d^1	Ex. 5a
↑4	2	♭	$c_1\ c_4$	g^1 / g	
	3	♮	$c_1\ c_4$	a^1 / a	Ex. 4a
	4	♮	$c_1\ c_4$	e^1 / e	Ex. 4b
↓4	5	♮	$c_1\ c_4$	c^2 / c^1†	
	6	♭	$c_1\ c_4$	f^1 / f	
↓5	7	♭	$c_1\ c_4$	d^1 / d^1‡	Ex. 5b
	8	♮	$c_1\ c_4$	g^1 / g	

† The cadential pitch class for tone 5 does *not* represent the *differentia* of psalm tone 5, but rather the final "of the antiphon," i.e., of the corresponding mode 5 (as transposed).

‡ As for tone 3, so also for tone 7 the pitch class at the final cadence represents the principal psalm-tone *differentia*, but now transposed "for the convenience of the choir," i.e., to bring the reciting tone of the psalm tone into a middle register (as also for tones 2 and 5). The tonal consequence, however is that there is little to distinguish tone 7 from tone 1 (v. Banchieri p. 82).

postulated as sufficiently conforming with polyphonic modal theory, first and foremost in the matter of their final sonority. The thematic material of his exemplary duo for mode 7, in fact, is almost neutral with respect to modal theory apart from its final; for example, the opening subject outlining the hard hexachord is virtually the same as the opening subject of his mode 8 duo (see ex. 2a). It is even partly contradictory with respect to the elementary modal requirements of mode 7, for that selfsame penultimate descent already mentioned, through the *la–sol–fa–mi–re* first species of the fifth, is a species of consonance ascribed in modal theory not to modes 7 and 8 but rather to modes 1 and 2; short as it is, this duo is in fact a fine instance of a "*tonus commixtus*."[20]

Turning back now to example 1a, Pontio's exemplary duo for mode 3, and comparing it with example 1b, his exemplary duo for psalm tone 3, one observes that here too the psalm-tone duo takes its *soggetti* from the the psalm tone, as again indicated with brackets (see line 3 of table 4a for the plainsong formulas). Nor does it make its final cadence to the final of the corresponding mode 3, which would be E, as in the duo representing mode 3 in example 1a; it makes its final cadence to A, the concluding degree of the principal *differentia* for psalm tone 3. Yet as with psalm tone 7, there is no warrant for ascribing Aeolian mode, ninth mode, or any mode at all, to this piece. Pontio's exemplary duo for psalm tone 4 has the same compass as his duo for psalm tone 3, but makes its final cadence to E, which is the termination of the principal *differentia* for psalm tone 4, and a fourth below the A that terminates psalm tone 3.

Examples 4a and 4b are from Adriano Banchieri's *Cartella musicale* of 1614. As with Pontio's duos embodying psalm tones 3 and 4, Banchieri's two duos exemplifying "church tones" 3 and 4 have the same compasses, while their concluding cadential degrees, like Pontio's, are to pitch classes A and E, respectively. The difference between Banchieri's duos and Pontio's duos—and this is consistent for all—is that the *soggetti* of Banchieri's duos, unlike those of Pontio's, have nothing to do with the melodic material of the respective psalm tones, as can be seen, for instance, by contrasting example 1a (Pontio's duo for psalm tone 3) and Example 4a (Banchieri's duo for psalm tone 3). Banchieri's duos do not *embody* the psalm tones, as Pontio's do, they merely *represent* them; they are not the psalm tones themselves, but rather merely tonal types recommended for polyphonic settings of psalm texts for practical use in the liturgy of the Office when the *soggetti* are not from the psalm tone but are instead freely invented.

How those tonal types are associated with psalmody can be illustrated from pages 71–72 of Banchieri's *Cartella musicale*, transcribed as table 4. On the left (table 4a) are the familiar psalm tones of plain chant, *canto fermo*; on the right (table 4b), the same contours are shown "transposed for compositions for the choir in polyphony." The purpose of the transposition is to bring the actual sung reciting

EXAMPLE 4 Adriano Banchieri, *Cartella musicale* (1614): tone 3 and tone 4

A. duo del terzo tuono ecclesiastico

B. duo del quarto tuono ecclesiastico

TABLE 4 Adriano Banchieri, *Cartella musicale* [3rd ed.], Venezia 1614
Psalmody in plainsong and polyphony

A. p. 70: Canto Fermo

Laudate pueri Dominum | Laudate | nomen Domini
[Psalm 112, the fourth psalm for Sunday Vespers, vs. 1]

1 brings the reciting tone from c[1] down to b♭, narrowing their overall range to a minor third.

2 changes the secondary cadences.

tones, the psalm-tone tenors, to written pitch levels within a somewhat narrower compass, for in *alternatim* psalmody the choir must sing its psalm verses at comfortable pitch levels that will also fit the organ with its fixed tuning; that is so whether they sing them in plainchant or polyphony, and if in polyphony, whether they do or do not use psalm-tone material as *soggetti*. Particularly noticeable are the ways Banchieri's transpositions raise the reciting tone of psalm tone 2, written f, up to b♭, and lower the reciting tone of psalm tone 7, written d^1, down to a, thereby reducing the written compass of the whole set of reciting tones from the major sixth f-d^1 to the perfect fourth f-b♭. Banchieri's alternative versions for psalm tones 2 and 8, shown as a second set of "cadenze" at the right of table 4b, reduce the compass of reciting tones yet further, to the minor third g-b♭.[21] Banchieri's transposition recommendations are followed immediately by eight duos exemplifying the "church tones," in the eight tonalities recommended, as may be seen by comparing table 4b with the tonal-type summaries of his duos in table 3b. Banchieri's "church keys," then, are written within the conceptual frame of the Guidonian diatonic, but they are also transpositions, in the modern sense of the term.

I want now to make two cautionary observations about the first of Banchieri's four transpositions, tone 2 up a fourth; after that I'll come to tone 3, with its final at a, then take note of the psalmodically anomalous final for tone 5, and go on to the transposition of tone 7 down a fifth, which results in a *cantus-mollis* tonality with its final at pitch class D.

Looking back at table 2 for a moment, consider the three authentic-plagal pairings, respectively, of modes 1 and 2 in Pontio's exemplary duos, Lasso's Penitential Psalms, and Lasso's *Sacrae cantiones* of 1562. Pontio's first pair of duos (see table 2a) follows chant theory: the two have the same final, they are both in *cantus durus*, and the contrast of authentic and plagal subsists in higher versus lower *ambitus*. Pontio also wrote out exactly the same pair of duos in *cantus mollis* with finals at pitch class G, describing them as transposed.

The authentic-plagal contrast in pieces representing modes 1 and 2 in the Lasso Penitential Psalms (see table 2b, c.1560) is handled differently: instead of contrasting high and low *ambitus*, Lasso kept the *ambitus* constant, and the contrast subsists in the differences in subsystem and final: mode 1 is represented in *cantus durus* at its proper pitch level and mode 2 is represented in *cantus mollis* as though transposed a fourth higher.[22] In the case of a collection representing modes in order, like Lasso's Penitential Psalms, this produces two tonalities based on the *re–mi–fa–sol–la* species of the fifth located at different levels within the same *ambitus*: one is authentic with final at D, the other plagal with final at G. In the case of Pontio's and Banchieri's exemplary duos, the effect is the same for polyphonic psalm-tone keys 1 and 2, since each of the psalm tones in question concludes with the final of its corresponding mode. But the only authentic psalm tone for which this is true is psalm tone 1; the other odd-numbered psalm tones never reach down as low as the final of their corresponding authentic modes.

* * *

Failure to make a firm distinction between the terminal degrees of psalm-tone *differentiae* and the finals posited by modal theory has been the cause of as much scholarly misdirection in the area of sixteenth- and seventeenth-century tonalities as the failure to distinguish authentic from plagal had been before Bernhard Meier's work appeared.[23] This misdirection unfortunately taints that part of the important historical study by Joel Lester which deals with the route to Mattheson's four minor and four major central tonalities.[24] Lester began by making the connection between Banchieri and the German part of the route that eventuated in Mattheson's scheme, and his first remarks suggest that by 1989 he might have come to sense not only that Banchieri's eight tonalities had a prehistory but also that they had some sort of connection with psalm tones.

> Italian musicians during the latter part of the sixteenth century began to organize the commonly used modal finals and key signatures into a list that was at first related to the eight psalm tones. . . . the lists are common in instrumental collections and treatises from the late sixteenth century through the mid eighteenth century. . . . Their earliest appearance in a treatise seems to be in *L'organo suonarino* (Venice 1605) by Adriano Banchieri (1567–1634).[25]

Shortly thereafter follows a tabulation corresponding to the one in my table 3b, except that there is no column for "*ambitus*"; then comes a definition of "this organization of tones as the *church keys*." For Banchieri's "eight tones of ecclesiastical chant" Lester preferred the term "church keys" to the term "pitch-key modes" used for them by Walter Atcherson in his comprehensive seminal essay of 1973, from which both Lester and I started along this particular route to the major / minor system of keys.[26]

The details in Lester's individual descriptions of Banchieri's "church keys," however, point up several sorts of confusion that arise from not observing distinctions, in this case not only between modes and psalm tones but also between authentic and plagal modes. The identity of the terminating pitch classes in psalm tones 1 and 2 and modes 1 and 2, for example, provides treacherously safe ground for saying that "thus the transposition of Dorian to a one-flat signature explains tones 1 and 2."[27] This is true, but by chance: the tonal types of Banchieri's first two polyphonic psalm-tone tonalities correspond with those of the most common mode 1 / mode 2 pairings of late sixteenth-century modal collections, the one with its D final in *cantus durus*, the other with its G final in *cantus mollis* (compare the initial pairs of tonal types on tables 3b and 2b, 1562). But the slipperiness of the ground is manifest in Lester's next comment.

> The same transposition of Phrygian results in tones 3 and 4, but the ordering is reversed, and there is no flat in the signature of the A mode.[28]

Lester has taken the *re*-tonality on A of Banchieri's tone 3 as a transposition by a fourth upward of mode 4, whose "regular" (according-to-rule) final is pitch class E.[29] He supposed that this was parallel with the transposition by a fourth upward that really does produce Banchieri's tone 2, even though on these grounds the absence of the upper leading-tone to the final that absolutely characterizes *mi*-tonalities—the so-called "Phrygian" tonalities—is inexplicable. And he has assumed that Banchieri's *mi*-tonality on E represents an untransposed mode 3 paralleling the untransposed tone 1. But Banchieri's tonalities are no more than the tonalities for polyphonic psalm tones 3 and 4, in their correct order.[30]

Of the next authentic-plagal pair Lester wrote that "Lydian was often changed to Ionian; here tone 5 is Ionian, tone 6 its transposition."[31] Here again is an instance of both the confusion of mode with psalm tone and the treachery built into "neo-modal" terminology, for in fact the transpositional relationship is the other way around: tone 5 is a tonality for polyphonic psalm tone 5 transposed down a fourth, bringing the reciting tone from C down to G, while tone 6 is a tonality for psalm tone 6 at its proper position. What really is anomalous in Banchieri's polyphonic duo for tone 5 is its final, for this is the only one of his odd-numbered "church keys" that has its final not on the psalm-tone termination (which would be E in this transposition down a fourth) but on the modal final; Banchieri did not explain why this was so, nor why it was done for tone 5 but not for tones 3 or 7.[32]

Lester's comment on the last two of Banchieri's "church keys" is that: "Tone 8 is Mixolydian; tone 7 the range of Hypomixolydian, but with D as final."[33] But Banchieri's tone 8 is psalm tone 8, not "Mixolydian"; if the familiar "pseudo-Greek" names were to be applied to psalm tones (which they never were) it would have to be "Hypomixolydian." To connect "Hypomixolydian" solely with the range of a D-to-D octave, with a terminating degree (D) independent of the modal final (G), would be a subtlety worthy of Pietro Aron, except that it ignores the one-flat signature that is given in Lester's tabulation of the "church keys" (as it is in table 3b here).

Lester continued with Banchieri's tone 7, postulating that

> at some point later in the seventeenth century the seventh mode was changed from D with one flat in the signature to D with one sharp in the signature, probably either to differentiate it more clearly from the first mode, or to present a true

> transposition of Mixolydian. With this change, the first four modes contain a minor triad on the final and the last four a major triad on the final. This listing of the church keys found its way into later treatises . . . [34]

Banchieri's duos for his "seventh mode . . . with one flat in the signature" and his "first mode" may be seen in example 5a/b, but the transformation of Banchieri's D-minor-like *re*-tonality for tone 7 in *cantus mollis* to D Major has nothing to do with making more of a contrast with his equally D-minor-like *re*-tonality tone 1 in *cantus durus* (in "neo-modal" terminology it would be called "Dorian," like J.S. Bach's "Dorian" Toccato and Fugue for organ). Nor is that D major that replaced Banchieri's tone 7 a "true transposition of Mixolydian." It is another way of treating psalm tone 7, as is shown below.

EXAMPLE 5 Adriano Banchieri, *Cartella musicale* (1614): Tone 1 and tone 7

A. duo del primo tuono ecclesiastico

EXAMPLE 5A (*cont.*)

B. duo del settimo tuono ecclesiastico

* f^1 in the print

† 4 in the print

Finally, Lester's general observation that each and every one of Banchieri's first four tones contains a minor triad, while obviously correct, is an oversimplification as applied to tones 3 and 4. It is true that tone 3 was a key whose final and other principal degrees did indeed form a minor triad—A, E, and C, an A-minor triad in our terms—but tone 4, as representing psalm tone 4, continued to be a *mi*-tonality; that is, a tonality whose final and principal degree was approached by an upper leading-note, never a lower leading-note as in all the others, and whose modal degrees E, A, and C were the same as those of tone three. Tonc 4 is more of a pseudo-A-minor tonality than an E-minor tonality, though unlike tone 3, it is an A minor that, in our modern terminology, always ends on its dominant—properly speaking, a *mi*-tonality ending with its usual E-major triad.

The construction of Banchieri's eight church tones is summarized on table 5. Table 5a shows the intervallic connection, for a choir singing plainchant, between the final tones of antiphons and the reciting tones and the by then standardized *differentiae* of the eight psalm tones. In table 5b are shown the *ambitus* (the octaves spanned) and the four finals (the white noteheads) with their associated secondary cadential points (the black noteheads), in octenary polyphonic modal theory of the time; the alternating upward and downward orderings of the noteheads index the respective authentic and plagal categories. That these designations were "in theory only" for Banchieri is confirmed in table 5c. One sees, for example, that the imitation points ("modo di fugare"), principal degrees ("corde"), and finals ("cadenze") in the tenor voice for the third tonality are those of psalmodic tonality 3 (see table 4b line 3), not of the theoretical authentic mode illustrated in the preceding column. Likewise, tone 4, as shown in table 5 line 4, is a *mi*-tonality for use in polyphonic psalmody, not the mode 4 of table 5b with its mechanical disposition of secondary degrees below and above the final. The signatures and principal degrees shown in table 5c line 7 are not those of the theoretical mode 7 shown in table 5b but rather those of Banchieri's psalm tone 7 "transposed for compositions for the choir in polyphony" (see table 4b line 7).

III

To trace out the route from Banchieri to Mattheson fully and correctly we need to account for each of the differences between Banchieri's psalm-tone tonalities and Mattheson's set of the eight principal keys. Most obviously, we need to suggest how Banchieri's D-minor-like tone 7 might have become D major, and how his "Phrygian" *mi*-tonality representing tone 4 might have become E minor. In these two transformations / replacements in particular one sees the keyboard model of tonal space, as concretely embodied in polyphonic psalmody or in organ versets

TABLE 5 Adriano Banchieri, *Cartella musicale* [3rd ed.], Venezia 1614 (Cf. Tables 3b and 6a)

C. *Modo di fugare, corde e Cadenze†

* tenor voice only, from pp. 84–87

† only the last note of the last cadence (in the tenor voice)

attached directly to liturgical practice, gradually taking over from the remaining shards of the Guidonian-diatonic vocal model.

In table 6 is outlined a route from Banchieri's psalm-tone tonalities (table 6a) to the major-minor scheme in the first set of eight tonalities in Georg Falck's *Idea boni cantoris* (table 6d).[35] These are item by item the same as Mattheson's first eight minor / major keys, as noted on table 1. Falck's second whole set of eight "feigned or transposed tones" is the same as Mattheson's second whole set of eight, but Falck's ordering is purely mechanical. The keys are simply listed in ascending order of tonics, starting with the first letter of the alphabet, and leaving out those keys already included in the first set; that they are also in alternated pairs of major and minor tonalities is a fortuitous though probably not unobserved coincidence. Mattheson's equivalent second set, as shown in the numbers to the left of his numbers in table 1, is a rearrangement of the keys in Falck's second set such that it is related to his own first set by systematic transposition, four down a tone and four up a tone.

The first three treatises summarized on table 6 are discussed in Walter Atcherson's comprehensive essay "Key and Mode," and though Atcherson did not take the connection as far as Mattheson—that was Joel Lester's contribution—he did provide some discussion of French treatises, including Nivers's *Traité* of 1667, depending largely on Almonte Howell's seminal essay from 1958.[36] Signature systems in table 6a–c are shown as branches in a tree bracket. Banchieri's tonalities need only the symbols for *cantus durus* and *cantus mollis*; the added signature systems using sharps in the two conspectus for mid-century French and Austrian treatises in table 6b and 6c are similarly symbolized. The pitch classes of the cadential degrees are shown in columns under the signatures, with letters so shaped as to indicate the quality of the modal triad as major or minor, or as a "Phrygian" modal dyad in the case of tone 4. The horizontal arrows on table 6 point towards the changing of tonal types as marked in the differences from one treatise to the next; the vertical arrows point towards the numbers of music examples provided in this essay that are meant to illustrate how Banchieri's system of eight psalm-tone keys gradually evolved into Mattheson's primary set of minor / major keys.

Like table 6d, table 6a also refers to material already looked at, the eight polyphonic tones from Banchieri's *Cartella musicale*. It is not based directly on the duos, however, but represents part of the information in Banchieri's tabulations, for each tonal type, of its imitation points, modal degrees, and cadential degrees as they would be used by all the voices in four-voice polyphony; those for the tenor voice may be seen in the last column of table 5c. Banchieri's cleffing is identical for all eight tonal types—c_1, c_3, c_4 and F_4—except that the alto for tone 4 has the c_4 clef, like the tenor; the cleffing for the eight transposed psalm tones and their exemplary duos is also uniform. That being so, it seemed more useful to tabulate

TABLE 6 From polyphonic / organ psalmody to major / minor tonalities

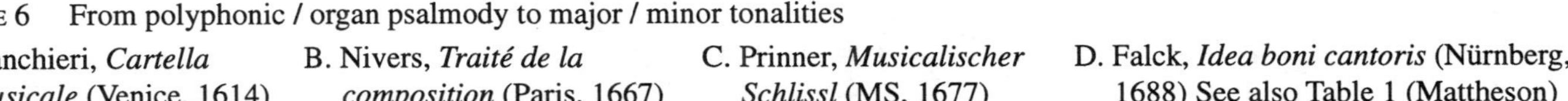

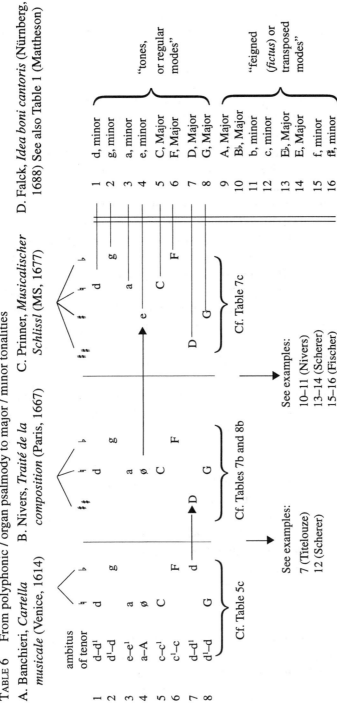

A. Banchieri, *Cartella musicale* (Venice, 1614)

B. Nivers, *Traité de la composition* (Paris, 1667)

C. Prinner, *Musicalischer Schlissl* (MS, 1677)

D. Falck, *Idea boni cantoris* (Nürnberg, 1688) See also Table 1 (Mattheson)

	A: ambitus of tenor	A: ♮	A: ♭	B: ♯♯	B: ♮	B: ♭	C: ♯♯	C: ♯	C: ♮	C: ♭	D	D: tonality	
1	d–d^1	d			d				d		1	d, minor	"tones, or regular modes"
2	d^1–d		g			g				g	2	g, minor	
3	e–e^1	a			a				a		3	a, minor	
4	a–A	ø			ø →			e			4	e, minor	
5	c–c^1	C			C				C		5	C, Major	
6	c^1–c		F			F				F	6	F, Major	
7	d–d^1		d →	D			D				7	D, Major	
8	d^1–d	G			G			G			8	G, Major	
											9	A, Major	"feigned (*fictus*) or transposed modes"
											10	B♭, Major	
											11	b, minor	
											12	c, minor	
											13	E♭, Major	
											14	E, Major	
											15	f, minor	
											16	f♯, minor	

A: Cf. Table 5c — B: Cf. Tables 7b and 8b — C: Cf. Table 7c

See examples (A–B):
7 (Titelouze)
12 (Scherer)

See examples (B–C):
10–11 (Nivers)
13–14 (Scherer)
15–16 (Fischer)

Letters (except ambitus): pitch class of final (ø = E)
upper-case: modal triad *ut–mi–sol* // major [*ut*] tonality
lower-case: modal triad *re–fa–la* // minor [*re*] tonality
ø: modal dyad *mi–la* // "phrygian" [*mi*] tonality

the actual *ambitus* according to Banchieri; the tenor voice is taken as representative of the whole polyphonic complex for each tone. The system signatures and final are exactly as in the duos (see table 3b).

* * *

I begin with the differences from Banchieri in tone 7. The D major in Nivers's *Traité de la composition* (tables 6b and 7b) reflects a different transpositional practice for polyphonic psalmody in tone 7, combined with an *alternatim* practice that took as the basis for organ-choir coordination in Vespers, Lauds, and other psalmodic liturgies not the standard *differentia* of the psalm tone itself, but rather the intervallic relationship of the final of the antiphon (i.e. the final of the corresponding modal category) with the immediately succeeding intonation of the psalm-tone verse. The particular transposition for psalmody in tone 7 and the use of the final of antiphons in the coordinate "mode" to conclude an organ verset, rather than the termination of its psalm-tone *differentia*, are both illustrated in Jean Titelouze's Organ *Magnificat*s of 1626, whose tonal types are symbolized in table 7a below; their significant scale degrees are listed in table 7a, where it may be seen that the final cadences for odd-numbered tones 1, 3, and 5 are to D, E, and F, the finals of the corresponding modes, and that while tone 2 is transposed up a fourth in the now familiar way, tone 7 is transposed down not by a fifth but by a fourth, bringing the reciting tone from d' down to a, rather than from d^1 down to g as in Banchieri's tone 7.

Titelouze's explanation for tone 7 in his foreword "to the reader" is paradigmatic for the whole, as to both his use of the modal final rather than the psalm-tone termination, and his reason for transposing.

> The Seventh [tone] makes five or six sorts of *differentia*; this is why I have treated it following the principal degree [i.e. the final] of its Antiphons, which resemble our Ninth Mode [the authentic G-tonality in Zarlino's revised *Istitutioni harmoniche* of 1573]; also, one ought not to play otherwise, the more so in that the Antiphons that precede the Canticle oblige the organ to give to that Canticle its intonation, mediation, and ending. Good composers have done it thus, and have finished on *Ut* [G] because the Choir would not be able to catch its intonation if one did not finish on that degree. I have transposed it a fourth lower for the convenience of the Choir.

Four points in Titelouze's note to the reader should be noted. First, giving the large number of traditional psalm-tone terminations as part of the reason for terminating with the final of the corresponding mode seems specious, for he also has tone 5 terminate with the modal final, despite the fact that

TABLE 7

A. Signatures and finals of Titelouze's *Magnificats* for organ (Paris 1626) (Cf. Table 8a)

[D soh re]

[G soh re]

E la mi

E la mi

F fa ut

F [fa] ut

[D] ut

[G] ut

"la principale dominante de son Antienne" [i.e. the modal final]

[psalm-tone dominant]

[termination of psalm tone]

B. G. G. Nivers, *Traité de la composition de musique* (Paris 1667), after Albert Cohen translation, p. 19 (Cf. Tables 6b and 8b)

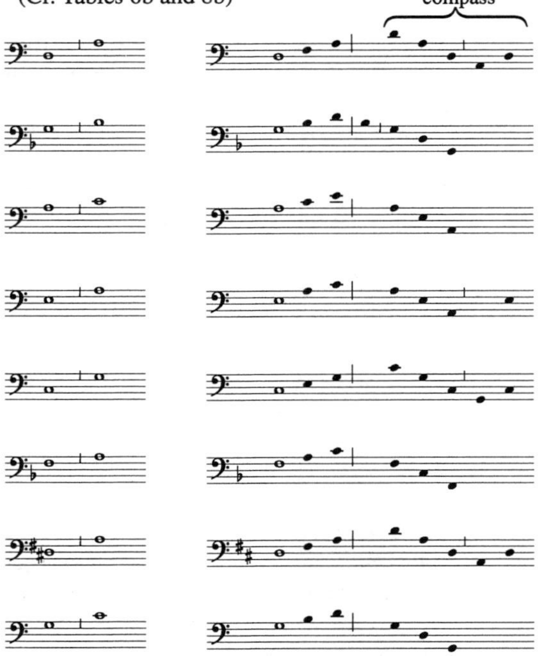

compass

Final of antiphon and dominant of psalm tone

Final

medial

dominant

C. J.J. Prinner (MS 1679) after H. Federhofer, "Eine Musiklehre," p. 49(Cf. table 6c)

D

G ♭

A

E ♯

C

F ♭

D ♯

G ♯

Table 8 Some seventeenth-century Catholic organ collections

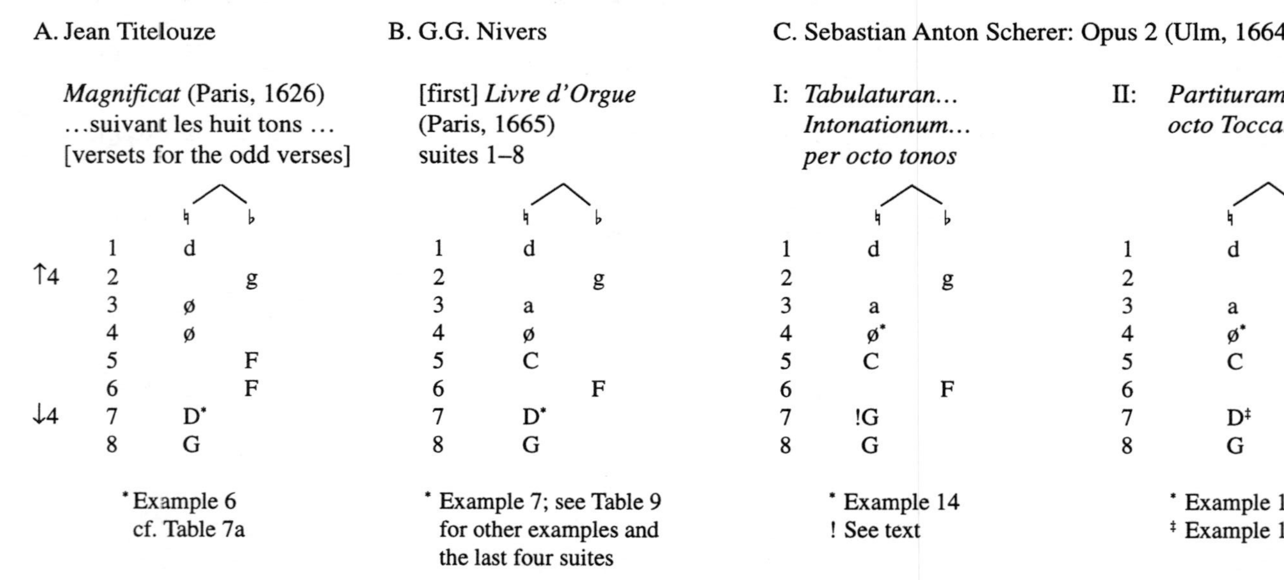

	A. Jean Titelouze			B. G.G. Nivers			C. Sebastian Anton Scherer: Opus 2 (Ulm, 1664)					
	Magnificat (Paris, 1626) …suivant les huit tons … [versets for the odd verses]			[first] *Livre d'Orgue* (Paris, 1665) suites 1–8			I: *Tabulaturan… Intonationum… per octo tonos*			II: *Partituram… octo Toccatarum…*		
		♮	♭		♮	♭		♮	♭		♮	♭
	1	d		1	d		1	d		1	d	
↑4	2		g	2		g	2		g	2		g
	3	ø		3	a		3	a		3	a	
	4	ø		4	ø		4	ø*		4	ø*	
	5		F	5	C		5	C		5	C	
	6		F	6		F	6		F	6		F
↓4	7	D*		7	D*		7	!G		7	D‡	
	8	G		8	G		8	G		8	G	

A: * Example 6; cf. Table 7a

B: * Example 7; see Table 9 for other examples and the last four suites

C I: * Example 14; ! See text

C II: * Example 13; ‡ Example 12

Letters denote the pitch class of the bass in the final $^5_3$ triad; ø = E
- upper-case: modal triad *ut–mi–sol* // Major [*ut*] tonality
- lower-case: modal triad *re–fa–la* // minor [*re*] tonality
- ø: modal dyad *mi–la* // "phrygian" [*mi*] tonality

> The Fifth Tone very seldom changes its ending; but one can observe that its Antiphons sometimes end in *Fa*, like our Seventh Mode, but more often in *Ut*, whence I have taken my reason for putting it in *F fa ut* with B-flat.

Second, references to "our Ninth Mode" (and "our Seventh Mode") are to the dodecachordal scheme favored in France, which originated from the 1573 edition, the second of Zarlino's *Istitutioni harmoniche*, where mode 9 was G-authentic and mode 7 was F-authentic.[37]

Third, to terminate organ versets based on the psalm tone not with the last note of a psalm-tone *differentia* but rather with the final of the corresponding mode—that is, with the final of whatever antiphon would have preceded the canticle in the Vespers liturgy of a particular day—was intended to help the choir to find the right pitch level for their alternate verses in plain chant, since the tonal conjunction between the end of the plainchant antiphon and the beginning of the plainchant psalm tone would be the first they would have heard or had to make on the occasion. And fourth, transposing downward on the organ does indeed bring the pitch level of the tenor for the *alternatim* plain chant, in terms of the fixed tuning of the organ, down to a level more comfortable for the Choir.

In Example 6 may be seen one instance of Titelouze composing in tone 7, and the kind of effect his particular approach has on the tonality.[38] An opening imitative point on a subject resembling the psalm-tone intonation—which would be *re–re–re–fa–mi–re–mi* in the hard and natural hexachords respectively—echoes the c^1 (*fa*) of the leading voice with f^1 (*fa*) in the answering voice. The succeeding passage adumbrates the psalm-tone *differentia* (in Titelouze's transposition it is a–a–b–a–g–f♯–e) and the accompanying figuration now uses only F♯, and so it continues in the following passage in triple meter. At the return to common time the reciting tone and *differentia* come in as a *cantus firmus*, beginning with repetitions of the reciting tone on a^1 and going on into the stepwise descent through the first species of the fifth that is the principal termination for psalm tone 7: *sol–sol–sol–sol, la–sol–fa–mi–re*, with a^1 as *sol* and e^1 as *re* (in the middle of the third system of ex. 9). As long as the reciting tone on a^1 is maintained the accompanying parts return to pitch class F, but when the *cantus firmus* begins the *differentia*, pitch class F♯ returns. It is to be noted also that Titelouze went to some trouble not to stabilize pitch class E, prolonged though it is, with cadential or other strong harmonic support. E-*re* is then brought down to D-*ut* in the final system, to end the verset with a fairly solidly stabilized D major.

According to Robert Frederick Bates,

> During the years between Titelouze's Magnificats of 1626 and Roberday's *Fugues et caprices* of 1660, no organ music was published in France. Beginning in 1660, however, a substantial number of books appeared.[39]

EXAMPLE 6 Jean Titelouze, *Magnificat ... 7me ton* [4] (Paris 1626)

EXAMPLE 6 (*cont.*)

EXAMPLE 7 G. G. Nivers, *Livre d'orgue* (1665), Suite No. 7
Prelude du 7e ton

The next collection to be published after Roberday's was the first of three organ collections by Guillaume Gabriel Nivers, his *Livre d'orgue contenant cent pièces de tous les Tons de l'Eglise* (Paris 1665).[40] The collection comprises twelve suites in as many tonalities, each beginning with a Prelude and including a number of other pieces such as fugues, pieces designated by organ registration, duos, and concluding with a Grand Jeu and/or Plein Jeu. The pieces were for *alternatim* use in the psalmody of the Office; the large number of tonalities were for the accommodation of the pitch level to the convenience of the choirs, primarily men's (for use in churches and monasteries) and women's (for nuns in cloisters), but also providing for exceptional needs.

Table 6b (p. 305) is a conspectus of the tonal types of the first eight of the twelve suites in Nivers's first *Livre d'orgue*. They are the same tonal types as those of his *Traité* (table 7b) except that the F-sharps and C-sharps in the signature shown for tone 7 in the *Traité* are written in as accidentals in the *Prelude* and other movements of the seventh suite. In the use of A-minor and C-major tonalities for tones 3 and 5, respectively, the tonalities of both Nivers's *Traité* and the first eight suites of his first *Livre d'orgue* correspond with Banchieri's tonalities rather than Titelouze's; but not so for tone 7 and suite 7. The quasi-D-major tonality of Nivers's seventh suite, conversely—as exmplifed by its Prelude reproduced as example 7—corresponds with the tonality of Titelouze's organ Magnificat in tone 7; in the deceptive cadence in Nivers's measure 4 there is a touch of that ambiguity regarding F-sharp and F-natural seen in Titelouze's music in example 6. There are, however, two very significant differences, one conceptual, the other musical.

First, Nivers's quasi-D-major tonality is not described by its author as a transposition of tone 7, as had been the case for Titelouze's seventh Magnificat; the rubric at the head of Nivers's seventh suite is simply "Prelude du 7. Ton." Second, there is no psalmodic *cantus firmus* actually present, although the emphasis on a^1 and the frequent stepwise descent, plain or ornamented almost beyond recognition, from a^1 to e^1 might suggest the reciting tone a^1 leading into the end of the *differentia*, (b^1)–a^1–g^1–$f\sharp^1$–e^1. The difference between Titelouze's tone 7 Magnificat movement shown in example 6 and Nivers's tone 7 Prelude shown in example 7 is the same as that between Pontio's and Banchieri's duos for psalm tone 3 (exx. 1b and 4a). The Pontio and Titelouze examples *embody* a psalm tone in a particular tonality, while the Banchieri and Nivers examples illustrate tonalities for use in psalmodic contexts, but in compositions with freely invented material having no explicit melodic origin in the psalm tone.

Nivers's assignment of tonalities for psalmody of even his first eight suites, however, is not like Titelouze's simple one-to-one correspondence with the eight psalm tones, since Nivers cites transposition for the convenience of a choir for some of the first eight suites, as well as for all four of suites nine through twelve.

The signature systems and the finals for the first eight suites of Nivers's first *Livre d'orgue* that are shown in table 8b are reprised in table 9, along with the signatures and finals for the last four suites; for all twelve, the ubiquitous written-in accidentals are noted in parentheses in the column of system signatures. The title rubrics for each suite are also shown, and one sees that the *cantus mollis* tonalities for tones 2 and 6 are also said to be available for use as transpositions for tones 1 and 5, respectively. The tonalities for suites 9 through 12 are designated for transposed tones only; the C tonality in *cantus mollis*, with its ubiquitous E-flats, is the only one whose title rubric mentions a second use. In the Guidonian diatonic psalm tone 4 usually ended at e, but in medieval practice some mode 4 antiphons required a psalm-tone *differentia* finishing at a; Nivers's termination at c^1 for tone 4 "at the dominant," therefore, implies a transposition for tone 4 up a minor third.[41]

The expressions in brackets on table 9 are taken from a "Table of the eight church tones, natural and transposed" provided by Nivers on the first of five unnumbered pages between the title page of the first *Livre d'orgue* and the Prelude of the first suite. Only those expressions adding new information or terms have been included on table 9; for instance, the word "diesé" in the heading for tone 7 calls attention to the ubiquitous sharping of pitch classes F and C in the *cantus durus* signature for the pieces in the seventh suite. Table 10 is a summary of Nivers's "Table of the eight church tones," in which he designates the keys of the twelve suites as suitable for different kinds of choirs.

> The organ was established in church for augmenting the solemnity and for comforting the heart. It is, therefore, appropriate to know which tones are for low voices and which for high voices, such as those of nuns. For nuns, transposition is necessary; one must choose a tone suitable for the range of their voices. . . . The exceptional tones are used in offices when chant is too high or too low; in this case, the organist plays in a transposed tone, choosing one suitable for the range of the voices.[42]

The title rubrics on the Preludes of each suite and the further indications for transposition in Nivers's table of eight tones and their transpositions, taken all together, result in a mélange of *re*-tonalities and *ut*-tonalities at various pitch levels, plus one *mi*-tonality at its standard Guidonian pitch level. On table 11 the twelve tonalities of Nivers's suites are reordered by their tonics and set forth in *re*, *mi*, and *ut* columns. Note that the tonics are the six degrees of the natural hexachord of the outgoing Guidonian diatonic model of tonal space; they are also the "white" keys of the incoming keyboard model, without B. In one or another choral context the *cantus mollis G-re* tonality can be associated with any of the first three tones and the *cantus mollis F-ut* tonality with any of the last four. There are two suites in

TABLE 9 Guillaume Gabriel Nivers, *Livre d'orgue contenant cent pièces de tous les Tons de L'Eglise* (Paris, 1665)

Suite		System ♮	System ♭	Title on Prelude
				[bracketed designations provide further transposition information contained in Nivers's "Table des 8 Tons..." (see Table 10)]
1		d		... du 1. Ton
2			g	... du 2. ou du 1 transposé [le 2. et Le 3. en G re sol ut, par ♭]
3		a		... du 3. Ton [le 2. et Le 3. en A mi la re]
4	Ex. 10	ø		... du 4. Ton
5		C		... du 5. Ton
6			F	... du 6. ou du 5. transposé [le 7. en F ut fa]
7	Ex. 7	D (+f♯ / c♯)		... du 7. Ton [le 7. eu D la re sol, diesé] [du 5. en D la re sol]
8	Ex. 8	G		... du 8. Ton [le 6. en G re sol ut, par ♮]
9			c (+e♭)	... du 1. transposé en C. Ou du 4. à la dominante, transposé
10	Ex. 11	e (+f♯)		... du 1. transposé en E [Du 1. ou du 2. en E mi la]
11	Ex. 9	G (+f♯)		... du 6. transposé en G
12		A (+f♯ / c♯ /g♯)		... du 6. transposé en A

♮ / ♭ designate system signatures (note names in parentheses designate accidentals almost always written in.

Lower-case or upper-case letters indicate the thirds as minor or major, respectively.

ø indicates a minor third and minor second ("Phrygian").

TABLE 10 After G.G. Nivers, *Livre d'orgue* (1665), *Table des 8 Tons de L'Eglise …*

… ordinary for low voices

		(organ suite)
1	♮–d	(1)
2, 3 }	♭–g	(2)
4	♮–ø	(4)
5	♮–C	(5)
6	♭–F	(6)
7	♮–D (+f♯ / c♯)	(7)
8	♭–F	(6)

… ordinary for high voices

		(organ suite)
1	♭–G	(2)
2, 3 }	♮–a	(3)
*4	♭–c (+e♭)	(9)
5	♭–F	(6)
6	♮–G	(11)
7	♭–F	(6)
8	♮–G	(8)

*[… à la dominante]

… extraordinary for low voices

1	♭–c (+e♭)	(9)
1, 2 }	♮–e (+f♯)	(10)
3	♮–a	(3)
5	♮–D (+f♯ / c♯)	(7)
6 {	♮–G (+f♯)	(11)
	♮–A (+f♯ / c♯ / g♯)	(12)
8	♮–G	(8)

… extraordinary for high voices

1 {	♮–a	(1)
	♮–e (+f♯)	(10)
2	♭–g	(2)
4	♮–ø	(4)
5 {	♮–c	(5)
	♮–D (+f♯ / c♯)	(7)
6	♮–A (+f♯ / c♯ / g♯)	(12)

two different *G-ut* tonalities, one for tone 8 and one for tone 6 transposed, and two suites with final at pitch class E; one is the *mi* tonality already noted, with F-natural, the other a *re*-tonality with F-sharp.[43]

Examples 8 and 9 are the Preludes to Nivers's suites in the two *G-ut* tonalities. The Prelude to suite number 8, for tone 8, reflects the psalm tone in that it constantly moves up to c^2 but never rises above it. C is the "dominant" of this *G-ut* tonality: the harmony constantly tends towards cadencing in C without ever fully doing so; and though F-sharp is used elsewhere than at cadences to G, F-natural is always used in descent. The Prelude to suite number 11, for tone 6 in transpositions "ordinary for high voices" and "extraordinary for low voices" (see table 10),

TABLE 11 Tonalities represented in G.G. Nivers's [first] *Livre d'orgue* (1665) (on the six degrees of the natural hexachord)

	re tonality (m3)		*mi* tonality (m3, m2)		*ut* tonality (M3)	
Final	Suite number	Tone	Suite number	Tone	Suite number	Tone
D	1	1	—	—	7 (+f♯ / c♯)	7 5 transp.
E	10 (+f♯)	1 transp. 2 transp.	4	4	—	—
F	—	—	—	—	6	6 5 transp. 7 transp. 8 transp.
G	2	2 3 transp. 1 transp.	—	—	8 11 (+f♯)	8 6 transp.
A	3	3 2 transp.	—	—	12 (+ f♯ / c♯ /g♯)	6 transp.
C	9 (+e♭)	1 transp. 4 with ending on the reciting tone, transp.	—	—	5	5

is very different. Melodic emphasis is on pitch class D, and F-sharp is frequently used in descent; it is a tonality very like the ordinary G major of the next century.

Examples 10 and 11 represent the two E-tonalities in Nivers's first *Livre d'orgue*. In the *mi*-tonality for tone 4 F-natural is the norm; F-sharp occurs only occasionally, and only once in descent in order to make a perfect fifth over B in the bass in the antepenultimate measure. Pitch class A is much emphasized, accompanied by E and C, there are several near-cadential approaches to a D-minor sonority—F accompanied by A and D—and a full cadence in C midway (mm. 7–8). The last full cadence is "Phrygian," five measures before the end, with the upper leading-tone F moving to E in the lowest voice, in the usual manner for a *mi*-tonality; the E-major triad of cadential arrival is then briefly abandoned before it is finally reaffirmed.

EXAMPLE 8 G. G. Nivers, *Livre d'orgue* (1665), Suite No. 8, Prelude du 8[e] ton

EXAMPLE 9 G. G. Nivers, *Livre d'orgue* (1665), Suite No. 11
Prelude du 6. transpose en G

EXAMPLE 10 G. G. Nivers, *Livre d'orgue* (1665), Suite No. 4, Prelude du 4e ton

EXAMPLE 11 G. G. Nivers, *Livre d'orgue* (1665), Suite No. 10
Prelude du 1. transpose en E

Nivers's E-tonality for the tenth suite, in "extraordinary" transposition from tone 1 for both high and low voices, is a *re*-tonality that comes near the normal E-minor tonality of the next century: F-sharp is ubiquitous in descent as in ascent, and the final cadence is made with a D-sharp lower leading-tone above B in the bass, in the usual form of cadential arrival for *re*-tonalities (and *ut*-tonalities). These two kinds of E-tonality and instances of transmutation of the *mi*-tonality into the *re*-tonality are discussed in some detail in the next section of this essay.

* * *

For an illustration of the French tone 7 as D major carried over into the realm of German Catholic organ practice, see the beginning and end of the seventh organ toccata by the South German composer Sebastian Anton Scherer, shown in example 12.[44] The tonal types of Scherer's set of eight toccatas are summarized in table 8c-II (p. 308); they conform to those of the first eight suites in Nivers's first *Livre d'orgue* (table 8b). Scherer's seventh Toccata moves from the initial D major shown at the beginning of example 12 to pedal G at measure 17, and on to similar harmonic prolongations over long pedals on C, D, E, then A and back to the final D as shown at the end of example 12. Though the tonal focuses established in the middle of the Toccata are not all those we would expect in the D major of eighteenth-century common practice, the D major itself, at the beginning and end, shows none of the ambiguity about F-natural and F-sharp that characterized Titelouze's tone-7 D major, or Nivers's somewhat less ambiguous tone-7 D major. These portions of Scherer's Toccata work with a D major that we know, Mattheson's seventh key of his first eight.

The existence of an E-tonality that is a transposition of the *cantus durus* D-*re* tonality, as found in the eleventh suite of Nivers's first *Livre d'orgue*, is certainly an important forerunner of the E-minor tonality of the eighteenth century. But in the first set of eight keys in Mattheson's scheme, as taken over from Georg Falck and other Germans, E minor is not a secondary tonality derived from a primary one elsewhere in the system. It is a primary tonality, occupying the position once occupied by psalm tone 4; it is, in short, not a transposition, genetically, but rather a replacement of the *mi*-tonality of tone 4. I know of no contemporaneous theoretical rationale for the replacement of the *mi*-tonality of tone 4 by the *re*-tonality E minor that is comparable to the explanation Titelouze provided in the foreword to his Organ Magnificats for his treatment of tone 7. It is an uneasy substitution at best: as already noted, tone 4 is the only instance of a *mi*-tonality in the set of eight, as seen for instance in Nivers's *Traité* and first *Livre d'orgue*; his tones 1, 2, and 3 are *re*-tonalities and tones 5 through 8 are *ut*-tonalities.

Table 6c (p. 305) summarizes the information in an Austrian manuscript treatise from 1677; the notated pattern from the treatise itself may be seen along with

EXAMPLE 12 Sebastian Anton Scherer, Opus 2 (Ulm, 1664), Liber II
Toccata Septima (mm. 1–4, 14–16, 85–end)

those from Titelouze's Magnificats and Nivers's *Traité* in table 8c.[45] The Prinner treatise may serve to mark the completed transformation of Banchieri's psalm-tone keys into Mattheson's first set of eight, including E minor in the position of tone 4 as well as D Major in the position of tone 7, with no additional tonalities.

Despite the absence of documented explication from seventeenth-century sources, a gradual transformation of tone 4 into E minor in the German-speaking lands can be illustrated from musical sources. Example 13, also taken from Scherer's set of eight toccatas, might be described as a piece trying to be in E minor that keeps backsliding into the ways of an ancestral *mi*-tonality. The first measure is E minor; the next two lean towards what we would call a strongly tonicized sub-dominant neighbor chord elaboration; E minor reasserts itself in measures 4 and 5, while in measure 6 the neighbor chord returns, followed by a kind of E minor in measures 7 and 8. Then the elaborated neighbor chord returns, and as the pedal heads towards its first move, from E to A, the ancestral Phrygian is finally in full command. All this of course turns on the inflection of certain scale degrees. The D-sharps in measures 1 and 5, in conjunction with G-natural having F-sharp as a lower neighbor note, establish E minor; G-sharp leading to or led to by A, with emphasis on pitch classes A and C in addition to E, establish the *mi*-tonality even though the characteristic F–E semitone of the old *mi*-tonality is assiduously avoided until after the pedal has made its move to A. At the end of the toccata, however, as the pedal makes its final move the other way, from A to E, there is no longer any trace of E minor: F-sharp always passes to G-sharp; the upper leading-tone and its resolution—the F–E semitone—is very much in evidence as long as the A is present in the pedal; and in only one of the six measures over the final pedal on low E are there any G-naturals.

Example 14 shows another piece by Scherer in tone 4 where E minor and the old *mi*-tonality cohabit uneasily, but here it is E minor that wins out. The last three measures are unambiguously E minor; so also are the cadences in measure 5 and measure 15, though they are what we would call deceptive cadences, making much of the half step B–C, thereby leaning towards that A-minor neighbor chord.

The tonality of the intonations for tone 7 in Scherer's tablatures, as may be seen from table 8c-I, is anomalous in the other contexts here under consideration. Like the intonations for tone 8, it is a G-*ut* tonality, but there is no difference in tonal quality between the two: both are a quasi-G-major, with secondary emphases on pitch class D, and the only distinction is that the intonations for tone 7 lie somewhat higher than those for tone 8, as though Scherer were suddenly reverting to the most ancient of paired distinctions, that of authentic and plagal by register.

Examples 15 and 16 below are Preludes and Fugues from J.C.F. Fischer's *Ariadne musica* (1702), a predecessor of J.S. Bach's *Wohltemperierte Clavier* in that the tonalities of its Preludes and Fugue pairs are arranged in ascending order

EXAMPLE 13 Sebastian Anton Scherer, Opus 2 (Ulm, 1664), Liber II
Toccata Quarta (mm. 1–15, 101–end)

EXAMPLE 13 (*cont.*)

EXAMPLE 14 Sebastian Anton Scherer, Opus 2 (Ulm, 1664), Liber I
Quarti Toni: Intonatio 2da (of 4)

up the keyboard through an octave of the total chromatic from C to C.[46] The tonal types of *Ariadne musica* are summarized in table 12. There are twenty tonalities in all, and every degree in the total chromatic is represented by at least one: each of the *claves* of *cantus durus*—the white keys of the keyboard—has a major *and* a minor tonality; the black keys each have a major *or* a minor tonality.

TABLE 12 Tonalities of the Preludes and Fugues in J.C.F. Fischer's *Ariadne Musica* (< 1715)

system:	♭♭♭	♭♭	♭	[♮]	♯	♯♯	♯♯♯	♯♯♯♯	♯♯♯♯♯
1				C (5)					
2								*c♯	
3				d (1)					
4						D (7)			
5	E♭								
6				*ø (4?)					
7						e (4?)			
8								E	
9	f								
10			F (6)						
11								f♯	
12			g (2)						
13					G (8)				
14	*A♭								
15				a (3)					
16							A		
17		B♭							
18							b		
19									B
20		c							

* tonalities not among Mattheson's 17 with affects (see Table 1).
(n) tonalities in Mattheson's first set of eight.

The white key E has three tonalities.[47] There is an E "Phrygian"—a *mi*-tonality in *cantus durus*—as well as an E minor, a *re*-tonality in the two-sharp transposition system, and an E major, an *ut*-tonality in the four-sharp transposition system. The *mi*-tonality Prelude and Fugue is shown as example 15; comparing it with Scherer's *Intonatio* (ex. 14), one sees that Fischer's "Phrygian" is much more aggressively so than Scherer's with its heavy admixture of E minor: only in three

EXAMPLE 15 J.C.F. Fischer, *Ariadne Musica*

6. Praeludium VI

EXAMPLE 15 (*cont.*)

EXAMPLE 16 J.C.F. Fischer, *Ariadne Musica*
7. Praeludium VII

EXAMPLE 16 (*cont.*)

TABLE 13 Tonalities in keyboard collections by J.C.F. Fischer

Pièces de clavecin (1696)
Preludes and French dance types, except Nos. 5 (Prelude and Aria with Variations) and 8 (Prelude and Chaconne)

	♯♯	♯	[♮]	♭	(Mattheson)
1			d		(1)
2				g	(2)
3			a		(3)
4			ø		[4]
5			C		(5)
6				F	(6)
7	D				(7)
8		G			(8)

Blumenstrauß (1732)
Sets of a Prelude, six fugues, and Finale, all very short

	♯♯	♯	[♮]	♭	(Mattheson)
1			d		(1)
2				F	(6)
3			a		(3)
4			C		(5)
5		e			(4)
6	D				(7)
7				g	(2)
8		G			(8)

Parnassus (1738)
each set is a series of French dance types preceded by a Prelude / Ouverture / Toccata etc.

	♯♯	♯	[♮]	♭	♭♭	(Mattheson)
Clio			C			(5)
Calliope		G				(8)
Melpomene			a			(3)
Thalia					B♭	
Erato		e				(4)
Euterpe				F		(6)
Terpsichore				g		(2)
Polymnia	D					(7)
Urania			d			(1)

measures of Fischer's Prelude are there any G-naturals with F-sharp as lower neighbor note; elsewhere F-sharp occurs only as lower neighbor to G-sharp, which is ubiquitous, as is the characteristic E–F–E of the *mi*-tonality in the natural hexachord and its structural reflection B–C–B in the hard hexachord. The "Phrygian" *mi*-tonality Fugue has G-natural much more prominently than the Prelude, but in neither the Fugue nor the Prelude is there any of that D-sharp that keeps creeping into the Scherer pieces for tone 4. In Fischer's Prelude and Fugue there is not even a whisper of E minor—and suitably so, for the subsequent Prelude and Fugue in his *Ariadne musica* are just as aggressively E minor, a *re*-tonality with D-sharp lower leading-tone and all, as may be seen in glancing through example 16. Fischer's E minor is not a transformed *mi*-tonality, far less so than the two Scherer examples in tone 4 that have some E-minor coloration; it is simply a *cantus durus* D minor transposed up a whole step, using the two-sharp transposition system.

The set of tonal types in Fischer's *Ariadne musica* has no direct connection with the sets of eight we have been looking at, notwithstanding the specious parenthetical noting in table 12 of the numbers of Mattheson's first eight. It is one step removed; the keys are already fully grounded in the new keyboard model of tonal space, and the ordering principal—upward a half-step at a time—has nothing to do with Mattheson's *Neu-eröffnete Orchestre* scheme. Its utility for our present concern is the survival of the *mi*-tonality E "Phrygian" alongside E minor, with E major as well. Fischer's other keyboard collections, however, do confirm the centrality of those first eight tonalities of Mattheson's scheme in the system of tonalities in effect in Mattheson's time; the tonal types of those collections are summarized in table 13. The sequence of tonalities in the suites of versets of Fischer's *Blumenstrauss* of 1732 coincides not with Mattheson's first eight tonalities but with older patterns for *alternatim* psalmodic use, as in Nivers's scheme of 1667 or the suites of his first *Livre d'orgue*; it differs from Nivers only in that Fischer's G major uses the one-sharp transposition system where Nivers's is in simple *cantus durus*. Fischer's first publication, his *Pièces de clavecin*, does use Mattheson's first eight keys; their different order only confirms their centrality as a group, and their separation, now complete, from their genetic origins. Fischer's *Parnassus* shows the same group of keys, with one extra for the ninth muse.

And in reaching Parnassus, we have completed a mapping of the route "from psalmody to tonality," a route that began with the psalm tones for Vespers in the liturgical practice of Counter-Reformation Italy, traveled in the hands of organists through France and Catholic South Germany, and ended in a Protestant North German treatise, having been transformed step by step into a partly patterned accounting of the twenty-four minor and major keys. It is not the only route from the tonalities of the sixteenth century to those of the eighteenth, but it is one relatively easy to follow, through the jungle of conflicting seventeenth-century musical practices and doctrines.

NOTES

*Work on this project was begun in 1974, in connection with research for my article "Mode" in *The New Grove* (1980). The first formal presentation was at the annual meeting of the Royal Musical Association, at Royal Holloway College (London) in April 1989. The work has been redone for the present publication, taking account of the appearance later that same year of Joel Lester's revision of his earlier "Major-minor Concepts" and "Emergence of Major and Minor Keys" in his *Between Modes and Keys*.

When I wrote the original paper I did not have access to Nivers's first *Livre d'orgue*, neither the facsimile nor the modern edition. As I was incorporating Nivers's material a year or two later I learned of Robert Frederick Bates's dissertation, "From Mode to Key," and I sent him the original version of this essay. His courteous and detailed reply has saved me from several errors and misapprehensions, and though my interpretations differ from his in some fundamental points, I am much more confident of my overall evaluation of the role of seventeenth-century French organ music in the route "from psalmody to tonality" in that it is by and large the same as that reached by Dr. Bates in his much more thorough investigation and reporting on the French organ sources, both theoretical and practical.

I'm most grateful to Cristle Collins Judd for the invitation to participate in her symposium "Tonal Structures in Early Music" (Philadelphia, March 29–30, 1996), for her encouraging me to return to and revise my work again for publication in this volume, and for her punctilious and patient preparation of a difficult manuscript. Thanks also to Dana Gooley for a thoughtful reading that led to several clarifications.

1. Powers, "Mode," 416.

2. There is a curious naiveté about modal theory in the English music-theoretical writings of the period. For instance, an English translation of the *Micrologus* of Ornithoparcus was published by John Dowland in 1609 more than half a century after its last known edition in 1555, and nearly a century after its first appearance in 1517, as though Glarean's *Dodecachordon* and Zarlino's *Istitutioni harmoniche* and their epigones had never existed. The only passage in Thomas Morley's *Plaine and easie Introduction* touching on modal theory for polyphony is his unpaginated "Annotations" tipped in at the end of the book at the suggestion of "some of better skill in letters than myself"; otherwise there is a discussion of the "eight tunes" in the body of the text, but that has to do only with polyphonic psalmody. On the positive side, in Thomas Campion's extraordinary *New way of making Fowre Parts in Counter-point* (c. 1615) what I have called "tonal focus" (I owe the term to Karol Berger) and allied topics are forthrightly treated with no reference whatever to any theory of modality. Given this English innocence of Continental modal theory, then, it is reasonable to suppose further that analyses of the music of such composers as William Byrd ought not to be burdened with modern-day adaptations of dodecachordal or other modal theories. These matters and much more are now thoroughly elucidated in Jessie Ann Owens's "Concepts of pitch" in this volume.

Given that Byrd's music is not all that different stylistically from that of his Continental contemporaries, moreover, one then begins to suspect that systematic "modality," of either a dodecachordal or octenary sort, is not an inherent and necessary compositional property of Continental polyphony either, but rather a theoretically ascribed and only sometimes compositionally contingent one. To be sure, one might argue that despite the English unfamiliarity with Continental modal doctrines, English music such as Byrd's is not all that different from Continental polyphony *grosso modo*, and therefore can perfectly well be construed according to Continental modal theory, or its modern "neo-modal" derivative (to use Owens's apt term): in her words, the "modern hybrid that reduces Glarean's twelve modes to five scale-types: Dorian, Phrygian, Mixolydian, Aeolian, and Ionian." But to suppose that is to suppose once again that Continental polyphony itself is rightly so to be construed. I have suggested in a number of writings (see for example "Is mode real?") that that is a gross oversimplification of the relationship between modal theory and compositional practice in Continental polyphony.

3. A full and detailed mapping of the French territory covered in the route "from psalmody to tonality" outlined in the second and third parts of my essay may be seen in Bates, "From Mode to Key." Bates sketches out a very general map in his first chapter:

> [1] Before about the mid-sixteenth century, the psalm tones were used melodically in all versets of continental organ Magnificats. [2] By mid-century, composers were inconsistent in their use of the psalm tones. . . . [3] Finally by the late sixteenth and early seventeenth centuries, some organ Magnificats were written with no reference whatsoever to the psalm tones . . . [4] With the abandonment of the direct use of the psalm tones came a new type of modal system appropriate to alternation with the sung formulas.

Bates's use of the expression "new type of modal system" to characterize the final phase of the French development, however, presumes an older type of "modal system," even though in the bulk of the dissertation the peculiar and patently unsystematic nature of the tonalities used for psalmody is thoroughly explored.

4. "Is mode real?"

5. Bent, "Diatonic *Ficta*," 10.

6. See Ellsworth, ed., *The Berkeley Manuscript*, 53–67.

7. Bent, "Accidentals, Counterpoint and Notation," 321.

8. Ibid., 322.

9. The so-called "enharmonic" equivalence of G♯ and A♭, F♯ and G♭, and so on, is not comparable to the dual nomenclature in the Guidonian system, since both names come from the same list; it is a consequence of the new conceptual model based on the keyboard.

10. Eventually, however, the new "*litterae*" proved not enough by themselves for efficient theoretical analysis. The introduction in German-speaking lands of Roman numerals I–VII for the scale degrees of a tonality the letter name of whose degree "I" comes from the

keyboard model—the beginnings, in short, of "Stufenlehre"—meant that once again the position of a tone in the general scale (of letters) and its function in any particular tonal context (by numbers beginning from a "tonal focus" designated by one of the letters) could be denoted with simple signs from two independent lists, one pansystemic (the letters) and the other musically functional (the numbers), like the *litterae* and the *voces* of the Guidonian system, respectively.

11. At the end of table 1, by way of contrast, is shown Heinichen's famous "Musicalischer Circul" of 1711, in which the 24 keyboard-oriented major and minor keys that lie at the base of eighteenth-century musical practice are laid out in a closed, rationalized scheme that accommodates both the burgeoning major / minor pairings with which we are familiar, and the older kind of pairings based on the two species of the fifth contained within a single hexachord (*ut–re–mi–fa–sol* and *re–mi–fa–sol–la*).

12. "Emergence of Major and Minor Keys." This essay was the continuation of Lester's "Major-Minor Concepts." The two essays, revised and extended, are the basis of his *Between Modes and Keys*, which will be cited hereafter.

An English version of the first passage on the 24 keys in Mattheson's *Das neu-eröffnete Orchestre* appears in Lester, *Between Modes and Key*, 114–15 (= Lester, "Emergence of Major and Minor Keys," 84–85.)

13. Steblin, *A History of Key Characteristics*; Auhagen, *Studien zur Tonartencharakteristik*. Though not specifically at issue here, tonal affect is a central factor in the histories of both continuities and disjunctions in European ideas about "tonality"—tonality in the fourfold sense in which Fétis used the term—and I expect to deal with it in that context on another occasion.

14. Meier, *The Modes*. Meier's demonstration of the distinction of authentic and plagal in polyphony was first presented in full in his "Bemerkungen."

15. For a comprehensive account of sixteenth-century polyphonic psalmody in Italy, see Armstrong, "How to compose a psalm." Armstrong did not concern himself in his essay with the distinction between modes and psalm tones, as illustrated by Pontio, but he documented and illustrated the great importance of

> polyphonic vesper music, which at the beginning of the seventeenth century had come to rival the Mass in musical opulence . . . the flowering of an extraordinarily rich and varied repertory of vesper music in Italy during the early years of the Counter-Reformation . . . it is impossible to consider this music apart from its liturgical surroundings (103–04).

Armstrong described various ways of making *alternatim* settings, and both cited and quoted excerpts of psalmodic polyphony by a number of the composers mentioned by Pontio and Cerone.

16. Cf. my "Tonal types," 438–40.

17. Pontio, *Ragionamento*, 117.

> I prattici . . . le cadenze principali, & terminate faranno l'istesse, che del Settimo Tuono, facendo Motetto, ò Madrigale, ò altra tale compositione. Vero è, che il diligente compositore piglierà per cadenza principale la corda di C sol fa ut; acciò sia meglio conosciuto, e distinto detto Tuono dal Settimo, per esser corda, che fà la mediatà del Salmo di detto Tuono.

18. Compositions representing two different "G major" tonalities, one of which represents tone 8 and the other a transposition of tone 6, may be seen in examples 8 and 9 below. Distinctions between varieties of other tonalities among the 24 major and minor keys may be perceivable, distinctions similarly arising from the sometimes multiple origins of the tonality in question. An E-minor tonality arising from the replacement of F-natural in the *mi*-tonality of E with F-sharp is not the same as an E-minor tonality arising from transposition up one degree of a D-minor tonality (as in exx. 10–11 and 15–16 discussed below). Similiarly, there may be two different kinds of A minor, one ultimately connected with tonal type g_2-♮-A, the other with tonal type c_1-♮-A.

19. The confusing of psalm-tone tonalities with modal categories is often accompanied in modern scholarship by the confusing of one or both with dodecachordal modal systems and the modern "neo-modal" version that uses Glarean's pseudo-Greek terminology without making the distinction between authentic and plagal. Pontio himself was aware of Zarlino's dodecachordal scheme but respectfully dismissed it, referring his readers to its inventor.

> There are in fact other modes [*tuoni*], so-called "irregular" by musicians from not finishing on the four degrees [D / E / F / G] where the aforesaid others finish. Not that they too are not formed regularly with their [species of the] Fifth and Fourth, such that rationally they cannot be called "irregular." But if they can rightly be called "regular," as Zarlino affirms in Part IV of his *Institutione di Musica* Chapter 27, because they observe the [same] rule as the others, yet through not finishing (as I told you) on the four degrees [D / E / F / G], they are called "irregular," finishing a fifth away from the former. And if you see a *cantilena* that finishes on A la mi re, the soprano in the g_2 clef [*chiave di G sol re*], that will be one of the aforesaid [irregular modes], about which I shan't elaborate, because if you want to have a fuller understanding of them, read Zarlino, Part IV, Chapters 26, 27, 28, and 29, where he has discussed them at length.
>
> [Vi sono veramente altri tuoni, così dalli prattici chiamati irregolari, per non finire nelle quatre corde, dove finiscono gli altri sopranomati; non già ch'ancora loro non siano formati regolarmente con la sua Diapente, & Diatessaron; talche ragionalmente non si potranno dire irregolari, ma si bene regolari potrian chiamarsi come gli altri, come afferma Zarlino nella quarta parte della sua Institutione di Musica nel capo vigesimo sesto; perche servano la regola, come gli altri; ma per

non finire (come v'hò detto) nelle quattro corde sono dette irregolari finendo per Quinta lontano dalli primi, & vedendo voi una cantilena, che finisca nella corda di A la mi re, essendo il Soprano per la chiave di G sol re ut, questo sarà un delli sopranomati, circa quali non mi estenderò; perche se voi desiderate più à pieno haverne cognitione, legete esso Zarlino nalla Quarta parte al vigesimo sesto, settimo, ottovo, nono capo, che diversamente n'ha trattato (Pontio, *Ragionamento*, 120–21).]

20. *Tonus commixtus* is one of five types of mode originally proposed by Marchetto of Padua in the early fourteenth century and subsequently carried on through more than three centuries of Italian modal theory. (For a summary of the bases of this tradition, which includes Tinctoris and of which Pontio was one of the last carriers, see Powers, "Mode," II.4.ii, iii, 392–96.)

21. Banchieri's alternative "cadenze" for tone 4 merely bring it in line with the traditional psalmody in which the reciting tone is a fourth above the terminal degree, the last note of the *differentia.*

Banchieri's transpositions have been effected within the subsystems of the Guidonian diatonic, but transpositions outside the Guidonian diatonic were theoretically possible, and the more the organ was involved in the sung liturgy, the more frequently they were recommended. (See further below on Nivers's first *Livre d'orgue*).

22. In Lasso's 1562 motets (see table 2b-1562), modes 1 and 2 are both transposed, so once again the authentic-plagal distinction is made by contrasted *ambitus*, as marked by the cleffing, but now within the *cantus-mollis* subsystem of the Guidonian diatonic.

23. Elsewhere I have called psalm-tone *differentiae* cited as though they they were modal finals, "pseudo-finals." See "Is mode real?", 25 ff.

24. Lester, *Between Modes and Keys*.

25. Lester, *Between Modes and Keys,* 77-78, but cf. Lester, "The Emergence of Major and Minor Keys," 71–72.

26. Atcherson, "Key and Mode."

27. Lester, *Between Modes and Keys*, 79, and cf. Lester, "The Emergence of Major and Minor Keys," 72.

28. loc. cit. I have corrected the obviously misprinted numbers "tones 4 and 5" in both Lester, *Between Modes and Keys* and "The Emergence of Major and Minor Keys."

29. For a full discussion of "*re*-tonality" and "*mi*-tonality" (and also "*ut*-tonality")—concepts originating in a threefold distinction made in passing by Glarean in five places in his *Dodecachordon*—see now Judd, "Modal Types."

30. For an instance of an A-final *mi*-tonality that genuinely does represent mode 3, translated from *cantus durus* to *cantus mollis*—that is, with a B-flat in the signature—see no. 5 in Lasso's *Cantiones* for two voices of 1577, now available in a convenient and correct modern edition (Orlando di Lasso, *The complete motets* 11, ed. Peter Bergquist). It uses

the g_2 and c_2 clefs from the high cleffing (the first six duos in this collection are for the two high voices) and contrasts with no. 6 in the same collection, also in an A-final tonality in *cantus mollis*, which uses the c_1 and c_3 clefs from the low cleffing. Thus, where no. 5 represents the authentic mode 3, no. 6 represents the plagal mode 4. For a summary of the tonal types and modal categories represented in this collection, see my "Tonal Types," Table VII (p. 452), and for further discussion of A-tonalities both with and without b♭, see now my "Anomalous modalities," 228-30.

31. Lester, *Between Modes and Keys*, 79.

32. And note that in his transposed psalm tones "for compositions for the choir in polyphony" as listed in table 4b, Banchieri actually does give *e* as the termination for psalm tone 5.

33. Lester, *Between Modes and Keys*, 79.

34. Lester, *Between Modes and Keys*, 80, almost identical with Lester, "Emergence of Major and Minor Keys," 73.

35. See Lester, *Between Modes and Keys*, 81, 83.

36. Howell, "French Baroque organ music." This essay was the starting point for Bates, "From Mode to Key," as it was for my own foray into this part of the route.

37. In Zarlino's 1573 dodecachordal construction both F-modes were *cantus durus*. Tonal types with their finals at F, however, were almost always set in *cantus mollis* in practice, so that the common species of the fifth for pieces representing modes 5 and 6 was not the third species, *fa–sol // re–mi–fa*, but rather the fourth species, *ut–re–mi–fa–sol*, and it is this usage that Titelouze was following. In a dodecachordal system of course an F-tonality with B-flat would have to be regarded as a transposition of the corresponding "Ionian" C-mode, and dodecachordal theorists were faced with the problem of finding (or inventing) representative musical instances for their "true" Lydian and Hypolydian, the F-modes with B-natural. See now my essay "The Lydian mode: Gregor Meyer reads Glarean," for the Symposium "Music as Heard: 1300–1600," organized by Rob Wegman, Princeton, September 27–28, 1997.

Relationships between octenary tonalities and their transpositions and one or the other of Zarlino's dodecachordal schemes and their transpositions are an important factor in all tonal routes between sixteenth-century and eighteenth-century music, including the route "from psalmody to tonality."

38. After *Titelouze: Oeuvres complètes*, ed. Guilmant.

39. Bates, "From Mode to Key," 98, and see his Table 4.1, 99.

40. Ed. Fuzeau; modern transcription by Dufourcq.

41. Though in medieval plainchant practice some of the psalm tones had many *differentiae*, this is the only designation in Nivers's elaborate scheme of transpositions suggesting that a French mid-seventeenth-century organist might need versets for more than one *differentia* ending for a single psalm tone in *alternatim* psalmody with the choir. Yet Titelouze accounted for his use of the modal final rather than the psalm-tone termination in his versets

for the Magnificat in tone 7 precisely because "the Seventh [tone] makes five or six sorts of *differentiae*," as quoted above in the text.

42. Nivers, *Livre d'orgue* (1665), from his "Table des 8 Tons de l'Eglise, au naturel et transposés" and "Remarques sur les 8 Tons de l'Eglise," translation from Bates, "From Mode to Key," 196, 197.

> L'orgue estant institué dans l'Eglise pour l'ornement de la Solemnité et pour le soulagement du Coeur; il est à propos de distinguer les Tons pour les Voix basses, des Tons pour les Voix hautes telles que sont celles des Religieuses en faveur desquelles il faut transposer; et choisir le ton convenable à la porteé des Voix. . . . L'on doibt se servir des Tons extraordinaires aux Offices dont le chant est trop haut ou trop bas, transposant pour cet effet et choisissant un Ton convenable selon la portée¡ des Voix.

43. Transpositions (in the modern sense) of both modes and psalm tones became an ever more significant affair with the growing use of the organ for *alternatim* practice in both Mass and Office from the fifteenth century on (see Bates, "From Mode to Key," and Armstrong, "How to Compose a Psalm"). The dissemination from mid-sixteenth century onward of dodecachordal modal theory, alongside the continuing octenary modal system of chant theory and the tonalities of the associated psalm tones as well, made for confusions in the interface of theory and practice in the seventeenth century too complex to sort out here.

44. Reproduced after *Archives des Maîtres de l'Orgue*, ed. Guilmant.

45. After Federhofer, "Eine Musiklehre."

46. See for instance Mendel and David, *The Bach Reader*, 28: " . . . Johann Caspar Ferdinand Fischer, who may have studied with Lully, and whose *Ariadne Musica* furnished Bach with themes for his Inventions and the idea for the *Well-Tempered Clavier*." Examples 15 and 16 are after Fischer's *Sämtliche Werke*.

47. I am indebted to Alexander Silbiger for calling this to my attention, and see also Bukofzer, *Music in the Baroque Era*, 386: "The independence of the Phrygian mode is clearly evident as late as Ferdinand Fischer who presented in his *Ariadne Musica* three preludes and fugues successively in Phrygian, *e*, and *E*."

Tonal Types and Modal Equivalence in Two Keyboard Cycles by Murschhauser

Michael R. Dodds

To the aspiring church musician around 1700, the many ways of thinking about tonal structure in music must at times have seemed bewildering. There were the traditional eight modes; various incarnations of the twelve-mode system; the set of keys arising from polyphonic psalmody; and an emergent system of only two modes, often still conceptualized in terms of solmization-based Ut and Re (or La) tonalities, that could each be situated on any chromatic degree. The young musician's task was made somewhat easier by correspondences between certain modal systems and musical repertories—such as that between the eight-mode system and plainchant—but such correspondences were hardly exclusive: some theorists, for example, thought there to be twelve modes in plainchant. It is plausible that four randomly selected musicians, asked to name the mode of a given polyphonic composition, might have invoked four different modal systems.

Two cycles of organ works by Franz Xaver Anton Murschhauser (1663–1738), organist at the collegiate church of Unser Lieben Frau in Munich, provide a unique opportunity to illuminate how two of these modal systems—the so-called church keys, arising from *alternatim* psalmody, and the twelve modes—could be correlated with one another on the basis of shared characteristics. *Octi-Tonium novum organicum* (Augsburg, 1696) contains nine sets of Magnificat or psalm versets ordered according to the church keys, with two sets for tone five; each set consists of a *praeambulum*, five fugal versets, and a finale. In addition, *Octi-Tonium* contains various works appropriate for Christmas (not modally labeled) and a suite in E minor. Murschhauser appears to have modeled *Octi-Tonium* closely upon the *Modulatio organica* (Munich, 1686) of his teacher Johann Kaspar Kerll, who held among other posts that of organist at the Vienna Stephansdom.[1]

Murschhauser's *Prototypon longo-breve organicum* (published in two volumes, Nürnberg, 1703 and 1707) presents an array of independent intonations, preludes, fugues, finales, toccatas, and canzonas, all "in the most frequently used tones" of the dodecachordal system (*super tonos figuratos magis usitatos*), as the extended title advertises. That these works are intended for liturgical use is indicated not only by their titles, but also by Murschhauser's provision of optional cuts and by his declaration in the preface that he employed few melodic leaps so as to facilitate transposition up or down a second;[2] coordination of pitch levels with a choir would be the most likely reason for transposing pieces that are already in the best-sounding and least difficult keys.[3]

The two modal systems according to which *Prototypon* and *Octi-Tonium* are labeled, the twelve-mode system and the church keys, respectively, differ markedly not only in their defining features but also in the ways they came to be recognized and described in writings about music. Glarean blended received theoretical doctrine with creative humanistic speculation and analysis to produce a system of twelve modes ordered on the basis of intrinsic characteristics: one authentic and one plagal mode with a final on each of the six diatonic pitches d, e, f, g, a, and c^1. The system could be transposed *in toto* up a fourth. The church keys, on the other hand—as Joel Lester and others have called them—originated from the practical constraints of performance. While they resemble the traditional eight modes of plainchant in some respects, the church keys' overall shape reflects the tonal features of the psalm tones and their most common transpositions, rather than application of theoretical criteria—a case of form following function.[4]

The church keys originated in the *alternatim* performance of psalms and canticles in Catholic offices, especially the office of Vespers. In this performance tradition, the psalm or canticle, preceded by an antiphon and followed by an antiphon or antiphon substitute, was performed in verse-by-verse alternation between two contrasting performance styles. These could be plainchant (with or without accompaniment); polyphonic organ versets; polyphonic versets for one or more choirs (either in *falso bordone* or through-composed alternate verses); and monodic versets for one or more soloists. In order to bring the psalm tones into a comfortable tessitura for the choir, musicians over time developed more or less standard transpositions for certain of them. In addition, they generally treated the psalm tones' last pitch as the final—a pitch class different, in some cases, from the final of the corresponding mode.

Although sixteenth-century theorists such as Aron, Zarlino, Pontio, and Zacconi address the tonal characteristics of polyphonic psalmody, the earliest description of the church keys in their standard seventeenth-century form is to be found in Banchieri's *L'Organo suonarino*. In this and later publications, such as *Cartella musicale*, Banchieri presents tables showing the finals, signatures, and interior cadential degrees for each tone, as well as numerous sets of examples showing the relationship between the psalm tones and polyphonic settings of them.[5] One of the chief differences between Banchieri and his predecessors is that while *Cinquecento* writers on psalmody in most cases tended to present transposition as merely an option available to the practitioner, Banchieri assumes it as a matter of course for tones 2, 5, and 7—to such an extent that the tonalities associated with those tone numbers were those of the most frequent transpositions, not of the natural forms as they would appear in a plainchant antiphoner. Figure 1 presents Banchieri's listing in *Cartella* of the finals for each mode, the corresponding psalm tones as they would be sung in plainchant, the psalm tones as typically transposed for polyphony, and the principal cadential degrees of the church keys. Figure 2 presents a comparison of the finals, signatures and ambitus of the traditional eight church modes with Banchieri's church keys, as well as listings of the dodecachordal system described by Glarean and Zarlino and the first eight of Mattheson's twenty-four major and minor keys.

It can be seen from figures 1 and 2 that, with respect to final and signature (but not necessarily ambitus), Banchieri's tones 1, 4, and 8 are equivalent to their traditional modal counterparts. Tones 2 and 5 are likewise congruent with traditional modes 2 and 5, but transposed up a fourth and down a fourth, respectively.[6] (Strictly speaking, were Banchieri's tone 5 a transposition downward by fourth of traditional mode 5, it would have a single sharp in the signature. In late sixteenth- and seventeenth-century music, however, a flat was often added to the mode 5 signature, or, to put it another way, the "Lydian" mode 5 was often supplanted by the "Ionian" mode 11, transposed down a fifth from its natural position on C in *cantus durus* to F in *cantus mollis*. Therefore, since *cantus mollis* would have been commonplace for mode 5 in Banchieri's day, transposition down a fourth entails a reversion to *cantus durus*.) Banchieri's tone 6 has the same final, F, as its traditional counterpart; the addition of a flat to its signature represents not transposition, but rather a conventionalized concession to the need to inflect the upper-neighbor B in the sixth psalm tone.[7] Two of Banchieri's tones have finals different from those of the like-numbered traditional modes or transpositions thereof: tone 3 derives its final from the third psalm tone's principal ending on A, and tone 7 likewise derives its final from the seventh psalm tone's principal ending, also on A, but transposed down a fifth to D in *cantus mollis*.

With some noteworthy variants upon Banchieri's scheme, the church keys are presented or discussed by more than thirty later writers, including Angleria, Titelouze, Stella, Nivers, Bononcini, Falck, Samber, and Mattheson. This chain of writings about the church keys is paralleled by a long succession of modally ordered cycles of keyboard works within which their history can also be traced. Figure 3 lists the tonal types of a selection of cycles from the Catholic German-speaking lands, along with one of the earliest Italian cycles to correspond exactly to Banchieri's set of finals and signatures, the anonymous *Intavolatura d'organo* of 1598.

FIGURE 1 Antiphon finals for each of the eight traditional modes, the corresponding psalm tones as sung in plainchant, the psalm tones as transposed for compositions in polyphony, and the principal cadential degrees of the church keys. Adriano Banchieri, *Cartella musicale*, 69–71, Venice, 1614.

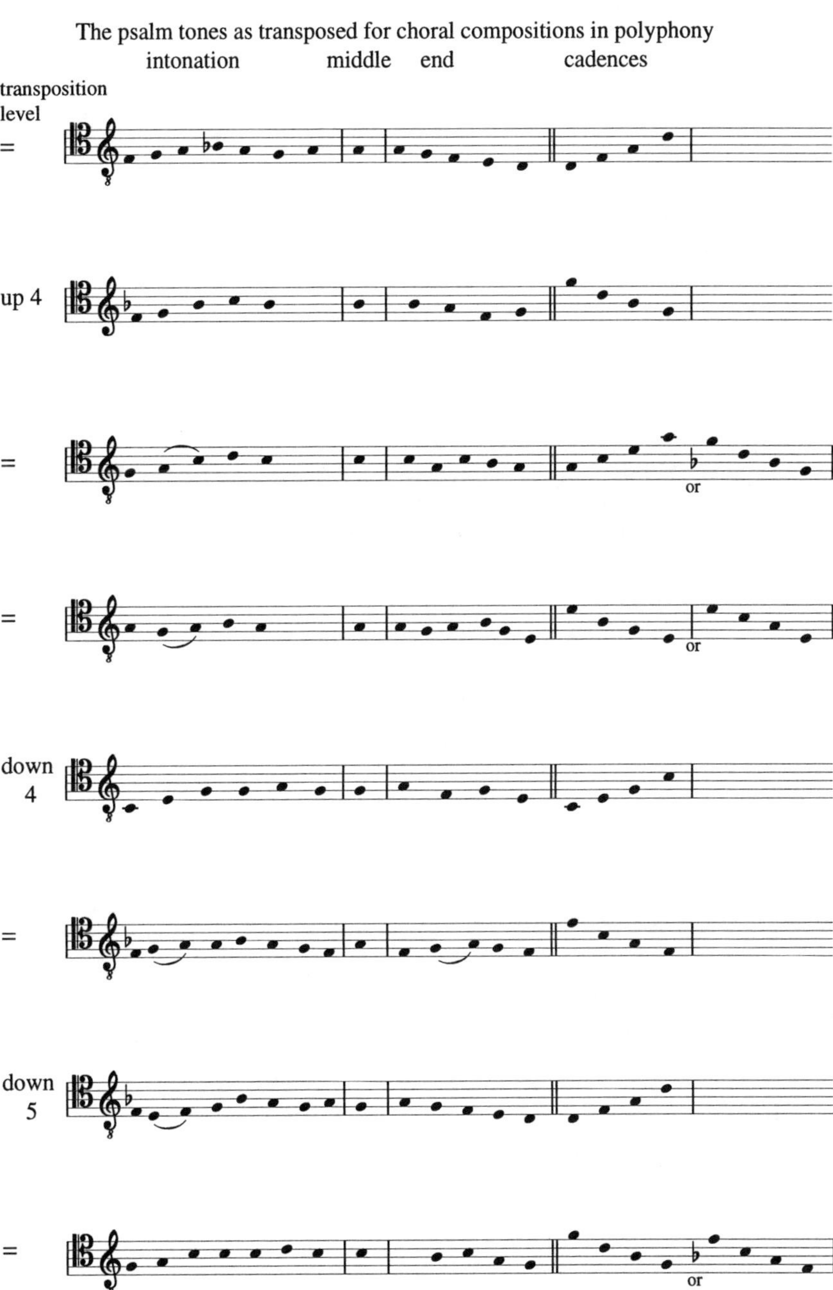
The psalm tones as transposed for choral compositions in polyphony
intonation
middle
end
cadences
transposition level
=
up 4
=
=
or
=
or
down 4
=
down 5
=
or

FIGURE 2 Overview of paradigmatic modal systems relating to keyboard music around 1700

Mode or Tone	Traditional church modes	Twelve-mode system*	Church keys†	Major-minor system‡
1	d–♮ authentic (Dorian)	d–♮ authentic (Dorian)	d–♮	*d f a* or D minor
2	d–♮ plagal (Hypodorian)	d–♮ plagal (Hypodorian)	g–♭	*g b♭ d* or G minor
3	e–♮ authentic (Phrygian)	e–♮ authentic (Phrygian)	a–♮	*a c e* or A minor
4	e–♮ plagal (Hypophrygian)	e–♮ plagal (Hypophrygian)	e–♮	*e g b* or E minor
5	f–♮ authentic (Lydian)	f–♮ authentic (Lydian)	c–♮	*c e g* or C major
6	f–♮ plagal (Hypolydian)	f–♮ plagal (Hypolydian)	f–♭	*f a c* or F major
7	g–♮ authentic (Mixolydian)	g–♮ authentic (Mixolydian)	d–♭	*d f# a* or D major
8	g–♮ plagal (Hypomixolydian)	g–♮ plagal (Hypomixolydian)	g–♮	*g b d* or G major etc.
9		a–♮ authentic (Aeolian)		
10		a–♮ plagal (Hypoaeolian)		
11		c^1–♮ authentic (Ionian)		
12		c^1–♮ plagal (Hypoionian)		

Both the traditional church modes and Glarean's system were recognized to exist at the pitch level shown (in *cantus durus*, i.e., with a blank signature) or transposed up a fourth (in *cantus mollis*, i.e., with a signature of one flat).

* Heinrich Glarean, *Dodecachordon*, 1547.

† Adriano Banchieri, *L'Organo suonarino*, 1605.

‡ First 8 of 24 keys in Johann Mattheson, *Neu-Eröffnete Orchestre*, 1713.

Figure 3 Some South German (and one Italian) keyboard cycles ordered according to the church keys

Cycle		1	2	3	4	5	6	7	8				
Anon., *Intavolatura* (Venice, 1598)		d–♮	g–♭	a–♮	e–♮	C–♮	F–♭	d–♭	G–♮				
Scherer, Op. 2 (1664)	Intonations	d–♮	g–♭	a–♮	e–♮	C–♮	F–♭	G–♮	G–♮				
	Toccatas	d–♮	g–♭	a–♮	e–♮	C–♮	F–♮	D–♮ (♯)	G–♮				
Poglietti, *Compendium* (1676)		d–♮	g–♭	a–♮	e–♮	C–♮	F–♭	D–♯♯	G–♮				
Kerll, *Modulatio organica* (1686)		d–♮	g–♭	a–♮	e–♮	a–♮	F–♭	d–♭	G–♮				
Anon., *Wegweiser* (1689)		d–♮	g–♭	a–♮	e–♮	C–♮	F–♭	D–♯ / ♯♯	G–♮				
Muffat (Georg), *Apparatus* (1690)		d–♮	g–♭	a–♮	e–♮	C–♮	F–♭	C–♭	G–♮	e–♯	D–♯	c–♭♭	B♭–♭♭
Speth, *Ars magna* (1693)	Toccatas	d–♮	g–♭	a–♮	e–♯	C–♮	F–♭	D–♯♯	G–♮				
	Magnificats	d–♮	g–♭	a–♮	e–♮	C–♮	F–♭	D–♯	G–♮	B♭–♭♭	A–♯♯		
Murschhauser, *Octi-Tonium* (1696)		d–♮	g–♭	a–♮	e–♮	a–♮ C–♮	F–♭	d–♭	G–♮				
Samber, *Continuatio* (1707)		d–♮	g–♭	a–♮	e–♮	C–♮	F–♭	d–♯	G–♮				
Fischer, *Blumen-Strauß* (1732)		d–♮	g–♭	a–♮	e–♮	C–♮	F–♭	D–♯♯	G–♯				
Kolb, *Certamen aonium* (1733)		d–♮	g–♭	a–♮	e–♮ e–♯	C–♮	F–♭	D–♯♯	G–♯				
Nauss, *Spielende Muse* (c. 1740)		d–♮	g–♭	a–♮	e–♯	C–♮	F–♭	D–♯♯	G–♯				
Eberlin, *IX Toccate e fuge* (1747)		d–♮	g–♭	a–♮	e–♮	C–♮	F–♭	D–♯♯	G–♯	e–♯			
Albrechtsberger, *Octo toni eccles* (c.1759-65)		d–♭	g–♭♭	a–♮	e–♮ e–♯	C–♮	F–♭	D–♯♯	G–♯				

Lower case pitch names denote minor third above final; upper case names denote major third above final.

Many of the church keys (specifically tones 3, 5, 6 and 7) correspond more easily to modes in the dodecachordal system (including transpositions) than to those of the traditional eightfold system. This prompted Banchieri, Bononcini, Nivers, Samber, and others to view the church keys as a conflation of, or reduction from, the most frequently used of the twelve modes or their standard transpositions, as can be seen in figure 4.[8] Their reasons for doing so were probably various: to make the church keys easier to understand, to have an integrated theory that accounted for wider repertories than just psalmody, and perhaps even to bolster the theoretical legitimacy of the seemingly unsystematic church keys. Not surprisingly, the particular twelve-mode equivalents vary from author to author.

Murschhauser himself published a two-part treatise, *Academia musico-poetica bipartita* (Augsburg, 1721), which addresses psalm-tone tonalities solely in the context of the psalm tones and *falso bordone*, but otherwise continues to promulgate, even at that late date, the dodecachordal system. Murschhauser's image as a hopelessly reactionary traditionalist is due at least as much to Mattheson's vituperative polemic against the first half of this treatise as it is to the conservative nature of the treatise itself.[9] While Mattheson's polemic in *Critica musica* against Murschhauser's presentation of the old dodecachordal system is characterized by contempt tinged with religious prejudice, he himself had incorporated the "Italian" church keys as the first eight of his own listings of the twenty-four major and minor keys in *Das neu-eröffnete Orchestre* and his *Exemplarische Organisten-Probe*, as can be seen in figure 2.[10]

Willi Apel's comments about *Prototypon* in his survey of keyboard music before 1700 will likely remove any remaining doubt about the need for a clearer understanding of modal theory and practice in the late seventeenth century.[11] Apel writes that "confusion and uncertainty in the concept of keys reaches its absolute zenith here," and then goes on to refer to the tonalities in question as "D Minor, G Minor, A Minor, E Minor," and so forth.[12] To be sure, some of the tonalities in this ostensibly dodecachordal cycle—such as tone 7 on D with a one-sharp signature—are certainly more "modern" than their classic counterparts in Glarean and Zarlino, not only in terms of final and signature, but also from the point of view of counterpoint and harmonic syntax. Nonetheless, the logic of their modal labeling is clear when transpositions (conventional ones in the seventeenth century, at that) are taken into account.

A more historically and analytically sensitive approach to seventeenth-century tonality may be derived from Harold Powers's work on mode in Renaissance vocal music. Powers, enlarging upon a distinction first made by Siegfried Hermelink, draws a sharp contrast between "mode," which he characterizes as a culturally contextual way of thinking about tonal structure, and "tonal type," which is "objectively observable completely apart from its musical or cultural context."[13]

FIGURE 4 Equivalencies between the church keys and dodecachordal modes according to three authors

	Banchieri, *Cartella musicale* (1614), p. 137	Bononcini, *Musico prattico* (1673) pp. 137–44	Samber, *Manuductio ad organum* (1704), pp. 165-66
1	mode 1 (d–♮)	[mode 1 (d–♮)][*]	mode 1 (d–♮)
2	mode 2, ↑4th (g–♭)	[mode 2, ↑4th (g–♭)][*]	mode 2, ↑4th (g–♭)
3	[none explicitly given, but 8ve species and primary cadential degrees on p. 136 are the same as mode 9, a–♮]	mode 10 (a–♮)	mode 9 (a–♮)
4	[none explicitly given, but 8ve species and primary cadential degrees on p. 136 are the same as mode 10, but ending on E]	mode 10 (a–♮) but ending on E	mode 4 (e–♮)
5	mode 11 ↓8ve (C–♮) or ↓5th (F–♭)	mode 11, ↓8ve (C–♮)	mode 11, ↓8ve (C–♮)
6	mode 12, ↓5th (F–♭)	mode 12, ↓5th (F–♭)	mode 12, ↓5th (F–♭)
7	mode 10, ↓5th (d–♭)	mode 9 [↓5th] (d–♭)	mode 8 (!), ↓4th (D–♯); mode 9, ↓5th (d–♭)
8	mode 8, (G–♮) or ↓5th (C–♭)	[mode 8 (G–♮)][*]	mode 8 (G–♮)
mixtus	mode 9, ↓5th (d–♭)	[(d–♭); no equivalent given]	[none given]

Lower case pitch names denote minor third above final; upper case names denote major third above final.

[*] In his textual explanation Bononcini offers no twelve-mode equivalents for church keys 1, 2, and 8, the categories with the most obvious kinship to their eight- or twelve-mode counterparts; he does provide musical examples, however, labeled according to the dodecachordal system but ordered in the sequence of the church keys.

Mode is "a music-theoretical construct, an inherited category in a fixed set of categories"; "tonal type" he specifies as the "particular combination of system signature, cleffing [reflecting ambitus], and final sonority" that "minimally characterize . . . a class of polyphonic compositions."[14] Powers goes on to argue that

> in given instances a tonal type may be intended to *represent* a mode in a categorical scheme; that is not to say, though, that the tonal type in question *is* that mode. The distinction is what an anthropologist of music might call a distinction between 'etic' and 'emic.'[15]

As Powers convincingly demonstrates, a modal category may be represented by more than one tonal type, and some tonal types may represent more than one modal category. Powers charges that

> the task of the music historian is to sort out the ways in which the many tonal types objectively found in Renaissance polyphonic compositions were correlated with modal categories in the traditional schemes.[16]

The distinction between tonal type and modal category may be fruitfully applied to Baroque keyboard music, even if the concept of tonal type is not itself strictly applicable—after all, in most Baroque keyboard music, cleffing does not "mark" or signal ambitus as reliably as it does in certain Renaissance vocal repertories. Indeed, a keyboard composer may choose not to observe traditional ambitus at all. Accordingly, in referring to the combinations of the two remaining modal markers, final and signature, I shall use the terms "tonality" or "tonalities." Powers's charge could be rephrased as follows: the music historian's task is to sort out the ways in which the many tonalities objectively found in Baroque keyboard music were correlated with modal categories in the traditional schemes—including the church keys. A second task is to determine the extent to which composers chose to observe ambitus or implicitly to regard it as a defining modal trait.

When one compares the tonalities found in *Prototypon* with those in *Octi-Tonium*, striking parallels emerge: they are, with one noteworthy exception, the same, for in *Prototypon* the composer includes only those eight of the twelve modes, or transpositions thereof, that possess an equivalent in the church keys. As one can see by comparing the two columns of figure 5, three sets of works in each cycle (tones 1, 2, and 8) share the same numbering, signature, and final; the sets of works in tone 7 have the same numbering and final, but different signatures; and the remaining sets of works are numberered differently but can be paired on the basis of finals, signatures, and, where applicable, ambitus.[17]

FIGURE 5 Two Keyboard Cycles by Murschhauser Compared

Octi-Tonium Novum Organicum (Augsburg, 1696) For each tone the composer presents a *praeambulum*, five fugues, and a *finale*, the items required for *alternatim* performance of the Magnificat or adaptible to psalms.		*Prototypon Longo-Breve Organicum* (Nuremberg, 1703, 1707) Vol. 1 contains the works in tones 1, 2, 3, and 7; vol. 2, the works in tones 8, 10, 11, and 12.	
Primi toni	D–♮ [Authentic]	*Primi toni* *Intonatio–Praeambulum–Fuga prima–Fuga secunda–Fuga finalis–Praeambulum*	D–♮ [Authentic]
Secundi toni	G–♭ [Plagal]	*Secundi toni* *Praeambulum–Fuga–Praeambulum aliud–Fuga alia–Fuga–Arpeggiata overo Toccata*	G–♭ [Plagal and authentic]
Tertii toni	A–♮ [Plagal]	*Decimi toni* *Praeambulum–Fuga–Praeambulum–Fuga* (2 parts)–*Finale*	A–♮ [Plagal]
Quarti toni	E–♮ [Authentic]	*Tertii toni* *Praeambulum–Fuga–Fuga brevissima–Praeambulum–Praeambulum brevissimum–Fuga*	E–♮ [Authentic]
Quinti toni regularis *Quinti toni irregularis*	A–♮ C–♮ [Predominantly authentic]	*Undecimi toni* *Toccata pro pedali–Fuga brevis–Fuga sive Canzon prima* (2 parts)–*Fuga sive Canzon secunda* (2 parts)–*Praeambulum–Arpeggiata*	C–♮ [Predominantly authentic]
Sexti toni	F–♭ [Plagal]	*Duodecimi toni* *Praeambulum–Fuga prima–Fuga secunda–Fuga tertia–Fuga quarta–Toccata (ped. ad lib.)–Toccata–Toccata*	F–♭ [Plagal and authentic]
Septimi toni	D–♭ [Authentic]	*Septimi toni* *Finale–Fuga prima–Praeambulum–Fuga secunda*	D–♯ [Authentic]
Octavi toni	G–♮ [Plagal]	*Octavi toni* *Intonatio–Praeambulum–Fuga prima–Fuga secunda– 351 Arpeggiata*	G–♮ [Plagal and authentic]

Ambitus naturally plays a different role in Baroque keyboard music than it does in Renaissance vocal music. In his recent monograph on mode in late sixteenth- and early seventeenth-century instrumental music, Bernhard Meier distinguishes between works based on vocal models, such as ricercars and canzonas, and more idiomatically instrumental works such as improvisatory toccatas and preludes that may not have a fixed number of voices and do not respect vocal ranges.[18] In the first sort of works, as Meier shows, composers usually observe correct ambitus both in terms of vocal ranges (particularly tenor and cantus) and the treatment of imitative subjects and answers. In non-vocally disposed works, ambitus in the sense of vocal range is of little or no relevance, leaving final, signature, and interior cadence degrees as the most objectively observable modal traits.[19]

What Meier found to be true about ambitus in the earlier repertory he studied applies most of the time to Murschhauser's works from the turn of the eighteenth century. A contrast is discernible between the contrapuntal works of Murschauser's two cycles, however: he usually observes ambitus quite strictly in the *alternatim* versets of *Octi-Tonium*, while in the generally longer, more discursive and idiomatically instrumental fugues in *Prototypon*, he sometimes exceeds the traditional ambitus considerably in either direction. Because ambitus is more distinguishable in contrapuntal than toccata-like works, and because one of the aims of this small study is to determine the extent to which ambitus acts as a defining modal trait in these two collections, in general I will focus more on the fugues than on the toccatas, preludes, and other nonvocally oriented pieces.

I will concentrate first on those modal categories that share tonalities but are numbered differently; in *Octi-Tonium* and *Prototypon*, respectively, these are tones 3 and 10, 4 and 3, 5 and 11, and 6 and 12. I will then address the works in tone 7, which share the same numbering but differ in their tonalities. I will not address the less problematic modal categories that share the same numbering and tonalities, namely tones 1 (on D in *cantus durus*, authentic), 2 (on G in *cantus mollis*, usually plagal in these collections), and 8 (on G in *cantus durus*, also usually plagal in these cycles).

* * *

The first pair of modal categories to be considered are tone 3 in *Octi-Tonium* and tone 10 in *Prototypon*, both of which end on A in *cantus durus*. In all of the tone 3 fugues in *Octi-Tonium*, the tenor and cantus span at least e to e^1 and e^1 to e^2, respectively; the ranges often exceed the octave species by a note or two at either extreme, as permitted by classic modal doctrine.[20] This octave species is actually that of traditional *mode* 3 (on E with authentic ambitus), in which the framing antiphon would be sung. Unlike most mode 3 antiphons, however, Murschhauser's versets in tone 3 possess a final of A in *cantus durus*, derived (as noted earlier) from the

FIGURE 6 Tonal features of *Octi-Tonium* tone 3 and *Prototypon* tone 10

Title	Final and signature	Tenor range	Cantus range	Subject outline	Ascribed ambitus
Octi-Tonium—Praeambulum tertii ton	a–♮	—	—	—	—
Fuga prima	a–♮	e–f^1	c^1–f^2	a^1–c^2–b^1–e^1	plagal
Fuga secunda	a–♮	e–e^1	c^1–f^2	a^1–e^2–e^1	plagal
Fuga tertia	a–♮	c–e^1	c^1–g^2	a^1–c^2–e^1	plagal
Fuga quarta	a–♮	d–g^1	c^1–g^2	a^1–c^2–a^1–e^2–f^2–e^2	plagal
Fuga quinta	a–♮	e–e^1	b–e^2	e^1–d^1–c–b–a	plagal
Finale	a–♮	—	—	—	—
Prototypon—Praeambulum decimi toni	a–♮	—	g^1–f^2	—	—
Fuga decimi toni	a–♮	c–f^1	b–a^2	alto: a^1–e^1–a	plagal
Praeambulum decimi toni	a–♮	—	—	—	—
Fuga decimi toni (2 parts)	a–♮	d–e^1	b–f^2	a^1–e^1–c^2–a^1–e^1–f^1–e^1	plagal
Finale decimi toni	a–♮	[B–e^1]	[e–a^2]	a^2–e^2–f^2–c^2	—

ending of the third psalm tone. With the octave species thus divided (arithmetically instead of harmonically), the ambitus becomes plagal, making the tone 3 pieces in *Octi-Tonium* equivalent in signature, final, and quality of ambitus (where applicable) to the *Prototypon* pieces in traditional mode 10. Murschhauser was hardly the first to correlate the third church key with the tenth mode: a generation earlier, Bononcini indicated that the tenth mode "served in place of" the third tone, and even in the sixteenth century, Zarlino, among others, regarded modal mixture between modes 3 and 10 as a commonplace.[21] The tonal features of *Octi-Tonium* tone 3 and *Prototypon* tone 10 are summarized in figure 6.

The next pair of modal labels are applied to works ending on E in *cantus durus*. Predictably, the tone 3 fugues in *Prototypon* exhibit authentic ambitus with occasional licenses. By analogy with traditional modal numbering, one would expect the tone 4 pieces in *Octi-Tonium* to evince plagal characteristics, but in fact the opposite is true: in each of the five fugues as well as in the imitative *finale*, the cantus and tenor parts adhere fairly strictly to authentic ambitus (see ex. 1, the fifth verset in tone 4). In short, Murschhauser employs the same combination of final, signature, and ambitus to represent tone 3 in *Prototypon* and tone 4 in *Octi-Tonium*. The tonal features of Murschhauser's pieces in these modal categories are outlined in figure 7.

EXAMPLE 1 *Octi-Tonium*, fifth fugue in tone 4

The authentic tone 4 of Murschhauser's *Octi-Tonium* is not without precedent. In Part 2 of *Il Transilvano*, Girolamo Diruta observes that "many composers and organists give the name of the fourth tone to that which is actually the third, since they do not use melodic motion different from the authentic tone."[22] In *Cartella musicale*, Banchieri presents the fourth *tuono ecclesiastico* as spanning e^1 to e in *cantus durus*, divided either harmonically (with principal interior cadences on g and b) or arithmetically (with principal interior cadences on a and c^1).[23] Echoing Banchieri, Bononcini equates the fourth *tuono ecclesiastico* with mode 10 (which has a theoretical tenor ambitus of e^1 to e) with an *affinales* ending on e—or, to be more precise, he specifies that the tenth mode "serves in place of" the fourth tone.[24] Banchieri's and Bononcini's equivalents contrast with that given by Samber, who equates the fourth *tuono ecclesiastico* with the fourth traditional mode (which, by

FIGURE 7 Tonal features of *Octi-Tonium* tone 4 and *Prototypon* tone 3

Title	Final and signature	Tenor range	Cantus range	Subject outline	Ascribed ambitus	Final cadence type
Octi-Tonium—Praeambulum quarti toni[6]	e–♮	—	—	—	—	$iv^{5-\sharp 6}_{3}$–I
Fuga prima	e–♮	e–e^1	e^1–e^2	e^1–b^1–c^2–a^1	authentic	Phrygian
Fuga secunda	e–♮	e–e^1	e^1–e^2	T: b–e^1–b–c	authentic	Phrygian
Fuga tertia	e–♮	e–e^1	d^1–e^2	b^1–g^1–c^2–b^1–a^1–g^1	authentic	Phrygian
Fuga quarta	e–♮	g–e^1	e^1–e^2	b^1–g^1–c^2–a^1	authentic	$iv^{5-\sharp 6}_{3-4}$–I
Fuga quinta	e–♮	f♯–e^1	e^1–e^2	b^1–e^2–b^1–c^2	authentic	Phrygian
Finale	e–♮	f♯–e^1	e^1–e^2	e^2–b^1–e^2	authentic	$iv^{5-\sharp 6}_{3-4}$–I
Prototypon—Praeambulum tertii toni	e–♮	e–d^1	b–g^2	—	authentic	$iv^{5-\sharp 6}_{3}$–I
Fuga tertii toni	e–♮	d–e^1	d♯^{1}–a^2	b^1–c^2–a^1–d^2–b^1	authentic	$iv^{5-\sharp 6}_{3-\sharp 4}$–I
Fuga brevissima	e–♮	f♯–e^1	d^1–e^2	b^1–c^2–a^1–b^1–e^2	authentic	iv–I
Praeambulum tertii toni	e–♮	—	—	—	—	Phrygian
Praeludium brevissimum	e–♮	B–g^1	b–e^2	—	[authentic]	iv–I
Fuga tertii toni	e–♮	e–e^1	f♯^{1}–f^2	b^1–c^2–b^1	authentic	iv–I

implication, would be plagal; see figure 4).[25] To summarize, the same tonality—E–♮ with authentic ambitus—is thus demonstrated in the examples just cited to represent three different modal categories: mode 3 (Murschhauser), tone 4 (Murschhauser, Banchieri, and Diruta), and mode 10 with an *affinales* ending (Bononcini).

Etic aspects of pitch-class collection are not a primary concern of this small study, but Apel's reference to the tone 3 pieces in *Prototypon* as "E minor" cannot pass completely unchallenged: Murschhauser certainly knew how to compose in modern E minor, as the "suite in the modern style" that concludes the *Octi-Tonium* shows.[26] Apel perhaps based his judgments about major-minor tonality too much on such non-fugal works in *Prototypon* as the *praeambulum tertii toni* (ex. 2); this prelude does indeed abound in F-sharps, with only a tenth as many F-naturals.

EXAMPLE 2 *Prototypon*, first preambulum in tone 3 (first 9 of 36 mm.)

Similarly, the *praeambulum* from *Octi-Tonium* contains not one single F-natural, but only F-sharps. Of course, such brute quantifications of pitch-class collections say nothing about the particular melodic or harmonic context (e.g., ascending or descending lines, neighbor-note figures, or secondary tonal areas) in which particular scale degrees appear; as indices of the extent to which a piece is objectively in "Phrygian" or "E minor," they must be employed judiciously. The *Octi-Tonium* piece just cited, for example, is simply an elaborated I-IV-I progression; F-natural non-harmonic tones would create undesirable tritones or diminished fifths against the frequently sounded fifth (B) over the bass pedal-point (E). In contrast to the toccata-like works on E in both collections, the fugal works exhibit far fewer inflections of scale degrees 2, 6, and 7; the frequently encountered B–C in fugal subjects is always answered by the emphatically Phrygian E–F. These characteristic differences in pitch-class collection between preludes and fugues are aptly illustrated by the first *praeambulum tertii toni* and first *fuga tertii toni* from *Prototypon* (exx. 2 and 3).

EXAMPLE 3 *Prototypon*, first fugue in tone 3 (first 7 of 29 mm.)

In *Octi-Tonium* Murschhauser offers two sets of versets for tone 5, which he labels *regularis* and *irregularis*, respectively. The pieces labeled *regularis* begin by outlining the modal fifth, F to C, in *cantus durus*, but conclude with an A-major sonority on the psalm-tone ending—making this form of the tone something of a modal manticore, with the head of one beast and the tail of another. Though tone 5 settings ending on A in *cantus durus* were common in the sixteenth century, seventeenth-century examples, such as those by Murschhauser and his teacher Kerll, are less frequently encountered (see fig. 3). The most common tonality for tone 5 in seventeenth-century music, that of C in *cantus durus*, Murschhauser labels *quinti toni irregularis*; it is "irregular" because, unlike all of the other church keys in *Octi-Tonium*, its final is not the psalm-tone ending but rather the corresponding final of the traditional eight-mode system, transposed down a fourth. This same tonality Murschhauser labels tone 11 in *Prototypon*, as figure 8 shows.

In his 1721 treatise, *Academia musico-poetica bipartita*, Murschhauser addresses the respective endings of tone 5, advising that while the *regularis* form (ending on the psalm tone's last pitch, A) is better for versets responding to the choir, the *irregularis* form (ending on the modal final, but not necessarily transposed) is better for the subsequent antiphon substitute, since the antiphon itself

FIGURE 8 Tonal features of *Octi-Tonium* tone 5 *irregularis* and *Prototypon* tone 11

Title	Final and signature	Tenor range	Cantus range	Subject outline	Ascribed ambitus
Octi-Tonium—Praeambulum quinti toni irregularis	C–♮	—	—	—	—
Fuga prima	C–♮	d–g^1	g^1–g^2	A: c^2–a^1–e^1–f^1–g^1	plagal
Fuga secunda	C–♮	c–c^1	c^1–d^2	scalar c^1–c^2	authentic
Fuga tertia	C–♮	T: c–e^1 B: G–c	C: d^1–g^2 A: g–g^1	T: c^1–b–d^1–g	authentic
Fuga quarta	C–♮	c–a	c^1–d^2	scalar c^1–a^1–e^1	authentic
Fuga quinta	C–♮	c–e^1	c^1–d^2	T: scalar c^1–c	authentic
Finale	C–♮	g–g^1	g^1–g^2	A: c^2–g^1; C: g^2–d^1	plagal
Prototypon—Toccata undecimi Toni pro Pedali	C–♮	—	—	—	—
Fuga brevis	C–♮	c–g^1	e^1–g^2	A: g^1–c^2–g^1; C: c^2–g^2–c^2	ambiguous
Fuga sive Canzon prima undecimi toni (2 parts)	C–♮	B–g^1	b–a^2	c^1–g^1–c^2	authentic
Fuga sive Canzon secunda undecimi toni (2 parts)	C–♮	d–a^1	a–a^2	c^2–d^1–g^1–e^1	authentic
Praeambulum undecimi toni	C–♮	—	—	—	—
Arpeggiata	C–♮	—	—	—	—

would end on the modal final.[27] He does not forbid use of the *regularis* form for antiphon substitutes, however, nor does he completely rule out the *irregularis* form for versets. Of course, were both forms to be employed for a single Magnificat and its antiphon, as Murschhauser indicates that he would prefer, they would need to be played at the same transposition level. At the time of publishing *Octi-Tonium*, he offered both tonal types in order to make his collection as useful as possible;[28] by the time he published *Academia musico-poetica bipartita* twenty-five years later, however, he had changed his mind about the suitability of the C in *cantus durus* (authentic) for *alternatim* use in tone 5:

> Nor are they correct, who transpose this fifth tone a fourth lower, because in its natural manner and melody it is quite suitable and comfortable for the choir to chant, as opposed to its transposition to C (particularly when the organ is tuned in *Chor-Ton*), which is so deep and difficult, that for many tenor voices (for it is to these that plainchant really pertains), this depth can be difficult to reach with full voice; from which then a feeble, weak, and disagreeable song must necessarily follow.[29]

As for ambitus, four of the five fugues in *tonus quintus irregularis* from *Octi-Tonium* are authentic; in the curiously anomalous *fuga prima* the ambitus of all voices appears to be reversed (ex. 4). A similar reversal of ambitus is to be observed in the *fuga brevis* in tone 11 of *Prototypon*. In both of these diminutive fugues, the subjects (spanning c^2 to e^1 and c^2 to c^1, respectively) are introduced by the alto, with the bass in stretto at the octave. The dual "answers" (to apply that term loosely) in stretto between cantus and tenor do not enter until the subject has been completely stated by alto and bass. In these two instances, the logic of the fugal design—a subject, authentic in range, presented in stretto at the octave followed by its answer a fifth higher, also in stretto at the octave—necessitated Murschhauser's reversal of these modal categories' normal ambitus. In both of *Prototypon*'s remaining fugues in tone 11 the subjects are strongly authentic in cast, though the cantus and tenor exhibit greater license with regard to range than in *Octi-Tonium*, sometimes exceeding the ambitus by as much as a sixth. Example 5, the beginning of *fuga sive canzon secunda undecimi toni* from *Prototypon*, and example 6, the second fugue in tone 5, *irregularis*, from *Octi-Tonium*, illustrate this tonal type.

All of the works labeled tone 6 in *Octi-Tonium* and tone 12 in *Prototypon* have a final of F with a signature of one flat. In the case of tone 12, this flat signifies transposition downward by a fifth from the natural form of the mode; in the case of tone 6, however, as observed earlier, the flat represents not transposition, but rather a conventionalized concession to the necessary B-flat inflection

EXAMPLE 4 *Octi-Tonium*, first fugue in tone 5, *irregularis*

EXAMPLE 5 *Prototypon*, second *fuga sive canzona* in tone 11 (*prima pars*)

t.

N.B.

EXAMPLE 6 *Octi-Tonium*, second fugue in tone 5, *irregularis*

in the sixth psalm tone. In *Octi-Tonium* all of the fugues are clearly plagal with respect to voice ranges; while cantus and tenor exceed the upper boundary by a fourth in some pieces, all but one of the fugue subjects delineate the complete octave species of the mode.[30] In *Prototypon*, however, the first and third fugues cannot really be described as anything but authentic with respect to their ranges, and their subjects (presented first in the cantus) delineate the fifth species of the mode; the bipartite fourth fugue displays such contradictory features that its *prima pars* can only very tentatively be labeled plagal, and its *secunda pars* authentic. The second fugue in *Prototypon* (ex. 7) is the only one in that set to feature a clearly plagal subject; the wide range of its tenor (more than two octaves) betokens its thoroughly instrumental conception. This example closely resembles the third fugue in tone 6 from *Octi-Tonium* (ex. 8) in the plagal contour of its subject, rhythm, and texture, if not in its scope and greater license of ambitus.

EXAMPLE 7 *Prototypon*, second fugue in tone 12 (first 25 of 83 mm.)

The parallels between the foregoing pairs of modal categories allow the conclusion that certain tonalities can represent both a mode in the dodecachordal scheme and a church key. The differences in ambitus between otherwise comparable categories of the two cycles, and even within individual modal categories of *Prototypon* (including in the latter case not only tone 12 but also tones 2, 8, and 11), point up differences in the use of mode touched on by Harold Powers in various essays.[31]

EXAMPLE 8 *Octi-Tonium*, third fugue in tone 6

Octi-Tonium exemplifies the use of mode (including the modal criterion of ambitus) as an *a priori*, pre-compositional decision, as is called for in composing a set of versets to respond to plainchant, while the apparently more randomly assembled, individual pieces in *Prototypon* implicitly illustrate the use of mode as an *a posteriori* criterion for collection within a modally ordered cycle.[32] Murschhauser's stricter observation in *Octi-Tonium* of ambitus in the sense of vocal range may indeed be a response to the organ's role as a substitute for the choir in *alternatim* performance.[33] It is also possible, however, that his close attention to ambitus reflects the didactic scrutiny of Johann Kaspar Kerll, with whom Murschhauser studied and under whose tutelage he may have begun to compose the cycle.

In *Prototypon*, inconsistencies of ambitus between fugues within individual modal categories indicate that Murschhauser—or his publisher, though I know of no evidence that Murschhauser himself did not assemble the collection—did not regard ambitus as an important criterion for modal labeling or inclusion within that collection. Since these are "practical" pieces intended for use by church organists, this implies that in composing or compiling this collection Murschhauser did not regard "correct" ambitus as a criterion for modal labeling, let alone liturgical usefulness: final and signature were sufficient.

Having compared the modal categories from *Octi-Tonium* and *Prototypon* that are represented by equivalent tonalities, I now turn to the modal categories that share the same number, 7, but are represented by two different tonalities. In *Octi-Tonium*, just like Banchieri's examples and the anonymous *Intavolatura* of 1598, works in the seventh tone end on D in *cantus mollis*. In *Prototypon*, however, the tone 7 pieces end on D with a signature of one sharp. The beginnings of two *finales* illustrating these tonalities, one from each cycle, are presented as examples 9 and 10. The tonalities' differences in signature stem from their different purposes, as both Murschhauser and Samber explain in their treatises. Murschhauser's explanation is clear enough, but Samber's more lucidly engraved illustration from *Manuductio ad Organum* (fig. 10), provides a better graphic summary of the derivation of these two tonalities.

EXAMPLE 9 *Prototypon, finale* in tone 7 (first 5 of 47 mm.)

The first three lines of Samber's figure show the derivation of D–♭ from psalm or Magnificat versets. The first line shows the seventh psalm tone in plainchant notation, untransposed, ending on A; at the beginning of the line is shown the corresponding antiphon final, G, and reciting tone, D. The second line presents the seventh psalm tone in plainchant notation, transposed down a fifth to end on D, as it would most frequently be sung in alternation with polyphony; once again, it is preceded by the antiphon final and reciting tone, C and G, respectively. The third line presents this same transposition of the seventh psalm tone, but in figural notation.

The last two lines of Samber's figure demonstrate the derivation of the tonal type ending on D–♯. Line 4 presents the final of an introit antiphon in mode 7,

EXAMPLE 10 *Octi-Tonium, finale* in tone 7 (first 8 of 16 mm.)

FIGURE 10 Facsimile of Johann Baptist Samber, *Manuductio ad Organum* (Salzburg, 1704), fig. 42 (By permission of the Sibley Library, Eastman School of Music)

No. 1. The seventh psalm tone in plainchant notation, untransposed, ending on a
No. 2. The seventh psalm tone in plainchant notation, transposed down a fifth, ending on d
No. 3. The seventh psalm tone in figural notation, transposed down a fifth, ending on d (d–♭)
No. 4. The seventh introit tone in plainchant notation, untransposed, ending on g
No. 5. The seventh introit tone in figural notation, transposed down a fourth, ending on d (D–♯)

followed in plainchant notation by the psalm tone to which the introit psalm verse would be sung. Unlike the seventh psalm tone employed for regular psalmody and canticles, however, the more ornate psalm tone used for mode 7 introits ends on the modal final, G. Line 5 presents this same introit tone in figural notation, transposed down a fourth to end on D with a signature of one sharp. According to Samber, this transposition level was used wherever the plainchant would normally end on the traditional modal final.[34]

Murschhauser approves of both of the transposition levels discussed by Samber for psalms and canticles:

> For the antiphon, together with its psalm tone, can be moved either a fourth lower, or (if it is more pleasing) can be transposed a complete fifth lower. If the first is pleasing, then end the antiphon on D, but the psalm (to which the organist must respond, according to the first *differentia*) on E. But if the other transposition to the fifth below is more befitting, end the antiphon on C, but the psalm on D.[35]

A somewhat rare instance among printed collections of tone 7 versets in E with a signature of one sharp is to be found in Sabbatini's keyboard manual, *Toni ecclesiastici*. Tone 7 works ending on C are similarly uncommon in seventeenth-century modally ordered keyboard cycles: Trabaci felt obliged to provide a lengthy justification for choosing C–♮ for the versets in his second book of ricercars,[36] and among South German keyboard cycles, Muffat's *Apparatus musico-organisticus* provides a rare example of C–♭. Interestingly enough, in that collection the ninth and tenth toccatas (which are not advertised as being in the ninth and tenth modes, however) are in E–♯ and D–♯, respectively—both being tonalities that can represent tone 7 in certain situations.

One fugue that stands out in the context of contrasting D tonalities for tone 7 is the third verset from *Octi-Tonium* (ex. 11). It is one of the more pronounced examples of chromatic *durezze e ligature* writing to be found in either of these cycles. The subject, d^2–a^1–$f\sharp^1$–$f\natural^1$–$b\flat^1$–a^1, almost seems to play upon the differences between the two tonalities most frequently used to represent the seventh church key, especially upon the difference between the all-important third degrees, F-natural and F-sharp.

As figure 3 attests, composers gradually came to prefer D with one or two sharps over D with a flat to represent tone 7. The effect on the church keys, as others have observed before me, is threefold: a greater differentiation between tones 1 and 7 (which, depending on the accidentals employed, can be aurally indistinguishable), greater congruence between tone 7 and mode 7, and a pattern of four minor-third tonalities followed by four major-third ones.[37]

EXAMPLE 11 *Octi-Tonium*, third fugue in tone 7 (first 9 of 16 mm.)

The two cycles' differing tonalities for tone 7, as well as the two tone 5 endings that Murschhauser includes in *Octi-Tonium*, suggest an important distinction that must be made. This distinction is between the church keys as a set of finals derived from specific *cantus firmi*, and the church keys as "the most frequently employed modes of figural music," as Murschhauser calls the modes he employs in *Prototypon*; seventeenth- and early eighteenth-century theorists present the church keys either or both ways. As byproducts of the psalm tones, the set of tonal types collectively identified as the church keys, and here exemplified by the works in *Octi-Tonium,* no more represent (in Powers's sense) the eight modes of plainchant than do the psalm tones themselves; rather, the church keys represent the tonal features of the psalm tones in their most common forms, much as polyphonic versets "represent" plainchant psalm tones in *alternatim* performance.

On the other hand, the tonalities included in *Prototypon* are labeled according to, and therefore do represent, the twelve modes—or, at least, two-thirds of them. But Murschhauser's inclusion of only "the most frequently used tones"—those that happen to correspond to the church keys—suggests that he intended for the organists using his collection also to be able to correlate them with the church keys if the need arose. For the practical church organist playing a *Vor-* or *Nachspiel* for a choral work, what really matters is not a work's modal label but its final and signature.

The coexistence around 1700 of a number of schemes for modal categorization—including the traditional eight modes, various forms of the twelve-mode system, the church keys, and major-minor tonality—suggests that while etic tonalities may in fact evolve, emic modal theories do not so much evolve as endure: they endure, jostling together, until at last the discrepancy between theoretically prescribed features and actual practice becomes too great, and musicians discard the old paradigm in favor of a newer one. This process is often a contentious one, as Mattheson's polemic against Murschhauser demonstrates. Murschhauser's treatise on composition was one of the last to treat the dodecachordal system prescriptively, yet as modal categories the church keys lasted throughout the eighteenth century and even to some extent into the nineteenth, thanks to their continued relevance to *alternatim* psalmody. Because Murschhauser's cycles in these two modal systems come from the same pen, they serve especially well to exemplify the pluralism in modal theory and practice around 1700 and to illustrate how two competing modal systems could be correlated on the basis of shared tonalities.

NOTES

1. For a more detailed discussion of Murschhauser's relationship to Kerll, see the forewords to the editions of *Octi-Tonium* by Seiffert, xl–xli and liv–lvi, and Walter, 2–3; see also Constantini, "Entwicklung der Versettenkomposition," 109–12.

2. "Super hos itaq. Fugas & Præambula construxi plurimorum genio (uti quidem confido) accommodata, tamq. brevitatis amantibus, quam patientibus moræ servitura; siquidem his per amplissimam thematum diductionem, illis vero per appositum NB. (quod expeditam ad Finale præbet manuductionem) omnimodo consulere, ac satisfacere studui, quin imo supra dicta Præambula & Fugas in secundam superiorem, aut inferiorem transponere volentibus pleraq. vel ad votum fluent, vel saltem parum negotii facessent." Murschhauser, *Prototypon*, vol. 1 (1703), preface.

3. The ability to effect such transpositions had been expected of skilled organists for well over a century by Murschhauser's time. Zarlino, in *Le Istitutioni harmoniche* (1558), 319–20, provides examples of transposition down a step (with a signature of two flats) and up a step (with a signature of two sharps), and notes that such transpositions are useful for the church organist accompanying choral music. Zarlino was followed by many seventeenth- and early eighteenth-century theorists who addressed transpositions eventually extending to every chromatic interval.

4. Lester, *Between Modes and Keys*, 77-82. The modal categories which I am collectively calling the "church keys" have been designated in various Baroque-era publications as, among other terms, "gli otto tuoni ecclesiastici" (anonymous, *Intavolatura d'organo*); "les huit tons de l'église" (Titelouze, *Le Magnificat*); and "acht tonos ecclesiasticos oder Kirchen Thon" (Fischer, *Blumen-Strauß*). Recent references to these modal categories have

employed various English terms, including "pitch-key modes" (Atcherson, "Key and Mode," 216–22); "church keys" (Lester, loc. cit.); or "psalm tone keys" (Powers, "Psalmody to Tonality," this volume). "Psalm tone keys" reflects most accurately the keys' origins, but it lacks a direct historical equivalent; in the present context, I prefer "church keys," a more or less direct translation of the most frequently encountered appellations in the original languages. As is often the case with seventeenth-century musical terminology, the cognates in European languages for the English word "tone" possess many alternate and often overlapping meanings, including pitch or pitch class, major second, mode, pitch level, timbre or voice quality, and recitation formula; even when translated contextually, some loss of nuance is unavoidable. On meanings of the word "tone" in seventeenth-century music, see the study of mode in French *alternatim* practice by Bates, "From Mode to Key," 151-55. For an examination of the church keys in Italian and German sources, see Dodds, "The Seventeenth-Century Church Keys."

5. See, for example, Banchieri, *L'Organo suonarino* (1605 ed.), 40–44 (tables), 45–59 (psalms), and 89–105 (Magnificats), and *Cartella musicale*, 70–71 (tables) and 72ff. (imitative duos).

6. Banchieri never makes explicit why he ends tone 5 on the modal final rather than on the psalm-tone ending, where Diruta and some other musicians end it.

7. In *Transilvano*, vol. 2 (1609), 11, Diruta admits to having previously employed a signature of one flat for untransposed tones 5 and 6 "out of common usage" and his own ignorance at the time, but acknowledges that he was in error to have done so. Few later musicians expressed such scruples.

8. Some authors—including Roddio, Picerli, and Berardi—in discussing polyphony present only the twelve-mode system but also address transposition, thus encompassing the tonalities of the church keys while not necessarily labeling them as such.

9. Recent research suggests that the second half of the treatise, which was long thought to have been suppressed before publication on account of Johann Mattheson's bitter polemic against it in the first half in *Critica musica* 1:74–83, *passim*, was indeed published but is simply lost. See Leuchtmann, "Ein wichtiger Neufund."

10. Mattheson, *Das Neu-eröffnete Orchestre*, 60; cf. 236–44ff. This has been noted by Powers, "Mode," 416, among others.

11. Apel, *Keyboard Music*, 586–89.

12. Ibid., 588.

13. Hermelink, *Dispositiones Modorum*; Powers, "Tonal Types," 439.

14. Powers, "Tonal Types," 439.

15. Ibid.

16. Ibid.

17. Both of the tonalities labeled tone 7 are included among the church keys in many other contemporary collections—so Murschhauser does indeed present those eight (not seven)

of the twelve modes, or transpositions thereof, that possess an equivalent in the church keys.

18. See Meier, *Alte Tonarten*, 38, 105. This is not to imply that Meier accepted Hermelink's and Powers's distinction between tonal types and modal categories, for he apparently did not; see op. cit.,12–14.

19. Due to the shortness of the pieces in *Octi-Tonium* and many of the pieces in *Prototypon*, as well as Murschhauser's tendency to construct toccatas using extended pedal tones, the number of internal cadences is too small to make possible a valid comparison of that parameter between the two cycles.

20. See, for example, Zarlino, *Le Istitutioni harmoniche* (1558), 314–15. Zarlino, reflecting a tradition going back to the Middle Ages, supplies a number of categories for classifying the ambitus and pitch content of a melody; in addition to authentic and plagal, these descriptive categories include perfect, imperfect, superfluous, common, mixed, and commixed.

21. Bononcini, *Musico prattico*, 138; Zarlino, *Le Istitutioni harmoniche* (1558), 336. To the best of my knowledge, Banchieri does not in his writings explicitly make a correlation between the third church key and the tenth mode, but in *Cartella musicale*, 74, he provides an exemplary duo for cantus and tenor in the third *tuono ecclesiastico* (Banchieri's term for the modal categories of polyphonic psalmody) that ends on A in *cantus durus* with plagal ambitus in both voices (with clefs c_1 and c_4)—a tonal type that in any context but psalmody would normally be labeled mode 10. In the same edition of *Cartella*, however (130–31), Banchieri correlates mode 10—at least as normally transposed "per voci humane"—with the seventh *tuono ecclesiastico* (on D in *cantus mollis* with plagal ambitus). Zarlino, loc. cit., discusses mixture at some length, noting that modes 3 and 10 are often mixed, and that, in mode 3 compositions admitting such mixture, the diapason e-e^1, common to both modes, is often mediated arithmetically (by a) rather than harmonically (by b). The concept of modal mixture within a single modal system is related to, but distinct from, correlations between different schemes of modal classification.

22. "Dico per conclusione del Quarto Tuono, che molti Compositori, & Organisti danno il nome di Quarto Tuono à quel che è Terzo, & non fanno le modulationi differenti dal suo Autentico." Diruta, *Transilvano*, part 2 (1609), bk. 3, 11; trans. Bradshaw and Soehnlen, *Transylvanian*, 2:117. Earlier, Diruta notes that proper *modulationi*, or melodic motion, should outline the mode's fifth and fourth species, and should employ ascending melodic motion in the case of authentic modes and descending melodic motion in the case of plagal ones. Banchieri, *Cartella musicale*, 72–87, establishes similar guidelines.

23. Banchieri, *Cartella musicale* 71, 75, 136. Banchieri makes the somewhat startling assertion that "the fourth tone, being plagal, has its octave from the note E to E" ("Il quarto tuono essendo plagale ha la sua ottava dalla corda E. alla E").

24. Bononcini, *Musico prattico*, 138, 140.

25. Samber, *Manuductio*, 165–66.

26. On the title page Murschhauser refers to the suite as a *Partía Genialis Styli moderni.* Seiffert contends in the preface to his edition of these works, p. lvi, that this one artful suite in a modern key refutes Mattheson's unfair and biased characterization of Murschhauser as a reactionary conservative. The suite is included in Seiffert's edition but not in Walter's.

27. Murschhauser, *Academia*, 108–09. Murschhauser does not employ the terms *regularis* and *irregularis* in this passage.

28. Murschhauser, *Octi-Tonium*, "Benevole Lector."

29. "Es sind auch diejenige nicht recht daran, welche eben diesen fünfften Tonum um ein Quart tieffer transponiren, dieweilen er in seiner natürlichen Weis und Melodey dem Chor gantz anständig, und bequemlich abzusingen, herentgegen indem C (absonderlich, wann die Orgel im Chor-Ton einstimmet,) so tieff und beschwerlich ist, daß manche Tenor-Stimm (dann dieser eigentlich das Choral-Gesang zuständig,) diese Tieffe schwerlich mit vollkommener Stimm erreichen kan; woraus dann nothwendig ein mattes, schwaches, und verdrießliches Gesang erfolgen muß." Murschhauser, *Academia*, 109.

30. The exceptional subject, that of the fourth fugue, is content to outline the modal diapente F-C. The successive fugues of tone 6 alternate between initially ascending and initially descending subjects: fugues 1, 3, and 5 begin with downward motion, while fugues 2 and 4 begin with upward motion.

31. Including "Tonal Types," 435.

32. I say "more randomly"; Constantini, "Entwicklung der Versettenkomposition," 110, has noted that the placement of many of the pieces in *Prototypon* suggests intentional pairings between adjacent preludes and fugues.

33. This is not to imply, however, that *Octi-Tonium* is vocally conceived in other respects; a subject such as that of fugue 3 in tone 6, featuring dance-like rhythms and wide skips, is clearly more instrumental than vocal in conception.

34. Samber, *Manuductio*, 176.

35. "Dann entweder kan die Antiphon samt seinem Psalm-Ton in ein Quart herunter versezt, oder (wann es gefälliger) gar um ein Quint tieffer transponirt werden. Gefällt das Erstere, so lässet die Antiphon in dem D. der Psalm aber (worzu [*sic*] der Organist zu respondiren hat, der ersten Differenz gemäß) in dem E. aus. So dann die andere Transposition in die Quint herab anständiger, endet sich die Antiphon in dem C, der Psalm aber in dem D." Murschhauser, *Academia*, 109.

36. Trabaci, *Secondo Libro de Ricercate*, 70.

37. See, for example, Lester, *Between Modes and Keys*, 77–82, and Powers, "From Psalmody to Tonality," this volume, *passim*.

Bibliography

MUSICAL SOURCES AND EDITIONS

Manuscripts

[D-Mbs 10] Munich. Bayerische Staatsbibliothek. Mus.Ms. 10. Facsimile with introduction by Howard Mayer Brown. New York, 1986.

[GB-Cfm 652] Cambridge. Fitzwilliam Museum. Ms. 652.

[GB-Lbl Add.31403] London. British Library. Ms. Add. 31403.

[GB-Lbl Add.34695] London. British Library. Ms. Add. 34695.

[GB-Lcm 1070] London. Royal College of Music Ms. 1070.

[GB-Och 49] Oxford. Christ Church. Ms. 49.

[GB-Och 1179] Oxford. Christ Church. Ms. 1179.

[I-CT 95–96 / F-Pn 1817] Cortona. Biblioteca Communale. Ms. 95–96. Paris. Bibliothèque National. Ms. Nouv. Acq. Françaises 1817.

[I-Rvat 42] Rome. Biblioteca Vatican. Cappella Sistina Ms. 42.

[I-Fn 232] Florence. Biblioteca Nazionale Centrale. Ms. II.I.232 (Magl. XIX.58).

[J-Tn MS n-3/35] Toyko. Nanki Music Library. Ms N-3/35.

Printed Anthologies

[RISM 1503[1]] *Motetti De passione De cruce De sacramento De beata virgine et huius modi. B*. Venice: Petrucci, 1503.

[RISM 1514[1]] *Motetti de la corona. Libro primo*. Venice: Petrucci, 1514.

[RISM 1538[6]] *Tomus primus psalmorum selectorum à praestantissimis musicis in harmonias quatuor aut quinque vocum redactorum*. Nuremberg: Petreius, 1538.

[RISM 1539[9]] *Tomus secundus psalmorum selectorum quatuor et quinque vocum*. Nuremberg: Petreius, 1539.

[RISM 1545[5]] *Officiorum (ut vocant) de Nativitate Circumcisione, Epiphania Domini, & Purificatione &c. Tomus primus*. Wittenberg: Rhaw, 1545.

[RISM 1553[8]] *Liber primus ecclesiasticarum cantionum quatuor vocum vulgo moteta vocant, tam ex Veteri quam ex Novo Testamento, ab optimis quibusque huius aetatis musicis compositarum. Antea nunquam excusus*. Antwerp: Susato, 1553.

[RISM 1554[10]] *Evangelia dominicorum et festorum dierum musicis numeris pulcherrime comprehensa & ornata. Tomi primi continentis historias & doctrinam, quae solent in Ecclesia proponi. De Nativitate. De Epiphanijs. De Resurrectione Jesu Christi.* Nuremberg: Montanus & Neuber, 1554.

[RISM 1555[10]] *Secundus tomus Evangeliorum, quatuor, quinque, sex, et plurium vocum. Continens historias & doctrinam, quae in Ecclesia proponi solet: de Ascensione Christi. De Missione Spiritus Sancti.* Nuremberg: Montanus & Neuber, 1555.

[RISM 1555[11]] *Tertius tomus Evangeliorum, quatuor, quinque, sex, et plurium vocum. Continens historias & doctrinam, quae in Ecclesia proponi solet: de Trinitate. De Dedicatione Templi. De Coena Dominica.* Nuremberg: Montanus & Neuber, 1555.

[RISM 1555[12]] *Quartus tomus Evangeliorum, quatuor, quinque, sex, et plurium vocum. Continens historias & doctrinam, quae in Ecclesia proponi solet: de Baptisato Christo a Ioanne. De Transfiguratione Christi. De Passione et Cruce Christi.* Nuremberg: Montanus & Neuber, 1555.

[RISM 1556[8]] *Quintus tomus Evangeliorum, et piarum sententiarum: quinque vocum. Continens historias & doctrinam, quae in Ecclesia proponi solet: de Poenitentia.* Nuremberg: Montanus & Neuber, 1556.

[RISM 1556[9]] *Sextus tomus Evangeliorum, et piarum sententiarum. Quatuor, sex, et octo vocum. Continens historias & doctrinam, quae in Ecclesia proponi solet: de Poenitentia.* Nuremberg: Montanus & Neuber, 1556.

[RISM 1559[2]] *Tertia pars magni operis musici, continens clarissimorum symphonistarum tam veterum quam recentiorum, praecipue vero Clementis non Papae, Carmina elegantissima. Quatuor vocum . . . .* Nuremberg: Montanus & Neuber, 1559.

Individual Prints and Modern Editions

Albrechtsberger, Johann Georg. *Octo toni ecclesiastici per Organo*. Vienna, n.d. (c. 1759–65). Edited by Rudolf Walter. Altötting, 1974.

[Anonymous.] *Intavolatura d'organo*. Venice, 1598. Edited by Macario Santiago Kastner as *Altitalienische Versetten.* Mainz, 1957.

Apel, Willi, ed. *French Secular Compositions of the Fourteenth Century*. 3 vols. Corpus Musicae Mensurabilis 53. American Institute of Musicology, 1970–72.

Archives des Maîtres de l'Orgue des XVIe, XVIIe et XVIIIe Siècles, Vol. 8. Edited by Alexandre Guilmant. Paris, 1907.

Byrd, William. *Keyboard Music*. Edited by Alan Brown. Musica Britannica 27, 28. London, 1971.

Eberlin, Johann Ernst. *IX. Toccate e fughe per l'organo*. Augsburg, 1747. Edited by Rudolf Walter. Altötting, 1958.

Fischer, Johann Caspar Ferdinand. *Blumen-Strauß*. Augsburg, 1732. Edited by Rudolf Walter. Altötting, 1956.

———. *Sämtliche Werke für Klavier und Orgel*. Edited by F. Werra. Leipzig, 1901.

Gibbons, Christopher. *Keyboard Compositions*. Edited by Clare G. Raynor. Corpus of Early Keyboard Music 18. American Institute of Musicology, 1967.

Gibbons, Orlando. *Keyboard Music*. Edited by Gerold Hendric. Musica Britannica 20. London, 1962; 2nd rev. ed. 1967.

Josquin des Prez. *Werken*. Edited by Albert Smijers, Myroslaw Antonowycz, and Willem Elders. 55 vols. Amsterdam, 1921–69.

Keitel, Elizabeth A., ed. *Seur toute creature humeinne*. Oxford, 1977.

Kerll, Johann Caspar. *Modulatio organica super Magnificat*. Munich, 1686. Edited by Rudolf Walter. Altötting, 1956.

Kolb, Carlmann. *Certamen aonium*. Augsburg, 1733. Edited by Rudolf Walter. Altötting, 1957.

Lasso, Orlando di. *The Complete Motets*. Edited by Peter Bergquist. Recent Researches in the Music of the Renaissance 103. Madison, 1995.

Ludwig, Friedrich, ed. *Guillaume de Machaut: Musikalische Werke*. Vol. 1, *Balladen, Rondeaux und Virelais*. Leipzig, 1926.

Lugge, John. *Three Voluntaries*. Edited by Susi Jeans and John Steele. London, 1956.

Muffat, Georg. *Apparatus musico-organisticus*. Salzburg, 1690. Edited by Michael Radulescu. Vienna, 1981.

Murschhauser, Franz Xaver Anton. *Octi-Tonium novum organicum*. Augsburg, 1696. Edited by Rudolf Walter. Altötting, 1961.

———. *Prototypon longo-breve organicum*. 2 vols. Nuremberg, 1703 and 1707. Edited by Rudolf Walter. Altötting, 1969.

———. Complete works for keyboard. In *Johann Krieger, Franz Xaver Anton Murschhauser, und Johann Philipp Krieger: Gesammelte Werke für Klavier und Orgel*. Edited by Max Seiffert. *Denkmäler Deutscher Tonkunst*, Zweite Folge, *Denkmäler der Tonkunst in Bayern*, 18. Leipzig, 1917.

Nauss, Johann Xaver. *Die spielende Muse*. Augsburg, c. 1740. Edited by Rudolf Walter. Altötting, 1983.

Ninot le Petit. *Opera Omnia*. Edited by Barton Hudson. Corpus Musicae Mensurabilis 87. Neuhausen-Stuttgart, 1979.

Nivers, Guillaume Gabriel. *Livre d'orgue contenant cent pièces de tous les Tons de l'Eglise*. Paris, 1665. Facsimile edited by Jean-Marc Fuzeau. Courlay, 1987. Modern edition by Norbert Dufourcq. Paris, 1963.

Poglietti, Alessandro. *Compendium oder Kurtzer Begriff* [A-KR L Ms 146]. Edited by Rudolf Walter as *Praeludia, Cadenzen und Fugen*. Heidelberg, 1970.

Sabbatini, Pietro Paolo. *Toni ecclesiastici colle sue intonationi.* Rome, 1650.

Scherer, Sebastian Anton. *Operum musicorum secundum.* Ulm, 1664. *Ouvres d'orgue de Sebastian Anton Scherer.* Edited by Alexandre Guilmant and Andre Pirro. Archives des maitres de l'orgue des XVIe, XVIIe et XVIIIe siècles 9. Mainz, [1907].

Schrade, Leo, ed. *The Works of Guillaume de Machaut.* 2 vols. Monaco, 1956.

Shaw, H. Watkins, ed. *John Blow Complete Organ Works.* London, 1958.

Speth, Johann. *Ars magna consoni et dissoni.* Augsburg, 1693. Edited by Gregor Klaus. Heidelberg, c. 1960.

Titelouze, Jean. *Oeuvres complètes d'orgue.* Edited by A. Guilmant. Archives des Maîtres d'Orgue 1. Paris, 1898.

Trabaci, Giovanni Maria. *Il secondo libro de ricercate, et altri varij capricci.* Naples, 1615. Facsimile, Florence, 1984.

Valente, Antonio. *Versi spirituali sopra tutte le note.* Naples, 1580. Edited by I. Fuser. Padua, 1958.

THEORY TREATISES

Agricola, Martin. *Musica choralis deudsch.* Wittenberg, 1533. Facsimile, Hildesheim and New York, 1969.

———. *Rudimenta musices, quibus canendi artificium compendiosissime complexum . . . traditur.* Wittenberg, 1539. Facsimile, New York, 1966.

Angelo da Picitono. *Fior angelico di musica.* Venice, 1547.

Angleria, Camillo. *La Regola del contraponto.* Milan, 1622.

[Anonymous]. *Kurtzer jedoch gründicher Wegweiser.* Augsburg, 1689.

[Anonymous]. *The Pathway to Musicke.* London, 1596. [STC 19464], with ("annexed to") *A New Booke of Tabliture.* London, 1596. [STC 1433].

Aron, Pietro. *Toscanello in musica.* Venice, 1523, 1529, 1539. Facsimile, New York. Translated by Peter Bergquist. 3 vols. Colorado Springs, 1970.

———. *Trattato della natura et cognitione di tutti gli tuoni di canto figurato.* Venice, 1525. Facsimile, Utrecht, 1966. Chapters 1–7 translated by Oliver Strunk. *Source Readings in Music History,* 205–18. New York, 1950.

Artusi, Giovanni Maria. *L'Artusi overo delle imperfettioni della moderna musica ragionamenti dui.* Venice, 1600. Facsimile, Bologna, 1968.

———. *Seconda parte dell'Artusi overo delle imperfettioni della moderna musica.* Venice, 1603. Facsimile, Bologna, 1968.

Banchieri, Adriano. *Cartella musicale.* Venice, 1614. [The only one of Banchieri's five *Cartella* publications to bear the exact name *Cartella musicale*, the 1614 edition contains a great deal more material than the other four editions: *Cartella overo regole utilissime* (Venice, 1601); *La Cartella del R.P.D. Adriano Banchieri* (Venice, 1610); *La Cartellina musicale* (Venice, 1615); and *La Banchierina overo cartella picciola* (Venice, 1623).] Facsimile of 1614 ed., Bologna, 1968.

———. *L'Organo suonarino*, op. 13. Venice, 1605. 2nd ed., op. 25, Venice, 1611. 3rd ed., op. 43, Venice, 1622. Reprint of 1622 ed., Venice, 1627. 4th ed., Venice, 1638. Facsimile of 1605 ed. and portions of 1611 and 1638 eds., Amsterdam, 1969.

Bathe, William. *A Brief Introduction to the True Art of Music*. Edited by Cecil Hill. Colorado College Music Press Critical Texts 10. Colorado Springs, 1979.

———. *A Briefe Introduction to the Skill of Song c. 1587*. Facsimile with introduction by Bernard Rainbow. Classic Texts in Music Education 3. Kilkenny, Ireland, 1982.

———. *A Briefe Introduction to the Skill of Song*. London: T. Este, n.d. [copy examined: Houghton Library] [STC 1589].

Berardi, Angelo. *Miscellanea musicale*. Bologna, 1689.

Bermudo, Juan. *Declaracion de instrumentos musicales*. Osuna, 1555. Facsimile, Kassel and Basel, 1968.

Beurhusius [Beurhaus], Friedrich. *Erotematum musicae libri duo*. 1573. 2nd ed., Nuremberg, 1580. Facsimile, edited by W. Thoene. Cologne, 1961.

Boethius, Anicius Manlius Severinus. *De institutione musica*. Edited by Gottfried Friedlein. Leipzig, 1867.

———. *Fundamentals of Music*. Translated, with an introduction and notes, by Calvin M. Bower; edited by Claude V. Palisca. New Haven and London, 1989.

Bononcini, Giovanni Maria. *Musico prattico*. Bologna, 1673. Facsimile, Hildesheim, 1969.

Burmeister, Joachim. *Musica poetica*. Rostock, 1606. Facsimile, Kassel and Basel, 1955. Translated with introduction and notes by Benito V. Rivera, as *Musical Poetics*. New Haven and London, 1993.

Butler, Charles. *The Principles of Musik in Singing and Setting*. London, 1636. Facsimile with an introduction by Gilbert Reaney. New York, 1970.

Calvisius, Sethus. *Excercitationes musicae duae*. Leipzig, 1600. Facsimile, Hildesheim and New York, 1973.

Campion, Thomas. *A New Way of Making Fowre Parts in Counter-point*. [n.d., c. 1613] [STC 4542, reel 726]. In *The Works of Thomas Campion*. Edited by Walter R. Davis. New York, 1967.

Coperario, Giovanni. *Rules How to Compose*. Facsimile with an introduction by Manfred Bukofzer. Los Angeles, 1952.

Dialogus de musica. GS 1:252–64.

Dionigi, Marco. *Li primi Tuoni*. Parma, 1648.

Diruta, Girolamo. *Il Transilvano*. Part 1: Venice, 1593; part 2: Venice, 1609. Translated by Murray C. Bradshaw and Edward J. Soehnlen as *The Transylvanian*. 2 vols. Institute of Medieval Music, 1984.

Dowland, John. *Andreas Ornithoparcus his Micrologus, or Introduction: Containing the Art of Singing*. London, 1609. Facsimile, Amsterdam and New York, 1969.

Effrem, Mutio. *Censure . . . sopra il sesto libro de madrigali di M. Marco da Gagliano. . . .* Venice, 1623.

Ellsworth, Oliver, ed. and trans. *The Berkeley Manuscript*. Lincoln and London, 1984.

Falck, Georg. *Idea boni cantoris*. Nuremberg, 1688.

Finck, Hermann. *Practica musica*. Wittenberg, 1556. Facsimile, Bologna, 1969.

Gaffurius, Franchinus. *Theorica musice*. Milan, 1492. Facsimile, Milan, 1934.

Galilei, Vincenzo. *Fronimo dialogo . . . sopra l'arte del bene intavolare*. Venice, 1584. Facsimile, Leipzig, 1969.

Glareanus, Heinricus Loritus. *Dodecachordon*. Basel, 1547. Facsimile, Hildesheim and New York, 1969. English translation by Clement Miller. 2 vols. Musicological Studies and Documents 6. N.p., 1965.

Guido of Arezzo. *Micrologus*. CSM 4.

Hawkins, Sir John. *A General History of the Science and Practice of Music*. London, 1776; edition cited here: London, 1875.

Lanfranco, Giovanni Maria. *Scintille di musica*. Brescia, 1533. Facsimile, Bologna, 1970.

Le Roy, Adrian. *A Briefe and Plaine Instruction to Set All Musicke of Eight Divers Tunes in Tableture for the Lute*. London, 1574. Edited by Jean Jacquot, Pierre-Yves Sordes, and Jean-Michel Vaccaro. Paris, 1977. Original edition (Paris, 1557) lost.

———. *Les instructions pour le luth (1574)*. Edited by J. Jacquot, P.-Y. Sordes, J.-M. Vaccaro. In *Oeuvres d'Adrian Le Roy*. Paris, 1977.

Lossius, Lucas. *Erotemata musicae practicae*. Nuremberg, 1563. Facsimile, Bologna, 1980.

Mattheson, Johann. *Das neu-eröffnete Orchestre*. Hamburg, 1713.

———. *Exemplarische Organisten-Probe*. Hamburg, 1719. 2nd ed. as *Grosse General-Baß-Schule*. Hamburg, 1731.

———. *Critica musica* I. Hamburg, 1722.

Milán, Juan de. *Libro de musica de vihuela a mano. Intitulado El maestro*. Valencia, 1536. Edited and translated by Charles Jacobs. University Park and London, 1971.

Morley, Thomas. *A Plaine and Easie Introduction to Practicall Musicke*. London, 1597. Facsimile, Amsterdam, 1969. [STC 18133].

———. *A Plain & Easy Introduction to Practical Music*. Edited by Alec Harman. New York, 1952; paperback ed., New York, 1973.

Muris, Johannes de. *Ars Discantus*. CS III.

———. *Cum notum sit*. CS III.

Murschhauser, Franciscum Xaverium. *Academia musico-poetica bipartita*. Nuremberg, 1721.

Nivers, Guillaume-Gabriel. *Traité de la composition de musique*. Paris, 1667.

[North, Francis (Baron Guilford)]. *A Philosophical Essay of Musick*. London, 1677.

North, Roger. *Memoirs of Musick*. Edited by Edward F. Rimbault. London, 1846.

Ornithoparchus, Andreas. *Musicae activae micrologus*. Leipzig, 1517. Facsimile, Hildesheim, 1977.

———. *A Compendium of Musical Practice*. Translated by John Dowland. Facsimile edited by Gustave Reese and Steven Ledbetter. New York, 1963.

Paumann, Conrad. *Fundamentum organisandi*. Corpus of Early Keyboard Music 1. [n.p.], 1963.

Picerli, Silverio. *Specchio primo di musica*. Naples, 1630.

———. *Specchio secondo di musica*. Naples, 1631.

Playford, John. *An Introduction to the Skill of Musick*. 5th ed. London, 1674. Reprint, Ridgewood, NJ, 1966.

———. *An Introduction to the Skill of Musick*. 12th ed. Revised by Henry Purcell. London, 1694.

Pontio, Pietro. *Ragionamento di musica*. Parma, 1588.

Prosdocimo de' Beldomani, Contrapunctus. Edited by Jan Herlinger. Lincoln and London, 1984.

Ravenscroft, Thomas. *Treatise of Musick*. London, British Library, Add. 19758.

Rhau, Georg. *Enchiridion utriusque musicae practicae*. Wittenberg, 1538. Facsimile, Basel, 1951 (incomplete).

Rodio, Rocco. *Regole di musica*. Naples, 1609.

Rossetti, Biagio. *Libellus de rudimentis musices*. Verona, 1529. Facsimile, New York, 1968.

Samber, Joannem Baptistam. *Continuatio ad manuductionem organicam*. Salzburg, 1707.

———. *Manuductio ad Organum*. Salzburg, 1704.

Scacchi, Marco. *Cribrum musicum ad triticum Syferticum*.Venice, 1643.

Siefert, Paul. *Anticribratio musica ad avenam Schachianam*. Gdansk, 1645.

Simpson, Christopher. *A Compendium of Practical Music in Five Parts*. Edited by Phillip J. Lord. Oxford, 1970.

Stella, Gioseppe Maria. *Breve instruttione*. Rome, 1665.

Tigrini, Orazio. *Il compendio della musica*. Venice, 1588. Facsimile, New York, 1966.

Tinctoris, Johannes. *Liber de natura et proprietate tonorum*. Edited by Albert Seay. *Opera theoretica*. Corpus Scriptorum de Musica 22. [n.p.], 1975.

Titelouze, Jean. Preface to *Le Magnificat*. Paris, 1626.

Vicentino, Nicola. *L'antica musica ridotta alla moderna prattica*. Rome, 1555. Facsimile, Kassel, Basel, London, and New York, 1959.

Zacconi, Lodovico. *Prattica di musica*. Venice, 1592. Reprinted with new title page, Venice, 1596. Facsimile, Bologna, 1967.

———. *Prattica di musica seconda parte*. Venice, 1622. Facsimile, Bologna, 1967.

Zarlino, Gioseffo. *Le istitutioni harmoniche*. Venice, 1558. Facsimile, New York, 1965.

———. *Le Istitutioni harmoniche*. Venice, 1573. Facsimile, Ridgewood, NJ, 1966.

———. *On the Modes: Part Four of Le istitutioni harmoniche, 1558*. Translated by Vered Cohen; edited with an introduction by Claude V. Palisca. New Haven and London, 1983.

———. *Theorie des Tonsystems* [Parts I and II of *Le istitutioni harmoniche*]. Translated by Michael Fend. Frankfurt am Main, 1989.

SECONDARY SOURCES

Agawu, Kofi. "Analyzing Music under the New Musicological Regime." *Music Theory Online* 2.4 (1996).

———. "Does Music Theory Need Musicology?" *Current Musicology* 53 (1993): 89–98.

———. "The Invention of 'African Rhythm'." *Journal of the American Musicological Society* 48 (1995): 380–95.

Aldrich, Putnam. "An Approach to the Analysis of Renaissance Music." *Music Review* 30 (1969): 1–21.

Andrews, H. K. *The Technique of Byrd's Vocal Polyphony*. London, 1966.

Apel, Willi. *The History of Keyboard Music to 1700*. Translated by Hans Tischler. Bloomington, 1972.

———. "The Partial Signatures in the Sources up to 1450." *Acta Musicologica* 10 (1938): 1–13 and 11 (1939): 40–42.

Apfel, Ernst. *Geschichte der Kompositionslehre von den Anfängen bis gegen 1700*. 5 vols. Wilhelmshaven, 1981. 3rd ed. with corrections, Saabrücken, 1989, with an additional volume, 1995.

Armstrong, James. "How to Compose a Psalm: Ponzio and Cerone compared." *Studi musicali* 7 (1978): 103–39.

Arnold, F.T., *The Art of Accompaniment from a Thorough-Bass*. Oxford, 1931. Reprint, New York, 1965.

Atcherson, W. T. "Key and Mode in Seventeenth-Century Music Theory Books." *Journal of Music Theory* 17 (1973): 204–33.

———. "Symposium on Seventeenth-Century Music Theory: England." *Journal of Music Theory* 16 (1972): 6–13.

Auhagen, Wolfgang. *Studien zur Tonartencharakteristik in theoretischen Schriften vom späten 17. bis zum Beginn des 20. Jahrhunderts*. Frankfurt, 1983.

Austern, Linda. *Music in English Children's Drama of the Later Renaissance*. New York, 1992.

Bailey, Candace. "English Keyboard Music, c. 1625–1680." 2 vols. Ph.D. diss., Duke University, 1992. University Microfilms 9303533.

Bates, Robert Frederick. "From Mode to Key: A Study of Seventeenth-Century French Liturgical Organ Music and Music Theory." Ph.D. diss., Stanford University, 1986. University Microfilms 8700725.

Beebe, Ellen S. "Tonal Type and Octo-Modal Classification." Paper read at the Symposium "Modus und Tonalität," Basel, March 1991.

Bent, Ian. "Analysis." *New Grove* 1:340–88.

Bent, Margaret. "Accidentals, Counterpoint and Notation in Aaron's *Aggiunta* to the *Toscanello in Musica.*" *The Journal of Musicology* 12 (1994): 306–344.

———. "Diatonic *Ficta.*" *Early Music History* 4 (1984): 1–48.

———."Diatonic *Ficta* Revisited: Josquin's *Ave Maria* in Context." *Music Theory Online* 2.6 (1996).

———."Editing Early Music: The Dilemma of Translation." *Early Music* 22 (1994): 373–94.

———."Fact and Value in Contemporary Scholarship." *Musical Times* 127 (1986): 85–89.

———. "Musica Recta and Musica Ficta." *Musica Disciplina* 26 (1972): 73–100.

Berger, Christian. *Hexachord, Mensur und Textstruktur: Studien zum französischen Lied des 14. Jahrhunderts.* Beihefte zum Archiv für Musikwissenschaft 35. Stuttgart, 1992.

Berger, Karol. *Musica Ficta.* Cambridge, 1987.

Berlin, Isaiah. "On Political Judgment." *New York Review of Books* October 3, 1996.

Besseler, Heinrich. *Bourdon und Fauxbourdon.* Leipzig, 1950.

Bielitz, Mathias. "Materia und Forma bei Johannes de Grocheo." *Die Musikforschung* 38 (1985): 257–77.

Boorman, Stanley. "False Relations and the Cadence." In *Altro Polo*, edited by Richard Charteris, 220–64. Sydney, 1990.

Boyd, Morrison Comegys. *Elizabethan Music and Musical Criticism.* Philadelphia, 1940. 2nd ed., 1962.

Braun, Werner. *Deutsche Musiktheorie des 15. bis 17. Jahrhunderts.* Zweiter Teil: Von Calvisius bis Mattheson. Geschichte der Musiktheorie, 8/II. Darmstadt, 1994.

Bray, Roger. "Music and Musicians in Tudor England: Sources, Composition Theory and Performance." In *Music in Britain: The Sixteenth Century*, ed. Roger Bray, 1–45. Oxford, 1995.

Brett, Philip. "Facing the Music." *Early Music* 10 (1982): 347–50.

Brett, Ursula. *Music and Ideas in Seventeenth-Century Italy: The Cazzati-Arresti Polemic.* New York, 1989.

Brown, Howard Mayer. *Instrumental Music Printed Before 1600: A Bibliography.* Cambridge, MA, 1965.

———. "The Mirror of Man's Salvation: Music in Devotional Life about 1500." *Renaissance Quarterly* 44 (1991): 744–73.

———. *Music in the Renaissance.* Englewood Cliffs, NJ, 1976.

Bujic, Boyan. "Josquin, Leonardo, and the Scala Peccatorum." *International Review of the Aesthetics and Sociology of Music* 4 (1973): 145–61.

Bukofzer, Manfred. *Music in the Baroque Era.* New York, 1947.

Burden, Michael, ed. *The Purcell Companion.* London, 1994 and Portland, OR, 1995.

Burney, Charles. *A General History of Music*. 3 vols. London, 1776–1789. Edited by Frank Mercer. Reprint (3 vols. in 2), London, 1935 and New York, 1957.

Caldwell, John. "Music in the Faculty of Arts." In *The Collegiate University. The History of the University of Oxford*, vol. 3, ed. James McConica, 201–12. Oxford, 1986.

Carpenter, Nan Cooke. *Music in Medieval and Renaissance Universities*. Norman, OK, 1958. Reprint, 1972.

———. "The Study of Music at the University of Oxford in the Renaissance (1450–1600)." *Musical Quarterly* 41 (1955): 191–214.

Casey, William S. "Printed English Lute Instruction Books 1568–1610." Ph.D. diss., University of Michigan, 1960. University Microfilms 6002514 .

Christensen, Thomas. "Fétis and Emerging Tonal Consciousness." In *Music Theory in the Age of Romanticism*, edited by Ian Bent, 37–56. Cambridge, 1996.

———. "Music Theory and its Histories." In *Music Theory and the Exploration of the Past,* edited by Christopher Hatch and David W. Bernstein, 9–39. Chicago and London, 1993.

Constantini, Franz Peter. "Die Entwicklung der Versettenkomposition vom ausgehenden Mittelbarock bis zum Rokoko." Ph.D. diss., University of Vienna, 1967.

Cook, Nicholas. *A Guide to Musical Analysis*. London, 1987.

———. *Music, Imagination and Culture*. Oxford, 1990.

Cooper, Barry. "Englische Musiktheorie im 17. und 18. Jahrhundert." In *Entstehung nationaler Traditionen: Frankreich, England*. Geschichte der Musiktheorie 9. Darmstadt, 1986.

———. *English Solo Keyboard Music of the Middle and Late Baroque*. Outstanding Dissertations in Music from British Universities. New York and London, 1989.

Cox, Geoffrey. *Organ Music in Restoration England: A Study of Sources, Styles, and Influences*. Outstanding Dissertations in Music from British Universities. New York and London, 1989.

Crocker, Richard L. "Discant, Counterpoint and Harmony." *Journal of the American Musicological Society* 15 (1962): 1–21.

Cummings, Anthony. "A Florentine Sacred Repertory from the Medici Restoration (Manuscript II.I.232 of the Biblioteca Nazional Centrale, Firenze)." Ph.D. diss., Princeton University, 1979. University Microfilms 8009530 .

———. "Toward an Interpretation of the Sixteenth-Century Motet." *Journal of the American Musicological Society* 34 (1981): 43–59.

Dahlhaus, Carl. "Aristoteles-Rezeption und Neuzeit in der Musikgeschichte." In *Wege in die Neuzeit*, edited by T. Cramer, 146–48. Munich, 1988.

———. *Über die Entstehung der harmonischen Tonalität*. Kassel, 1967. Translated by Robert O. Gjerdingen as *Studies on the Origin of Harmonic Tonality*. Princeton, 1990.

Damschroder, David and David Russell Williams. *Music Theory from Zarlino to Schenker*. Stuyvesant, NY 1990.

Dart, Thurston. Review of *Lute Music of Shakespeare's Time. William Barley: A New Booke of Tabliture*, ed. Wilburn W. Newcomb. In *Journal of the American Musicological Society* 20 (1967): 493–95.

A Dictionary of Philosophy. Editorial consultant Antony Flew. Second, revised edition. London, 1984.

Dodds, Michael R. "The Seventeenth-Century Church Keys in Theory and Practice." Ph.D. diss., University of Rochester, forthcoming.

Elders, Willem. "Plainchant in the Motets, Hymns, and Magnificats of Josquin des Prez." In *Josquin des Prez*, Proceedings of the International Josquin Festival-Conference, 21–25 June 1971, edited by Edward E. Lowinsky in collaboration with Bonnie J. Blackburn, 523–42. New York, 1976.

Everist, Mark, ed. *Models of Musical Analysis: Music before 1600*. Oxford, 1992.

Fallows, David. "The Performing Ensembles in Josquin's Sacred Music." *Tijdschrift van de Vereniging voor Nederlands muziekgeschiedenis* 35 (1985):32.

Federhofer, Hellmut. "Eine Musiklehre von J. J. Prinner." In *Festschrift Alfred Orel zum 70. Geburtstag*. Vienna and Wiesbaden, 1960.

———. "Zur handschriftlichen Überlieferung der Musiktheorie in Österreich in der zweiten Hälfte des 17. Jahrhunderts." *Die Musikforschung* 11 (1958): 264–79.

Fétis, François Joseph. *Esquisse de l'histoire de l'harmonie*. Translated with introduction and annotations by Mary I. Arlin. Stuyvesant, NY, 1994.

Fellowes, Edmund H. *William Byrd*. London, 1936. 2nd. ed., 1963.

Fenlon, Iain and John Milsom. "'Ruled Paper Imprinted': Music Paper and Patents in Sixteenth-Century England." *Journal of the American Musicological Society* 37 (1984): 139–63.

Flynn, Jane E. "The Education of Choristers in England During the Sixteenth Century." In *English Choral Practice, 1400–1650*, ed. John Morehen, 180–99. Cambridge, 1996.

———. "A Reconsideration of the Mulliner Book (British Library Add. MS 30513): Music Education in Sixteenth-Century England." Ph.D. diss., Duke University, 1993. University Microfilms 9416896.

Forte, Allen. Letter to the Editor, *Music Analysis* 51(1986): 335.

Foster, Joseph. *Alumni Oxoniensis, The Members of the University of Oxford, 1500-1714 . . . Being the Matriculation Register of the University, Alphabetically Arranged, Revised, and Annotated*. Oxford, 1891–92.

Freis, Wolfgang. "Perfecting the Perfect Instrument. Fray Juan Bermudo on the Tuning and Temperament of the vihuela de mano." *Early Music* 23 (1995): 421–35.

Frost, Maurice. *English and Scottish Psalm and Hymn Tunes, c. 1543–1677*. London, 1953.

Fuller, Sarah. "Guillaume de Machaut: *De toutes flours*." In *Models of Musical Analysis: Music before 1600*, edited by Mark Everist, 41–65. Oxford, 1992.

———. "Line, *Contrapunctus*, and Structure in a Machaut Song." *Music Analysis* 6 (1987): 37–58.

———. "Machaut and the Definition of Musical Space." *Sonus* 12 (1991): 1–15.

———. "On Sonority in Fourteenth-Century Polyphony." *Journal of Music Theory* 30 (1986): 35–70.

———. "Tendencies and Resolutions: The Directed Progression in *Ars Nova* Music." *Journal of Music Theory* 36 (1992): 229–58.

Fuller-Maitland, John Alexander. *Contemporaries of Purcell.* Vol. 7. London, 1921.

Gehrenbeck, David Maulsby. "Motetti de la corona: A Study of Ottaviano Petrucci's Four Last-Known Motet Prints (Fossombrone, 1514, 1519), with 44 Transcriptions." 4 vols. Ph.D. diss., Union Theological Seminary, 1971. University Microfilms 7112440.

Göllner, Theodor. *Die Mehrstimmigen Liturgischen Lesungen.* 2 vols. Tutzing, 1969.

Graduale Romanum. Edited by Dom Jacques-Marie Guilmard. Solesmes, 1991.

Greer, David. "Manuscript Additions in 'Parthenia' and Other Early English Printed Music in America." *Music & Letters* 77 (1996): 169–81.

Hansen, Finn Egeland. *The Grammar of Gregorian Tonality: An Investigation Based on the Repertory in Codex H 159, Montpellier.* 2 vols. Copenhagen, 1979.

———. "Tonality in Gregorian Chant Based on an Investigation of the Melodies in Codex H 159, Montpellier." In *IMS Report of the Eleventh Congress Copenhagen, 1972*, 425–31. Copenhagen, 1974.

Harper, John. *The Forms and Orders of Western Liturgy from the Tenth to the Eighteenth Century*. Oxford, 1991.

Harrison, Frank Ll. *Music in Medieval Britain.* 4th edition. Buren (GLD), The Netherlands, 1980.

Hartley, L. P. *The Go-Between.* London, 1953.

Harwood, I. "On the Publication of Adrian Le Roy's Lute Instructions." *Lute Society Journal* 18 (1976): 30–36.

Hasselman, Margaret Paine. "The French Chanson in the Fourteenth Century." Ph.D. diss., University of California at Berkeley, 1970. University Microfilms 719830.

Henderson, Robert V. "Solmization Syllables in Musical Theory 1100 to 1600." Ph.D. diss., Columbia University, 1969. University Microfilms 7017017.

Hermelink, Siegfried. *Dispositiones modorum: die Tonarten in der Musik Palestrinas und seiner Zeitgenossen*. Tutzing, 1960.

Horace. *Satires, Epistles and Ars Poetica.* Edited and translated by H. Rushton Fairclough. 2nd rev. ed. Loeb Classical Library 194. Cambridge and London, 1929.

Howell, Almonte C. "French Baroque Organ Music and the Eight Tones." *Journal of the American Musicological Society* 11 (1958): 106–18.

Howes, Frank. *William Byrd.* London, 1928. Reprint, London, 1978.

Illing, Robert. *The English Metrical Psalter 1562: A Catalogue of Early Editions.* Adelaide, 1983.

———. *Est-Barley-Ravenscroft and the English Metrical Psalter*. Adelaide, 1969.

Jalowetz, Heinrich. "On the Spontaneity of Schoenberg's Music." *Musical Quarterly* 30 (1944): 385–408.

Johnson, Timothy A. "Solmization in English Treatises Around the Turn of the Seventeenth Century: A Break from Modal Theory." *Theoria* 5 (1990–1): 42–60.

Josephson, Nors. "Formal Symmetry in the High Renaissance." *Tijdschrift van de Vereniging voor Nederlandse muziekgeschiedenis* 41(1991): 105–33.

Judd, Cristle Collins. "Aspects of Tonal Coherence in the Motets of Josquin." 2 vols. Ph.D. diss., King's College, University of London, 1993. University Microfilms 9501876.

———. "Josquin des Prez: *Salve regina* (à 5)." In *Models of Musical Analysis: Music before 1600*, edited by Mark Everist, 114–53. Oxford, 1992.

———. "Modal Types and *Ut, Re, Mi* Tonalities: Tonal Coherence in Sacred Vocal Polyphony from about 1500." *Journal of the American Musicological Society* 45 (1994): 428–67.

———. "Reading Aron Reading Petrucci." *Early Music History* 14 (1995): 121–52.

———. "Some Problems of Pre-Baroque Analysis: Josquin's *Ave Maria . . . virgo serena.*" *Music Analysis* 4 (1985): 201–39.

Just, Martin. "Josquins Vertonungen der Genealogien nach Matthäus und Lukas. Textgestalt und musikalische Struktur." In *Zeichen und Struktur in der Musik der Renaissance*, edited by Klaus Hortschansky, 87–106. Kassel, 1989.

Kallberg, Jeffrey. *Chopin at the Boundaries: Sex, History, and Musical Genre*. Cambridge, MA and London, 1996.

Kellman, Herbert. "Josquin and the Courts of the Netherlands and France: The Evidence of the Sources." In *Josquin des Prez*. Proceedings of the International Josquin Festival-Conference, 21–25 June 1971, edited by Edward E. Lowinsky in collaboration with Bonnie J. Blackburn, 181–216. London, 1976.

Kerman, Joseph. *Contemplating Music: Challenges to Musicology*. Cambridge, MA, 1985.

———."How We Got into Analysis and How to Get Out." *Critical Inquiry* 7 (1980–81): 311–31.

———. *The Masses and Motets of William Byrd*. Berkeley, 1981.

———. "On William Byrd's *Emendemus in melius*." *Musical Quarterly* 49 (1963): 431–49. Revised version in *Hearing the Motet*, edited by Dolores Pesce, 329–347. New York, 1997.

———."A Profile for American Musicology." *Journal of the American Musicological Society* 18 (1965): 61–69 and 426–27.

Krantz, Steven Charles. "Rhetorical and Structural Functions of Mode in Selected Motets of Josquin Des Prez." 2 vols. Ph.D. diss., University of Minnesota, 1989. University Microfilms 9005239.

Krebs, Wolfgang. *Die Lateinische Evangelien-Motette des 16. Jahrhunderts: Repertoire, Quellenlage, musikalische Rhetorik und Symbolik*. Frankfurter Beiträge zur Musikwissenschaft 25. Tutzing, 1995.

Krummel, D. W. *English Music Printing 1553–1700*. London, 1975.

Lavin, J. "William Barley, Draper and Stationer." *Studies in Bibliography* 22 (1969): 214–23.

Leech-Wilkinson, Daniel. *Machaut's Mass*. Oxford, 1990.

———. "Machaut's *Rose, Lis* and the Problem of Early Music Analysis." *Music Analysis* 3 (1984): 9–28.

Leeson, Daniel and Robert Levin. "On the Authenticity of K. Anh.C14.01(297b), a Symphonia Concertante for Four Winds and Orchestra," *Mozart-Jahrbuch 1976/77*, 97–107. Kassel, 1978.

Lefferts, Peter. "Signature-Systems and Tonal Types in the Fourteenth-Century French Chanson." *Plainsong and Medieval Music* 4 (1995): 117–47.

Lerdahl, Fred and Ray Jackendoff. *A Generative Theory of Tonal Music*. Cambridge, MA, 1983.

Lester, Joel. *Between Modes and Keys: German Theory 1592–1802*. Stuyvesant, NY, 1989.

———. "The Emergence of Major and Minor Keys in German Theory: 1680–1730." *Journal of Music Theory* 22 (1978): 65–103.

———. "Major-Minor Concepts and Modal Theory in Germany: 1592–1680." *Journal of the American Musicological Society* 30 (1977): 208–53.

Leuchtmann, Horst. "Ein wichtiger Neufund: Murschhauser's Opus 7, *pars secunda*, wiederentdeckt." *Musik in Bayern* 26 (1983): 35–36.

Levin, Robert. *Who Wrote the Mozart Four-Wind Concertante?* New York, 1988.

Lewis, Christopher. "Incipient Tonal Thought in Seventeenth-Century English Theory." *Studies in Music from Western Ontario* 6 (1981): 24–47.

Lidov, David. " The *Lamento di Tristano*." In *Models of Musical Analysis: Music before 1600*, edited by Mark Everist, 66–92. Oxford, 1992.

Lindley, David. *Thomas Campion*. Leiden, 1986.

Lloyd, Angela Jane. "Modal Representation in the Early Madrigals of Cipriano de Rore." Ph.D. diss., Royal Holloway and Bedford New College, University of London, 1996.

Lockwood, Lewis. "Josquin at Ferrara: New Documents and Letters." In *Josquin des Prez*. Proceedings of the International Josquin Festival-Conference, 21–25 June 1971, edited by Edward E. Lowinsky in collaboration with Bonnie J. Blackburn, 103–37. London, 1976.

———. *Music in Renaissance Ferrara, 1400–1505*. Cambridge, MA, 1984.

Loge, Eckhard. *Eine Messen- und Motettenhandschrift des Kantors Matthias Krüger aus der Musikbibliothek Herzog Albrechts von Preussen*. Kassel, 1931.

Lowbury, Edward, Timothy Salter, and Alison Young. *Thomas Campion: Poet, Composer, Physician*. New York, 1970.

Lowinsky, Edward E. "Canon Technique and Simultaneous Conception in Fifteenth-Century Music; a Comparison of North and South." In *Essays on the Music of J.S. Bach and Other Divers Subjects*, edited by Robert L. Weaver, 181–222. New York, 1981.

———. "Character and Purposes of American Musicology: A Reply to Joseph Kerman." *Journal of the American Musicological Society*, 18(1965): 222–34; Kerman response 426–27.

———. "The Function of Conflicting Signatures in Early Polyphonic Music." *Musical Quarterly* 31 (1945): 227–60.

———. *Tonality and Atonality in Sixteenth-Century Music*. Berkeley, 1962.

———. ed. *The Medici Codex of 1518*. Monuments of Renaissance Music 3. Chicago, 1968.

Macey, Patrick. "Josquin as Classic: *Qui habitat*, *Memor esto*, and Two Imitations Unmasked." *Journal of the Royal Musical Association* 118 (1993): 1–43.

———. "Josquin's *Misericordias Domini* and Louis XI." *Early Music* 19 (1991): 163–77.

Mathiassen, Finn. *The Style of the Early Motet (c. 1200–1250): An Investigation of the Old Corpus of the Montpellier Manuscript*. Translated by Johanne M. Stochholm. Studier og publikationer fra Musikvidenskabeligt Institut Åarhus Universitet, 1. Copenhagen, 1966.

Mattfeld, Jacquelyn. "Cantus Firmus in the Liturgical Motets of Josquin des Pres." Ph.D. diss., Yale University, 1959. University Microfilms 6606841.

McClary, Susan. "The Transition from Modal to Tonal Organization in the Works of Monteverdi." Ph.D. diss., Harvard University, 1976. University Microfilms 7711168.

McGuinness, Rosamond. "Writings about Music." In *Music in Britain: The Seventeenth Century*, edited by Ian Spink, 406–20. Oxford, 1988.

McNaught, W. G. "The History and Uses of the Sol-Fa Syllables." *Proceedings of the Musical Association* 19 (1893): 35–51.

Meier, Bernhard. *Alte Tonarten: Dargestellt an der Instrumentalmusik des 16. und 17. Jahrhunderts*. Kassel, 1994.

———. "Bemerkungen zu Lechners 'Motectae Sacrae' von 1575." *Archiv für Musikwissenschaft* 14 (1957): 83–101.

———. "The Musica Reservata of Adrianus Petit Coclico and its Relationship to Josquin." *Musica Disciplina* 10 (1956): 67–105.

———. *Die Tonarten der klassischen Vokalpolyphonie*. Utrecht, 1974. Translated by Ellen S. Beebe, with revisions by the author, as *The Modes of Classical Vocal Polyphony, Described According to the Sources*. New York, 1988.

———. "Zur Tonart der Concertato-Motetten in Monteverdi's 'Marienvesper'." In *Claudio Monteverdi: Festschrift Reinhold Hammerstein*, edited by Ludwig Finscher, 359–67. Laaber, 1986.

Mendel, Arthur. "Towards Objective Criteria for Establishing Chronology and Authenticiy: What Help Can the Computer Give?" In *Josquin des Prez*. Proceedings of the International Josquin Festival-Conference, 21–25 June 1971, edited by Edward E. Lowinsky in collaboration with Bonnie J. Blackburn, 297–308. London, 1976.

Mendel, Arthur and Hans David. *The Bach Reader*. New York, 1945.

Meyer, Jeff. "Tonal Structures in the Lute Songs of John Dowland." Paper presented at "Analyzing Early Music," Brandeis University, July 1995.

———. "Tonality in John Dowland's Lutesongs: English Theory and the Constructive Use of Airs." Ph.D. diss., University of Minnesota, forthcoming.

Miller, Gertrude. "Tonal Materials in Seventeenth-Century English Treatises." Ph.D. diss., Eastman School of Music, 1960.

Milsom, John. "The Eloquent Cantus Firmus." Paper read at the Royal Musical Assocation, London, April 1989.

Missale Romanum Mediolani. 1474. Edited by Robert Lippe. London, 1899–1907.

Moser, Hans Joachim. *Die mehrstimmige Vertonung des Evangeliums.* Wiesbaden, 1931. Reprint, Leipzig, 1968.

Narmour, Eugene. *Analysis and Cognition of Basic Melodic Structures: The Implication-Realization Model.* Chicago, 1990.

———. "The Top-Down and Bottom-Up Systems of Musical Implication: Building on Meyer's Theory of Emotional Syntax," *Musical Perception* 9 (1991): 1–26.

Neighbour, Oliver. *The Consort and Keyboard Music of William Byrd.* Berkeley, 1978.

Nixon, Paul J. "William Bathe and His Times." *Musical Times* 124 (1983): 101–02.

Noble, Jeremy. "The Function of Josquin's Motets." *Tijdschrift van de Vereniging voor Nederlandse muziekgeschiedenis* 35 (1985): 9–31.

Novack, Saul. "The Analysis of Pre-Baroque Music." In *Aspects of Schenkerian Theory,* edited by David Beach, 113–33. New Haven, 1983.

———. "Fusion of Design and Tonal Order in Mass and Motet." *Music Forum* 2 (1970): 187–263.

———. "The History of the Phrygian Mode in the History of Tonality." *Miscellanea Musicologica* 9 (1977): 82–127.

Nowacki, Edward. "The Latin Psalm Motet 1500–1535." In *Renaissance-Studien: Helmuth Osthoff zum 80. Geburtstag,* edited by Ludwig Finscher, 159–184. Tutzing, 1979.

Ó Mathúna, Seán P. *William Bathe, S. J., 1564–1614. A Pioneer in Linguistics.* Amsterdam Studies in the Theory and History of Linguistic Science 37. Amsterdam, 1986.

Osthoff, Helmuth. *Josquin Desprez.* 2 vols. Tutzing, 1962–65.

Owens, Jessie Ann. *Composers at Work: The Craft of Musical Composition 1450–1600.* New York, 1997.

———."Palestrina as Reader: Motets from the Song of Songs." In *Hearing the Motet,* edited by Dolores Pesce, 307–28. New York, 1997.

———. "Waelrant and Bocedization: Reflections on Solmization Reform." Forthcoming in the yearbook of the Alamire Foundation.

Page, Daniel Bennett. "Uniform and Catholic: Church Music in the Reign of Mary Tudor (1553–1558)." Ph.D. diss., Brandeis University, 1996. University Microfilms 9626001.

Palisca, Claude V. "The Artusi-Monteverdi Controversy." In *The New Monteverdi Companion,* edited by Denis Arnold and Nigel Fortune, 127–58. London and Boston, 1985.

———. *Baroque Music*. 3rd ed. Englewood Cliffs, NJ, 1991.

Payne, Ian. "Thomas Ravenscroft: A Biographical Note." *Musical Times* 127 (1987): 707–09.

Perkins, Leeman. "Modal Species and Mixtures in a Fifteenth-Century Chanson Repertory." In *Modality in the Music of the Fourteenth and Fifteenth Centuries*, edited by Ursula Günther, Ludwig Finscher, and Jeffrey Dean, 177–202. American Institute of Musicology, 1996.

———. "Mode and Structure in the Masses of Josquin." *Journal of the American Musicological Society* 26 (1973): 189–239.

———. Review of Joseph Kerman, *The Masses and Motets of William Byrd* and Oliver Neighbour, *The Consort and Keyboard Music of William Byrd* in *Musical Quarterly* 70 (1984): 134–39.

Pinker, Steven. *The Language Instinct*. Harmondsworth, 1994.

Plumley, Yolanda. *The Grammar of 14th Century Melody: Tonal Organization and Compositional Process in the Chansons of Guillaume de Machaut and the Ars Subtilior*. New York and London, 1996.

Powers, Harold S. "Anomalous modalities." In *Orlando di Lasso in der Musikgeschichte*, edited by Bernhold Schmid. Munich, 1996.

———."Il do del baritono." *Opera e Libretto* II, 267–81. Florence, 1993.

———. "Is Mode Real? Pietro Aron, the octenary system, and polyphony." Proceedings of the colloquium "Modus und Tonalität" at the Schola Cantorum in Basel, March 1991. *Basler Jahrbuch für historische Musikpraxis* 16 (1992): 9–52.

———. "Language Models and Musical Analysis." *Ethnomusicology* 24 (1980): 1–60.

———."Modal Representation in Polyphonic Offertories." *Early Music History* 2 (1982): 43–86.

———. "Modality as a European Cultural Construct." In *Secondo convegno europeo di analisi musicale: atti*. Edited by Rosanna Dalmonte and Mario Baroni, 207–19. Trent, 1992.

———. "The Modality of 'Vestiva i colli'." In *Studies in Renaissance and Baroque Music in Honor of Arthur Mendel*, edited by Robert L. Marshall, 31–46. Kassel, 1974.

———. "Mode." *New Grove* 12: 376–450.

———. "Monteverdi's Model for a Multimodal Madrigal." In *In cantu et Sermone: For Nino Pirrotta on His 80th Birthday*, edited by Fabrizio Della Seta and Franco Piperno, 185–219. Florence, 1989.

———. "Reading Mozart's Music: Text and Topic, Syntax and Sense." *Current Musicology* 57 (1995): 5–44.

———. Review of A. Merriam, *The Anthropology of Music*. *Perspectives of New Music* 4 (1966): 161–71.

———. "Three Pragmatists in Search of a Theory." *Current Musicology* 53 (1993): 5–17.

———."Tonal Types and Modal Categories in Renaissance Polyphony." *Journal of the American Musicological Society* 34 (1981): 428–70.

Preußner, Eberhard. "Solmisationsmethoden im Schulenunterricht des 16. und 17. Jahrhunderts." In *Feschrift Fritz Stein zum 60. Geburtstag*, edited by Hans Hoffmann and Franz Rühlmann, 112–28. Braunschweig, 1939.

Pruett, James. "Charles Butler—Musician, Grammarian, Apiarist." *Musical Quarterly* 49 (1963): 498–509.

Rainbow, Bernarr. "Bathe and his Introduction to Musicke." *Musical Times* 123 (1982): 243–47.

———. *English Psalmody Prefaces: Popular Methods of Teaching 1562–1835*. Kilkenny, 1982.

Randel, Don. "Dufay the Reader." In *Music and Language*, 33–78. Studies in the History of Music 1. New York, 1983.

———."Emerging Triadic Tonality in the Fifteenth Century." *Musical Quarterly* 57 (1971): 73–86.

Reese, Gustave. *Music in the Renaissance*. New York, 1954. 2nd ed. 1959.

Reese, Gustave and Jeremy Noble. "Josquin Desprez." In *The New Grove High Renaissance Masters*, edited by Stanley Sadie, 1–90. London, 1984.

Rifkin, Joshua. "Problems of Authorship in Josquin: Some Impolitic Observations, with a Postscript on Absalon, fili mi." *Proceedings of the International Josquin Symposium Utrecht 1996*, edited by Willem Elders. Utrecht, 1991.

Rivera, Benito. "Harmonic Theory in Musical Treatises of the late 15th and early 16th Centuries." *Music Theory Spectrum* 1 (1979): 80–95.

Ruff, Lillian. "The 17th Century English Music Theorists." Ph.D. diss., University of Nottingham, 1962.

Ruwet, N. "Methodes d'analyse en musicologie." *Revue belge de musicologie* 2(1966): 65–90. Translated with introduction by Mark Everist as "Methods of Analysis in Musicology." *Music Analysis* 6 (1987): 3–36.

Sachs, Curt. *The Rise of Music in the Ancient World East and West.* New York, 1943.

Salzer, Felix. *Structural Hearing*. New York, 1962.

———. "Tonality in Medieval Polyphony: Towards a History of Tonality." *Music Forum* 1 (1967): 35–98.

Schubert, Peter. "Authentic Analysis." *The Journal of Musicology* 12 (1994): 3–18.

Schulenberg, David. "Modes, Prolongations, and Analysis." *Journal of Musicology* 4 (1985): 303–29.

Shaw, H. Watkins. "Tradition and Convention in John Blow's Harmony." *Music and Letters* 30 (1949): 136–45.

Silbiger, Alexander. "Music and Crisis in the Seventeenth Century." In *Music and Science in the Age of Galileo*, edited by Victor Coelho, 35–44. University of Western Ontario Series in Philosophy and Science 51. Dordrecht and Boston, 1992.

———. "Tipi tonali nella musica di Frescobaldi per strumenti a tastiera" ("Tonal Types in the Keyboard Music of Frescobaldi"). In *Girolamo Frescobaldi IV. centenario della nascita*, edited by Sergio Durante and Dinko Fabris, 301–14. Florence, 1986.

Simpson, Adrienne. "A Short-Title List of Printed English Instrumental Tutors up to 1800 Held in British Libraries." *Royal Musical Association Research Chronicle* 6 (1966): 24–50.

Smits van Waesberghe, Joseph. *A Textbook of Melody*. N.p., 1955.

Snow, Robert. "Toledo Cathedral MS 'Reservado 23': A Lost Manuscript Rediscovered." *The Journal of Musicology* 2 (1983): 246–77.

Sparks, Edgar. *Cantus Firmus in Mass and Motet 1420–1520*. Berkeley, 1963.

———. "Problems of Authenticity in Josquin's Motets." In *Josquin des Prez*. Proceedings of the International Josquin Festival-Conference, 21–25 June 1971, edited by Edward E. Lowinsky in collaboration with Bonnie J. Blackburn, 345–59. London, 1976.

Stainer, Sir John. "On the Musical Introductions Found in Certain Metrical Psalters." *Proceedings of the Musical Association* 27 (1900–01): 1–50.

[STC]. *A Short-title Catalogue of Books Printed in England, Scotland and Ireland, and of English Books Printed Abroad, 1475–1640*. First compiled by A. W. Pollard and G. R. Redgrave. 2nd ed. begun by W. A. Jackson and F. S. Ferguson, completed by Katharine F. Parker. London, 1976–91.

Steblin, Rita. *A History of Key Characteristics in the Eighteenth and Early Nineteenth Centuries*. Ann Arbor, 1983.

Steele, Robert. *The Earliest English Music Printing*. London, 1903. Reprint, 1965.

Steele, Timothy Howard. "The Latin Psalm Motet, c. 1460–1520: Aspects of the Emergence of a New Motet Type." 2 vols. Ph.D. diss., University of Chicago, 1993. University Microfilims T032202.

Stern, David. "Schenkerian Theory and the Analysis of Renaissance Music." In *Schenker Studies*, edited by Hedi Siegel, 45–59. Cambridge, 1990.

———."Tonal Organization in Modal Polyphony." *Theory and Practice* 6 (1981): 5–39.

Stevenson, Robert. "Thomas Morley's 'Plaine and Easie' Introduction to the Modes." *Musica Disciplina* 6 (1952): 177–84.

Strahle, Graham. *An Early Music Dictionary. Musical Terms from British Sources, 1500–1740*. Cambridge, 1995.

Strainchamps, Edmund. "Theory as Polemic: Mutio Effrem's Censure . . . Sopra il Sesto Libro de Madrigali di Marco da Gagliano." In *Music Theory and the Exploration of the Past*, edited by Christopher Hatch and David W. Bernstein, 189–216. Chicago and London, 1993.

Strohm, Reinhard. "Musical Analysis as Part of Musical History." In *Tendenze e Metodi nella Ricerca Musicologica. Atti del Convegno Internazionale (Latina 27–29 Settembre 1990)*, edited by Raffaele Pozzi, 61–81. Florence, 1995.

Strunk, Oliver. "Some Motet-Types of the Sixteenth Century." In *Essays on Music in the Western World*, 108–13. New York, 1974.

Temperley, Nicholas. "The Adventures of a Hymn Tune—2," *Musical Times* 112 (1971): 488–89.

———. *The Hymn Tune Index: A Census of English-Language Hymn Tunes in Printed Sources from 1535 to 1820.* Oxford, forthcoming.

———. *Music of the English Parish Church.* Cambridge, 1979.

———. "The Old Way of Singing: Its Origins and Development." *Journal of the American Musicological Society* 34 (1981): 511–44.

Thompson, Robert. "'Francis Withie of Oxon' and His Commonplace Book, Christ Church, Oxford, MS 337." *Chelys* 20 (1991): 3–27.

Tomlinson, Gary. "The Web of Culture: A Context for Musicology." *Nineteenth-Century Music* 7 (1984): 350–62.

Treitler, Leo. "Music Analysis in an Historical Context." *College Music Society Symposium* 6 (1966): 75–88. Reprinted in *Music and the Historical Imagination*, 67–78. Cambridge, MA and London, 1989.

———. "On Historical Criticism." *The Musical Quarterly* 53 (1967): 188–205. Reprinted in *Music and the Historical Imagination*, 79–94. Cambridge, MA and London, 1989.

———. "The Present as History." *Perspectives of New Music* 7 (1969): 1–58. Reprinted in *Music and the Historical Imagination*, 95–156. Cambridge, MA and London, 1989.

———. "'To Worship That Celestial Sound': Motives for Analysis." *Journal of Musicology* 1 (1982). Reprinted in *Music and the Historical Imagination*, 46–66. Cambridge, MA and London, 1989.

———. "Tone System in the Secular Works of Guillaume Dufay." *Journal of the American Musicological Society* 18 (1965): 131–69.

Turbot, Richard. *Tudor Music: A Research and Information Guide*. New York, 1994.

———. *William Byrd: A Guide to Research.* New York, 1987.

Urquhart, Peter. "Cadence, Mode, and Structure in the Motets of Josquin." M.A. thesis, Smith College, 1982.

———. "Canon, Partial Signatures, and 'Musica Ficta' in Works by Josquin DesPrez and His Contemporaries." Ph.D. diss., Harvard University, 1988. University Microfilms 8909017.

Van der Werf, Hendrik. *The Chansons of the Troubadours and Trouvères: A Study of the Melodies and their Relation to the Poems*. Utrecht, 1972.

Ward, John M. "Barley's Songs Without Words." *Lute Society Journal* 12 (1970): 5–22.

Werbeck, Walter. *Studien zur deutschen Tonartenlehre in der ersten Hälfte des 16. Jahrhunderts.* Kassel, Basel, London, and New York, 1989.

Wessely, Othmar. "Bruck, Arnold von." *New Grove* 3: 351–52.

Westendorf, Craig J. "Glareanus' Dodecachordon in German Theory and Practice: An Expression of Confessionalism." *Current Musicology* 37–38 (1984): 33–48.

Whythorne, Thomas. *The Autobiography*. Edited by James M. Osborn. Oxford, 1961. Modern Spelling Edition, London, 1962.

Wienpahl, Robert W. "English Theorists and Evolving Tonality." *Music and Letters* 36 (1955): 377–93.

———. *Music at the Inns of Court*. Ann Arbor, 1979.

Wiering, Frans. "The Language of the Modes: Studies in the History of Polyphonic Modality." Ph.D. diss., University of Amsterdam, 1995.

Williams, Peter. "Spurious Purcell." *Musical Times* 102 (1961): 371.

Wilson, Christopher. *Words and Notes Coupled Lovingly Together: Thomas Campion, a Critical Study*. New York, 1989.

Woodfill, Walter L. *Musicians in English Society from Elizabeth to Charles I*. Princeton, 1953. Reprint, 1968.

Woodley, Ronald. *John Tucke: A Case Study in Early Tudor Music Theory*. Oxford, 1993.

Woods, Isobel. "A Note on 'Scottish Anonymous'." *Royal Musical Association Research Chronicle* 21 (1988): 37–39.

Zimmerman, Franklin B. "Air, A Catchword for New Concepts in Seventeenth-Century English Music Theory." In *Studies in Musicology in Honor of Otto E. Albrecht*, edited by John W. Hill, 142–57. Kassel, 1980.

———. "Advanced Tonal Design in the Part-Songs of William Byrd." In *Kongress Bericht über den siebenten Internationalen Musikwissenschaftlichen Kongress Köln 1958*, 322–26. Kassel, 1959.

Contributors

Candace Bailey is an Associate Professor at Louisburg College in North Carolina. She completed her PhD at Duke University in 1992 with a dissertation entitled "English Keyboard Music, c. 1625–1680." Her edition *Late Seventeenth-Century English Keyboard Music* is volume 81 of Recent Researches in Baroque Music (A-R Editions, 1997).

Margaret Bent is a Fellow of All Souls College, Oxford. A former President of the American Musicological Society, she previously taught at Brandeis and Princeton Universities and has published on many aspects of late medieval music.

Michael Dodds is an Assistant Professor at Southern Methodist University. His dissertation, *The Seventeenth-Century Church Keys in Theory and Practice* (Eastman School of Music), addresses the intersection of liturgical practice and mode in Italian and South German keyboard music.

Sarah Fuller teaches music history and history of theory at the State University of New York at Stony Brook. Her previous articles on analysis of fourteenth-century French music have appeared in *Journal of Music Theory, Music Analysis, Current Musicology*, and *Sonus.*

Cristle Collins Judd is Assistant Professor of Music Theory at the University of Pennsylvania. She received her PhD from King's College, University of London in 1993. Her work has appeared in *Music Analysis, Journal of the American Musicological Society*, and *Early Music History*. Current projects include a monograph, *"Harmonic Institutions": Theory, Practice, and Printed Repertories (1501-1558).*

Jessie Ann Owens is Professor of Music and former Dean of the College at Brandeis University. She received her BA from Barnard College in 1971 and her MFA and PhD in 1975 and 1978 from Princeton University. Her study of compositional process in Renaissance music—*Composers at Work: The Craft of Musical Composition 1450–1600*—was published in 1997 by Oxford University Press. She is currently Vice President of the American Musicological Society.

Harold Powers is Scheide Professor of Music History at Princeton. He has published widely in Indic musicology, Italian opera studies, and history of (Western) music theory.

Timothy H. Steele is Associate Professor of Music at Covenant College. His 1993 University of Chicago dissertation on the early sixteenth-century psalm motet was recently honored by the American Choral Directors Association. He is currently at work on the second edition of *Josquin Des Prez: A Guide to Research*, forthcoming from Garland Publishing.

Frans Wiering studied biology and musicology at the University of Amsterdam where he completed his dissertation "The Language of the Modes: Studies in the History of Polyphonic Modality" in 1995. At the Department of Computing and Humanities of Utrecht University he is currently working on the *Thesaurus musicarum italicarum*, a corpus of electronic, multimedia editions of music treatises by Gioseffo Zarlino and other Italian theorists from the late Renaissance.

Index